Revolutionary Transformations

Using firsthand material from Chinese archives that are no longer open to researchers, and bringing together a leading team of international scholars, this volume is a major contribution to the study of the People's Republic of China. Calling into question existing narratives on the foundational decade of the PRC, these essays present a nuanced consideration of China in the 1950s by integrating two periods that are often considered separately: the relatively "happy" years 1949–1956 and the relatively "unhappy" years from 1957 onwards. Exploring the challenges faced in constructing socialism, the transnational context, and early modes of PRC governance, the contributors highlight the ways in which China was shaped by diversity on all levels and scales in how socialism was enacted and experienced. These essays clearly demonstrate how the unevenness of Party control created discrepancies and variations between different regions and between the center and the locale.

Anja Blanke is a Research Fellow at Zeppelin Universität.

Julia C. Strauss is Professor of Chinese Politics at SOAS, University of London.

Klaus Mühlhahn is President and Chair of Modern China Studies at Zeppelin Universität.

Revolutionary Transformations

The People's Republic of China in the 1950s

Edited by

Anja Blanke
Zeppelin Universität

Julia C. Strauss
School of Oriental and African Studies, University of London

Klaus Mühlhahn
Zeppelin Universität

CAMBRIDGE
UNIVERSITY PRESS

CAMBRIDGE
UNIVERSITY PRESS

Shaftesbury Road, Cambridge CB2 8EA, United Kingdom

One Liberty Plaza, 20th Floor, New York, NY 10006, USA

477 Williamstown Road, Port Melbourne, VIC 3207, Australia

314–321, 3rd Floor, Plot 3, Splendor Forum, Jasola District Centre, New Delhi – 110025, India

103 Penang Road, #05–06/07, Visioncrest Commercial, Singapore 238467

Cambridge University Press is part of Cambridge University Press & Assessment, a department of the University of Cambridge.

We share the University's mission to contribute to society through the pursuit of education, learning and research at the highest international levels of excellence.

www.cambridge.org
Information on this title: www.cambridge.org/9781009304108

DOI: 10.1017/9781009304146

First published 2023

A catalogue record for this publication is available from the British Library.

Library of Congress Cataloging-in-Publication Data
Names: Blanke, Anja, editor. | Strauss, Julia C., editor. | Mühlhahn, Klaus, editor.
Title: Revolutionary transformations : the People's Republic of China in the 1950s / edited by Anja Blanke, Zeppelin Universität, Julia C. Strauss, School of Oriental and African Studies, University of London, Klaus Mühlhahn, Zeppelin Universität.
Description: Cambridge ; New York, NY : Cambridge University Press, 2023. | Includes bibliographical references and index.
Identifiers: LCCN 2022062034 | ISBN 9781009304108 (hardback) | ISBN 9781009304092 (paperback) | ISBN 9781009304146 (ebook)
Subjects: LCSH: China – History – 1949–1976. | China – Politics and government – 1949–1976.
Classification: LCC DS777.55 .R463 2023 | DDC 951.05–dc23/eng/20230111
LC record available at https://lccn.loc.gov/2022062034

ISBN 978-1-009-30410-8 Hardback

Contents

List of Figures   *page* vii
List of Contributors   viii
Acknowledgments   xii

Introduction: Revolutionary Transformations in 1950s
China
JULIA C. STRAUSS, ANJA BLANKE, AND KLAUS   1
MÜHLHAHN

Part I   Revolution and the Transnational

Introduction to Part I   17

1   International Relations and China's Position in the
    Socialist Camp   22
    SUSANNE WEIGELIN-SCHWIEDRZIK

2   Sino–Soviet Anxiety: Science and Chinese Conditions
    in the PRC Coal Industry (1949–1965)   44
    ANNA BELOGUROVA

3   Producing Socialist Bodies: Transnational Sports
    Networks and Athletes in 1950s China   69
    AMANDA SHUMAN

4   Asia's Fourth Rome: Cultural Industries and Cultural
    Diplomacy in the International Legitimization
    of the People's Republic of China, 1949–1953   97
    MATTHEW D. JOHNSON

Part II   Domestic Governance: Inheriting Empire, Revolutionizing Society

Introduction to Part II   121

5   Modalities of State Building: Bureaucracy, Campaign, and Performance in Sunan, 1950–1953   127
    JULIA C. STRAUSS

6   The Wilds of Revolution: Anti-localism and Hainanese Women in the Early People's Republic of China   153
    JEREMY A. MURRAY AND ALEXANDER J. SERRANO

7   Reconstruction and Solidification: The Restructuring of "Peasant" Status in the 1950s Dispersal of Shanghai's Urban Population   175
    RUAN QINGHUA

Part III   Legitimacy and Local Agencies

Introduction to Part III   195

8   Anxiety in the Revolutionary Turn: Shanghai Film Personnel in the 1950s   198
    ZHANG JISHUN

9   Letters from the People: The Masses and the Mass Line in 1950s China   212
    AMINDA M. SMITH

10 Cadres, Grain, and Rural Conflicts: A Study of Criminal Cases in a Village during the Great Leap Forward   231
    JING WENYU

11 How the CCP Has Failed to Obtain Control over China's Collective Memory on the 1950s   256
    ANJA BLANKE

12 Postscript: Rethinking China under Mao   275
    KLAUS MÜHLHAHN

    Index   289

Figures

1.1 Models of triangularity   *page* 27
1.2 Bipolarism and triangularity combined   28
3.1 The front of a Soviet postcard from a WFYS event (undated)   82
3.2 Huang (left) and Wu (right) with a German coach in East
    Berlin, 1951   86
3.3 "A greeting from the Indonesian swimmers"   87
3.4 The Indonesian delegation in Beijing, October 1951   88
3.5 Photographs of the Chinese national swim team in 1953   90
3.6 Wu Chuanyu, model athlete   91
3.7 Photograph of Erich Jolig next to a swimming pool (A) with
    a message on the back   94
5.1 A mass accusation session   146

Contributors

ANNA BELOGUROVA (PhD in Chinese history, University of British Columbia, 2012) is a research fellow at the Institute for the Chinese Studies, Freie Universität Berlin, holding an individual research grant from Deutsche Forschungsgemeinschaft "The World of Socialist Coal: Technology, Economy, and Environment in China in the Context of the Cooperation with the Eastern Bloc (1945–1991)." She has published in the *Journal of Global History*, *Modern Asian Studies*, and the *Cambridge Handbook of the History of Communism*. Her first monograph is *The Nanyang Revolution: The Comintern and Chinese Networks in Southeast Asia, 1890–1957* (Cambridge University Press, 2019). She also edited *Naming Modernity: Rebranding and Neologisms during China's Interwar Global Moment in East Asia*, special issue of *Cross-Currents: East Asian History and Culture Review*, September 2017, No. 24. Her latest publication is "China, Anti-imperialist Leagues, and the Comintern (1926–1937): Visions, Networks, and Cadres," in Carolien Stolte, Heather Streets-Salter, and Michele Louro, eds., *The League against Imperialism: Lives and Afterlives* (Leiden University Press, 2020)

ANJA BLANKE is a researcher and lecturer at Zeppelin Universität in Friedrichshafen. She received her PhD in sinology from Freie Universität Berlin in 2020. Her research interests are historiography and competing narratives in the PRC and the history of the CCP.

JING WENYU is a PhD candidate at the Institute for East Asian Studies at the University of Cologne, Germany. Her research interests are rural society and criminal punishment in 1950s China.

MATTHEW D. JOHNSON is an independent researcher and advisor, and a visiting fellow at the Hoover Institution. He was a co-founder and director of the PRC History Group, and co-editor of *Maoism at the Grassroots: Everyday Life in China's Era of High Socialism* (Harvard University Press, 2015). He previously led the Faculty of Arts and Social Sciences at Taylor's

University in Malaysia. He started his career at the Weatherhead Center for International Affairs at Harvard University; earned a PhD in history from the University of California, San Diego; and taught at the University of Oxford, Renmin University of China, and Grinnell College. His primary research areas include the Chinese Communist Party, comparative propaganda studies, US-China relations, and state and independent media in China.

KLAUS MÜHLHAHN is a professor of modern China studies and president at Zeppelin Universität. He studied sinology at Freie Universität Berlin and National Taiwan Normal University, and graduated in 1993 with a master's degree. He obtained his PhD in 1998 at the Institute of Chinese Studies at Freie Universität Berlin. From 2002 to 2004 he was a visiting fellow at the Center for Chinese Studies, University of California, Berkeley. In 2004, he accepted a position at the University of Turku in Finland, where he taught as a professor of contemporary Chinese and Asian history at the Institute of History and at the Center for East Asian Studies. In 2007 he was appointed (full) professor of modern Chinese history at Indiana University, Bloomington. From 2010 to 2020 he taught at Freie Universität Berlin as professor of history and culture of modern China. Between 2014 and 2020 he was vice president of Freie Universität Berlin. He has published widely on modern Chinese history in English, German, and Chinese and is a frequent commentator on China for the German media. His most recent book, *Making China Modern*, published by Harvard University Press in January 2019, rewrites China's history, telling a story of crisis and recovery, exploring the versatility and resourcefulness essential for China's survival as well as its future possibilities.

JEREMY MURRAY teaches and writes about modern China at California State University, San Bernardino. He received his doctorate in history from the University of California, San Diego, and has published work on China's Hainan Island, Asian cultural traditions, and pop culture. His monograph on the history of the Communist revolution on Hainan is *China's Lonely Revolution: The Local Communists of Hainan Island, 1926–1956* (State University of New York Press, 2017). He also edited and contributed to *China Tripping: Encountering the Everyday in the People's Republic*, with Perry Link and Paul G. Pickowicz (Rowman and Littlefield, 2019).

RUAN QINGHUA holds a PhD in history from Fudan University. He is an associate professor of the History Department of East China Normal University, engaged in modern Chinese history and the history of the People's Republic of China. He mainly focuses on the development of

and changes in Chinese traditional nongovernmental charity organizations, as well as the urban grassroots social transformation and urban
population migration after 1949. He has published more than twenty
professional papers, and published two monographs: *Reforming
Vagrants in Shanghai (1949–1958)* and *The Difficulty of Cihang:
Charity and Modern Shanghai Urban Society.*

ALEXANDER J. SERRANO is a doctoral student of East Asian languages and
culture studies at the University of California, Santa Barbara, under the
guidance of Dr. Mayfair Yang and Dr. Hangping Xu. He earned his BA
and MA in history from California State University, San Bernardino,
under the supervision of Dr. Jeremy Murray. His master's thesis examined the cultural and societal impact of the Manchu queue hairstyle on
Chinese identity during the Qing and early Republican China.

AMANDA SHUMAN is a researcher and lecturer at the University of
Freiburg (Germany). She received her PhD in East Asian History
from the University of California, Santa Cruz. She has published a
number of articles on sport, politics, and diplomacy, and is currently
working on a book manuscript that examines the politics of transnational and international sport and physical culture in Mao's China.
She is also the primary administrator for the Maoist Legacy Database
and maintains a wiki that provides information on historical archives
and other resources for researching the People's Republic of China.

AMINDA M. SMITH is codirector of the PRC History Group and associate
professor in the Department of History at Michigan State University.
She specializes in the social and cultural history of Chinese Communism,
with a particular interest in the grassroots histories of political thought. She
has researched and written on brainwashing and thought reform, global
Maoism and leftist politics, and China's petition system.

JULIA C. STRAUSS is professor of Chinese politics at SOAS, University of
London, where she served as editor of the *China Quarterly* from 2002 to
2011. She works on twentieth-century state building and institution
building in China and Taiwan, with her monograph *State Formation in
China and Taiwan: Bureaucracy, Campaign and Performance*
(Cambridge University Press, 2020) her most recent publication on
this topic. She also publishes on performance in politics, BRI (particularly China–Africa), and Chinese forestry.

SUSANNE WEIGELIN-SCHWIEDRZIK completed her PhD in 1982 and was
appointed full professor of modern China studies at Heidelberg
University in 1989. From 2002 to 2020 she was chair professor of sinology

at the University of Vienna. After studying at Beijing Yuyan Xueyuan and Beijing University from 1975 to 1977 she had multiple affiliations with such universities as the University of California, Berkeley, Tsinghua University, Beijing University, Kyoto University, Hong Kong University of Science and Technology, Brandeis University, the Chinese Academy of Social Sciences, National Chengchi University, and the Chinese University of Hong Kong. Her research has been focused on the writing of modern and contemporary Chinese and East Asian history and the politics of memory in the PRC. In addition, she publishes on Chinese politics, with a more recent focus on international relations.

ZHANG JISHUN is professor of history and a senior researcher at the Si-Mian Institute for Advanced Studies in the Humanities at East China Normal University in Shanghai. Her main research interest is modern Chinese history, especially metropolitan social culture and Shanghai history. She has published *Zhongguo Zhishi Fenzi de Meiguo Guan* (Comments on Chinese Intellectuals' Outlook on United States) (Fudan University Press, 1999), *Yuanqu de Dushi: Yijiuwuling Niandai de Shanghai* (A City Displaced: Shanghai in the 1950s) (Social Sciences Academic Press, 2015), and numerous articles in *Social Sciences in China, Historical Research, CCP History Studies, China Quarterly,* and *Twentieth-Century China*.

Acknowledgments

The last decade has witnessed an explosion of work on China in the 1950s, prompting many to begin to rethink the history of that decade. In order to carry the conversation further, Anja and Klaus brought together more than twenty colleagues from China, Europe, and the USA to call into question existing narratives on the foundational decade of the PRC. To this end, the Volkswagen Foundation generously supported two workshops entitled "Rethinking 1950s China: New Materials, New Challenges, New Approaches" in Berlin in August 2017 and Hannover in October 2018. We were overwhelmed by the abundance of new ideas and approaches, much of which was based on archival material collected in the 2000s and early 2010s, when it was still possible to get access to Chinese archives. The volume that has emerged from these meetings is truly a collective project based on the exchanges, debates, and perspectives of all our participants. We would like to take this opportunity to thank our participants, Felix Boecking, Feng Xiaocai, Fabio Lanza, Daniel Leese, Liu Jianping, Liu Yajuan, Liu Yanwen, Lu Tian, Nicolas Schillinger, Glenn Tiffert, Stig Thøgersen, Martin Wagner, Felix Wemheuer, Xiao Yanzhong, Xu Xilin, Yang Kuisong, and Zhou Shuxian.

As editors, our most difficult task was in bringing all these new research approaches together: how to tell the story of 1950s China? After intensive and fruitful discussions, at meetings at UCLA and in La Quinta in October 2019, we decided that we wanted to tell the story of 1950s China by integrating aspects that are usually considered separately: (1) the relatively "happy" 1949–1956 period and the relatively "unhappy" period of 1957 and after, and (2) the different scales at which history was articulated, from the systems level of bipolarism to the most local articulations of how individuals functioned within socialism.

It has been a pleasure as editors to work together. Our wonderful contributors from all over the world made this book a reality. We thank the three anonymous reviewers who urged us to sharpen our thinking and better integrate the substantive chapters. Lucy Rhymer at Cambridge University Press supported the project through the review and publishing processes. Helena Rothfuss, finishing her BA at Zeppelin Universität, and Ole Bekaan, finishing his MA at Zeppelin Universität, provided organizational help and excellent copyediting well beyond the call of duty.

Finally, we would like to thank our families for their support and for allowing us the time to complete the work on the volume.

Introduction
Revolutionary Transformations in 1950s China

Julia C. Strauss, Anja Blanke, and Klaus Mühlhahn

The history of the People's Republic of China as a field of study has changed beyond recognition over the last quarter-century. Once covered primarily by political scientists and the occasional sociologist, PRC history now is a recognized area of study in the West, with its own e-journals, Facebook groups, and hires in history departments. A generation of superb historians and their graduate students also have emerged, albeit more cautiously, in the PRC itself. Both Chinese and foreign scholars have produced what has amounted to a remarkable explosion of work in the last two decades, much of it in Chinese, some of it in English or German. The combination of increasingly accessible Chinese archives and individuals within China increasingly willing to speak openly about the post-1949 period created a research environment in which it was not long before thoughtfully edited volumes ensued that confounded old understandings and shed new light on specific periods of PRC history.[1] We now have a wide range of monographs and edited volumes that provide new insights into the history of post-1949 China. Since full books invariably take somewhat longer than edited volumes, it wasn't until the early 2010s that a series of monographs on the broad sweep of post-1949 history emerged. Some of the most notable authors of these works include Yang Kuisong, Shen Zhihua, and Zhang Jishun, all of whom offer new insights into such topics as the establishment of the key institutions of the PRC, the implementation of campaigns carried out in the early 1950s, and the urban history of Shanghai.[2] Felix Wemheuer's new

---

[1] Early works included Jeremy Brown and Paul Pickowicz, eds., *Dilemmas of Victory: The Early Years of the PRC* (Cambridge, MA: Harvard University Pres, 2007); Julia C. Strauss, *The History of the PRC 1949–1976* (Cambridge: Cambridge University Press, 2007); Joseph Esherick, Paul Pickowicz, and Andrew Walder, *The Chinese Cultural Revolution as History* (Stanford: Stanford University Press, 2006); somewhat later works are Kimberly Ens Manning and Felix Wemheuer, *Eating Bitterness: New Perspectives on China's Great Leap Forward and Famine* (Vancouver: University of British Columbia Press, 2012).

[2] Yang Kuisong, ed., *Zhonghua renmin gongheguo jiangou shi yanjiu* (A Study of the History of the Establishment of the PRC), vol. 1 (Nanchang: Jiangxi renmin chubanshe, 2009); Shen Zhihua, *Chuzai shizilukou de xuanze: 1956–1957 nian de Zhongguo* (Decision at the Crossroads: China in 1956–1957) (Guangzhou: Guangdong renmin chubanshe, 2013);

social history of China focuses on questions of class, gender, ethnicity, and the urban–rural divide, thus analyzing the experiences of a range of social groups under Communist rule – workers, peasants, local cadres, intellectuals, "ethnic minorities," the old elites, men and women – between 1949 and 1976. Yang Kuisong's most recent work has a similarly broad sweep that draws on the dramatic social transformations at all levels after the establishment of the PRC in 1949.[3]

Some of this turn to PRC history revises the conventional received wisdom: work on land reform suggests that it was not nearly as popular or demanded from below as the standard histories suggest.[4] Daniel Leese's study provides new insights into the question of how the state has dealt with the injustices of the Mao era between 1976 and 1986.[5] After a first monograph on the Republican period, Ralph Thaxton built on his access in one village in north China to produce two more incredibly detailed studies that delve into the specifics of how local power holders acquired and maintained their status, how ordinary villagers survived the appalling conditions after the Great Leap Forward, and how they negotiated the assorted depredations of officials thereafter.[6] Jie Li provides new insights into societal activities which contest the official narratives by the Chinese Communist Party (CCP) on Maoist China.[7] Unofficial histories published in Chinese and translated into English, such as *Tombstone*, have viscerally brought to light the suffering engendered by the mass starvation

Zhang Jishun, *Yuanqu de dushi: 1950 niandai de Shanghai* (A City Displayed: Shanghai in the 1950s) (Beijing: Shehui kexue wenxian chubanshe, 2015).

[3] Felix Wemheuer, *A Social History of Maoist China: Conflict and Change, 1949–1976* (Cambridge, MA: Harvard University Press, 2019); Yang Kuisong, *Eight Outcasts: Social and Political Marginalization in China under Mao* (Oakland: University of California Press), 2020.

[4] Luo Pinghan, *Tudi gaige yundongshi* (A History of the Land Reform Movement) (Fuzhou: Fujian renmin chubanshe, 2005); Wang Youming, *Geming yu xiangcun: Jiefang qu tudi gaige yanjiu: 1941–1948. Yi Shandong Liinan xian wei ge'an* (Revolution and the Countryside: Land Reform in Liberated Areas, 1941–1948. A Case Study on Liinan County, Shandong) (Shanghai: Shanghai shehui kexueyuan chubanshe, 2006); Yu Liu, 'Why Did It Go So High? Political Mobilization and Agricultural Collectivization in China,' *China Quarterly* 187 (2006): 732–742; Brian De Mare, *Land Wars: The Story of China's Agrarian Revolution* (Stanford: Stanford University Press, 2019).

[5] Daniel Leese, *Maos langer Schatten: Chinas Umgang mit der Vergangenheit* (Mao's Long Shadow: China's Association with the Past) (Munich: C.H. Beck, 2021). See also Daniel Leese and Puck Engman, eds., *Victims, Perpetrators, and the Role of Law in Maoist China: A Case Study Approach* (Berlin: DeGruyter Oldenbourg, 2018).

[6] Ralph Thaxton, *Catastrophe and Contention in Rural China: Mao's Great Leap Forward Famine and the Origins of Righteous Resistance in Da Fo Village* (Cambridge: Cambridge University Press, 2008); and Ralph Thaxton, *Force and Contention in Contemporary China: Memory and Resistance in the Long Shadow of the Catastrophic Past* (Cambridge: Cambridge University Press, 2016).

[7] Jie Li, *Utopian Ruins: A Memorial Museum of the Mao Era* (Durham, NC: Duke University Press, 2020).

after the Great Leap Forward.[8] And the Cultural Revolution period has given rise to an entire cottage industry of publication, including memoirs, edited volumes, microhistories, and monographs.[9] The openness of China in the 2000s and early 2010s also made it possible to engage in telling the story of PRC history from the bottom up. Access to archives, the ability to interview, and the ready availability of materials in flea markets have all contributed to a wave of articles, edited volumes, and monographs of microhistories geared to in-depth analyses of the variety of different local realities and personal fates.[10] Access to individuals willing and able to tell their stories has opened up a whole new level of historical texture and immediacy: Felix Wemheuer's and Wang Ning's studies, for example, draw from personal memories of witnesses and other grassroots' sources such as labor farm archives.[11] There are also journals published in China – with and without official publication licenses – with articles based on the oral histories of those who were variably implementers of and witnesses to the great policies unleashed over the course of the Mao years.[12]

---

[8] Yang Jisheng. *Tombstone: The Great Chinese Famine, 1958–1962* (London: Penguine Books, 2013).

[9] Liu Ping, *Wo de Zhongguo meng* (My Chinese Dream) (Beijing: Zhongguo yanshi chu-banshe, 2014); Esherick, Pickowicz, and Walder, *The Chinese Cultural Revolution as History*; Roderick MacFarquhar and Michael Schoenhals, *Mao's Last Revolution* (Cambridge, MA: Harvard University Press, 2006); Hu Ping, *Mao Zedong weishenme hui fadong Wenhua dageming?* (Why Did Mao Zedong Launch the Cultural Revolution?) (Taipei: Yunchen wenhua, 2016); Andrew Walder, *Fractured Rebellion: The Beijing Red Guard Movement* (Cambridge, MA: Harvard University Press, 2012); and Andrew Walder, *Agents of disorder: inside China's Cultural Revolution* (Cambridge, MA: Harvard University Press, 2019).

[10] Jeremy Brown and Paul G. Pickowicz, eds., *Dilemmas of Victory: The Early Years of the PRC* (Cambridge, MA: Harvard University Press, 2010); Dong Guoqiang and Andrew G. Walder, "Factions in a Bureaucratic System: The Origins of Cultural Revolution Conflict in Nanjing," *China Journal* 65 (2011): 1–25; Jeremy Brown and Matthew Johnson, eds., *Maoism at the Grassroots: Everyday Life in China's Era of High Socialism* (Cambridge, MA: Harvard University Press, 2015); Andrew G. Walder, *Agents of Disorder: Inside China's Cultural Revolution* (Cambridge, MA: Harvard University Press, 2019); Yang Jisheng, *The World Turned Upside Down: A History of the Chinese Cultural Revolution* (New York: MacMillan Publishers, 2021).

[11] Felix Wemheuer, *Steinnudeln: Ländliche Erinnerungen und staatliche Vergangenheitsbewältigung der "Großen Sprung"-Hungersnot in der chinesische Provinz Henan* (Stone Noodles: Rural and Official Memories of the Great Leap Famine in the Chinese Province Henan) (Vienna: Peter Lang, 2007); Manning and Wemheuer, *Eating Bitterness*. Wang Ning, *Banished to the Great Northern Wilderness: Political Exile and Re-education in Mao's China* (Vancouver: University of British Columbia Press, 2017).

[12] Before 2016 the history magazine *Yanhuang Chunqiu* contained countless critical articles about the campaigns of the 1950s and the Cultural Revolution; the magazine *Bashan Yeyu* (Night Rains on Mount Ba), about the Anti-Rightist Campaign (1957–1958), was published by former rightists and their relatives. See http://prchistory.org/night-rains-on-mount-ba.

With this wealth of new sources and different perspectives, scholars have also begun to integrate PRC history with other historical subfields in two distinct ways. First, historians whose early work was on the Republican period in such distinct areas as gender history and environmental history have definitively crossed the historical divide of 1949 and extended their work into the post-1949 era.[13] Second, the collapse of the Marxist–Leninist regimes of Eastern Europe and the Soviet Union, in combination with a generation of distance from the politics and personalities of the pre-1989 period, has led to an outpouring of work in English and Chinese on Cold War history, reconsideration of the wider global socialist order of which China was a part, and comparative and transnational work on East Asia as a region.[14]

Our volume makes two contributions to the field of PRC studies. First, it provides a more nuanced consideration of the foundational decade of the PRC by integrating two aspects that are usually considered separately: the relatively "happy" 1949–1956 period and the relatively "unhappy" period of 1957 and after; second, it considers the different scales at which history was articulated, from the systems level of bipolarism to the most local articulations of how individuals functioned within socialism.

With such a broad range of work already done on PRC history, it is surprising that until now there has been no overall consideration of the 1950s as the foundational decade of the PRC. The decade of the 1950s reveals, in all its contradictions, the ways in which the young PRC

[13] See Gail Hershatter, *The Gender of Memory: Rural Women and China's Collective Past* (Berkeley: University of California Press, 2011), which is based on some eighty oral histories of rural women in Shaanxi; Micah Muscalino, "'Water Has Aroused the Girls' Hearts': Gendering Water and Soil Conservation in 1950s China," *Past & Present* (forthcoming 2021); and Micah Muscaliano, "The Contradictions of Conservation: Fighting Erosion in Mao-Era China, 1953–66," *Environmental History*, April 2020: 237–62.

[14] Odd Arne Westad, *Cold War and Revolution: Soviet–American Rivalry and the Origins of Chinese Civil* War (New York: Columbia University Press, 1993); Masuda Hajimu, *Cold War Crucible: The Korean Conflict and the Postwar World* (Cambridge MA: Harvard University Press, 2015); Shen Zhihua and Xia Yafeng, *A Misunderstood Friendship: Mao Zedong, Kim Il-sung, and Sino-North Korean Relations, 1949–1976* (New York: Columbia University Press, 2018); Zhihua Shen and Yafeng Xia, *Mao and the Sino-Soviet Partnership 1945–1959: A New History* (Lanham: Lexington Books, 2015); Zhihua Shen and Danhui Li, *After Leaning to One Side: China and Its Allies in the Cold War* (Stanford: Stanford University Press, 2011); Lorenz M. Luethi, *Cold Wars: Asia, the Middle East, Europe* (Cambridge: Cambridge University Press, 2020); Harry Verhoeven, ed., *Marx and Lenin in Africa and Asia: Socialism(s) and Socialist Legacies*, special issue of *Third World Quarterly* 42, no. 3 (2021); Kristen Looney, *Mobilizing for Development: The Modernization of Rural East Asia* (New York: Cornell University Press, 2020); and Sheena Chestnut Greitens, Dictators and Their Secret Police: Coercive Institutions and State Violence (Cambridge: Cambridge University Press, 2016).

was a period of revolutionary transformations that were replete simultaneously with progressive enthusiasm and hope and with cruelty and waste. The progressivism and the cruelty both were inherent to the fundamental processes of revolutionary transformations, and were in clear evidence from the beginning, even as the ways in which we assess that mix continue to be debated today. The 1950s were indeed a foundational *and* a "swing" decade that began with optimism and ended in mass starvation. Attention needs to be paid to both the foundation and the swing. Insofar as the PRC still has a master history, it agrees on the importance of the early to mid-1950s as a positive period of high legitimacy and significant regime accomplishment. In this reckoning, the young PRC was enormously successful both externally and internally between 1949 and 1956. Externally, it fought the world's then only superpower to a standstill in Korea, decisively reversing a century of military weakness and international humiliation. It also enjoyed high prestige in the developing world and was an important diplomatic presence both in Bandung for the inauguration of the nonaligned movement and in Geneva for the Geneva Accords of 1954. Domestically it tackled long-standing social problems (prostitution, opium addiction, mass unemployment), stabilized the economy by bringing hyperinflation under control, implemented such key revolutionary programs as land reform and the New Marriage Law, established the basic institutions of socialism (the planned economy, the work unit, the unified purchase and sale of grain), and managed to collectivize agriculture and nationalize urban enterprises without the violent resistance that had been so characteristic of collectivization in the Soviet Union. These processes of revolutionary transformation, and their putative successes, are inextricably linked with a wider narrative of how revolutionary China, and its people, rightfully "stood up" with socialism under the leadership of the CCP. Official histories do acknowledge that, after 1956, things went pear-shaped: starting with the Anti-Rightist campaign of 1957, worsening with the Great Leap Forward, and ultimately culminating in the ten years of chaos of the Cultural Revolution.[15] But there is little in the literature, particularly in the official literature, that integrates the "enthusiastic" early to mid-1950s with the "deeply tragic" post-1956 period of escalating tensions with the Soviet Union, domestic witch hunts, out-of-control campaigns, utopianism gone wrong, and mass starvation after the Great Leap Forward.

---

[15] "Resolution on Certain Questions in the History of Our Party since the Founding of the People's Republic of China," June 27, 1981, History and Public Policy Program Digital Archive, trans. *Beijing Review* 24, no. 27 (July 6, 1981): 10–39, at http://digitalarchive .wilsoncenter.org/document/121344.

Because most of the studies published on the 1950s only look at one period (the early years of the People's Republic or the later catastrophes such as the Great Leap Forward), one campaign, one locale, or one sector, there is a disconnect that runs through much of the literature that this volume seeks to rectify. Most of our chapters, even if they focus only on one period, locale, or sector, demonstrate how deeply connected the happier early 1950s were with the unhappier late 1950s.

What emerges is not simply a China, dominated by the CCP or its great leaders, but diversity on all levels and scales in how socialism was enacted and experienced. But this does not mean that we can forgo the CCP entirely. Mao's and the Party's vision of the world and their goals continued to set the conditions and agenda of the 1950s. Whereas Mao and his party were once seen as great (as, for instance, in Li Rui's portrait of the young Mao) for their ability to muster power in the service of truth, the leadership of the CCP in this volume comes across as a distant, tragic hero forced by circumstances to place power ahead of truth. Ambitious and uncompromising, for the quarter-century before 1949 the CCP had fought from a position of disadvantage and uncertainty and won preeminence by taking enormous chances. For better, and also for worse, this *Weltanschauung* continued to shape choices throughout the foundational 1950s.

We also highlight the ways in which the unevenness of Party control led to discrepancies all across China, resulting in differences between different scales, from region to region and between the center and the locale. The lofty-sounding rhetoric of the "Resist America/Aid Korea" campaign may well have engendered mass rallies in urban China, but it did not resonate with the peasants in the north China countryside when it came to the recruitment of village youths to serve in the military. Basic expectations were often broken: Korean War POWs (prisoners of war) went home by routes of contingency, to circumstances beyond promises or logic. "Model woman worker" status did not guarantee any of the honored individuals a career of correctness with the people. Meanwhile, local cadres had agendas and priorities of their own. Local people deployed Party-sanctioned quasi-religious rhetoric in fights over economic gains. Provincial cadres overseeing coal projects bent world news to promote work unit objectives through the publication of leaflets. A growing number of people – from a multitude of subject positions inscribed by the Party – learned to play their parts in a master script that was expressly designed to privilege some over others.

When we turn to a global scale, it is clear that the new government faced equally daunting challenges such as a Western trade embargo and international isolation. In principle, the government articulated that it would rather perish than accept a position of subjugation. At the same time, the CCP demonstrated impressive skills and foresight with regard to the exploitation of USA–USSR strategic conflicts for China's own gains. It seemed, for instance, to come out on top of a Korean War in which its soldiers were sacrificed in "human-wave" tactics, and in Bandung it gained respect by claiming to represent the Third World. But in practice, the new government was also frequently not experienced enough to effectively handle international affairs. PRC foreign policies, personally directed by Mao, appeared to be improvised and reactive. China's international thinking fused elements of national interest and socialist brotherhood. On matters of territoriality or nationality, it continued to retain residues of Qing imperial assumptions about the relationships between the suzerain and tributary states. For instance, in Xinjiang or Tibet, the CCP continued without hesitation the nationalist policies of previous governments and without mercy enforced Chinese rule over non-Han Chinese ethnic groups.

China in the 1950s was an embattled country fighting for Mao's vision of socialism, but this vision was replete with cross-cutting imperatives and irreconcilable internal tensions. Coastal cities in general – and Shanghai in particular – were understood as sites of corruption to be extirpated even as they were admired and needed for their high level of industrialization and economic productivity. The CCP both needed an extensive government bureaucracy to implement revolutionary programs and establish a planned economy, and deeply mistrusted all forms of hierarchical authority. The government implemented campaigns such as the Three Antis, the Four Cleanups, and the Cultural Revolution for the rectification and continued revolutionary purity of the CCP, but insisted that this be done through maintaining "close links to the people." "The people" were imagined to be naturally revolutionary. Many urbanites indeed were, but there were also many groups that were hesitant or defiant. According to the Party, these "elements" needed to be either educated or, *pour encourager les autres*, made an example of and repressed. The 1950s, in short, was a decade of many challenges and much uncertainty. The PRC was able, by and large, to stabilize its control as a new regime. The CCP leadership continued, however, to see enemies and agents of subversion everywhere. The government was eager, by 1956, to declare the triumph of socialism in China, and, by its own lights, it had good reason to do so. But the very methods that led to its successes also sowed the seeds of larger, and eventually catastrophic, consequences. Powerful as the Central Committee of the CCP had become, power at the top, did not protect the center from the systemic falsification of information (thanks to the socialization of the cadres through rectification campaigns) coming up from the bottom. And, more prosaically, the government's drive to establish control led either to the abandonment of its earlier principles or to the imposition of standard categories, which then led to profound suffering and waste.

Many of our chapters detail ways in which the government's mania for uniform classification and direct control led to policies that diverged sharply from its own revolutionary rhetoric on such themes as gender equality and self-reliance (Murray and Serrano, Jing), that dispersed the long-term unemployed and the undesirable from big cities on the specious ground that they were really peasants (Ruan), or that imposed ill-conceived class categories on people in order to implement a land reform that was, contrary to regime proclamations, not particularly popular or desired from below (Strauss). Others point to the sheer difficulty of implementing the ideals of the revolution in the face of either technical realities (Belogurova) or the messily unreconstructed former cultural elites that the regime wanted to reform (Zhang). Here some of the smaller details in these chapters are especially telling. Belogurova illustrates how, even at the height of Sino-Soviet technical co-operation in the early to mid-1950s, Chinese technicians were reluctant to hand over the survey information on coal deposits that could have helped Soviet technicians devise the most appropriate technology transfer. Zhang draws out the frustration of the committed Party cadre at the rapidity with which the CCP's cultural establishment not only was willing to accommodate and absorb decidedly non-revolutionary, if not outright decadent, pre-1949 film stars, but also stored up a world of trouble for exactly those stars when the campaigns of the later 1950s blew up. The unhappy late 1950s did not emerge suddenly out of nowhere; the very elements that gave rise to them were in evidence from very early in the history of the PRC. But unless one were of a bad class (e.g., landlords or local bullies), or were otherwise marginalized (female revolutionary fighters far away from Beijing, the urban unemployed), the sharper edges of the revolution were kept in check, only appearing in full force once the visible enemies (landlords, Guomindang holdovers, capitalists, and unreliable intellectuals) had been vanquished and the key institutions of socialism fully established.

The picture of the PRC in the 1950s that emerges from our volume is thus one of unfulfilled promises and departures from the ideals of socialism at the micro level: from the local cadres who didn't ensure clean toilets to the tough female revolutionaries in Hainan who, once the revolution was won, were told to go home and bear children, to the elite swimmer who, having bought into the opportunity and promise of a career in New China, ended up quietly retiring to the Netherlands. In one way or another, all of our chapters illustrate in ways large and small that Chinese socialism under Mao didn't quite work out the way things were supposed to. Perhaps this isn't surprising. China's scale, its poverty, and its recent history of civil war and foreign invasion laid down conditions that any government would have struggled with. But in addition to these structural challenges, the goal of establishing a revolutionary state and implementing revolutionary programs aimed at nothing less than the total transformation of society according to Marxist–Leninist principles was bound to run up against additional difficulties: how to determine friend from enemy, how to balance the need for a developed bureaucracy to manage a planned economy with the revolutionary impetus for continued close links to the people, and how to maintain revolutionary élan once the usual suspects had been rounded up and dispatched after 1953. It is clear that the leadership of the CCP deserved a fair share of the blame for how things unfolded in the later 1950s and after. But it is far from certain that the Party's foibles (and its inability to control a larger domestic and international context) prove that socialism was doomed to fail in China – or that socialism was not the correct path to follow. Certainly, there were many within the CCP who were deeply committed to implementing what they understood to be socialism, and there were many more, likely the vast majority of the population of the PRC, who went along with these principles either because they were themselves convinced, because socialism gave them opportunities to rise in their careers or make claims on the state, or, more prosaically, because they had no choice in the matter.

Beyond the internal complexities of the 1950s, there was the larger issue of space in which the revolution was implemented. History – for the PRC as for anywhere – simultaneously plays out at different scales. Depending on sources, the research question, and personal bent, researchers tend to focus on very different slices of spatial reality. International theorists focus on international systems, those interested in state formation focus on the level of the central nation-state, those concerned with the emergence of social movements focus on the municipality or locality, those working on rural history or peasant resistance focus on the sub-county or village, and so on. Most of the historiography on the history of the PRC privileges the notion of China as a sovereign nation-state, and even many of the local studies we have revolve around central–local issues – either how central-government directives were implemented or deflected by local governments, or how individuals in particular localities experienced and adapted to the impact of those directives. Clearly, trends and events occurring at particular spatial scales reverberated well beyond their immediate domain. Most obviously, the rising tensions in Korea were both a cause and a consequence of deepening Cold War in a bipolar world and had a dramatic impact on China's central government (what it could reasonably expect to push through in terms of land reform and anti-counterrevolutionary campaigns), and on a range of local governments, from those who were net suppliers of soldiers (e.g., Yunnan) to those who were net recipients of Korean War veterans (e.g., villages in north China).[16] But at present, there is still vanishingly little that integrates the different spatial levels in which the revolutionary PRC operated in its first decade.

For these reasons, we explicitly cover different scales of revolutionary transformation, from the most systemic of the macro to the smallest of the micro. Our first scale encompasses the global and the transnational. The bipolar global system so accurately sketched out by Weigelin-Schwiedrzik encompassed not only triangles and balancing but also China's participation in two forms of transnationalism: the socialist ecumenical and the regional. The socialist world of the 1950s was a transnational system characterized by a commitment to principles of world socialism and fraternal assistance (Belogurova on coal, Shuman on transnational sport, and Johnson on transnational film in the East Asian and Southeast Asian region). But Shuman and Johnson's chapters on sport and film also highlight how China interacted at two different transnational levels simultaneously: in a wider socialist ecumene, with an "inner" geography of sinophone and ethnic closeness in a quite different regional system.

Our next scale engages directly with the problems faced by the centralizing party-state as it attempted to grapple with a very significant problem of domestic governance: how to revolutionize society when its cadres were spread thin over a vast area inherited from a large agrarian empire. Although the subject matter is very different for each, Strauss on shifting modalities of bureaucracy and campaign, Murray on the central party-state's insistence that women fighters in Hainan cede their positions to cadres sent down from the center, and Ruan on urban government bureaucratic classification of people it wanted to offload as "peasants" all point to the larger problem of the difficulty of governing a territory that was large, diverse, and resource-short. One shortcut was through posting

---

[16] Jeremy Brown, "From Resisting Communists to Resisting America: Civil War and Korean War in Southwest China, 1950–51," in Jeremy Brown and Paul Pickowicz, eds., *Dilemmas of Victory: The Early Years of the People's Republic of China* (Cambridge, MA: Harvard University Pres, 2007), 105–129; Thaxton, *Catastrophe and Contention in Rural China*; Ralph Thaxton, *Salt of the Earth: The Political Origins of Peasant Protest and Communist Revolution in China* (Berkeley: University of California Press, 1997); David Cheng Chan, *The Hijacked War: The Story of Chinese POWs in the Korean War* (Stanford: Stanford University Press, 2020); Covell F. Meyskens, *Mao's Third Front: The Militarization of Cold War China* (Cambridge: Cambridge University Press, 2020.

and then implementing simplifying bureaucratic rules. Another, related, shortcut was to replace key cadres thought to be too sympathetic to "localist" concerns with those who would be more responsive to central dictates without arguing for undue sensitivity to messy local realities that confounded categories and suppositions already decided on from above.

Our final scale considers the local and the individual: how, within the constraints established by the system, local states and individuals enmeshed in local networks engaged in efforts to chart a path within new socialist structures of authority. Sometimes this led to great frustration on the part of idealistic cadres who wanted to imbibe recalcitrant subjects with the ideals of socialism (Zhang). Others directly engage how individuals quickly adapted to the language, forms, and institutions of socialism to press for everything from cleaner toilets (Smith) to more equitable grain rations (Jing). And, of course, the party-state's language of grievance and oppression, in combination with its formula of investigation of cases, opened doors for individuals to pursue very local grievances (Jing).

Most of our chapters cover more than one of these scales. A few – notably Belogurova's and Shuman's – incorporate almost all of them. But even when they are not explicitly considered in a particular chapter, bringing together this evidence in one volume prompts us to begin to integrate these different scales of revolutionary transformation in surprisingly different ways: transnational socialism certainly provided both blueprints for action and immediate assistance and solidarity, but it didn't prevent Chinese revolutionaries from shopping around for the best technology from the enemy capitalist West even as the selfsame Chinese revolutionaries claimed to be adapting technology to their local circumstances. Even as the Cold War in East Asia hardened some geographical boundaries as China restricted out-migration and direct contact between the mainland and Taiwan was shut down, questions of citizenship and belonging remained surprisingly porous in others, as when ethnically Chinese elite athletes who had never even been to China proper were invited to become national representatives of the People's Republic.

Because we cover a wide range of topics, the range of the sources used by our authors is similarly wide-ranging: from personal diaries and interviews with family members to collections of letters, to the more familiar archives and publicly available documents. In a world in which archival access is increasingly restricted, in which semiprivate collections that were circulating entirely legally in the last decade are now suddenly off-limits, and in which scholars of PRC history within China must be increasingly guarded and careful, creativity with available sources inside and outside China is clearly the way forward.

Despite the wealth of work that has come out on the history of post-1949 China, we believe that there is still a need for ongoing discussions and new knowledge about this period. Blanke and Mühlhahn demonstrate how important the historiography of the CCP and the PRC continues to be, even as the Xi Jinping government continues to rewrite official narratives and follow a more authoritarian approach to alternative discourses and historiographies on the CCP history.

Of late, access to archives in China has become increasingly limited for Chinese and foreign scholars alike. To take but one example, in the well-used Shanghai Municipal Archive, any number of materials on "non-sensitive" subjects that were for years open and readily reproducible have become less available and at best only partially reproducible, and now in many cases are not accessible at all. This partial closing down has been replicated in universities, in which critical discourse on history has become increasingly sensitive and monitored. Unavoidably, not only will these trends change the way scholars can conduct research in China, but also this is going to change the way scholars are able to understand China. Many of the studies in this volume are based on archival materials collected and oral histories conducted when it was more possible to do so. But things are, at present, highly uncertain. We simply don't know when, or even whether, it will be possible for the next generation of young scholars to work with the kinds of material that so many of the authors in this collection have been so fortunate in being able to have used. But we hypothesize that there are usually ways to work around obstacles, insurmountable though they might seem to be. There are collections in such venerable repositories as the Hoover Institution. Archives and collections in libraries or in private hands outside China remain untapped; careful use of gazetteers and *wenshi ziliao* still offers a wealth of concrete information about local histories. Retired scholars who collected materials that were at the time current events but are now in the process of being re-evaluated as history are often willing to pass them on. Those who work on Southeast Asia, Taiwan, Korea, or Japan might well have access to sources that are hiding in plain sight, and the archives of the GDR and other Soviet satellites are, to varying degrees, open to scholars.

We suspect that greater attention to the different scales of history, and to the ways in which these different levels are mutually constitutive, is the way forward. The revolutionary foundational 1950s cannot be understood apart from the Cold War, but at the same time, the very uncompromising nature of the revolutionary transformations of China in the 1950s reinforced the hardening of Cold War boundaries. At the outset of the 1950s, the hardening of those boundaries, China's reasonable fear of invasion from abroad, and a popular wave of mass nationalism made its claims to necessarily rid the country of counterrevolutionaries, landlords, and class enemies plausible. The waves of campaigns in the early 1950s against counterrevolutionaries, landlords, private businesses, holdover officials, and unreconstructed intellectuals simultaneously removed any organized dampener on the CCP and extended the power of the party-state down to the level of the village. At the same time, we suggest that the so-called "Bamboo Curtain" remained porous in surprising ways. China's impact on and engagement with the transnational did not cease in 1949. Indeed different scales of the transnational – from the socialist ecumene, to the region, to the Chinese ethnic diaspora – continued to shape, and be shaped by, revolutionary China in the 1950s.

The ways in which the transnational, the national (from central, to regional, to local), and the micro (family historical, autobiographical) were all recipients of and actors in the same swirl of revolutionary transformation represents one of the most promising avenues in which PRC history can move forward, and we hope that the next generation of scholarship will take on what we have only begun to explore here.

Part I

Revolution and the Transnational

Introduction to Part I

In a very influential and frequently cited article published twenty-five years ago, William Kirby compellingly argued that Chinese history before 1949 was defined and shaped by the nature of its foreign interactions.[1] This would appear to be all the more true of China under Communist rule in the 1950s. If the Guomindang regime styled itself "Nationalist", the CCP was, from its conception, internationalist in premise and in promise. Indeed, when Mao Zedong declared that the Chinese people had finally "stood up" with the establishment of the PRC in 1949, he made it clear that they would not stand alone but would stand by the Union of Soviet Socialist Republics (USSR) and its allies.[2] Stalin and Mao may often have been "uncertain partners,"[3] but the PRC in its formative years would be Moscow's most faithful and self-sacrificing ally, a distinction earned in blood in Korea and by the fact that, unlike the Eastern European "people's democracies," the PRC's allegiance was not bought by force.

The history of the PRC is thus simply incomprehensible without a strongly transnational or global perspective. Its ruling party, the CCP, was the creation of a foreign power and it began its rule of the country under foreign protection. Internally its system of government was deliberately modeled on that of its foreign allies. The consequences of "leaning to one side" were far-reaching and can hardly be exaggerated. China became part of a larger web of co-operative relationships with all the "brother countries" of the socialist bloc. In numerous respects – including city planning, agricultural reform, higher education, labor camps, nationalist policies, economic models, propaganda, and intelligence work – the new state in China was closely modeled on Eastern European and, above

---

[1] William Kirby, "The Internationalization of China," *China Quarterly*, 150 (June 1997): 443–458.
[2] Mao Tse-tung, *Selected Works*, vol. 5 (Peking: Foreign Language Press, 1977), 17.
[3] Sergei N. Goncharov, John W. Lewis, and Xue Litai, *Uncertain Partners: Stalin, Mao and the Korean War* (Stanford: Stanford University Press, 1993).

all, Soviet experiences. The life of the population would be changed profoundly by the transfer of foreign models for social, political, and even cultural transformation.

For China, the Soviet Union and the world of state socialism represented an appealing alternative form of modernity. The socialist model aspired to achieve industrial progress free of the darker aspects of exploitation, inequality, and imperialism that marred Western modernity.

It was also the most obvious choice as the model that offered effective solutions to a wide range of pressing domestic political, economic, and social challenges. In economics as in culture or politics, it was never the aim of the PRC leadership to build "socialism in one country." That phrase summed up the model of Stalinist autarky, when the Soviet Union survived "capitalist encirclement" as the world's only communist country during the interwar years. The PRC would not have to build socialism alone: the "fraternal partnership" with the states of the socialist community, and above all with the Soviet Union, would facilitate and ease integration into the socialist system. The early PRC was a leading actor in the global socialist system. This socialist world stretched from Berlin to Canton and included one-third of the world's population. There can be no doubt that China's links to Eastern bloc countries and the Soviet Union led to the most systematic transfer of knowledge and technology in its modern history.

As the chapters in this section demonstrate, it is indeed impossible to separate the internal from the external when we study this era of China's history. Rather we should aim to systematically connect the processes in China and on the global level. This was in part the result of a unique international configuration. True, the world was divided into two bipolar blocs, but the two blocs were both diverse and extended to several world regions. Hence, like the Western or capitalist bloc, the global socialist system was made of several formally independent and sovereign nation-states, middle powers, and smaller actors. It is therefore insufficient to see the Cold War exclusively through the lens of a bipolar conflict between the two systems. In fact, we need to redirect the interpretive focus from the global, or systemic, Cold War to the multitude of regional, subsystemic, cold wars.

This unique and complex structure, as Susanne Weigelin-Schwiedrzig shows in her contribution, offered China as one actor within the socialist bloc both opportunities and risks. It gave way to a dynamic triangular relationship linking the USA, the USSR, and China that opened up room for maneuvering and manipulation. This offers a new perspective on the bipolarity within the Cold War world. The great powers, such as the Soviet Union, might have believed that they were in control pulling strings across the world. They were indeed able to intervene and exercise considerable influence, but states like the PRC also followed their own agendas and frequently succeeded at their end in pursuing their own national interests. Concentrating on national developments within the socialist camp illuminates the impact of states like the PRC on structural change in the international system throughout the course of the whole global Cold War.

This tension between internationalism and the national re-emerges in the chapter by Matthew Johnson. Johnson focuses on the construction and definition of Chineseness in the early PRC. Despite the fact that the PRC saw itself as part of the socialist world, sharing the same values, aesthetics, and acumen, it also stressed its historical role in the great mission to rejuvenate the Chinese nation and to make China strong and prosperous again. The broader cultural dimensions in the early PRC are profoundly contradictory. On the one hand, the PRC promoted a "shared socialist culture," but it also actively redefined what it meant to be Chinese, especially when speaking to an audience outside China. Socialist China portrayed itself above all as the legitimate heir of the Great State of the Chinese Empire.

One of the areas that the new state concentrated its energies on was sports. Building a healthy and physically fit Chinese nation required taking part in international events and transnational networks that connected competitions, athletes, coaches, and even audiences. The PRC also sent overseas Chinese, even those hailing from capitalist countries, to represent China at international sports events, as long as they promised to win. As Amanda Shuman argues, not only did the very national mission of physical strengthening depend on taking part in the exchanges within the socialist world, but also it required precisely delineating Chinese nationality. And here it is fascinating to note that the PRC applied a historic concept that slowly gained traction during the late nineteenth century in China and was promoted not only by the Qing empire but also by the Nationalist government. In this perspective, Chinese born and raised outside China were considered Chinese nationals when their families could trace their descent back to China. In other words, bloodline, not place of birth or any other category, was used to determine nationality. Within the progressive world of socialism, older prerevolutionary notions of race, ethnicity, and national belonging obviously prevailed.

In many ways, at the center of the socialist bloc was the economy. China became a member of one of what Stalin called "two parallel world markets . . . confronting one another."[4] But how did this socialist

---

[4] Joseph Stalin, *Economic Problems of Socialism in the USSR* (New York: International Publishers, 1952), 26.

world economy work (or not)? To what degree was it genuinely "internationalist," even as it was negotiated by formally sovereign states? Focusing on coal, Anna Belogurova describes the Soviet assistance to China to develop the coal industry. Soviet aid was large, essential, and ambitious, but frequently encountered problems. One of the thorniest issues that came up time and again was the role of Chinese conditions. Soviet engineers and their Chinese counterparts recognized that China lacked some of the necessary conditions for adopting the Soviet model. China's economy was huge, complex, and very diverse. War and civil war had left the economy highly decentralized and regionalized, and different economic areas emerged that were almost autarkic. The Soviet model also rested on assumptions about the energy and transportation sectors that were wholly incompatible with the Chinese realities of the 1950s. China faced bottlenecks in transport, energy, and construction materials that emerged as a consequence of rapid industrialization. By the mid-1950s, many in the bureaucracy had started to realize that the implementation of Eastern European development concepts threatened to overwhelm the economic system. They surmised from their daily work that it would take China a long time to acquire the necessary technical expertise for a planned economy. In Russia there were many more engineers and trained technicians per capita than the PRC education system could produce – it would take decades to close the knowledge gap – yet, without those engineers, mathematicians, technicians, and planners, the planned economy could simply not operate. The idea that China could quickly develop a Soviet-style system had never been realistic given its size, complexity, and uneven development. The attempt to duplicate the Soviet strategies of development in China ran up against significant structural hurdles and created general economic instability. Again, Sino-Soviet co-operation ran up against the contradiction between national circumstances and transnationally transferred assumptions.

The chapters in this part show also that, within the world of socialism, national and international dimensions were difficult to reconcile. This perhaps explains the sudden end in 1960 of the most self-consciously international age of Chinese political, cultural, and economic development. From the perspective of the early 1950s, it would have been difficult to imagine that Chinese co-operation with the Eastern bloc, which had appeared so promising, would founder so quickly, never to be revived. The Sino-Soviet alliance was in some sense preordained by the tutelary role of the USSR in international communism in general and over the CCP in particular. It began with grand dreams and clear blueprints, not just for "red factories" but for the path to a better world of communism.

Perhaps there is one conclusion: that the ambitious, high-spirited, and idealistic alliance of socialist brother states was unlikely, from the start, to fulfill the expectations: not just for joint security and economic development, but for the path to a shared, indeed universal, utopia. More concretely, since the entire system of the socialist world was founded on the presumption of shared political, ideological, and military needs in the creation and defense of international communism, if the contradictions within the socialist political or cultural world could not be reconciled, then everything else was thrown into uncertainty. In this world, too, far removed from that which Marx and Engels had imagined, politics and culture were not simply *Überbau* (superstructure); it was just the reverse.

1 International Relations and China's Position in the Socialist Camp

Susanne Weigelin-Schwiedrzik

This chapter will revisit Sino-Soviet relations and develop a model explaining the structure of state-to-state relations within the socialist camp.[1] It is aimed at contributing to our understanding of the positioning of the PRC within the realm of the socialist camp, and the influence that this positioning had on the global setting of the Cold War. To achieve these aims, I am going to discuss the idea of triangularity in international relations, a topic which is usually disregarded by political science. I will argue that triangularity is a hidden structure within the bipolar structure of the Cold War world. While the bipolarity of the structure helps us to explain the mechanisms of long-term relative stability, triangularity helps us to understand the changes in the system and its eventual collapse.

So far, research into the relationship between the countries of the so-called socialist camp has not been very much the focus of political scientists. There is much research on Sino-Soviet relations, and to some extent we know what was going on between China and Eastern Europe as well as between China and other countries belonging to the socialist camp in Asia and Africa. But to the best of my knowledge, specialists in international relations have refrained from trying to develop a theoretical framework as a model to help us understand the complicated structures inside the socialist camp.

In order to come to terms with the complicated relationships to be observed among the countries belonging to the socialist camp, this chapter will focus on triangularity and thus take a structuralist approach to international relations. This perspective is fundamentally shaped by assumptions stemming from the neorealist approach to Chinese foreign

---

[1] When I use the word "model" here, I am referring to a set of interrelated logical assumptions which cannot be tested empirically. Instead, a model gains in plausibility by its inherent coherence and its capacity to explain complex constellations. Models are reductionist and at the same time work on the basis that actors act rationally. As we all know, this is not always true in the real world. See Alexei D. Voskresenskiĭ, *Russia and China: A Theory of Inter-state Relations* (London: RoutledgeCurzon, 2003), 40.

policy, and thus implicitly rejects recent trends in the research on Chinese foreign policy during the Maoist era which focus on ideological and internal policy issues.[2] However, as this chapter is positioned between political science and history, it will strive to establish a plausible relationship between the structural focus on triangularity and the historical approach to important events in post-World War II PRC history, focusing on developments in the realm of international relations within the socialist camp during the 1950s.[3]

Triangularity as a Theoretical Concept

The concept of triangularity is often regarded by political scientists as vague and theoretically not decisive enough. However, we have to face the fact that triangularity is a common setting in human behavior and a widespread phenomenon in state-to-state relations. Every once in a while, dealing with triangularity becomes a pragmatic necessity, and this is usually when researchers start getting interested. Morgenthau published the first prominent contribution to the debate on triangularity in his famous book *Politics among Nations* in 1948.[4] The next time we encountered scholarly interest in this topic was during the USA–China rapprochement in the 1970s when the *strategic triangle* between the USA, the USSR, and China attracted attention.[5] Since the end of the Cold War, the constellation in Northeast Asia has been looked at in terms of triangularity focusing on the relationship between China, Russia, and Japan.[6] But we also find interest in the changing *strategic triangle* in which, according to Burakov, we should expect the emergence of a new alliance of Russia with China against the USA.[7]

---

[2] For the focus on the relationship between internal policy issues and foreign policy, see Chen Jian, *Mao's China and the Cold War* (Chapel Hill and London: The University of North Carolina Press, 2001); and Chen Jian, "The Chinese Communist Revolution and the World," in Norman Naimark, Silvio Pons, and Sophie Quinn-Judge, eds., *The Cambridge History of Communism* (Cambridge: Cambridge University Press, 2017), vol. 2, 87–11. For the focus on ideology, see Lorenz Lüthi, *The Sino-Soviet Split: Cold War in the Communist World*, Princeton Studies in International History and Politics (Princeton: Princeton University Press, 2008).
[3] Lowell Dittmer, "The Strategic Triangle: An Elementary Game-Theoretical Analysis," *World Politics* 33, no. 4 (July 1981): 485–515, 47.
[4] Hans J. Morgenthau, *Politics among Nations: The Struggle for Power and Peace* (New York: Alfred A. Knopf, 1948).
[5] Dittmer, "The Strategic Triangle."
[6] Lowell Dittmer, "The Sino-Japanese-Russian Triangle," *Journal of Chinese Political Science* 10, no. 1 (April: 2005): 1–21.
[7] Denis Burakov, "The Strategic Triangle in the 21st Century: Implications for Sino-Russian Relations," *Journal of China and International Relations* 1, no. 1 (May 2013): 46–65.

One article which tries to overcome the theoretical vagueness of triangularity was written by Lowell Dittmer in 1981. Dittmer defines the strategic triangle as a "transactional game between three players,"[8] explaining that there are three different ideal types of relationship between the three players: the *ménage à trois* in which all three players collaborate in amity and symmetry with each other; the *romantic triangle* in which the pivot player has friendly relations with two wing players, but the two wing players see each other as enemies; and finally the *stable marriage* relationship, in which two players are friends and both regard the third player as their enemy.[9]

According to Dittmer's typology, the relationship between the USSR and the PRC was one of *stable marriage* between 1949 and 1960,[10] as the two socialist brother countries were close friends and had chosen the USA as their common enemy. However, because the situation was commonly perceived as a bipolar relationship between the USSR and the USA at the time, observers did not recognize the autonomy that the PRC had or was trying to develop in its relationship with the USSR.

During the decade from 1960 to 1969, the *stable marriage* between the USSR and the PRC deteriorated while the relationship between the USA and the USSR changed to détente, without reaching the level of *stable marriage*, however. Dittmer calls this type of relationship an affair.[11] At the same time, relations between the USSR and the USA were improving the PRC and the USSR were competing for leadership within the socialist camp and used ideology as a tool to voice their different claims to power. "By the end of the decade, Chinese foreign policy had moved from an autonomy based on ideological principles to one based on national interest,"[12] and the "Sino-Soviet conflict was transformed from an intra-bloc dispute to an international altercation."[13] This is when the *strategic triangle* came into being. It was the result of the PRC breaking out of the socialist bloc and starting to strive for support among the so-called Third World countries instead.

Under these conditions, the US leadership realized that there was room for using triangularity to approach the PRC and develop a *romantic triangle* based on the principle that "triangular diplomacy must avoid the impression that it is 'using' either of the contenders against the other."[14] Consequently, ideal-type triangularity only came into existence, according to Dittmer, when the PRC left its subordinate position within the socialist bloc and became an independent player.

For Dittmer, triangularity is only of interest in the context of the relationship between the USSR, China, and the USA. It is a new structure

---

[8] Dittmer, "The Strategic Triangle," 485.   [9] Ibid., 489.   [10] Ibid., 491.
[11] Ibid., 493.   [12] Ibid., 496.   [13] Ibid., 497.
[14] Quote from Henry Kissinger, *White House Years* (Boston: Little, Brown and Company, 1979), 65, quoted in ibid., 499.

which emerges as a consequence of the growing Sino-Soviet conflict and the Sino-US rapprochement. He also observes earlier developments inside the socialist camp which made the USA move toward establishing the strategic triangle possible, but he is not interested in a further analysis of intra-bloc relations. However, what we do see from his analysis is a relationship between what is going on inside the socialist bloc (between the USSR and the PRC) and the way the three players of the strategic triangle relate to each other.

Inter-state Relations inside the Socialist Camp

Belkin and Blight published an article on the Cuban crisis ten years later in which they analyze a triangular setting with one of the three players – Cuba – participating as a member of the socialist bloc in the triangle from a position of a client state whose vital interests were hurt by the "patron" state, the USSR. In this paper, the focus of attention is on Cuba suddenly confronted with the USA and the USSR forming an alliance against Cuba's security interests. As a result, "the Cuban leadership felt abandoned by the Soviets, threatened by the United States, and more desperate than ever we knew."[15]

Belkin and Blight draw our attention to the fact that "leaders of third parties experiencing a sense of abandonment and/or loss of control may turn to desperate measures that might seem irrational, even suicidal."[16] As both the USA and the USSR at the time perceived the international situation as bipolar rather than triangular, they did not take the third player's perspective into account. The USA saw Cuba as a *slave state* in the socialist camp, and the USSR regarded its relationship to Cuba as asymmetric to a point where Cuba had no choice but to submit its own interests to those of the USSR.

Belkin and Blight's article is of interest with regard to two important questions. On the one hand, they show that inside the socialist bloc the hierarchy of state-to-state relations was taken for granted both by the USSR as the pivot country and by the USA as the perceived opponent. The USSR urged the members of the socialist bloc to accept its leadership by drawing on structures it had established in the Communist International (COMINTERN). In this context, the interests of the USSR were to be served by all member countries even to the point of harming their own security interests, as we see from the article by Belkin and Blight.

---

[15] Aaron Belkin and James G. Blight, "Triangular Mutual Security: Why the Cuban Missile Crisis Matters in a World beyond the Cold War," *Political Psychology* 12, no. 4 (December 1991): 731.

[16] Ibid., 740.

On the other hand, we see how constellations combining a patron–client relationship within the socialist bloc involve a player outside the bloc, and how this *stable-marriage* situation changes as a result of the client being abandoned by its patron. In this situation, the triangularity does not change from one ideal type to another, as Dittmer suggested, but the positions of the players in the game of *stable marriage* change. This example shows again how intra-bloc relations are related to the overall strategic-triangle relationship between the USSR, China, and the USA.

Both constellations referred to in the article by Belkin and Blight need to be taken into consideration when developing our own model of triangular relations during the Cold War era.

Models of Triangularity Re-visited

Summing up the state of the art, we see three basic constellations of triangularity in inter-state relations. What Dittmer calls a *ménage à trois* is, drawing on geometrical terminology, an equilateral triangle. In this constellation, all players perceive each other as friends but never know whether or not two will unite against the third. Because, in this constellation, the distribution of power among the three tends to be symmetric (which is why we refer to it as an equilateral triangle with all sides the same length), an alliance of two against the third player must always be expected. If this happens, the combined power of two exceeds the power of the third player.

The *romantic triangle* that Dittmer refers to is, geometrically speaking, an obtuse or wide triangle with two of its three sides forming a wide angle and having the same length. This constellation seems to imply the highest degree of stability among the three players as the pivot player has an asymmetrical relationship with the wing players, that is, the pivot player is the most powerful among the three, and the combined power of the two wing players does not exceed the potential of the pivot player.

Finally, Dittmer's *stable marriage* can be symbolized as an acute or narrow triangle. In this constellation, two players form a close relationship (and for that matter a narrow angle) by uniting against the third player as the common opponent. This constellation looks stable but has the potential to provoke the third party to try to wedge the two friends apart. That is why the *narrow-triangle constellation* needs good incentives for the two to stay together, and very often their relationship to each other is a *patron–client relationship* in which patron and client stay together by pursuing their respective interests.[17]

---

[17] Dittmer, "87–112 rategic Triangle," 489–490.

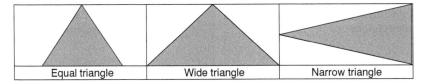

| Equal triangle | Wide triangle | Narrow triangle |

Figure 1.1 Models of triangularity
Source: Illustration by the author

State-to-state relations inside the socialist bloc can also be understood in terms of the three ideal types of triangular setting mentioned above; however, what is not included in these considerations is the fact that inside the socialist bloc state-to-state relations are hierarchical. In order to understand this constellation, we have to add to the models mentioned above (which are two-dimensional; see Figure 1.1) an additional dimension reflecting the hierarchy of intra-bloc relations in the socialist camp.

Bipolarism and Triangularity Combined

Chen Jian claims that China was a competitor for leadership in the socialist camp right from the moment the PRC was founded in 1949. He explains the Sino-Soviet rift as a consequence of the radicalization of CCP internal policies but at the same time analyzes the necessity for radicalization as stemming to a high degree from the aim of taking over leadership among the countries and communist parties of the socialist camp.[18] If China was indeed a competitor for the leadership position, the socialist camp needs to be conceived as a bipolar system with two potential *centers* containing and provoking each other in their striving to eliminate the competitor and take over the leadership position. And if we can show that the socialist camp was indeed structured by two competitors for the pivot position, we can hypothesize that it had a hidden triangular structure just as much as the global Cold War system worked with an explicit bipolar structure combined with an implicit triangular one. While the overall global setting was explicit in its bipolar structure combined with implicit triangularity, the socialist camp had an explicit hierarchical structure and implicit bipolarity combined with triangular relationships (see Figure 1.2).

The PRC and the USSR were in a *narrow triangular* constellation as long as their common enemy was the USA, but at the same time they played the game of *wide triangle* with the USA, that is, they created the

[18] See Chen, *Mao's China and the Cold War*; and Chen, *The Chinese Communist Revolution and the World*, 87–112.

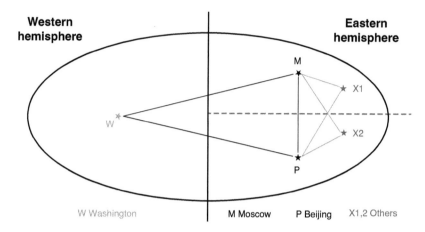

Figure 1.2 Bipolarism and triangularity combined
Source: Ilustration by the author

USA as a pivot and acted as wing players competing with each other. By creating the USA as their pivot, they threatened each other constantly by building a possible alliance with the USA against their former friend.[19] Simultaneously, in order to be able to assure each other of their functioning patron–client relations, they made their enmity vis-à-vis the USA visible to each other as well as to their respective populations.[20]

If this hypothesis can be shown to be true then we can expect other countries in the socialist camp to make use of this constellation. Globally, they regard the PRC and the USSR as equal as they are both part of the strategic triangle with the USA, and inside the socialist camp they recognize Moscow as the center of the international communist movement and thus regard the PRC as a client state in its relation to the USSR. On this basis, they grant the PRC a special position inside the socialist camp which is, in terms of hierarchy, lower than the position of the USSR and higher than their own respective positions. When they opt to unite with the PRC, the USSR's power is contained; when they submit to the USSR, the PRC's power is limited. Consequently, they use the competition between the two centers of the bloc and bargain for all kinds of bonuses that they would not receive without the competition between the USSR

[19] This is more than obvious during the Brezhnev era. See Nancy Bernkopf Tucker, "China as a Factor in the Collapse of the Soviet Empire," *Political Science Quarterly* 110, no. 4 (Winter 1995–1996): 501–518.

[20] For an explanation of internal and external factors, see Voskresenskiĭ, *Russia and China*, 36.

and the PRC.[21] As they regard the USA as their common enemy, however, the aim of this game is not to wedge the two bigger players apart. The game is aimed at ameliorating the conditions for participant client countries and at using the instability of the partnership between the USSR and the PRC only to the extent that it does not break apart.

To sum up, within the binary world of the Cold War, the USSR and the USA needed the third player, the PRC, in order to add an extra deterrent factor and avoid hot wars. As long as the USSR and the PRC cultivated a patron–client relationship against their common enemy, the USA was not only deterred by the USSR's growing nuclear and conventional military capacity, but also had to consider the possibility that the joint power of the USSR and the PRC might exceed its own capacities. When the conflict between the USSR and the PRC gained momentum, the USSR realized that it had to enter a period of détente with the USA because with this move it made the other alternative impossible: the PRC was deprived of the opportunity to align with the USA against the USSR. For the PRC, Khrushchev's policy of "peaceful coexistence" posed a major threat because, with friendly relations between the USSR and the USA, China ran the risk of turning into the common enemy or at least losing its special position in the socialist camp and in the world at large.

When China left the socialist camp, the bipolarity of internal camp structures no longer existed, with the effect that the client countries could not play the game of triangularity anymore and therefore had to squarely confront the USSR or else act in absolute obedience. The so-called Brezhnev doctrine was the logical consequence. In this situation, developing relations with client countries from the Western hemisphere was the only escape and often much needed as economic problems became more and more difficult to solve.[22] The PRC, in contrast, strengthened its position within the strategic triangle and gradually established political and economic relations with the Western hemisphere.

For this theoretical model to strengthen its plausibility, we have to deal with two major questions. First, we have to discuss whether or not there was competition between the PRC and the USSR for leadership in the socialist camp, and, if so, from what time on we can observe this competition. In order to answer this question, we will draw on recently published secondary

---

[21] For a similar view and an important case study, see Nicholas Khoo, *Collateral Damage: Sino-Soviet Rivalry and the Termination of the Sino-Vietnamese Alliance* (New York: Columbia University Press, 2011), 3. Khoo develops his theoretical concept by drawing on the triangular relationship between the Moscow, Peking, and Hanoi; however, he does not seem to be interested in theorizing the triangle as such. See ibid., 11–12.

[22] I am borrowing here Arne Westad's terminology in Odd Arne Westad, *The Cold War: A World History* (London: Penguin Books, 2018).

sources for the period between 1949 and 1953. The second question we need to answer is whether or not client countries within the socialist camp indeed used the PRC as an opportunity to establish triangular constellations within the socialist camp and thus ameliorate their terms of trade in their relationship with the USSR. In order to answer this question, we will use existing research on the Khrushchev era and look at the PRC's reaction to the revolts in Poland and Hungary.

Patron–Client Relations between the USSR and the PRC and the Emergence of Multiple Triangularities in East Asia (1947–1953)

From the beginning of the Civil War in China until Stalin's death, the CCP hoped for Soviet recognition at eye level while Stalin pushed the CCP into a client position in its relationship to Moscow, albeit one more elevated than that of other countries of the socialist bloc. Thus multiple triangularities started evolving in East Asia.

In June 1949, Mao launched his "leaning to one side" approach to foreign policy in a lengthy article called "On the Democratic Dictatorship of the People." He declared that the socialist state to be founded in China needed equality in its relationships with foreign countries and that only by uniting with the Soviet Union and its allies, the people's democratic countries, could China be safe as part of an international united front against US imperialism.[23] This announcement was the logical consequence of decisions which had been taken earlier on.

The 2nd Plenary Session of the 7th Chinese People's Political Consultative Conference (CPPCC) of February 1949 had decided not to seek diplomatic recognition by the USA or any other "capitalist" country.[24] Arguments that, before the summer of 1949, the CCP was still open to diplomatic contacts with the USA are based on reports from the then US ambassador John Leighton Stuart, who was in contact with representatives of the democratic forces close to the CCP at the time. He held the view that China, if it turned communist, should not be rejected by the USA in order to make sure that the CCP would include democratic personalities in its future government.[25] For a certain time, Mao Zedong had, indeed, contemplated the possibility of learning from Yugoslavia's successful attempt to gain support from Great Britain and the USA. However, he had also learned that this policy had aroused Stalin's suspicion and criticism. Rumors reached

---

[23] See Chen, *Mao's China and the Cold War*, 50.   [24] Ibid., 40.   [25] Ibid., 41.

Mao that he was already called "half a Tito" in Moscow.[26] He therefore had to come up with additional demands such as cutting relations with the Guomindang (GMD) as a precondition to diplomatic ties with the USA,[27] and to setting up higher hurdles as a precondition for good relations with countries having a colonial past in China. "In Mao's opinion, America's willingness to change its attitude toward China represented a pass-or-fail test for policymakers in Washington; and he simply did not believe they would pass the test."[28] During the summer of 1949, Mao repeatedly wrote articles explaining that the USA was China's main enemy.

In contrast, relations with the USSR and the Communist Party of the Soviet Union (CPSU) had been developing positively during the Civil War period. From 1947 on, Mao prepared to go to Moscow and show the CCP's inclination to be part of the emerging socialist camp.[29] However, he was not met with enthusiasm from Stalin's side, as Stalin was unsure of his strategy in China and East Asia and doubtful about the "class charac-ter" of the CCP, with its unconventionally strong relations to the peas-antry. Finally, he decided to send Anastas Mikoyan, a CPSU Politburo member, to the CCP headquarters at Xibaipo.[30] During his visit from January 31 to February 7, 1949, Mikoyan gathered information on the CCP's policies and strategies. In his talks with the CCP leadership, he suggested that the CCP should take over responsibility and leadership among the communist organizations in East Asia. He flattered his inter-locutors by explaining to them that the imminent victory of the Chinese revolution was due to Mao Zedong creating a model of resistance against foreign incursion under Communist leadership. It could be successful not only in China but also in other countries suffering from colonialism. Therefore China should act as the center of revolutions in East Asia.[31]

Subsequently, Liu Shaoqi was sent to Moscow to meet Stalin. He left Xibaipo, accompanied by Gao Gang, Wang Jiaxiang, and the Soviet Union's vice minister for transport, Ivan Kovalev, for a secret journey to Russia on June 21, 1949.[32] After arriving in Moscow, Liu Shaoqi

---

[26] Yang Kuisong, *Mao Zedong yu Mosike de enen yuanyuan* (Mao's Gratitude and Resentment towards Moscow) (Nanchang: Jiangxi Renmin Chubanshe, 2008), 257.

[27] Ibid., 181–182.

[28] Ibid., 43. Mao either did not know or deliberately overlooked the fact that the USA and Great Britain had already retreated from the "unequal" treaties during the Cairo confer-ence in which Chiang Kai-shek participated in 1943.

[29] Yang, *Mao Zedong yu Mosike de enen yuanyuan*, 254–262.   [30] Ibid., 44.

[31] Niu Jun, *The Cold War and the Origins of Foreign Relations of the People's Republic of China*, trans. Zhong Jijing (Leiden: Brill, 2018), 82.

[32] See Li Wendong, n.d. "Liu Shaoqi de liuci Mosike zhi hang" (Liu Shaoqi's Six Journeys to Moscow), *Zhongguo gongchandang xinwen* (News of the Communist Party of China), at http://cpc.people.cn/GB/85037/8385148.html, accessed April 4, 2020.

submitted a long report on the situation in China in which he informed Stalin that the CCP was close to victory and would soon be taking over leadership in China. He also explained that the CCP agreed to Stalin's assessment of the general meaning of the Chinese revolution for anticolonialist movements in East Asia. On July 11, Stalin met Liu Shaoqi and his comrades, showing regret for past misunderstandings and support for CCP plans.[33] Stalin was very interested in having China stick to collaboration with the "national bourgeoisie" and in maintaining trade relations with capitalist countries. He assured Liu that the USSR would be the first country diplomatically to recognize the PRC once its founding had been proclaimed. Before leaving the USSR, Liu Shaoqi signed an agreement with Malenkov on a US$300 million loan for Communist China on July 30.

In addition, Liu Shaoqi also talked to the CPSU about the future party-to-party relations. According to Chinese-language secondary sources, he reached an agreement on the two parties' acknowledging each other's merits and forgiving each other's mistakes.[34] It must have been in this context that they also talked about the situation of other communist parties in East Asia. With regard to Japan, Stalin showed his discontent about the policies pursued by the Japanese Communist Party (JCP) and especially its prominent leader and long-held friend of the CCP, Nosaka Sanzō. Stalin wanted the CCP, which during the war had given shelter to Nosaka Sanzō, who had had intensive contacts with Mao Zedong during his sojourn at Yan'an, to exert influence on the JCP so that it would give up its policy of using parliamentary means to come to power. He told Liu Shaoqi again that the CCP should take over responsibility for the revolutions in East Asia.[35] As Russia had entered the Pacific war theatre quite late, Stalin did not want to show too much activity in that region. Leaving it to the CCP to organize the revolution in East Asia seemed a good way to support communist organizations and at the same time not create the

---

[33] Ibid.; also Lüthi, *The Sino-Soviet Split, Cold War in the Communist World*, 30.

[34] Chen Kexin and Xia Yuansheng, *Xiangji kaiguo renwu zhuanlüe* (Biographies of Personalities of the Time of the Founding of the Country of Hunanese Background) (Changsha: Hunan Renmin Chubanshe, 2009).

[35] Liu Jianping, *Zhanhou zhongri guanxi: "Bu zhengchang" lishi de guocheng he jiegou* (Sino-Japanese Relations after the War: The Process and Structure of an "Abnormal" History) (Beijing: Shehui Kexue Wenxian Chubanshe, 2010), 64. Interestingly, the CCP did not criticize the JCP immediately for its *parliamentary* way to socialism. This attitude did not change even after Stalin had published an article straightforwardly criticizing the Japanese comrades. Later, when the ideological conflict between the CCP and the CPSU became more and more articulate, the CCP accused the USSR of revisionism because it propagated the *parliamentary* way to socialism for capitalist countries with parliamentary systems. This was an astonishing turnaround as the CCP had propagated the *parliamentary* way for a long time. See Ibid., 65–70.

impression that the USSR was competing with the USA by expanding its sphere of influence in East Asia.

Immediately after the founding of the PRC, the CCP accepted the task of organizing the Trade Union Conference of the Asian–Oceanic Region in November 1949. Liu Shaoqi gave the opening address and propelled the idea that the Chinese revolution was the model for other colonized and partly colonized countries. In a later speech during the meeting, he declared that China would be willing to support revolutionary movements in Europe. The enthusiasm for the Chinese revolution was widespread among the delegates, and the idea that the center of revolutionary activities would move to Asia was met with much support.

Similar activities had been going on in 1947 already. At the time, the CCP organized a meeting of representatives from communist parties of the Far East (*Yuandong gongchandang daibiao da hui*) in Harbin. The aim of this meeting was to decide whether or not Asia should follow the example of communist parties in Europe which had founded the Information Bureau of the Communist and Workers' Parties (Cominform) in Szklarska Poręba, Poland, on October 5, 1947. On the side of the CCP, former general secretary of the Party Li Lisan acted as Chinese representative meeting delegates from Manchuria, North Korea, Mongolia, Indochina, and Indonesia. At the time Stalin did not support the idea of founding an Asian version of the Cominform. According to Shen Zhihua, he did not want to risk provoking the USA with revolutionary movements which, according to his assessment, did not have a chance of decisive victory soon. Mao also did not show any enthusiasm for this idea. When the issue was raised during Mikoyan's visit to Xibaipo, Mao did not show too much interest in strengthening the relationship with other communist parties in East and Southeast Asia. Nevertheless, Mikoyan proposed the plan to start an Eastern Cominform by collaborating with a small number of communist parties from Japan, North Korea, and Indonesia. At the same time, he made clear that Stalin did not want the CCP to join the already existing European version of the Cominform.[36]

Looking at the situation described above, we see that there were several triangles in the making. On the one hand, the global triangle consisting of the USA, the USSR, and China was being used in the form of an *equilateral triangle* by all three players.[37] Initially, the CCP, as the weakest among

---

[36] Shen Zhihua, "Mao Zedong yu 'Dongfang Qingbaoju'" (Mao and the "Eastern Cominform"), *Ai Sixiang*, at https://m.aisixiang.com/data/48542.html, accessed March 17, 2022.

[37] Interestingly, we observe time and again that China is used as a third player by the USA and the USSR, despite the fact that China was much weaker in every respect.

the three, used the constellation to ameliorate its position by making the two others compete for China's alignment. It tried to gain more support from the USSR by threatening to align with the USA. By allowing its middlemen to contact the US ambassador it showed the USSR that China had an alternative to leaning on the side of the USSR exclusively; and by propelling the idea that the USA was China's main enemy, it made it clear that it wanted a close relationship with the USSR. Once the USSR sent Mikoyan to Xibaipo and showed that it was interested in a *narrow-triangle* constellation with China under Communist rule, the CCP agreed to enter into a patron–client relationship with the USSR and build a *narrow-triangle* relationship against the common enemy, the USA. From this change from *equilateral triangle* to *narrow triangle*, the CCP emerged as the winner, and the USA ended up as the loser.[38]

The USSR regarded the *narrow-triangle* constellation with the CCP and Communist China as both a challenge and an opportunity. The reason for its ambivalent attitude was the CCP's tactic of using the *strategic-triangle* constellation for its own benefit and pushing the USSR into a position where it could only act according to the wishes of the weakest player on the team. By threatening to side with the USA, the CCP generated the result it had been hoping for and forced the USSR into a *narrow-triangle* constellation. Nevertheless, the USSR saw this result also as advantageous in terms of its own interests because, by aligning with the PRC, the USSR expanded its sphere of influence in Asia enormously without having to assume responsibility for the CCP's takeover. However, with the CCP victorious without direct USSR military intervention, Stalin anticipated having a new member on the team which would be as difficult to handle as Tito's Yugoslavia.

It is in this context that yet another triangle came into play. Stalin suggested a certain "division of labor" to the CCP leadership. On the one hand, he downgraded China by forcing it to accept the idea that it had not yet reached socialism but had to undergo preparations by going through a period of "new democracy." On the other hand, he gave China the honor of acting as the center for revolutionary movements in East Asia. This "division of labor," while paying proper respect to the conspicuous size and impact of the PRC within the international communist movement and to the awe and enthusiasm that the victory of the Chinese revolution had generated worldwide, was at the same time

---

[38] See Yang, *Mao Zedong yu Mosike de enen yuanyuan*, 262. "Striving for absolute consensus with the USSR was the issue the Central Committee of the CCP spent most of its time thinking about during the period before the founding of the PRC." (Unless otherwise noted, all translations are my own.)

a clever tool to contain China's ambitions as a major player within the socialist camp. The triangle that was created by Stalin's suggestion was a constellation in which the USSR and China entered into a *wide-triangle* relationship to which we need to add the dimension of hierarchy. Inside the socialist bloc, the USSR was the pivot, and the two wing countries, the PRC and some other member countries of the socialist bloc, were positioned on different levels of the hierarchy. The other communist movements' reaction to this setting is not well known to us as the archival situation is not clear.[39] The Korean War, however, shows that the players in East Asia learned to use the game of triangularity. If we take the example of the Cuban crisis and transfer it to the situation in East Asia before the beginning of the Korean War, we come to realize that here, the weakest player, that is, North Korea, acted as a player conscious of the inherent competition between the USSR and the PRC, using this constellation to push the other actors into the war.[40] For China, the only solution was to join North Korea and forestall the USA, as the perceived major enemy, from drawing close to its border. As the intermediary between North Korea and the USSR, the PRC tried to hold the USSR responsible, but because of Stalin's proclaimed division of labor China was sandwiched into entering the war.

No wonder Mao Zedong was not too enthusiastic about Stalin's division of labor. On the one hand, the fact that the USSR had acknowledged the general meaning of what the CCP regarded as Mao Zedong Thought elevated the Chinese communist movement to a level of recognition it had long hoped for. On the other hand, the center position for East Asia put a heavy burden on the shoulders of the young People's Republic. The Korean War was the first test to this constellation, and the CCP had to give up plans to "liberate" Taiwan in order to fulfil its duty as the center of the revolution in East Asia. As we know today, this was a major sacrifice with long-term consequences. In addition, the fact that Stalin did not "allow" the CCP to become a member of the European-based Cominform indicated to Mao that Stalin was dividing the socialist camp into a European and an Asian part, refusing to grant equality to China and to treat the CCP at eye level.

Competing for Leadership (1954–1964)

With Stalin's death, the whole socialist camp moved into a period of reshuffling relationships between the respective countries and the leadership in Moscow. In contrast to the times when Stalin was telling

---

[39] Ibid.   [40] Belkin and Blight: "Triangular Mutual Security."

everybody what was right and wrong, Khrushchev neither had the standing nor the stature to convince or coerce the member states of the socialist bloc to obedience.[41] He had to retrench a more collective leadership style at home and in relation to the other member countries of the socialist camp. As a consequence of the leadership crisis in the USSR, the situation in Eastern Europe did not generate the kind of regime consolidation that Stalin had expected to take place and instead led to unrest, especially in Poland and Hungary. It was under these conditions that Khrushchev needed China, and China had the chance to compete with the USSR for leadership in the socialist camp.

The first years after Stalin's death saw a deepening of collaboration between the Soviet Union and China. Soviet foreign policy tried to strengthen the relationship to China and to solve the problems generated by Stalin's tendency to push the PRC into a minor position. Instead, Khrushchev wanted to re-establish China as a world power. All rights which the Soviet Union had been claiming in Manchuria were returned to the PRC, and the Soviet military base in Port Arthur (Dalian) was handed over to the Chinese side. China received support in developing its own nuclear program,[42] Khrushchev agreed to deploy military personnel to China, and more than 10,000 Chinese military staff were undergoing training in the Soviet Union.[43]

In 1954, Khrushchev visited China and participated in the festivities to commemorate the founding of the PRC five years earlier. He signed agreements that elevated support for industrialization in China to the level of 7 percent of Soviet national revenue.[44] During the short period of two years from 1954 to 1956, Khrushchev consulted on all important foreign-policy issues with the CCP leadership and received in exchange support from the CCP on important issues concerning the inner fabric of the socialist bloc, such as the founding of the Warsaw Pact.[45] They collaborated closely when convincing the Vietnamese comrades that they had to accept the division of their country. The question that the two countries could not agree upon, however, was whether their future relationship to the USA should follow the *equal-triangle* model of amity among the three or the *narrow-triangle* model of two friends against one enemy. Taiwan played the decisive role in this development.

[41] Yang, *Mao Zedong yu Mosike de enen yuanyuan*, 379.
[42] Vladislav M. Zubok, *A Failed Empire: The Soviet Union in the Cold War from Stalin to Gorbachev* (Chapel Hill: University of North Carolina Press, 2009), 110–111.
[43] Westad, *The Cold War: A World History*, 237–239.
[44] This is a figure given by Zubok, *A Failed Empire*, 111; Westad, *The Cold War: A World History*, 237, reports that during the years from 1946 to 1960, Soviet aid to China amounted to US$25 billion (according to current prices).
[45] Chen, *Mao's China and the Cold War*, 62.

On his way back from the Geneva conference, Zhou Enlai made a statement revealing that the end of the First Vietnam War would make it possible for other issues in East Asia to be settled. When he reached Moscow on his way back to Beijing, he had received orders from the CCP Politburo to brief the Soviet leadership on China's intention to bring the Taiwan issue to a close soon. On July 26, 1954, two People's Liberation Army (PLA) airplanes had been taken down by the US Army near Hainan Island, and the CCP leadership decided it had to attend to the Taiwan issue immediately. Zhou Enlai "told them that the United States was instigating new conflicts in East Asia and this time directly against China ... To fight against US instigations, the CCP Central Committee would propose 'liberating Taiwan' to prevent the United States and Taiwan from signing the treaty."[46] According to Zubok's account, the USSR agreed to provide military support to China despite the fact that it assessed its military capacities in a direct confrontation with the USA as minor and the danger of a nuclear attack on the USSR as imminent.[47] While the PLA bombarded Quemoy Island the USA–ROC (Republic of China) talks on a military alliance gained momentum, and the PLA had to fulfill the duty of seizing the exterior islands near Zhejiang Province in order to avoid their being included in the USA–Taiwan treaty. Consequently, tensions across the Taiwan Strait were rising; however, diplomatic contacts with the USA which had first started during the Geneva conference facilitated by the USSR's foreign minister, Molotov, were still regarded as possible by both sides. The USSR even offered to raise the Taiwan Strait issue during a summit meeting with the USA, Great Britain, and France in early 1955. Its aim was to use the military pressure the PLA had built up to enter into diplomatic talks in order to avoid a military takeover of Taiwan and a possible confrontation with the USA.[48]

After the Geneva conference and before the Bandung conference, the situation in East Asia was of high concern, and the collaboration between the USSR and the PRC seemed to function very well. The USSR supported the agenda of the PRC and avoided a direct military clash with the USA. It used the PRC to contain the USA and used the USA to contain the PRC. "The 1954–55 period shined as the golden age of the Sino-Soviet alliance."[49] The patron–client relationship between the two biggest communist parties and their respective countries had finally generated the kind of equality Mao had so long hoped for.

[46] Niu, *The Cold War and the Origins of Foreign Relations*, 261.
[47] Zubok, *A Failed Empire*, 111.
[48] Niu, *The Cold War and the Origins of Foreign Relations*, 269–270.
[49] Zubok, *A Failed Empire*, 62.

The year 1956 painted a totally different picture. With Khrushchev's pressing ahead and criticizing Stalin during the 20th Party Congress of the CPSU without prior notice to the international delegates, the situation changed dramatically. The Central Committee of the Chinese Communist Party (CCCCP) reacted with deep concern, fearing that Khrushchev's criticism might hurt the consolidation process in the PRC. It saw its authority and legitimacy weakened by Khrushchev's de-Stalinization and anticipated that "class enemies" would make use of the situation to attack the CCP. Nevertheless, Mao Zedong also voiced his grievances about Stalin. When he met the then Soviet ambassador in Beijing, he talked to him for three hours, explaining all the mistakes Stalin had made in forcing the CCP to submit to his will. Especially did he articulate his concerns about the lack of equality in the relations between the CCP and the CPSU. In this context, Mao also criticized the Soviet Union's tendency toward "great-nation chauvinism" and the CPSU's interference in the internal affairs of other communist parties. While the USSR and the PRC had issued a joint statement during the Geneva conference in October 1954, declaring that the "Five Principles of Peaceful Coexistence" formed the basis of their relationships to countries in the Afro-Asian world, "Zhou Enlai, with Mao's authority, [now] sponsored the same principles in Eastern Europe in the hope of ameliorating pent-up post-Stalinist nationalist tensions that were threatening the future of socialism in that region."[50] As Deng Xiaoping said in revisiting the Sino-Soviet rift many years later, "The basic problem was that the Chinese were not treated as equals and felt humiliated."[51]

Khrushchev realized immediately that times had changed fundamentally when 100,000 people took to the streets in Warsaw in June of 1956. The protesters demanded a better life with lower quotas to fulfill and more consumer products on the market, as well as the right to form their own organizations. They were brutally repressed by the Polish Army but continued to fight until the leadership of the Polish communists split and elected Władysław Gomułka as their reform-oriented leader. The protests spread to the whole country, demanding religious freedom, free elections, and the retreat of the Soviet Army. In response, the Soviet Army was put on alert. Gomułka finally rescued the situation by allowing for a number of reforms while sticking to membership of the Warsaw Pact.[52]

Interestingly, Mao's first reaction to the situation in Poland was to relate it to Stalin's "great-nation chauvinism." On October 19, 1956,

---

[50] Ronald C. Keith, *Deng Xiaoping and China's Foreign Policy* (London: Taylor & Francis Group, 2018), 172.
[51] Deng Xiaoping quoted in ibid., 175.
[52] Westad, *The Cold War: A World History*, 200–201.

the then Soviet ambassador informed Liu Shaoqi that Poland might leave the socialist bloc and that the CPSU would send a high-ranking delegation under the leadership of Khrushchev to Warsaw. Simultaneously, reports were received informing the Chinese leadership about the deployment of Soviet troops at the Eastern and Western borders of Poland. During a Politburo meeting the next day, Mao is reported to have said,

When the son fails to obey, the rude father picks up a stick to beat him, when a socialist power uses military forces to intervene in the internal affairs of a neighboring socialist country, this is not only a violation of the basic principles of international relations; this is also a violation of the principles governing the relations between socialist countries. This is serious big-power chauvinism, which should not be allowed by any circumstances.[53]

Mao's assessment of the situation and his threat of an open protest against a possible invasion of Poland by Soviet troops met with unanimous support by the CCP leadership. The Soviet ambassador was informed immediately.

Subsequently, the CPSU asked the CCP to send a delegation to Moscow. In response, Liu Shaoqi and Deng Xiaoping, together with other high-ranking members of the Party leadership, were sent to Moscow. They were instructed never to participate in discussions between the Polish and the Soviet sides, but only to speak to them in a bilateral setting.[54] Their way of handling the situation was welcomed by the parties from Eastern Europe, which is why the CCP delegation was asked by Khrushchev to help dealing with the Polish comrades.

While the situation in Poland was calming down without Soviet intervention, the protests in Hungary were becoming more and more articulate. During a meeting of the CPSU Presidium on October 24, 1956, Liu Shaoqi was asked to give his view on the situation both in Poland and in Hungary. He answered by stressing that both unrests were a logical consequence of great-power chauvinism, which had not yet been totally eradicated from the relationships between Moscow and the other countries of the socialist camp. However, he rejected the so-called "multi-centrality thesis" propelled by the leader of the Communist Party of Italy, Palmiro Togliatti, and stressed, "The center can only be the Soviet Union."[55]

On October 29, 1956, Liu Shaoqi and Deng Xiaoping met with Khrushchev, Molotov, and Bulganin again. Liu conveyed a message which Mao had passed on to him. He explained that Moscow should abstain from interfering in the economic, political, and military situation

---

[53] Mao Zedong quoted in Chen, *Mao's China and the Cold War*, 147.   [54] Ibid., 150.
[55] Liu Shaoqi quoted in ibid., 153.

in the Eastern European countries and allow them to construct socialism according to their own necessities. Again, he referred to the "Five Principles of Peaceful Coexistence" and argued that they should be regarded as guiding principles for the relationships between the members of the socialist camp. The meeting lasted all through the night, and in the morning of October 30 an agreement was signed based on the ideas Liu had proposed. The same day, the Soviet government issued a "declaration on developing and enhancing the friendship and co-operation between the Soviet Union and other Socialist countries."[56]

At the end of October 1956, 200,000 people demonstrated in the streets of Budapest asking for an end to Soviet occupation and demanding civil rights. When the number of protesters had grown to 2 million a statue of Stalin was taken down, and the building of the State Broadcasting Service was occupied. Khrushchev did not dare to take a decision single-handed and summoned the leaders of all Eastern European communist parties to Moscow. When the party secretary of the Hungarian Party, Ernő Gerő, asked for the support of the Soviet Army, the decision was taken collectively to have the Soviet Army cross the border.[57] Nevertheless, the protest still did not die down and instead became increasingly violent. Khrushchev finally decided to use the army massively and suppress the rebellion. He knew that leaders from all communist countries, including China, were backing his decision.[58] "Mao gave priority to bloc unity and claimed that 'all other countries in the socialist camp have learned a lesson'. He appeared to forget the domestic and international problems associated with the 'export of revolution'."[59]

Looking at the situation described above from the point of view of triangularity, we realize how Khrushchev was hoping to elevate the global status of China to the level of world power so that China could strengthen the strategic triangle with the USSR and the USA. According to the USSR's assessment, its military and nuclear capacities were still lagging behind those of the USA and needed to be supported by the PRC. From Khrushchev's perspective, there was no contradiction between going for détente with the USA and strengthening China. Instead, he had decided to establish an *equilateral-triangle* relationship and for that *equilateral triangle* to function he needed a more powerful PRC to enter the game.

In addition, Khrushchev needed the CCP to handle the difficult situation with other member states of the socialist bloc. That is why he had to

---

[56] Ibid., 155.   [57] Ibid., 229.   [58] Ibid., 231.
[59] Mao Zedong quoted in Keith, *Deng Xiaoping and China's Foreign Policy*, 174.

solve the equality problem and agree to the suggestions made by the CCP. When the other communist parties in the socialist bloc realized that the CCP pushed for more equality, they were open to aligning with the PRC in order to force the USSR into a more benevolent attitude toward its allies. The more they opted for this strategy, the more the CCP and the PRC gained in standing, authority, and power.

However, the CCP leadership, while feeling flattered by the new attitude Khrushchev displayed, did not agree to enter into an *equilateral-triangle* relationship with the USA unless the Taiwan problem were solved. The reason why Khrushchev had to agree to supporting the PRC during the Taiwan crisis of 1954–1955 is simple. He had to convince the PRC that his inclination toward "peaceful coexistence" with the USA would not inhibit the PRC from reaching its aim of "liberating" Taiwan. He knew that the USA could only be talked into "peaceful coexistence" if the USSR and China united and established a "balance of power" in which the combined power of the two equaled the power of the USA. But the PRC wanted to preserve the *narrow-triangle* situation of friendly relations between the USSR and China against the common enemy, the USA. Only in this constellation could the PRC count on the USSR backing its moves toward "liberating" Taiwan. The USSR could not but support China's claim on Taiwan while containing the Chinese military from taking over Taiwan by military means.

Liu Shaoqi's insistence that Moscow should be the center of the socialist bloc was his tribute to the USSR. His precondition, however, was that China expected Moscow to get rid of its great-power chauvinism. Beijing spoke on its own and on behalf of the client states in the socialist bloc with the aim of ameliorating the position of the minor players. By strengthening the position of the minor players, Beijing enhanced its own position in the socialist bloc. At the same time, it used Moscow's wish to establish an *equilateral triangle* between the USSR, China, and the USA to elevate its own global position, and finally it intended to push Moscow into a *narrow-triangle* relationship against the USA in order to come to a solution of the Taiwan problem as soon as possible.

In contrast to Chen Jian, who argues that in this situation China was already claiming to be the center of the socialist bloc,[60] I would argue that the PRC leadership realistically assessed the situation and knew that militarily it did not possess the capacity to take over Taiwan without the support of the USSR . In order to compel the USSR to support China's Taiwan plans it made use of the opportunity of the USSR's enormous trouble in Eastern Europe to gain leverage inside the socialist bloc and to

[60] Chen, *Mao's China and the Cold War*, 148, 168.

weaken the leading role of the Soviet Union. To claim leadership, however, would have been disadvantageous as this would have meant insulting the patron and consequently losing Soviet military and economic support. At this point, China was not yet ready for this step.

Conclusion

The idea of hidden triangularity inside the bipolar system of the Cold War generated plausible explanations with regard to the decisions taken by the USSR and China in their relations with the USA and with members of the socialist camp. Concerning the PRC's position inside the socialist camp, we have been able to show that the global strategic triangle was used by the CCP to convince the USSR to accept the emerging PRC as a client in a *narrow-triangle* constellation against the USA. The USSR accepted this idea, but as long as Stalin was still alive China was held in a minor position. In exchange, China was elevated to a higher level within the hierarchy of countries belonging to the Eastern hemisphere by handing over to it the task of acting as *center* for East Asian revolutionary movements. This elevation was simultaneously a downgrading. China was put into one category together with other anticolonial revolutionary movements which could not move directly on to socialism but needed to pass through a transitional period of "new democracy" first. Simultaneously, Stalin made China accountable for these movements to avoid repercussions from the USA for expanding the USSR's sphere of influence in East Asia.

Mao Zedong and the CCP voiced their disagreement with this position in the socialist camp openly only after Stalin had died. They used the relative weakness of Khrushchev to enhance their standing inside the socialist camp, and Khrushchev was willing to collaborate as he was heading for an *equilateral-triangle* situation of détente with the USA, for which the USSR needed the PRC to be recognized as a world power. The uprisings in Poland and Hungary saw the CCP actively involved in conflict resolution with Eastern European countries striving for the support of the PRC against what was called the great-power chauvinism of the USSR at the time. The *wide-triangle* constellation with the USSR as the undisputed pivot in a strictly hierarchical relation with all other socialist countries could no longer be upheld. The combined power of the PRC and other socialist countries threatened to outperform the USSR. This is how Khrushchev realized that he had to get rid of China. The different constellations analyzed in this chapter show how our theoretical assumption of bipolar and triangular structures coexisting at both the global and the regional levels can help to clarify complicated decision-making processes and their political outcomes.

While Dittmer, as many other authors, does not give an explanation of why the PRC was accepted in the strategic triangle despite the fact that, in terms of economic and military capacity, it was inferior to the USSR and the USA, the model of implicit triangularity in explicit bipolarity helps to identify the need for a third player, especially on the side of the USSR. The USSR invested in China's economic development, building up its nuclear capacity and training its military. It did everything it could afford to make China rise to world power status as quickly as possible. The aim of its strategy was to reach détente with the USA and to slow down the arms race between the two superpowers in order to be able to develop its economy. The USA overlooked the importance of China during the early 1950s, as getting China involved was of no advantage to the USA during this period. The PRC, in contrast, was conscious of the implications of the strategic triangle. It did not follow Khrushchev's strategy, however, as détente with the USA seemed unfeasible to the PRC as long as the Taiwan issue was not resolved.

The PRC very rapidly moved on from a client position of inferiority to that of a competitor for a leadership position in the socialist camp. The fact that the Soviet Union had been weakened after Stalin's death, and that Khrushchev's move to de-Stalinization had brought turmoil to the socialist camp, provided a window of opportunity for the PRC to increase its leverage within the socialist camp. Multiple crises over the Taiwan Strait showed, however, that the PRC needed the USSR to deter the USA from interfering in the relationship across the Taiwan Strait. Because of this dependence on the support of the USSR, the PRC found itself in a vulnerable position. It was not able to pursue the so-called liberation of Taiwan as this move would have been to the detriment of the USSR's seeking détente with the USA.

The CCP eventually decided to leave the socialist camp. Only by asserting itself as an independent player in the game of strategic triangle could the PRC escape from being contained by the USSR in its moves toward Taiwan. When it left the socialist camp, the bipolar constellation within the socialist bloc dissolved. In order to benefit from triangularity, the client countries of the Eastern hemisphere could not but seek support from a third player outside the bloc. The loser of this game would turn out to be the USSR; the winners were both China and the USA.

2   Sino–Soviet Anxiety
Science and Chinese Conditions in the PRC Coal Industry (1949–1965)

Anna Belogurova[*]

Coal was not only a fuel for industrialization during the twentieth century, but also a projection of modernity. As such, problems in the Chinese coal industry in the 1950s, such as the low proportion of coal mined by open-cast methods and issues with ventilation and the extraction of gas, persisted into the 2010s.[1] In Mao's China, where coal was the main source of heating, fuel, and electricity, its shortage limited industrialization and economic growth.[2] Under the conditions of a Western embargo, the adoption of Soviet mining technology in accordance with the Sino-Soviet Treaty of Friendship, Alliance, and Mutual Assistance (1950) was the only choice when the Chinese coal mining industry was predominantly manual and needed mechanization to increase its output.[3]

This chapter provides new insights into China's position in the Eastern bloc and vis-à-vis the Soviet Union by showing that "self-reliance" did not preclude the PRC from expanding contacts with the Western world, in both trade and technology transfers, wrapping up this co-operation in socialist ecumene. The Soviet technology did not work as intended, and, as in other industries,[4] the technology that worked was phased out because Chinese mining personnel had already been trained by the Soviets.[5] While Soviet and Eastern bloc countries felt anxiety over the

[*] I thank Tim Wright for his feedback, as well as the editors of this volume for their suggestions. I gratefully acknowledge the funding of Deutsche Forschungsgemeinschaft for this project. I thank Diana Nikolaevna Savelieva for introducing the sources on Soviet visits to Chinese universities to me and Xue Yi and Zhang Jiucheng for help identifying and accessing some sources, as well as Mechthild Leutner and Ouyang Zhesheng for support.
[1] I thank Tim Wright for this point.
[2] Elspeth Thomson, *The Chinese Coal Industry: An Economic History* (London: RoutledgeCurzon, 2003),1; Christopher Howe, *China's Economy: A Basic Guide* (London: Granada, 1980), 107.
[3] Eric Hillis Carlsen, "Soviet Aid and the Development of Communist China's Coal Industry, 1949–1960" (PhD diss., Cornell University, 1969), 169.
[4] Lorenz M. Lüthi, "Sino-Soviet Relations during the Mao Years, 1949–1969," in Thomas P. Bernstein and Li Hua-Yu, eds., *China Learns from the Soviet Union, 1949– Present* (Lanham: Rowman & Littlefield, 2010), 27–59, esp. 44.
[5] Carlsen, "Soviet Aid and the Development of Communist China's Coal Industry," 15.

nonreciprocal exchange with China, the Soviets nonetheless were eager to adapt Soviet technology to Chinese geological and economic conditions and willing to go on with the co-operation. Yet the PRC turned to the West for technology in the coal industry. This confounds our understanding of this period as one of deep ideological hostility on the part of the PRC party-state toward the capitalist West, showing instead that in international trade and co-operation, the priority was not ideology but economic development.

This chapter examines suggestions from 1958 to 1959 for Sino-Soviet co-operation in science and technology in the coal industry, which were submitted to the Soviets for feedback in 1957 with the twelve-year PRC science and technology development plan (1956–1967) and Soviet responses to that, as well as reports about Soviet coal specialists' visits to China in 1952 and 1965. The documents are held in the Russian National Archive of Modern History (Rossiiskii gosudarstvennyi arkhiv noveishei istorii – RGANI) and the Russian National Archive of Economics (Rossiiskii gosudarstvenniy arkhiv ekonomiki – RGAE). Unprecedented in scale for China, the plan aimed to allow the PRC to catch up with "world levels" in science and to speed up national development. Coming at a time when Mao had rejected the Soviet model, the intentions of the plan were nonetheless to attract more Soviet assistance, including nuclear technology.[6] The PRC's responses to Soviet policy advice are quoted in Soviet texts, and the PRC's positions are gathered from Chinese publications.

The Soviet and Chinese documents examined in this chapter reveal a genuine sense of fraternal co-operation but different managerial cultures within the socialist ecumene, with not only different expectations but very different ways of doing things – which overlaid very different resource bases. Sino-Soviet co-operation in the coal industry ended because, while both sides wanted "adaptation to local conditions" (as in every technology transfer),[7] each understood this differently in practice. The Soviets promoted a feasible introduction of world state-of-the-art technology in accordance with the geological conditions of each mine, but the Chinese wanted both state-of-the-art technology and the application of human labor to overcome all difficulties. By 1958, this notion was in full swing, touted also as a solution to the unemployment problem in

---

[6] Zuoyue Wang, "The Chinese Developmental State during the Cold War: The Making of the 1956 Twelve-Year Science and Technology Plan," *History and Technology* 31, no. 3 (2015): 180–205.

[7] Christopher Howe, "Introduction," in Charles Feinstein and Christopher Howe, eds., *Chinese Technology Transfer in the 1990s* (Cheltenham: Edward Elgar Publishing, 1997), esp. 2–6.

China. These different ways of doing things in the coal industry first became obvious in the mid-1950s, when both Soviet technology and the Soviet model did not work as planned in China.

Soviet Aid in the PRC's Coal Industry

Foreign involvement in China's mining industry was nothing new. From the early twentieth century, many coal mines were operated by foreign interests, including Russian.[8] In the post-1949 period, Japanese technical staff,[9] along with advisers from the Soviet Union and "newly democratic countries,"[10] worked in the Chinese coal industry. Much of the scarce Japanese, American, and British mining hardware in China had been destroyed by the Civil War; what remained had been removed by the Soviets from the former occupied Japanese territories in northeast China. In the early 1950s, the PRC's coal industry became dependent on received Soviet aid.[11] Of the "156 projects" launched with Soviet aid during the first five-year plan (FYP) (1953–1957), twenty-four were large- and medium-sized coal projects. During this period, on average, one new coal mine became operational every ten days.[12] According to PRC sources published in the 2000s, these industrial projects, based on the Soviet model but incorporating features of "socialism with Chinese characteristics," jump-started China's entry into the world market.[13] Across industries and in coal mining,[14] Soviet technology became a stepping-stone for China's "self-reliance" (*zili gengsheng*) policy. Building on the Soviet experience, the PRC created new branches in mining production.[15] Based on the Soviet Union's record of fast postwar

---

[8] Tim Wright, *Coal Mining in China's Economy and Society 1895–1937* (Cambridge: CUP Archive, 1984). On the Fushun coal field see Victor Seow, *Carbon Technocracy: Energy Regimes in Modern East Asia* (Chicago: The University of Chicago Press, 2021).

[9] Amy King, "Reconstructing China: Japanese Technicians and Industrialization in the Early Years of the People's Republic of China," *Modern Asian Studies* 50, no. 1 (2016): 141–174.

[10] Carlsen, "Soviet Aid and the Development of Communist China's Coal Industry," 73.

[11] Ibid., 91, 190.

[12] "Dandai Zhongguo" congshu bianjibu ed., *Dangdai Zhongguo de meitan gongye* (The Contemporary Chinese Coal Industry) (Beijing and Hong Kong: Dangdai Zhongguo chubanshe and Xianggang zuguo chubanshe, 2009), 25–26.

[13] Dong Zhikai and Wu Jiang, *Xin Zhongguo gongyede jiandishi: 156 xiang jianshe yanjiu* (The Cornerstone of the Industry of the New China: 156 Projects) (Guangdong: Jingji chubanshe, 2004).

[14] Zhang Baichun, Yao Fang, Zhang Jiuchun, and Jiang Long, "Sulian jishu xiang Zhongguo de zhuanyi 1949–1966" (Technology Transfer from the Soviesostavn to China: 1949–1966), in *Zhongguo jin xiandai kexue jishu shi yanjiu congshu* (Jinan: Shandong jiaoyu chubanshe, 2004), 407.

[15] Polozhenie v syr'evykh otrasliakh promyshlennosti KNR (The State of the Raw Materials Industry in the PRC), 18 October 1961, RGANI 5/49/260.

economic reconstruction and its successful consolidation of power over society, the CCP adopted Soviet policies and "high Stalinist" methods of stimulating production.[16] The Soviets followed the PRC's decisions in setting goals for the PRC's coal industry. Those were to increase coking coal output for steel production and to build a base for the construction of Chinese machinery for the coal industry so the PRC would be able to fulfill its policy of self-reliance and become independent of imports from the Soviet Union in the future.[17] In May 1950, the Ministry of Natural Resources announced that modern methods of coal mining should substitute for backward ones.[18] More efficient longwall mining was introduced in place of the room-and-pillar method dominant in China; thus the number of mines using longwall mining reportedly increased from 34 percent of all mines in 1949 to 75 percent in 1952.[19] The number of accidents fell. The percentage of mines using exclusively manual labor fell from fifty in 1951 to twenty-two in 1952. Soviet hardware for mechanizing different stages of mining was introduced, as were complex combines performing several operations. The Soviets equipped mines with mechanical cutters, pneumatic picks, and mechanized conveyors, as well as combined cutting, crushing, and loading machines.[20] During the first five-year plan (FYP) of 1953–1957, output increased through intensified use of plants.[21] In 1955, Soviet advisers suggested transferring control of the mines from provincial authorities to a central authority,[22] and stressed planning in science too, proposing central co-ordination of mining research.[23] In 1956, as the full socialization of the economy was

[16] Deborah Kaple, "Agents of Change: Soviet Advisers and High Stalinist Management in China, 1949–1960" *Journal of Cold War Studies* 18, no. 1 (Winter 2016): 5–30.
[17] Carlsen, "Soviet Aid and the Development of Communist China's Coal Industry," 169.
[18] Zhongguo meitan zhi (China Coal Gazetteer), *Zhongguo meitan zhi zuanweiyuanhui* (Beijing: Meitan gongye chubanshe, 1999), 627.
[19] Howe, *China's Economy*, 108; Carlsen, "Soviet Aid and the Development of Communist China's Coal Industry," 56.
[20] Carlsen, "Soviet Aid and the Development of Communist China's Coal Industry," 59, 66–68, 96, 99, 129–130.
[21] Howe, *China's Economy*, Preface, xxxv, xxv.
[22] V. Shkirev, Perspektivy dobychi uglei dlia koksovania v KNR i predlozhenia po obespecheniiu imi chernoi metallurgii v 1957–62–67 gg. (Perspectives of Coking Coal Mining and Supply Suggestions for Black Metallurgy in the PRC 1957–62–67), 1955, RGAE 8225/2/2643/5–32, esp. 30.
[23] Institut gornogo dela Akademii Nauk SSSR (Institute of Mining, Academy of Sciences of the USSR (hereafter IMAS USSR)), Ekspertnoe zakliuchenie po zadache No 11. Razrabotka vysokoproizvoditelnykh sposobov dobychi poleznykh iskopaemykh, sostavlennoi komitetom po planirovaniiu nauki pri gosudarstvennom komitete KNR [hereafter KPNGKKNR]. Po probleme No 1101 Issledovanie novykh, bolee effektivnykh system razrabotki otkrytym sposobom (Expert opinion [hereafter EO] on Task No. 11. Development of Highly Efficient Method of Mining, Prepared by the Science Planning

accomplished, including the nationalization of private mines,[24] the way for the party-state to run small and medium mines was free.

By the mid-1950s, it had become clear that Soviet methods were not applicable or feasible in medium and small Chinese mines, yet the coal shortage prompted the party-state to stimulate the development of such mines. Soviet-funded projects were, as a rule, capital-intensive, as they required complex mechanization for all steps of the mining operation and took years to become operational. However, due to low worker skills and resistance on the part of Chinese engineers, much of this new Soviet equipment was not installed or used. Soviet technology could be introduced only where there were trained technicians and miners to operate, maintain, and repair it. Because of the lack of mechanization, Soviet coal mining technology, sophisticated for the time, could be applied only in big mines. Moreover, in the Soviet system of mine management, the chief engineer, who was most often a Soviet adviser, achieved the de facto first-person role in the mine. This created a sharp conflict with the Chinese collective management mode and fueled Chinese anxieties over Soviet domination.[25]

As these problems with Soviet aid in the Chinese coal industry became increasingly obvious, another problem had emerged by 1956–1957: China's poor agricultural performance meant that it was no longer able to finance imports of Soviet industrial goods through exports of agricultural products.[26] The relatively happy story of co-operation, albeit already not idyllic in the early 1950s, had by the mid-1950s begun to fray and then unravel, undercut by a combination of internal and external factors. One was the aforementioned financing issue. At the same time, Mao rejected significant parts of the Soviet model and turned instead to campaigns of labor mobilization. Following the net receipt of a US-$1.4 billion Soviet loan, after 1955 the PRC's repayments exceeded new loan income. A 60 percent increase in industry investment led to an unplanned tripled number of workers and shortages of consumer goods, including coal. The government called for a 15 to 25 percent reduction in the use of coal for heating and cooking by government offices, the army, and schools.[27] The Soviet Union was unable to provide

Committee at the State Committee of the PRC [hereafter SPCSCPRC]. Moscow 1957. On Problem 1101 "Study of New Effective Systems of Open Mining), RGAE 9480/3/1760/284–342, esp. 289–91.

[24] *Zhongguo meitan zhi* (China Coal Gazetteer), 453.

[25] Carlsen, "Soviet Aid and the Development of Communist China's Coal Industry," 159, 54, 101,67, 196–201.

[26] Howe, *China's Economy*, 94, 134.

[27] Roderick MacFarquhar, *The Origins of the Cultural Revolution: Contradictions among the People, 1956–1957*, vol. 1 (Kuala Lumpur: Oxford University Press, 1974), 198.

considerable medium-term trade credits for the needs of the second FYP, as these credits had instead been diverted to belligerent Hungary and Poland. This led the Soviets to abandon their own sixth FYP. In the words of Roderick MacFarquhar, this "helped the Chinese decide to abandon Soviet-style planning altogether" and made inevitable the mobilization of labor, China's only substantial surplus resource.[28] Co-operation in the coal industry decreased in 1958–1959, and in 1960 all Soviet specialists were withdrawn from China.

Soviet Policy Recommendations in the Chinese Coal Industry: World Science, PRC Goals

Meanwhile, in the 1957 science development plan, Soviet advisers and PRC specialists made suggestions for research to fulfill the needs of the Chinese economy, provide economically effective state-of-the-art technology, and ultimately create a research foundation that would transform science in the PRC into a world-class knowledge production system. Soviet advisers in the PRC's coal industry promoted state-of-the-art technologies and the development of internationally competitive science. Yet the Soviets recommended the introduction of those technologies only where they were economically feasible and suitable to the geological characteristics of specific mines. A lack of detailed geological surveys of each coal deposit and possibly the unwillingness of the PRC to make existing surveys available to the Soviets – since the Chinese specialists themselves criticized their own surveying efforts in 1957[29] – impeded further development and left Soviet specialists anxious about the reciprocity of Sino-Soviet co-operation altogether.

In 1952, Soviet advisers in China discovered that expectations that Chinese coking-coal deposits would be enough to meet steel production needs often depended on hazy estimates (*nedostatochno tochnykh i proverennykh materialakh*) "because of the lack in the country of any kind of coal classification and chemical map of coal deposits [*uglekhimicheskoi karty prognosa uglei*]." The geographic location of coking-coal deposits in the northeast did not correlate with historically developed coal production sites, providing an output of only 30 percent of the

---

[28] MacFarquhar, *The Origins of the Cultural Revolution*, vol. 1, 293, 313–4; Roderick MacFarquhar, *The Origins of the Cultural Revolution, The Great Leap Forward*, vol. 2 (New York: Columbia University Press, 1983), 19.
[29] Carlsen, "Soviet Aid and the Development of Communist China's Coal Industry," 93–4. On pre-1949 geological surveys in China see Wu Shellen Xiao, *Empires of Coal: Fueling China's Entry into the Modern World Order, 1860–1920* (Stanford: Stanford University Press, 2015); Grace Yen Shen, *Unearthing the Nation* (Chicago: The University of Chicago Press, 2014).

required amount of coal, whereas demand was for 80 percent, Soviet engineers explained. Geological explorations to define the quality of coal in various deposits, prepare coking coal to increase output, and construct mines were planned for 1958–1967.[30]

According to Jersild, citing a conversation between Wang Jiaxiang and A. A. Gromyko in 1950, bloc advisers "at times would push their Chinese colleagues to pay more attention to the establishment of a local Chinese foundation for future industrial, technological, and cultural development."[31] Kong Hanbing has pointed out that high adaptability to Chinese conditions and an ability to centrally distribute resources and mobilize the population were the strengths of the Soviet model.[32] Indeed, Soviet advisers in the Chinese coal industry stressed both central distribution and the need to adapt, as well as to achieve international levels of science by connecting international experiences with the needs of the PRC's coal industry.

Georgiy Seliatitskiy, who had discovered coal deposits and then designed a mining system in the Kuznetsk coal deposit to meet the needs of the Soviet wartime economy,[33] was sent to oversee the results of the survey that the USSR had designed for the PRC. He dismissed the results as an insufficient basis for mine design,[34] citing a lack of geological surveys, cadres, technical literature, manuals (especially in design), standardized technical terminology, and systems to determine the lifespan of equipment or how it should be repaired. These problems, along with many others – such as deliveries of equipment without co-ordination with factory needs, resulting in large backlogs of unused equipment; breaches of technical exploitation rules and a lack of basic safety rules; insufficient mine ventilation because of a lack of equipment; and no precautionary measures or accident analysis – all impeded the development of the industry.[35]

---

[30] V. Shkirev, Perspektivy dobychi uglei; Technicheskiy otchet geologa Seliatitskogo G.A., komandirovannogo v KNR, v sostave brigady proektirovschikov MUP–SSSR dlia sbora materialov dlia proektirovania ugolnykh shakht i razreza na S[evero]V[ostoke] KNR. 1952. (Technical Report of Geologist Seliatitski G.A. Dispatched to the PRC in the Brigade of Engineers, Ministry of Coal Industry of the USSR, for Designing Coal Mines in the PRC Northeast, 1952), RGAE 8688/1/123.

[31] Austin Jersild, *The Sino-Soviet Alliance: An International History* (Chapel Hill: University of North Carolina Press, 1959), 215.

[32] Kong Hanbing, "The Transplantation and Entrenchment of the Soviet Economic Model in China," in Bernstein and Li, *China Learns from the Soviet Union*, esp. 154.

[33] "Seliatitskiy Georgiy Aleksandrovich (1918–1987)," Znamenitye novokuznechane (Famous Residents of Novokuznezk), at https://xn–400-eddplucwdhb0e2b.xn–p1ai/per sons/242-seljatitskij.html, accessed March 19, 2022.

[34] Technicheskiy otchet geologa Seliatitskogo G.A. (Technical Report of Geologist Seliatitski G.A.).

[35] V. Shmygol', Otchet o rabote sovetskikh spetsialistov, rabotaiushchikh v ugolnoi pro-myshlennosti KNR za 1953 g. (Report of the Soviet Specialists Working in the PRC Coal Industry in 1953), 20 April 1954, RGAE 8225/2/2591/13–46.

The Soviets warned that information provided by the Chinese side was not enough to determine whether a particular Soviet technology was applicable to Chinese conditions. This affected the work on joint research projects in coal preparation planned for 1956–1960,[36] open and hydraulic methods of coal mining,[37] gas emission control, mine ventilation, and the excavation of coal from explosion-prone mines. Soviet advisers were unsuccessful in their request for a survey report from the PRC's state planning committee on which deposits were suitable for open mining methods.[38]

Soviet consultants stressed the economic effectiveness of technology in Chinese conditions, advising that underground coal gasification, an advanced technology at the time, would be too expensive in the PRC in view of significant technical and economic problems. They suggested instead learning from experiences in other countries, such as the USSR.[39]

---

[36] IMAS USSR, EO on Task No. 11. Razrabotka vysokoproizvoditelnykh sposobov dobychi poleznykh iskopaemykh, sostevlennoi KPNGKKNR. Moskva 1957. On problem 1106 "Issledovanie ventiliatsii rudnikov" (Development of Highly Efficient Method of Mining, Prepared by the SPCSCPRC. Moscow 1957. "Study of Mine Ventilation"), RGAE 9480/3/1760/284–342, esp. 307.

[37] Perechen' problem, dlia uchastia v razrabotke kotorykh SSSR napravliaet v KNR v 1960 godu sovetskikh uchenykh i spetsialistov v naucnuiu komandirovku po priglasheniu kitaiskoi storony vo ispolnenie soglashenia, zaklyuchennogo mezhdu pravitel'stvami SSSR and KNR 18 ianvaria 1958 g. o sovmestnom provedenii vazhneishikh issledovaniy v oblasty nauki i tekhniki i okazanii pomoschi Sovetskim Soyuzom Kitaiu v etoi rabote (hereafter Soglashenie 18.01.1958) (List of Topics for the Design of Which the USSR Sends to the PRC in 1960 Soviet Scientists and Specialists at the Invitation of Chinese Side in Accordance with the Agreement Concluded by the Governments of the USSR and the PRC on 18 January 1958 about Joint Research in the Most Important Fields of Science and Technology and Soviet Aid to China) (hereafter Agreement 18.01.1958), 27.II. 1960, RGAE 9480/3/1760.

[38] Perechen' nauchno-tekhnicheskoi dokumentasii i obraztsov, peredavaemykh KNR SSSR v 1960 g. vo ispolnenie Soglashenia 18.01.1958. (List of Technical Documentation Handed by the PRC to the USSR in 1960 in Accordance with Agreement 18.01.1958), 22 October 1959, RGAE 9480/3/1760/108; Perechen' problem, po kotorym Sovetskiy Soiuz primet v 1960 g. kitaiskikh spetsialistov dlia uchastia v soveschaniiakh i sovmestnoi razrabotke nauchno-tekhnicheskikh problem vo ispolnenie Soglashenia 18.01.1958 (List of Topics on Which the USSR Will Receive in 1960 Chinese Specialists for Participation in Meetings and Co-operation on Scientific and Technical Problems in Accordance with Agreement 18.01.1958), 22 October 1959, RGAE 9480/3/1760/111; Perechen' problem po kotorym organizatsii Sovetskogo Soiuza v 1960 g. vypolniat po pros'be kitaiskoi storony issledovania i ekspertizy po otdelnym rabotam vo ispolnenie Soglashenia 18.01.1958 (List of Topics on Which Soviet Organizations at the Request of the Chinese Side will Carry Out Some Research and Expertise in Accordance with Agreement 18.01.1958), 22 October 1959, RGAE 9480/3/1760/112.

[39] Zakliuchenie po zapiske KPNGKKNR "Komleksnoie toplivo-khimicheskoie ispol'zovanie goriuchikh iskopaemykh (zadacha No 19)" (Assessment of the Report by the SPCSCPRC: Comprehensive Fuel-Chemical Usage of Fossil Fuel (Task No. 19)), 9.X.1957, RGAE 9480/3/1701/1–5.

In approving research topics suggested by PRC scientists, Soviet specialists assessed whether such proposals reflected state-of-the-art technology from the USSR and the USA and their relevance to the PRC's economic development program.[40] The authors of PRC reports on the goals of the coal industry were, in the opinion of the Soviets, familiar with most state-of-the-art technology in the Soviet Union, the USA, Western Europe, the Czech Republic, Poland, and Hungary. The study of such technologies, especially concerning open extraction, was suggested on the basis of Soviet reviews of Soviet and world experiences, as well as directly from Eastern bloc countries such as Romania, the Czech Republic, and Poland when the Soviet experience was insufficient.[41] In 1956, the PRC planned on receiving blueprints for coal preparation equipment from the USSR and adapting them to Chinese needs, with the goal of gaining the skills to develop and produce its own equipment in the second FYP. One recipient was the Institute for the Preparation of Ore and Coal in Changsha.[42] The Soviets also suggested that the PRC study and build

[40] Zakliuchenie po zapiske o zadache no 12 (Conclusion on Problem 12), RGAE 9480/3/1701/262–272 esp. 262; IMAS USSR. EO on task No 11. Razrabotka vysokoproizvoditelnykh sposobov dobychi poleznykh iskopaemykh, sostavlennoi KPNGKKNR. On problem 1101 "Issledovanie novykh, bolee effektivnykh system razrabotki otkrytym sposobom" (Development of Highly Efficient Method of Mining, Prepared by the SPCSCPRC. "Study of New More Effective Systems of Open Mining Method"), Moscow, 1957, RGAE 9480/3/1760/284–342.

[41] Zakliuchenie po zapiske KPNGKKNR: "Komleksnoie toplivo-khimicheskoie ispolzovanie" (Assessment of the Report Produced by the SPCSCPRC: Complex Fuel-Chemical Usage); Zakliuchenie po zapiske o zadache nomer 12, RGAE 9480/3/1701/262–272; SPCSCPRC, Annotatsia k probleme 1206: izuchenie veshchestvennogo sostava rud i produktov obogashchenia (Assessment of the Report on Theme 1206: Study of Content of Ores and Products of Preparation), Beijing, June 1956, RGAE 9480/3/1701/179–190, esp. 181,188; on problem 1104 "Issledovania vysokoproizvoditelnykh system razrabotki s otboikoi rudy" (Study of Highly Efficient System of Mining and Ore Breaking), RGAE 9480/3/1701/301–302; Zakliucheniie po zapiske KPNGKKNR: "Komleksnoie toplivo-khimicheskoie ispolzovanie" (Assessment of the Report Produced by the SPCSCPRC: Complex Fuel-Chemical Usage); Vsesoiuznyi nauchno-issledovatelskiy ugolniy institut. Zakliuchenie po zadache No 11 "Razrabotka vysoko-proizvoditelnykh sposobov dobychi poleznykh iskopaemykh i problemam nomer 1101, 1102, 1103, 1105, 1106, 1107, 1109, 1111–14. (All-Soviet Scientific Research Coal Institute. Assessment of Task No. 11, "Development of Highly Efficient Method of Mining and Questions 1101, 1102, 1103, 1105, 1106, 1107, 1109, 1111–14), September 1957; director of the Coal Institute Dokukin A. to the chairman of Gosudarstvennogo nauchno tekhnicheskogo komiteta soveta ministrov SSSR (National Science and Technology Committee of the Council of Ministers of the USSR), Zakluichenie po proektu osnovnykh polozhenii plana razvitia nauki i tekhniki KNR na 1956–67 gg. (Assessment of Draft Outline of the Plan of the Development of Science and Technology of PRC in 1956–1957), 30 October 1957. EO about technical co-operation with the PRC, report to the Council of Ministers, RGAE 9480/3/1760/345–431.

[42] SPCSCPRC, Annotatsia k probleme 1208 konstruirovanie i vnedrenie novogo vysokoef-fektivnogo oborudovania dlia obogashchenia, aglomeratsii i briketirovania. (Assessment of the Report on Theme 1208: Design and Implementation of New Highly Efficient

on the technology experiences of nonsocialist Sweden, the Netherlands, Germany, Canada, Belgium, Britain, France, and the Ruhr region,[43] especially stressing US technology and the technology that had been effective in the PRC's own experience.[44] The Soviets formed their opinion of the PRC's propositions in accordance with Chinese conditions, such as difficulties in the preparation of most coking coals in China, low mechanization levels, and high output of small-particle-size coal.[45] Thus, while the Chinese wanted the "state of the art," the Soviets were willing to promote only that state-of-the-art technology which they believed was suitable for specific mine conditions. This was a point of tension. The Soviets were, however, much more amenable to promoting another aspect of technology transfer requested by the Chinese: building state-of-the-art research foundations.

Practice-Based Research Models

In line with stated PRC goals, the ultimate goal of Soviet advisers was for the PRC to build a world-level research basis in the coal industry to provide for nationally developed technologies and equipment, which would then be applied in each mine according to its geological conditions. For this, the Soviets promoted what they called a practice-based research model, suggesting that theoretical investigations should be aimed toward swiftly providing solutions to practical problems, as in coal preparation, by developing research questions unique to the PRC's economy.[46] This was, of course, in total alignment with Chinese requests and indeed replicated very closely what Zhou Enlai had long proposed as a set of guidelines for Sino-Soviet co-operation.

Equipment for Preparation, Agglomeration, and Briquetting), Beijing, June 1956, RGAE 9480/3/1701/208–229 esp. 181, 220, 207.

[43] "Problem 1201. Intensifikatsia suschestvuiuschikh i razrabotka novykh, bolee effektivnykh osnovnykh i vspomogatelnkykh protsessov obogaschenia poleznykh iskopaemykh" (Task 1201. Improvement of Existing and Design of New More Effective Main and Auxiliary Processes of Raw-Materials Preparation), RGAE 9480/3/1701/236–238; Problem 1202. "Razrabotka metodov obogaschenia trudnoobogatimykh i bednykh rud i kompleksnogo ispolzovania soputstvuiuischykh metalov pri obogaschenii" (Design of New Methods of Preparation of Poor Ores and Complex Usage of Metals during Ore Preparation), RGAE 9480/3/1701/239–240.

[44] Zakliuchenie po zapiske po zadache 11. Razrabotka vysokoproizvoditel'nykh sposobov dobychi poleznykh iskopaemykh, RGAE 9480/3/1701/347–360, esp.351.

[45] "Problema 1204, Usovershenstvovanie suschestvuiushchikh i razrabotka novykh sposobov ugleobogashchenia s tsel'iu povyshenia kachestva i vykhoda kontsentrata (Task 1204, Improvement of Existing and Design of New Method of Coal Preparation to Improve the Quality and Quantity of Concentrate), 247–250, esp. 247.

[46] Zakliuchenie po zapiske o zadache no 12 (Assessment of the Report on Theme 12), RGAE 9480/3/1701/262–272.

The Soviets promoted a close connection between academic research and industry, that is, producing economic benefits by introducing industrial technology, improving the organization of design and engineering projects, and increasing safety.[47] The Soviets maintained that only by making theoretical conclusions based on industry experience could research institutions quickly develop valuable results which could later be used for building theories. Theoretical research unimportant for solving practical problems was not to be conducted in mining institutions. Advisers promoted research based on industrial experiments in mines, and research labs were established to fulfill the needs of the industry.[48] This is, of course, completely in line with the early to mid-1950s Maoist acceptance of pragmatism, "seeking truth from facts." Indeed, this was the outlook of the government until the mid-1950s.

The goal was to survey PRC and world experience and choose strategies that had been economically effective and useful in the PRC, which would also allow for the forward movement of world science. The Soviets tasked themselves with bringing science in PRC mining to par with world levels.[49] The Soviets also approved Chinese propositions to establish labs in the coal and metallurgy ministries and in the Academy of Science with semi-industrial rather than purely laboratorial equipment,[50] to involve the Faculty of Mining Institutes in research and to expand its institutions, to send Chinese specialists abroad for study, and to involve Soviet

---

[47] "Zakliuchenie po zadache No 11, Razrabotka vysokoproizvoditel'nykh sposobov dobychi poleznykh iskopaiemykh i problemam no 1101, 1102, 1103, 1105, 1106, 1107, 1109, 1111–14" ([All-Soviet Scientific Research Coal Institute,] Assessment of Task No. 11, Development of Highly Efficient Method of Mining and Questions 1101, 1102, 1103, 1105, 1106, 1107, 1109, 1111–14). Dokukin, Zakliuchenie po proiektu osnovnykh polozhenii plana (Assessment of the outline of the Draft of the Plan) Nauchno-issledovatel'skie raboty po naucho-tekhnicheskomu sotrudnichestvu mezhdu SSSR i KNR po zadache no. 11. IMAS USSR. EO on Task No. 11. Razrabotka vysokoproizvoditelnykh sposobov dobychi poleznykh iskopaemykh, sostavlennoi KPNGKKNR. On problem 1106, "Issledovanie ventiliatsii rudnikov" (Development of Highly Efficient Method of Mining, Prepared by the SPCSCPRC. Moscow 1957. "Study of Mine Ventilation"), RGAE 9480/3/1760/284–342, esp. 396, 398.

[48] On problem 1107, "Issledovanie zakonomernosty povedenia rudnichnogo gaza, vnezapnykh vybrosov uglia i gaza, a takzhe primeniaemykh meropriiatiy po bor'be s nimi pri razrabotke ugol'nykh plastov," 312–321, esp. 312, 314.

[49] Zakliuchenie po zadache No 11 "Razrabotka vysokoproizvoditel'nykh sposobov dobychi poleznykh iskopaemyh i problemam no 1101, 1102, 1103, 1105, 1106, 1107, 1109, 1111, 1112, 1113, 1114 (All-Soviet Scientific Research Coal Institute. Assessment of Task No. 11, Development of Highly Efficient Method of Mining and Questions 1101, 1102, 1103, 1105, 1106, 1107, 1109, 1111, 1112, 1113, 1114); Dokukin, Zakliuchenie po proiektu osnovnykh polozhenii plana (Assessment of the Outline of the Draft of the Plan), 358.

[50] Zakliuchenie po zapiske o zadache No 12 (Assessment of the Report on Theme No. 12), RGAE 9480/3/1701/262–272, esp. 270.

specialists in consultations in the PRC. In this, the Soviets followed Zhou Enlai's guidelines for co-operation.[51] The Soviets promoted a nationwide survey of raw-material deposits on the basis of which research institutions would determine what equipment should be prepared for China, grounding solutions in international research results and practical observations.[52] Equipment was to be improved and adapted for conditions in each Chinese mine.[53] Soviet advisers stressed that research should be organized around economic effectiveness.[54]

When commenting on research programs regarding effective extraction methods proposed by PRC research institutions, the Soviets based their assessment on how common the problems were, what would be beneficial for the PRC's economy, and whether those programs were practically applicable and effective. The Soviets suggested using the Chinese experience to improve techniques which had been successfully used in China and were feasible, such as in the Fushun field, and to expand the use of cheap open extraction methods, which were suitable on many sites.[55] The Soviets stressed that they lacked specific information on Chinese deposits and mining and on how specific research topics would benefit the PRC's economy. These topics included comprehensive mechanization, transportation, elimination of dust, labor and research organization, and equipment. The documents pertaining to the twelve-year science plan, which include drafts that the Chinese submitted, contain Soviet review responses proposing the use of only those strategies and technologies which were suitable for Chinese conditions. This necessitated the study of conditions in specific mines before any given technology could be applied there.

---

[51] Wang, "The Chinese Developmental State during the Cold War."
[52] IMAS USSR. EO on Task No. 11. Razrabotka vysokoproizvoditelnykh sposobov dobychi poleznykh iskopaemykh, sostevlennoi KPNGKKNR. On problem 1101 "Issledovanie novykh, bolee effektivnykh system razrabotki otkrytym sposobom" (Development of Highly Efficient Method of Mining, Prepared by the SPCSCPRC. Moscow 1957. "Study of New, More Effective Systems of Open Mining Method"), RGAE 9480/3/760/284 –342, esp. 289–91.
[53] On Problem 1109, 408.
[54] Problema 1203 "Izuchenie i razrabotka teoreticheskikh osnov obogashchenia rud i uglei, osobenno teorii flotatsii" (Study and Design of the Theoretical Basis of the Preparation of Ore and Coal, Especially Flotation Theory), RGAE 9480/3/1701/241–246.
[55] Zakliuchenie po zadache No 11 "Razrabotka vysokoproizvoditelnykh sposobov dobychi poleznykh iskopaemykh i problemam no 1101, 1102, 1103, 1105, 1106, 1107, 1109, 1111, 1112, 1113, 1114" (All-Soviet Scientific Research Coal Institute. Assessment of the task No 11 "Development of highly efficient method of mining and questions 1101, 1102, 1103, 1105, 1106, 1107, 1109, 1111–14"). Dokukin A. Zakliuchenie po proektu osnovnykh polozhenii plana (Assessment of Outline Draft of the Plan), RGAE 9480/3/1760/345–431.

Yet despite all these points of convergence between the Soviets and the Chinese in mining co-operation, the unsuitability of Soviet technology and equipment to geological conditions became the ground on which the Chinese side declined to adopt Soviet advisers. Meanwhile, the PRC began to see co-operation with the Soviet Union as no longer feasible.

The Leap: Chinese Conditions

By 1956–1957, the Soviet Union was no longer able to meet the PRC's expectations for substantial aid, as Sino–Soviet trade had become financially burdensome for the PRC and was no longer profitable. At the same time, Soviet technology and equipment were often not suitable for conditions in China. The PRC increasingly turned to a policy of self-reliance based on the use of what China possessed in abundance: an excess of labor. However, while the Soviet Union and Eastern bloc countries were anxious about the nonreciprocal exchange with China, the Soviets were nonetheless eager to adapt Soviet technology to Chinese geological and economic conditions and were willing to continue the co-operation.

As "local conditions" became crucial for policy making in the PRC, since the Great Leap Forward reflected Mao's determination to solve China's problems using different methods than Soviet ones, the Soviets were preoccupied with forming policy advice for the PRC which would suit "Chinese conditions." Mao's determination to follow a path appropriate for a country that had become the new center of the world revolution, and his conviction that central bureaucrats did not know "local conditions," resulted in the encouragement of local initiatives.[56] In December 1956, the CCCCP stated that the goal for science and technology workers was self-reliance, learning from fraternal countries but combining that learning with the Chinese experience. In 1957, as a result of China's unfulfilled obligations in Sino–Soviet co-operation, the Academy of Science of the USSR voiced concerns about the parity of exchanges with China. To explain the lack of success of the co-operation, they referred to a lack of information about "Chinese conditions," which the PRC did not provide despite Soviet requests.[57]

Co-operation in science declined further due to the lack of financial resources that the PRC was willing to provide in exchange for Soviet advice, technologies, and hardware. In 1957, the Chinese side justified

---

[56] Howe, *China's Economy*, xxvii.
[57] Isabella Goikhman, "Soviet–Chinese Academic Interactions in the 1950s," in Bernstein and Li, *China Learns from the Soviet Union*, esp. 287, 289.

the decrease in the number of topics open for scientific and technical co-operation with a need to save foreign currency. Therefore Chinese specialists could obtain only gratis Soviet documentation.[58] In an effort to save foreign currency, the Beijing Coal Mining Institute (*Beijing meikuang shejiyuan*) introduced guidelines to use Chinese-produced equipment rather than much-needed foreign equipment.[59] This was despite the 1957–1958 equipment shortage, caused by the dilapidation of equipment production plants.[60]

By 1957, not only was Soviet aid no longer needed, but the Soviet experience was not applicable to the geographical and geological conditions in various deposits in China. Indeed, some Soviet equipment was unsuitable for specific "Chinese conditions"; for example, large and immobile tunneling machines led to a loss of hard coal.[61] Conditions in Kuzbass and in the Zhunnan and Kailuan mines were different, so Soviet experience was not always beneficial for China, with its abundant labor resources and limited investment capital. The PRC's leadership, there-fore, pronounced mechanization not beneficial, because thus far it had not increased productivity. The foremost goal was to increase coal output and only then to mechanize mining.[62] Published technical documenta-tion for Soviet equipment included remarks that the experience of recent years had shown that only with comprehensive mechanization, which was not approved, could the introduction of new equipment bring improve-ments. Hence no new equipment was to be adopted.[63] This idea echoes discussions about mechanization in agriculture, given the difference of

---

[58] I.V. Turitsyn, "Nauchno-tekhnicheskie sviazi SSSR i KNR v 1949–1960 gg: po materialam kitaisko-sovetskoi komissii po nauchno-tekhnicheskomu sotrudnichestvu" (Soviet–Chinese Exchanges in Science and Technology in 1949–60: According to the Sino-Soviet Commission on Scientific–Technical Co-operation), in I.V. Turitsyn, ed., *Druzhba naveki: Ocherki istorii sotrudnichestva sovetskogo soiuza I kitaiskoi narodnoi respubliki (1949–1960)* (Friendship Forever: Historical Sketches of Sino-Soviet co-operation (1949–1960)) (Moskva: Nauchno-issledovatel'skiy institut istorii, ekonomiki i prava 2018), esp. 145.

[59] Beijing meikuang shejiyuan zengchan jieyue cuoshi (Beijing Coal Engineering Institute Increases Stringency Measures), *Meitan sheji* 4 (1957): 3–4.

[60] Zhong buzhang zai quanguo meitan gongye ganbu huyi zhunye huiyi shang de jianghua zhaiyao (Deputy Minister Zhong's Address at the All-China Conference of Coal Industry Cadres), *Meitan sheji* 5 (1959): 2–6; Ning Huan and Zhang Xinan, Guanyu meitan gongye biaozhun sheji gongzuo de jidian yijian (Suggestions on the Standardization Work in the Coal Industry), *Meikuang sheji* 8 (1957): 1–2, 4; Henansheng meitangongye touzi wenti de chubu fengxi (Preliminary Analysis of the Coal Industry in Henan), *Tongji gongzuo* 5 (1958): 20–22.

[61] *Zhongguo meitan zhi* (China Coal Gazetteer), 278.

[62] Qiao Fuxiang and Woguo Zhunnan, "Kailuan yu Sulian Kucibasi shuiping fenceng caimei fangfa de bijiao he chubu fenxi" (Preliminary Comparison of the Horizontal Slicing Mining in Zhunan and Kailuan and Kuzbass), *Beijing kuangye xueyuan xuebao* 4 (1957): 3–16.

[63] Fu Yi Lazujin, "Sulian he waiguohuicai gongzuo mian zhijia de xianzhuang ji qi fazhan qianjing" (Current Situation and Perspectives with Soviet and Foreign Surface Scaffolding in Extraction Work), *Beijing kuangye xueyuan xuebao* 1 (1960): 32–64.

proportion of land to labor between China and the Soviet Union, and Mao's statement in 1958 that in a country as big as China, achieving comprehensive mechanization was not possible.[64] In 1959–1960, the Anshan Steel and Iron Plant had to expand production in a way that did not put the government under pressure to provide new equipment.[65] In 1958, the journal *Meikuang sheji* published an overview of the British coal industry, stating that Britain had achieved impressive results in the coal industry by relying on its people – and so too should China.[66]

Soviet advice to utilize new technologies in accordance with conditions in each mine thus did not fit the aspirations of the Great Leap Forward (GLF), the PRC's policy being to rely on manpower productivity while also improving employment rates.[67] To make use of underutilized local resources, such as coal and iron ore, the second FYP planned to expand small-scale industry and increase local self-sufficiency. Similarly, the goal of increasing the output of small-scale mines via better production was to ease the transportation bottleneck through local consumption.[68] However, instead it created a problem of low quality and an imbalance between mining and processing.[69] Small mines were meant also to solve the problem of unemployment, as in Henan, where abundant coal was cheap to mine and thus surface mining would provide enough work for the residents.[70] Coal was therefore central to the development of the countryside and the whole economy because of a growing demand for coal and abundant coal and labor resources.

In the development of the coal industry, as this chapter has shown so far, the PRC leaders over the course of the 1950s adopted some Soviet recommendations and rejected others as they saw fit. Generally, the emphasis on coal was also in tune with the Soviet emphasis on the coal industry as the basis for targets in all other branches of the economy.[71] However, the twelve-year science plan received a blow during the GLF, and basic technological research stopped.[72]

---

[64] MacFarquhar, *The Origins of the Cultural Revolution*, vol. 2, 43–5.

[65] Howe, *China's Economy*, 43.

[66] Yang Zhen, "Yinggu meitan gongye qingkuang jieshao" (The British Coal Industry: An Introduction), *Meitan sheji* 3 (1958): 1–3.

[67] He Bingzhang, "Dali zhengdun laodong zuzhi, buduan tigao laodong shengchanlü, duo kuaihao shengdi fazhan meitan gongye" (Forcefully Consolidate Labour Organizations, Constantly Increase Labour Productivity, Develop the Coal Industry in More Provinces), *Laodong* 15 (1959): 4–9.

[68] Thomson, *The Chinese Coal Industry*, 39,40.

[69] Howe, *China's Economy*, 108.

[70] Henansheng meitan gongye (Preliminary Analysis of the Coal Industry in Henan); Zhang Linzhi, "Meitan gongye mingnian ganshang Yingguo" (The Coal Industry Will Catch Up with England Next Year), *Meitan sheji* 7 (1958): 1–3.

[71] Thomson, *The Chinese Coal Industry*, 37.

[72] *Zhongguo meitan zhi* (China Coal Gazetteer), 570.

The Maoist "mass line," which stressed the application of human labor, was not entirely in conflict with Soviet methods and advice. For example, in 1958, during the technical-revolution movement, students were sent to the mines to study in order to improve research and the quality of mining equipment design.[73] This, as the Soviets advised, made a connection between research and production. After the start of the GLF, the second FYP, which had originally included the development of scientific research and technology in the coal industry, changed. The new goal was to surpass Britain within five years and America within fifteen years, including in technology – that is, by widely employing the most advanced technology in the world.[74] The Soviet Union was not where the PRC could obtain such technology: some of it the Soviet Union was not ready to give, claiming that their equipment was in the experimental stage.[75] Moreover, Soviet specialists advised against the introduction of the most advanced technology of the time, hydraulic mining, although it was emphasized in the PRC's plan. Despite Soviet warnings to investigate its feasibility in Chinese conditions before its introduction, hydraulic mining was adopted indiscriminately during the GLF.[76] The Chinese side wanted the equivalent of being tall and short at the same time. They wanted to go their own way and, through the application of human labor and revolutionary fervor, vastly expand steel production, which meant a greater capacity for coal production. But they also wanted the latest technology, without having to pay for it.

In July 1958, the national conference on the hydraulic method resolved that this method should become the center of a technical revolution in coal mining and produce 60 percent of mined coal. Technological procedures were simplified, and a number of advanced technologies proved impossible to introduce. In the haste of the GLF, when politics were in command, in the face of Soviet advice to the contrary, new hydraulic mines were built fast and equipment was used beyond its capacity.

---

[73] Wu Zimu, Wang Taikui, "Xuexiao he guangkuang banzuo shi kaizhan kexue jishu gongzuo de zhongyao fangfa" (Co-operation between University and Mines Is an Important Way of Developing Science and Technlogy Work), Ge Shouqin, "Tigao jiqi sheji zhiliang de jige wenti" (Several Points Regarding Improvement of Equipment Design), *Beijing kuangye xuexiao xuebao* 2 (1959): 20–23, 24–28.

[74] *Zhongguo meitan zhi* (China Coal Gazetteer), 590, 569.

[75] Zakliuchenie na annotatsiu k probleme no 1113, "Issledovanie usloviy razrabotki na glubine" (Assessment of the Report on Theme 1113), 421–423.

[76] IMAS USSR EO on Problem 11. Razrabotka vysokoproizvoditelnykh sposobov dobychi poleznykh iskopaemykh, sostevlennoi KPNGKKNR. Moskva 1957. On problem 1101 "Issledovanie novykh, bolee effektivnykh system razrabotki otkrytym sposobom" (Development of Highly Efficient Method of Mining, Prepared by the SPCSCPRC. Moscow 1957. "Study of New, More Effective Systems of the Open Mining Method"), RGAE 9480/3/1760/284–342, esp.289–91; on problem 1103, "Izuchenie podzemnoi dobychi uglia gidravlicheskim sposobom" (Study of Underground Hydraulic Mining), 298.

Damage ensued, and production dropped. In 1960, because of the failure of newly introduced technologies, the Chinese authorities in the coal mining sector reintroduced traditional mining, abolished regulatory systems and the position of the chief engineer, and seriously disrupted the process of production.[77] Yet during the GLF, output increased from new plants constructed with Soviet assistance.[78]

As late as 1958, co-operation, albeit reduced, was occurring. Although the Soviets approved the Chinese twelve-year plan of research with the stipulation that the required information regarding "Chinese conditions" would need to be provided,[79] in 1958 the plan for a specialist exchange was not fulfilled by either side,[80] and no joint research or equipment supply was planned. However, specialist and student exchanges continued somewhat, and the Soviets passed along half the number of planned handover blueprints for mining and road construction equipment.[81] The PRC provided some reports on geological conditions required by the Soviets, but these were not sufficient for the Soviets to provide further advice. Despite declining Sino-Soviet relations, the PRC provided a co-operation plan for 1959, which was approved by the Soviets.[82] In 1958, the PRC had also passed on to the USSR blueprints for melting furnaces as well as equipment that would produce quick explosions for mining.[83]

Despite the Sino-Soviet rift, PRC specialists discussed the hydraulic mining method in the Soviet Union,[84] and Soviet surveys on the coalfields were published and discussed during a conference

---

[77] *Zhongguo meitan zhi* (China Coal Gazetteer), 253–254, 224–225, 569–570.

[78] Howe, *China's Economy*, xxxv, xxv.

[79] Zakliuchenie na annotatsiu k probleme no 1113, "Issledovanie usloviy razrabotki na glubine" (Assessment of the Report on Theme 1113, "Study of the Conditions of Underground Mining"), 421–423.

[80] Spravka po vypolneniiu napravlenia VII 4 (Report on the Fulfillment of Plan VII 4), 17.X 1958 RGAE 9489/3/1701/440.

[81] Omelchenko, "Chlenu Gosudarstvennogo nauchno technicheskogo komiteta sovieta ministrov SSSR Uskovu A.A." (To the Member of the Technology Committee of the Council of Ministers USSR Uskov A.A.), 29.X.1958, RGAE 9489/3/1701/492.

[82] Otchet o vypolnenii soglashenia 18.01.1958 za 9 mes. 1958g. (Report on Carrying Out the Agreement between the Governments of the USSR and the PRC about Joint Research in the Most Important Fields of Science and Technology and Soviet Aid to China over 9 Months in 1958), RGAE 9489/3/1701/493–8.

[83] Otdel stran narodnoi democratii AN USSR (Department of the Countries of the People's Democracy of the Soviet Academy of Science), Otchet o vypolnenii Soglashenia 18.01.1958 za 1958 g. (1958 Report about Carrying Out Agreement 18.01.1958), RGAE 9489/3/1701/466–470.

[84] B.B. Salabofu, Guan Fenglian and Sun Zhenyi, shuili caimei she Sulian meitan gongye wancheng qinian jihua de zhongyao fangfa zhi yi (Hydraulic Mining Is One of the Main Methods in the Soviet Coal Industry to Accomplish the Seven-Year Plan), *Meitan sheji* 6 (1959): 26–31.

on coal-deficient provinces in 1959.[85] In that year, a celebratory article by the head of the Coal Engineering Institute, Lu Zezhong, acknowledged Soviet aid since 1952, including thirty specialists in three delegations and 4,200 pieces of documentation. In 1954, Lu claimed, Soviet specialists had helped to establish design procedures and collected materials in the field. They were encouraged to adapt to Chinese conditions, policies, and needs, helping to set rules and correct mine surveys, improve administrative and technical management, and explain theories and technologies. Without the joint work of Soviet and Chinese specialists in the mining field to establish hydraulic mining, the GLF would have been impossible in the coal industry.[86] This reliance on hydro-mechanical coal mining technology – in which, from 1954 to 1959, the USSR claimed to "have given a lot of aid" to the PRC – was despite Soviet suggestions that underground hydraulic extraction could not become the main method of developing coal mining in China.[87]

Despite this somewhat reduced co-operation in 1958–1959, in 1960 the PRC refused Soviet aid in the coal industry on the ground that it was often not suitable and it had fulfilled its goals. Although the PRC was not happy with large-scale Soviet projects, which were slow to become operational,[88] Soviet aid in the PRC's coal industry also started to "phase itself out," as mentioned. At the same time, the most effective method of mining, open mining, comprised only 10 percent of mining projects in the PRC, while the Soviets planned to build eleven mines of this kind, with a production capacity of 76 million tons per year.[89] Yet by the time of the GLF, the termination of Soviet assistance in 1960 with the withdrawal of all Soviet specialists was a major setback for the coal industry.[90]

---

[85] Quemei shengqu meitian dizhi gongzuo huiyi wenjian xuanbian (Conference on the Geology of Coal Fields in Coal-Deficient Provinces), *Dizhibu dijuansi bian* (Beijing: Dizhi chubanshe, 1960).

[86] Ma Guanying, "Meikuang sheji huihuang chengjiu" (Glorious Successes of the Coal Industry), *Meitan sheji* 10 (1959): 2–6.

[87] "Zakliuchenie po annotatsii k probleme No 1108. Izuchenie podzemnoi dobychi uglia gidravlicheskim sposobom, sostavlennoi komitetom po planirovaniu nauk pri gosudrstvennom sovete KNR" (Assessment of the Report on Theme 1108. The Study of Underground Mining by the Hydraulic Method Prepared by the SPCSCPRC), RGAE 9489/3/1701/379–384.

[88] Thomson, *The Chinese Coal Industry*, 39.

[89] Goskomitet po toplivnoi promyshlennosti pri gosplane SSSR. Otchet delegatsii sovetskikh spetsialistov o poseshchenii ugolnykh predpriatiy i drugikh ob'ektov KNR (State Committee for Fuel at the State Planning Committee of the Council of Ministers of the USSR. Report of Soviet Specialists about Their Visit to Coal and Other Enterprises in the PRC), August 1965, RGAE 23/1/810/1–112, esp. 15–16.

[90] Thomson, *The Chinese Coal Industry*, 42–43.

At the same time, PRC professionals watched the development of American technology closely.[91] There was interest in the experience of the European Coal and Steel Community's investment policy, transmitted via translation of a Soviet publication.[92] In fact, as seen, Soviet coal industry specialists had promoted technologies from both the Soviet Union and capitalist countries which were determined suitable for Chinese conditions. In 1957, the PRC had planned to send specialists to learn about agglomeration and briquetting in Sweden as well as in the Soviet Union and other "people's democracies."[93] However, relations with socialist bloc countries also soured.

Turning Westward: Sino-Soviet Bloc Anxiety

Aside from the "colonial ethos," which contributed to the inefficacy of co-operation, other sources of anxiety for the Soviet Union and Eastern bloc over souring economic relations were the PRC's tilt to science and trade with the West because of the Soviet refusal to provide nuclear bomb technology,[94] the Chinese side downplaying Soviet bloc assistance, and a decline in the PRC's trade volume with Eastern Europe.

The PRC, despite rigid ideological pronouncements, pursued profitability in international trade and co-operation. Vladimir Pavlovich Fedotov, who was in China from 1953 to 1959 and worked as a translator in the Soviet embassy from 1957 to 1958, cited Mao in suggesting that, at the current pace, China would need 100 years to catch up with advanced Western countries. Although this makes absolutely no sense, because the PRC had just finished destroying private enterprise and markets, the Soviet side perceived the PRC's economic policies as a promotion of the market, a divergence from the Marxist model of industrialization and planning, instead of yielding to the market and private ownership. The Soviets were concerned with the inadequacy of exchanges with China, having detected

---

[91] Austin Jersild, "The Great Betrayal: Russian Memories of the 'Great Friendship'," *Cold War History* 12, no. 1 (July 2012): 164.

[92] Wen Sha, "Ouzhou meigang lianying guojia dui zhijin ji meitan gongye de touzi" (Investment Policy in the Coal Industry of the European Steel and Coal Union), *Shijie jingji wenhui* 12 (1958): 58–59.

[93] KPNGSKNR Annotatsia k probleme 1207, izuchenie i razrabotka teoreticheskikh osnov aglomeratsii rudnoi melochi chernykh metalov i novoi tekhnologii proizvodstva aglomeratov (Assessment of the Report on Theme 1207. Study and Design of the Theory of Agglomeration of Small Particle Ore of ferrous Metals), Beijing, June 1956, RGAE 9489/3/1701/192–207, esp. 204.

[94] Jersild, *Sino-Soviet Alliance*, 215. "Report by Nie Rongzhen to Mao Zedong Regarding Science and Technology (Abridged)," July 3, 1960, History and Public Policy Program Digital Archive, Dang de wenxian (Party Historical Documents), 1 (1996): 8–9 (trans. Neil Silver), at https://digitalarchive.wilsoncenter.org/document/114348.

from the beginning an "orientation on prospective co-operation with the West and Japan" in the Chinese Academy of Science and seeing further proof of this orientation in Mao's 1956 call to study both the Soviet experience – in order to avoid that inefficient path – and the advanced science of capitalist countries,[95] after which the number of Soviet specialists in China started to decline.[96] Even before Soviet advisers left China in 1960, the PRC had started to import oil-refining equipment from Italy.[97] In 1960, amidst the tragedy of the GLF, as in other industries, research on technology in the coal industry was to be resumed, and industries were to learn advanced technology from Western countries in accordance with the changed international situation; that is, the Sino-Soviet split.[98]

A lack of appreciation by the PRC for the assistance of the Eastern bloc further harmed strained relations. In 1961, during Romanian diplomat I. Dorobantsu's visit to a major heavy-machinery plant in Wuhan, he saw large amounts of equipment from different countries, mainly from the Soviet Union, and asked what percentage of equipment was nationally produced versus imported. He was told 80/20, because the ratio was calculated by unit rather than by weight and size, from large Soviet equipment to the modernized carts produced at the plant. This split, according to Dorobantsu, created a wrong opinion among the workers regarding aid from socialist countries to China.[99] Moreover, the movement for innovation and technical revolution in 1959, which promoted the connection between industry and research, led in some cases to the destruction of equipment produced in the Soviet Union. According to a Chinese translator disappointed in the policy of the Chinese Communist Party, in 1962 the PRC Ministry of Geology appeared mistrustful of foreign specialists both Western and Eastern. After it became obvious that the oil deposits that Hungarian specialists had found in northeast China were enormous, especially in Daqing, the Chinese side started to give those specialists insignificant work, indicating that they were no longer needed, and downplayed their role in the discovery of the deposits.[100]

---

[95] Vladimir Pavlovich Fedotov, *Polveka vmeste s Kitaem:* vospominania, zapisi, razmyshlenia (Half a Century together with China) (Moscow: ROSSPEN, 2005), 100, 85–86, 69–71.
[96] Shen Zhihua, *Sulian zhuanjia zai zhongguo* (Soviet Specialists in China) (Beijing: Xinhua chubanshe, 2009), 307–311.
[97] Selig S. Harrison, *China, Oil, and Asia: Conflict Ahead?* (New York: Columbia University Press, 1977).
[98] *Zhongguo meitan zhi* (China Coal Gazetteer), 570.
[99] Zapis besedy s attashe posolstva Rumynii v KNR I. Dorobantsu (Record of Conversation with Attaché of the Rumanian Embassy in PRC I. Dorobantsu), 20 May 1961, RGANI 5/39/531/120–123.
[100] Zapis besedy c poslom Vengerskoi narodnoi respubliki v KNR F. Martinom (Record of Conversation with Ambassador of the Hungarian People's Republic F. Martin), 15 October 1962, RGANI 5/39/531/411–414, esp. 413.

Around the same time, the PRC further developed connections with the capitalist world. General Electric visited China, and a PRC trade delegation headed by the minister of foreign trade, Li Qiang, was dispatched to Britain.[101] Although by 1964 the focus in coal production had shifted back from the small pits to large Soviet-constructed and -designed mines,[102] in the mid-1960s China started to "shop for technology throughout Western Europe."[103] Fedotov, reflecting on the PRC's external relations following Chinese marketization reforms, surmised that the PRC had never given up its market orientation and had always had ties to the capitalist world through Macao, Hong Kong, and the affluent Chinese diaspora and Western-educated intelligentsia.[104] In 1957–1958, fixed and long-term foreign-trade commitments to export and import were abandoned, and more flexible planning was adopted depending on the stabilization of domestic food consumption. In 1959, 70 percent of China's trade was with Soviet bloc countries and the Soviet Union. However, the break with the Soviet Union and the disaster of the GLF forced the PRC to decrease foreign trade and to import grain, thus abandoning the strategy of importing machinery for industrial growth.[105] Fedotov saw the policies of these years as the search for China's own "exit point" to the world market and its independently constructed political ties, including with the United States.[106] From 1950, the PRC was willing to trade with both socialist and capitalist countries.[107] This practical approach became evident in the economic relations of the PRC during the difficult times of the GLF. In 1962, speaking on the prospective establishment of economic relations with France, the acting head of the Department of Western European Countries within the Ministry of Foreign Affairs, Song Zhiguang, said that the PRC was open to establishing economic relations when doing so was profitable for the PRC.[108] Indeed, in 1964 Japan became the leading trade partner of the PRC.[109] In the energy industry, too, after the

---

[101] Zapis besed s rabotnikami nekotorykh posol'stv (Record of Conversation with Staff of Some Embassies), 7 noiabria 1962 g. iz dnevnika Zhdanovicha B.G., RGANI 5/39/531/511–513.

[102] Thomson, *The Chinese Coal Industry*, 42–43.

[103] Howe, "Introduction," 4.

[104] Fedotov, *Polveka vmeste s Kitaem*, 71.

[105] Howe, *China's Economy*, 144, 165, 152.

[106] Fedotov, *Polveka vmeste s Kitaem*, 1, 83.

[107] Shu Guang Zhang, *Economic Cold War: America's Embargo against China and the Sino-Soviet Alliance, 1949–1963* (Stanford: Stanford University Press, 2001), 73.

[108] Zapis besedy s sovetnikami posol'stva VNR v KNR K. Sigeti i la. Kukuchka (Record of the Conversation with Diplomats of the Hungarian People's Republic in the PRC K. Sigeti and J. Kukuchka), 15 September 1962, RGANI 5/39/531/327–337, esp. 336.

[109] Amy King, "Reconstructing China: Japanese Technicians and Industrialization in the Early Years of the People's Republic of China," *Modern Asian Studies* 50, no. 1 (2016): esp. 174.

installation of a 400-volt Soviet generator in 1963, a 2,000-volt British generator was installed in Juda, in Inner Mongolia, in 1964.[110] Soviet diplomatic memos and reports from the Beijing embassy about their exchanges with Eastern European embassies shed further light on this connectedness of the PRC with the nonsocialist world.[111] From 1961 to 1962, as the staff of the Soviet embassy were compiling reports on the PRC's economy and their meetings with staff from the embassies of Eastern bloc countries, they saw in the Chinese reluctance to trade with the Eastern bloc an interest in trading with the West. In 1960, the PRC decreased its export of legumes to Poland, failing to fulfill its contracts, while, according to the West German press, in the same year, trade between the PRC and West Germany, Britain, and Italy grew by 60 to 80 percent, mainly because of the increased export of food products.[112] In 1961, the PRC withdrew from Council for Mutual Economic Assistance (COMECON), where it had had an observer status.[113] PRC leaders explained decreased trade with the German Democratic Republic (GDR) in 1961 by citing economic difficulties due to natural disasters and the need to export a number of goods to capitalist countries in order to gain the hard currency necessary to import other goods – that is, the need to repay the Soviet loan. In the PRC's rejection of increased ties with the Academy of Sciences of the GDR, GDR diplomat Wenning saw a political motivation to become more economically independent.[114] A Czech diplomat likewise complained that the trade plan with China for 1961 was not satisfactory. However, he supposed that the PRC had built its relations with socialist countries based on how they behaved at the Moscow meeting of communist parties in 1960, where, in the ranks of who supported China the most, Albania had been first and the Czech Republic had been last.[115]

---

[110] *Zhongguo meitan zhi, NeiMenggu juan* (China Coal Gazetteer, Inner Mongolia) (Beijing: Meitan gongye chubanshe, 1999), 222.

[111] Roberto Peruzzi, "Leading the Way: The United Kingdom's Financial and Trade Relations with Socialist China, 1949–1966," *Modern Asian Studies* 51, no. 1 (2017): 17–43; Valeria Zanier, "'Energizing' Relations: Western European Industrialists and China's Dream of Self-Reliance. The Case of Ente Nazionale Idrocarburi (1956–1965)," *Modern Asian Studies* 51, no. 1 (2016): 133–169.

[112] Zapis′ besedy s pervym sekretarem posolstva PNR v Pekine Frantishekom Stakhanoviakom i attashe etogo posolstva Kazimirov Kramazhem (Record of Conversation with First Secretary of the Embassy of the Polish People's Republic in Beijing Frantishek Stachowiak and Attaché of That Embassy Kazimir Kramar), 8 January 1961, Iz dnevnika lashina G.V. (From the diary of lashin G.V.), RGANI 5/39/531/49–52, esp. 50.

[113] Howe, *China's Economy*, 135.

[114] Zapis′ besedy s vremennym poverennym v delakh GDR V. Venningom (Record of the Conversation with Acting Representative of German Democratic Republic V. Wenning), 3 March 1961, RGANI5/39/531/166–8.

[115] Zapis′ besedy s poslom Polskoi narodnoi respubliki Knote (Record of Conversation with Polish People's Republic's Ambassador Knote), 4 August 1961, RGANI 5/39/531.

Successful Technology Transfer?

By 1965, the Soviets had reported on the PRC's achievements in the coal industry. After visiting the PRC in August of that year, Soviet engineers reported that on the basis of "creatively adapting" Soviet technology in mining, Chinese specialists had developed hydro-mechanization coal technology, and the practice of connecting research with production had become embedded in educational and research institutions by the late 1950s. The Soviet specialists evaluated this as worth borrowing. The Fushun Research Institute for Safety in Coal Mining, created in 1953, established labs that in 1964 worked in close co-operation with production.[116] At Qinghua University, connections had been established between production and research done by students in the Hydro-technical Department.[117] The president of Yunnan University stated to a visiting Soviet delegation that a wise educational process comprised 70 percent practice and 30 percent theory, and this model was based on Soviet advice.[118] Soviet visitors, in their reports to the Council of Ministers, recommended that this practice be studied and adopted in the Soviet education system and that Sino–Soviet co-operation be pitched as a two-way street,[119] but the contacts soon stopped.

Conclusion

Anxieties about the PRC's orientation to the West among the Soviets and other "peoples' democracies" are, of course, hard to square with the stated ideological differences over peaceful coexistence with imperialist countries promoted by the USSR and rejected by the PRC. According to Susanne Weigelin-Schwiedrzik's chapter in this volume, "The idea of hidden triangularity inside the bipolar system of the Cold War generated plausible explanations with regard to the decisions taken by the USSR

[116] GKTPGP SSSR, Otchet delegatsii sovetskikh spetsialistov (SCFSPC CM USSR) (Report of Soviet Specialists), August 1965, RGAE 9606/1/1253.
[117] Otchet o rabote prof[essora] d[oktora]. t[ekhnicheskikh]. n[auk]. F.F. Gubina v politekhnicheskom institute Tsinhua, tiantsin'skom politekhnicheskom institute i drugikh organizatsiiakh KNR v period 6/11/1959–20/1/60 g. (Working Report by Professor Doctor of Technical Sciences F.F. Gubin at Qinghua Polytechnic University and Other PRC Organizations from 6/11/1959–20/1/60), July 1960, RGAE 9606/1/1253/91–113, esp.103.
[118] USSR ambassador to PRC S. Chervonenko, Poseschenie iun'nan'skogo universiteta (Visit to Yunnan University), 31 May 1961, RGANI 5/39/531/143 –146.
[119] Moscow Institute of Engineering and Construction V.V. Kuibyshev, Department of Water Resources, Head of the Department, Doctor of Technical Sciences, Professor F. F. Gubin, Ministru vysshego i srednego spetsial'nogo obrazovania SSSR V.P. Leliutinu (To the Minister of Higher and Vocational Education of the USSR V.P. Leliutin), 1 March 1960, RGAE 9606/1/173.

and China in their relations with the USA and with members of the socialist camp." She argues that the three players acted according to their respective national interests beyond ideological considerations.[120] This chapter has demonstrated the point of Weigelin-Schwiedrzik with regard to the aid provided by the Soviet Union and other members of the socialist camp to the Chinese coal industry in the 1950s.

Sino-Soviet co-operation in science provided the "academic foundation for China's policy of self-reliance" in the coal industry.[121] Moreover, the Soviet Union promoted in the PRC the undertaking of internationally compatible research that would be closely connected to industry and based on adaptations of world experience, both socialist and capitalist, to PRC conditions and needs. This promotion was successful, yet most didn't think it was successful at the time; the Chinese were dissatisfied with what the Soviet Union had provided, and the Soviet Union and Soviet bloc countries were anxious about the insufficient reciprocity of the exchange with China.

The cornerstone of pre-reform PRC science development, *renwu dai xueke* ("let tasks guide disciplines"), was adopted by the PRC government in 1957 under Soviet influence during discussions of the twelve-year plan and in the spirit of worldwide debates on basic versus applied research.[122] In the coal industry, the Soviets mediated, at least in part, the transformation of science in China from basic to applied.[123]

This story paints co-operation between China and the Soviet bloc and the Soviet Union in a new light. The case study of the PRC's coal industry and Soviet advisers shows the eagerness of the Soviets to adapt to Chinese conditions. The Soviet preoccupation with "Chinese conditions" was, of course, a response to the PRC's stress on "local conditions" in the mid-1950s. However, it also echoed earlier Communist International (Comintern) indigenization policies reaching back to the 1920s to 1930s, which promoted reliance on local cadres and local resources as a manifestation of interwar ideological globalization.[124] There was no contradiction between the PRC wanting world-level technologies and desiring to adapt those technologies to local conditions; the Soviets and

---

[120] See Weigelin-Schwiedrzik's chapter, above.
[121] Goikhman, "Soviet–Chinese Academic Interactions in the 1950s," 276–7.
[122] Wang, "The Chinese Developmental State during the Cold War," 195; Zhang Jiucheng, *Ziran ziyuan zonghe kaocha weiyuanhui yanjiu* [A Study of the Natural Resources Survey Committee] (Beijing: kexue chubanshe, 2013), 262.
[123] For the discussion of the nature of this transformation in the PRC, see Sigrid Schmalzer, "Self-Reliant Science: The Impact of the Cold War on Science in Socialist China," in Naomi Oreskes and Johan Krige, eds., *Science and Technology in the Global Cold War* (Cambridge, MA: The MIT Press, 2014), 75–106.
[124] Anna Belogurova, *The Nanyang Revolution: The Comintern and Chinese Networks in Southeast Asia, 1890–1957* (Cambridge: Cambridge University Press, 2019), 41.

the Comintern had earlier promoted the same. The point of contention was the different views of the PRC and the Soviet Union of what "local conditions" consisted of: the Soviets wanted technologies applied feasibly in accordance with each deposit's geological and technological conditions, while the PRC wanted utilization of its most abundant resource, human labor, to solve unemployment without having to rely on the Soviet Union. This was the ultimate reason for the demise of co-operation in the coal industry. Yet, at least rhetorically, despite all the issues with co-operation, both sides had an interest in positively spinning things: where it was beneficial for the PRC, co-operation with the Soviet Union continued, such as in gratis exchanges of technical documentation during the watershed years of 1957–1959.

Although the introduction of hydraulic coal mining failed during the GLF, by the time of the last visit by a Soviet delegation in 1965, mining technology had been further developed and had become a desired item for reverse transfer to the Soviet side. This example of socialist China's successful creative adaptation of foreign technology invites us to rethink PRC history from the vantage point of its current place in the world in order to identify the precursors of the PRC's success.[125] This chapter has told one story of successful Chinese adaptation of foreign technology and of the practical approach to the "socialist brotherhood" that allowed the PRC to attain more "modern" technology than the socialist bloc could provide.

---

[125] Klaus Mühlhahn, *Making China Modern: From the Great Qing to Xi Jinping* (Cambridge, MA: Harvard University Press, 2019).

3 Producing Socialist Bodies
Transnational Sports Networks and Athletes in 1950s China

Amanda Shuman

"Bau auf, bau auf, bau auf, bau auf! Freie Deutsche Jugend, bau auf!
Für eine bessr'e Zukunft richten wir die Heimat auf ... "[1]
Huang Hongjiu sings "Song of the Freie Deutsche Jugend [FDJ, Free
German Youth]," the youth movement of the German
Democratic Republic (GDR, East Germany)

Sixty-six years after his participation at the 1951 World Festival of Youth
and Students held in East Berlin, eighty-eight-year-old Huang Hongjiu,
or "Oom Julius" ("Uncle Julius," in Dutch), as he is known to his family
these days, launches into a spontaneous rendition of the chorus to the
Free German Youth song "Bau auf" during our interview. In the middle
of the conversation, which took place in Amsterdam and in which he
switched at times between four languages (English, Chinese, Dutch,
and Indonesian), his sudden memory of this song caught me by surprise
(not least because the German is also flawless).[2] My plan going into the
interview was simply to ask him about his experiences as a PRC athlete in
the 1950s – aside from locating his name in official publications like *Sports
Yearbooks*, he is virtually unknown outside his personal affiliation to
a famous swimmer named Wu Chuanyu. In fact, Huang was only brought
to my attention by the president of the International Swimming Hall of
Fame (ISHOF) in Florida, who contacted me after reading a short blog

---

[1] "Build up, build up, build up, build up! Free German Youth, build up! For a better
future, we'll focus on the homeland!" (Unless otherwise noted, all translations are
my own.)
[2] The interview took place on the morning of April 21, 2017, at Huang's home in
Amsterdam. Two of Huang's family members were present at the time of the interview
and helped fill in the family story in Indonesia as well as the later migration story following
his departure from the PRC in 1972. I thank Huang deeply for this interview and for
graciously welcoming me into his home. I also want to thank his family not only for
meeting me at the tram station and helping interpret during the interview when he
spoke Indonesian, but also for providing me with scans of all of Huang's wonderful
photographs. This chapter is dedicated to Huang, who passed away in February 2022,
prior to final publication.

post I had previously written about Wu[3] – Wu was posthumously inducted into the ISHOF in 2017.[4] Huang attended the ceremony and provided the organization with information on Wu, but otherwise he remains fairly anonymous in his retirement community in Amsterdam.

Huang's responses to my questions constantly challenged my idea of what it meant to be an athlete for the PRC in these years – especially because it seemed to me that he displayed no obvious identification with the PRC. He identified, first and foremost, as a former swimmer and an ethnically Chinese Indonesian. I call him Huang Hongjiu because that is his name in the Chinese records, but in person at least, he does not identify with this name, preferring instead his Dutch or even Indonesian name (Oei Hong Kioe). His reluctance to discuss the PRC per se at any length (especially its politics) is likely a result of his treatment during the Cultural Revolution – when those who were, or had connections to, overseas Chinese were often targeted as alleged spies, counterrevolutionaries, revisionists, or traitors[5] – but I began to wonder whether there was something more to it. Huang constantly brought up the international connections he had in the 1950s, especially his friendships with swimmers and coaches in the socialist bloc. He fondly remembered his training days as part of the first national swimming team in the PRC, after being recruited by sports leaders from an Indonesian sports delegation. But within those memories,

---

[3] Amanda Shuman, "A Champion for Socialist China," in *Afro-Asian Visions: New Perspectives on Decolonisation, the Cold War, and Asian–African Connections, Medium*, June 6, 2016, at https://medium.com/afro-asian-visions/a-champion-for-china-d22b771111ab, accessed January 31, 2020. I thank Bruce Wigo, ISOHF president, not only for bringing Huang's story to my attention but for also putting me in contact with Huang's family through email.

[4] "Honorees: Wu Chuanyu (CHN) 2017 Honor Pioneer Swimmer," ISHOF honorees, International Swimming Hall of Fame, at https://ishof.org/wu-chuanyu.html, accessed January 31, 2020.

[5] Michael Godley, "The Sojourners: Returned Overseas Chinese in the People's Republic of China," *Pacific Affairs* 62, no. 3 (Autumn 1989): 330. The best-known case in the world of sport is that of three famous table tennis players and coaches from Hong Kong – Fu Qifang, Jiang Yongning, and Rong Guotuan (the 1959 world champion for the PRC) – who were apparently attacked as "traitorous spies" and committed suicide consecutively over three months in 1968. Some biographies, books, and memoirs of former athletes mention persecution specifically. For example, Lin Huiqing, an Indonesian-born PRC table tennis player in the 1960s and 1970s, was likewise persecuted as a "revisionist seedling." Liang Yingming, *Pingbo yu fengxian: Yindunixiya guiqiao Lin Huiqing de pingpangqiu rensheng* (Beijing: Overseas Chinese publishing house, 2015), 28. Those who had family living overseas, such as former basketball player Kai Chen, whose relatives included former Guomindang (Nationalist Party) members in Taiwan, consistently ran into trouble or encountered persecution for their so-called "black" family backgrounds. Kai Chen, *One in a Billion: Journey toward Freedom* (Bloomington, IN: AuthorHouse, 2007).

competing for the PRC as such holds little importance – so long as he could do what he loved to do, not much else mattered. This chapter seeks to understand such athletes and the networks within which they were embedded, and the relationship of both to the Chinese party-state's national project of the early 1950s. In these years, the new state began to invest in an unprecedented project: to remake the physical fitness of the nation as a whole, down to the individual body of each citizen, while establishing China as an active contender in international athletic competition. The production of the socialist body politic and individual socialist bodies through *tiyu* (translated variously as "sports and physical culture," "body culture," "physical education," or simply "sport") became a nationwide project embedded in transnational sports networks and central to the Communist Party's legitimization f its rule. National sports development over these years vacillated in its focus between transforming the masses into active socialist subjects and building an elite cadre of internationally competitive athletes. Athletes like Huang were part of and invested in these networks.

Through the example of sport, this chapter also argues that to understand the national project within the early PRC we need to bring in a transnational perspective – that is, a refocus on "researching and writing a history with nations that is not a history of nations."[6] Current histories of PRC sport (and, I would contend, other social realms) tend to erase the complexity of this period in favor of reifying the nation-state. A linear, pro-Olympic narrative dominates much of this work.[7] I have argued elsewhere that the institutionalization of sport in the early 1950s required the involvement of Communist cadres (such as Rong Gaotang), Republican-period experts (such as Ma Yuehan), and Soviet and socialist bloc expertise.[8] But it goes beyond this, especially when one traces the athletic networks or athletes, who tend to leave behind fewer written sources. As I will show below, I am not arguing that we ignore the nation; indeed, these athletic networks can sometimes only be traced through official sources produced within specific national contexts. But in creating

---

[6] Pierre-Yves Saunier, *Transnational History* (London: Palgrave Macmillan, 2013), 8.

[7] One prominent example in English is Xu Guoqi, *Olympic Dreams* (Cambridge, MA: Harvard University Press, 2008), unsurprisingly released the same year as the Beijing Olympics. Most sports histories in English and Chinese (体育史) even more starkly follow a pro-PRC and pro-Olympic linear narrative of progression. In Chinese, for example, Xiong Xiaozheng, *Zhong Bingshu, xin zhongguo tiyu 60 nián* (60 Years of Sports in New China) (Beijing: Beijing tiyu chubanshe, 2010) or Wu Shaozu, *Zhonghua renmin gongheguo tiyi shi (1949–1998), zhonghe juan* (The History of Sports of the People's Republic of China (1949–1998), Comprehensive Volume) (Beijing: Zhongguo shuji chubanshe, 1999).

[8] Amanda Shuman, "The Politics of Socialist Athletics in the People's Republic of China, 1949–1966" (PhD diss., University of California, Santa Cruz, 2014), Chapter 1.

a history *of* the nation, the vast majority of sports histories of China have in turn marginalized anything that does not neatly fit or support a national narrative. Competitive athletes, for example, tend to appear in the media or in secondary publications (including academic scholarship) only when they are or have been exceptional at national and/or international levels.[9] In short, these sports narratives focus almost exclusively on athletic achievement and promote an international image of the nation.

A transnational perspective can help us trace the movements and connections between athletes, coaches, and other (state, substate, non-state) actors in order to map out a history that has mostly been rendered "invisible or at best peripheral" because it existed "between, across and through polities and societies."[10] This is essential when one considers that, in addition to regular state-to-state delegation visits, the socialist bloc also sponsored numerous non-Olympic international sports events, including competitions held during the World Festivals of Youth and Students (WFYS). Yet present histories on such events are few and far between, drowned out by the Olympic movement and its affiliates. Thus this is not an easy task, and this chapter provides just one glimpse into the complexities present. I rely on a diverse set of sources that encompasses archives, official media, oral history, and personal collections; some of these sources are in Chinese and some are not.[11]

---

[9] Nevertheless, the names of many athletic participants are often given in *Sports Yearbooks*, but without context. I have found this useful in tracing the movements of individual athletes internationally, though it is nearly impossible to pinpoint an athlete's origins within or beyond China.

[10] Saunier, *Transnational History*, 3.

[11] Although I have previously worked in the archives of the International Olympic Committee (IOC) in Lausanne, Switzerland, and in Chinese archives, this chapter includes few sources from these institutions because of the difficulties described in pursuing a topic that does not follow the mainstream, nation-based, Olympic-centered narrative in international sport. Archival materials on the World Festival of Youth and Students that I use in this chapter primarily come from the International Institute of Social History (IISH) in Amsterdam and are publicly accessible. I am enormously grateful to Bruce Wigo, the ISOHF president, for reaching out to me, and to Huang Hongjiu, who graciously shared not only stories, but also his personal collection of photographs. The Chinese-language materials I use in this chapter include newspapers, magazines, and yearbooks, many of which I found in major libraries outside China or purchased myself (yearbooks can sometimes be found in the ChinaMaxx database, but sports periodicals from the Mao era have not been digitized and are not available online). In 2010–2011, I spent several months in the Chinese Foreign Ministry Archives (before it mysteriously closed in 2013 and then reopened with most materials reclassified) and the Beijing Municipal Archives broadly researching "sports and physical culture" (*tiyu*) under Mao; that is how I obtained a few documents related to the Olympic committee from the early 1950s that are discussed in this chapter. However, to date, the Chinese State Sports Commission's archives were not and have never been made publicly accessible, even during the decade prior to Xi Jinping – what is now considered to be a time in which most archives were relatively "open." Since then, the situation has deteriorated

Finally, a transnational perspective also helps to provide a voice to, and sketch out an understanding of, an oft-forgotten group in early PRC history: ethnically Chinese athletes who, in official language, had "returned" to the motherland (*hui guo*) to help build a new China. The CCP, like the Guomindang (GMD), had been interested in and forged links with the overseas Chinese community in the decades prior to 1949, in part through the "united front" policy.[12] After 1949, the early PRC government strengthened the united front policy into an institution that included handling domestic overseas Chinese.[13] In late 1953, the government began to officially give overseas Chinese preferential treatment and privileges, in the hope that they would invest and participate in the larger project to transform China into a socialist state.[14] In the case of athletes, as this chapter will show, preferential treatment began earlier for those with crucial skills that the new government needed for this project.

The choice given to overseas Chinese to return (i.e., migrate to mainland China) must be put in the context of the post-Civil War and early Cold War moment in which, as Taomo Zhou notes, overseas Chinese were "at the center of a global battle for hearts and minds fought between the Chinese Communists and Nationalists."[15] Recent scholarship has looked at how this rivalry played out among ethnic Chinese communities located in Indonesia, the Philippines, Malaysia, Mexico, and the United States.[16] In Indonesia, the Sukarno government forged diplomatic relations with the PRC following its own independence, even while the local

and it is likely that, since early 2020, some or all of the documents I previously accessed at the Foreign Ministry archives have been reclassified. This makes it incredibly difficult to research the inner workings of state-sponsored sports institutions at the central level.

[12] Originally adopted by the CCP in the 1920s and then in the 1930s for the purposes of allying with the GMD to defeat Japan, this policy, Glen Peterson notes, was one of the major ways prior to 1949 in which the CCP interacted with overseas Chinese communities, especially in Hong Kong. Glen Peterson, *Overseas Chinese in the People's Republic of China* (London: Routledge, 2012), 18, 19.

[13] For a detailed discussion of the pre-1949 history of the united front policy and its transformation in the transition to socialism, see Gerry Groot, *Managing Transitions: The Chinese Communist Party, United Front Work, Corporatism and Hegemony* (London: Routledge, 2003).

[14] Glen Peterson notes that this included, among other things, exclusive investment opportunities and access to consumer goods unavailable to the public, and that it protected them from larger "social and economic transformations" at the time. Peterson, *Overseas Chinese in the People's Republic of China*, 55–56.

[15] Taomo Zhou, *Migration in the Time of Revolution: China, Indonesia, and the Cold War* (Ithaca: Cornell University Press, 2019), 12.

[16] This topic has proliferated in the last decade. For politics in Indonesia, see Zhou, *Migration in the Time of Revolution*. For other countries, see, for example, Kung Chien-Wen, "In the Name of Anticommunism: Chinese Practices of Ideological Accommodation in the Early Cold War Philippines," *Modern Asian Studies* 53, no. 5 (2019): 1543–1573; Fujio Hara, *Malayan Chinese and China* (Singapore: NUS Press, 2003); Fredy Gonzalez, *Paisanos Chinos: Transpacific Politics among Chinese Immigrants in*

Chinese population continued to experience discrimination; internally, the local ethnic Chinese community also split into pro-Beijing and pro-Taipei contingents. For those who decided to migrate to mainland China, I agree with Zhou's assessment that they displayed agency and autonomy in their decisions to do so during a rare time of fluid identities, contested citizenships, and wavering political loyalties.[17] This chapter is the first attempt to investigate the lives, agency, and autonomy of the overseas Chinese athletes that the early PRC government recruited for their strong sports skills. It attempts to answer a series of basic questions: who were these athletes and what kind of athletic work did they engage in? Why did the new state recruit them, and why did they want to go to the PRC? What kinds of training did they receive and what kind of networks did they help build? How did these experiences change their lives and, conversely, how did their athletic work change sport in China?

I start by outlining the broader historical context within which these athletes were situated. First, the participation of overseas Chinese representing China at the 1948 London Olympics helps lay groundwork for continuities and discontinuities between the Republican wartime pre-1949 and the post-1949 early PRC period. I then discuss the early PRC project to invest in sport, focusing on reasons behind the agenda to join the socialist bloc in sport and China's interest in the 1951 World Festival of Youth and Students. Using Huang Hongjiu and his now-famous teammate, Wu Chuanyu, as examples, I show how such "returned" Chinese helped build transnational networks and competitive water sport programs in the early PRC. PRC sports leaders were not the first to recruit such ethnically Chinese athletes from elsewhere to represent China on the world stage, but the PRC government was the first to label them "returned" Chinese athletes and provide them with training and amenities, all under a patriotic rubric of creating state-sponsored sports programs as part of building a "new" China. Above all, PRC sports leaders hoped that such athletes would serve at least two immediate goals: building China's elite sports programs and raising the international image of China and Chinese sport, especially within the socialist bloc but also more broadly. This was accomplished through providing these recruited athletes with everyday, on-the-ground training (and, especially later in the 1950s and into the 1960s, coaching), and in having them

---

Mexico (Berkeley: University of California Press, 2017); Meredith Oyen, *The Diplomacy of Migration: Transnational Lives and the Making of U.S.–Chinese Relations in the Cold War* (Ithaca: Cornell University Press, 2015); and Charlotte Brooks, *Between Mao and McCarthy: Chinese American Politics in the Cold War Years* (Chicago: The University of Chicago Press, 2015).

[17] Zhou, *Migration in the Time of Revolution*, 4.

represent China in the bustling socialist bloc sports network, which included large-scale international events like the biannual World Festival of Youth and Students. Such events had both symbolic importance for the new socialist nation – to be recognized internationally as a member of the socialist bloc – as well as a concrete purpose in connecting these athletes with those in the socialist bloc to exchange technical sports skills.

Overseas Chinese Athletes at the 1948 London Olympics

There is a history of overseas Chinese (*huaqiao*) representing China at international sports events prior to the establishment of the PRC. It was quite easy, in fact, for many ethnic Chinese to participate in such events because of the 1909 Nationality Law. The law, based on the principle of *jus sanguinis*, stated that "any person born of a Chinese father, or of a Chinese mother where the nationality of the father was unknown or indeterminate, was a Chinese citizen, regardless of place of birth."[18] Those in charge of the Republic of China's representation at sporting events clearly took advantage of this law as needed; the delegation sent to the 1948 London Olympics is a prominent example.

At least one contemporary observer considered China's participation in the 1948 London Olympics to be a feat in itself.[19] The country was in the midst of a Civil War following the end of the war against Japan, and personnel and resources for sports programs were in short supply. Moreover, international sport was hardly the top priority either of the fledgling Nationalist government (in which some officials were already fleeing to Hong Kong, Taiwan, and other countries) or of a Communist Party focused on its own guerrilla warfare tactics and land reform efforts in the countryside. It thus seems unsurprising that, as Andrew Morris has noted, China's participation at the London Olympics was an epic failure. In addition to winning no medals, as had previously happened at the 1936 Berlin Olympics, the underfunded delegation attempted to save money by bringing its own food along and there were insufficient funds to buy return tickets home, leaving the delegation to sell its remaining food and ask for small donations.[20]

In spite of this failure, however, the delegation itself was quite unique. It was not, as the same contemporary observer noted, "athletes from all over

---

[18] Stephen Fitzgerald, *China and the Overseas Chinese: A Study of Peking's Changing Policy, 1949–1970* (Cambridge: Cambridge University Press, 1972), 6.
[19] Hsieh Chang-an, "Development of Physical Education in China," *China Weekly Review*, June 19, 1948.
[20] Andrew Morris, *Marrow of the Nation: A History of Sport and Physical Culture in Republican China* (Berkeley: University of California Press, 2004), 236–237.

the country,"[21] but rather a group of ethnically Chinese athletes cobbled together from "Greater China" (Hong Kong, Taiwan, and Singapore), the Philippines, Indonesia, and even the Netherlands. In contrast to the delegation of more than 200 athletes that had attended the 1936 Berlin Olympics, only twenty-six athletes from mainland China went to London.[22] The football team was primarily Hong Kong players, hailing from clubs like Sing Tao SC and Kowloon Motor Bus. Only one of the three in athletics came from mainland China ("deaf and mute" Lou Wenao);[23] the other two came from Taiwan (Chen Ying-long or Chen Yinglang) and Singapore/Malaysia (Ng Liang-Chiang). Howard Wing was a half-Chinese Dutch cyclist who had never even been to China when he first competed for the country at Berlin in 1936. The basketball team, which did include a few mainland Chinese players, such as Wu Chengzhang and Li Zhenzhong,[24] also included players from the Philippines (Edward Lee and Jose Yee) and Wee Tian-Siak – a Singaporean player who went on to compete for the Republic of China at the Helsinki Olympics in 1952 and then for Singapore at the Melbourne Olympics in 1956.[25] And then there's one of the main subjects of this

[21] Hsieh, "Development of Physical Education in China."

[22] Some sources cite a delegation of thirty-one, but according to Olympic documents five of these were in the arts competition and did not compete in sport; twenty-six were listed as "competitors." Organising Committee for the XIV Olympiad, *The Official Report of the Organising Committee for the XIV Olympiad* (London: Organising Committee for the XIV Olympiad, 1948), 546, at https://digital.la84.org/digital/collection/p17103coll8/id/5717/ , accessed February 25, 2020.

[23] Lou's case is somewhat tragic in that he seems to have been taken advantage of by a former teammate Wang Zhenglin and then ultimately ended up as a janitor in Hong Kong for the rest of his life, passing away possibly sometime in the 1960s – but this is according to online sources of questionable repute. I have been unable to find any trace of him after 1949 in reputable secondary sources.

[24] "1948 Chinese Basketball Player Revisits London," *BBC News*, August 4, 2012, at http://www.bbc.com/news/world-asia-china-19117763; and "64 Years Later, a Chance to Relive London Memories," *China Daily*, August 8, 2012, at http://europe.chinadaily.com.cn/europe/2012-08/08/content_15652624.htm. Li Zhenzhong remained on the mainland, where he is remembered for his significant contributions to basketball. Du Chenglin, "Li Zhenzhong de lanqiu shengya ji qi dui wo guo lanqiu yungong de gongjian," *Lantai shijie*, December 2014, 121–122. Later a professor at Shanghai Normal University, he celebrated his 100th birthday in 2015 on the campus and Yao Ming apparently made an appearance. "Professor Li Zhenzhong's 100th Birthday Celebrated by 100 people, Yao Ming Included," *Shanghai Normal University*, at http://host.shnu.edu.cn/Default.aspx?tabid=5169&ctl=Details&mid=10176&ItemID=157492&SkinSrc=%5BL%5DSkins/english_2_news/english_2_news.

[25] This is somewhat surprising and speaks volumes about the state of sports programs in China at the time because basketball was clearly one of the sports in which China had significant experience and long-standing programs for both men and women. See Morris, *Marrow of the Nation*; and Gao Yunxiang, *Sporting Gender: Women Athletes and Celebrity-Making during China's National Crisis, 1931-45* (Vancouver: UBC Press, 2013). It is

chapter – whom I will discuss in further detail below – Indonesian swimmer Go Tjoan-Giok, known also by his Chinese name, Wu Chuanyu.[26] In short, being an ethnically Chinese athlete in 1948 meant that one could, at least from a technical standpoint, fluidly change national identity in order to compete. The more pressing issue had to do with money and long-term training: who, or which nation, would pay for someone to pursue a career in sport and compete internationally?

China Joins the Socialist World of Sport

Following the establishment of the PRC in 1949, the new leadership worked hard to establish its control nationwide, while also rebuilding a country devastated by years of war and still sending off soldiers to fight in the campaign to "Resist America/Aid Korea." An oft-told story about PRC sport in the early 1950s concerns the battle with the Republic of China (Taiwan) for sole recognition by the International Olympic Committee (IOC).[27] This is an important story, to be sure, but as far as the PRC leadership was concerned, competitive sport in these years was less about the Olympics and much more about strengthening the new socialist state's legitimacy domestically, while also reaffirming political solidarities with its allies.[28] The state-sponsored sports system was still

unclear exactly why mainland China had trouble finding athletes and coaches at the time – was it a question of organization or were these people unavailable (in areas heavily affected by the Civil War, or where families had already fled, and so on)? Further research will be required to determine what happened to those involved in these earlier programs, but we know about a few from memoirs and oral histories. Former basketball player and coach Tang Mingxin, for example, was in Taiwan already and remained there following the Communist takeover. Chang Chi-hsiung, Pan Kwang-che, and Wang Ching-ling, *Tang Mingxin xiansheng fangwen jilu* (The Reminiscences of Mr. Tang Ming-hsin) (Taipei: The Institute of Modern Chinese History Academia Sinica, 2005), 275.

[26] The 1948 London games program lists him under his Indonesian name, while histories of Chinese sport list him as Wu Chuanyu. Organising Committee for the XIV Olympiad, *The Official Report of the Organising Committee for the XIV Olympiad*. Tang Mingxin, *Wo guo canjia aoyunhui congshi (shang bian)* (The History of Our Country's Participation in the Olympics 1949–1996 (Part 1)) (Taipei: Zhonghua taibei aolinpike weiyuanhui, 2000), 393.

[27] During these years the PRC's policy in sport was to refuse joining any international sports organization that also recognized the Republic of China (Taiwan) (the so-called "two-Chinas" issue). Given the battle for PRC recognition in the International Olympic Committee, which remained unresolved in the first half of the 1950s, this essentially meant that PRC participation in sport outside the socialist bloc was quite limited. Xu Guoqi, *Olympic Dreams: China and Sports, 1895–2008* (Cambridge, MA: Harvard University Press, 2008), especially Chapter 5, "The 'Two Chinas' Question"; and Susan Brownell, "'Sports and Politics Don't Mix': China's Relationship with the IOC during the Cold War," in Stephen Wagg and David Andrews, eds., *East Plays West: Sport and the Cold War* (London and New York: Routledge, 2007).

[28] In fact, as I have shown elsewhere, deference to the Soviet Union's position on sport was common in these early years. When PRC leaders received an invitation in February 1951

under development, and sports interactions with the socialist bloc offered crucial opportunities not only to compete but also both to learn from existing socialist models and to solidify China's place in a Soviet-led socialist world.

The PRC leadership was focused on adopting mass sports programs based on Soviet models, while also interested in understanding Soviet competitive programs and the country's athletic ranking system. One of the most prominent examples of this was the "Ready for Labor and Defense" *tiyu* system. This system (abbreviated as the GTO in Russian and as the *laoweizhi* in Chinese) aimed to extend sports participation and raise the level of all-around physical fitness among ordinary citizens. The system's main goal was ostensibly to cultivate physically fit individuals who in their spare time voluntarily engaged in regular exercise. To accomplish this, participants trained regularly in order to pass fitness tests and receive badges at various levels. But it was more than just fitness: the system included the development of paramilitary skills, as well as courses on hygiene, health, and first aid.[29] Although the system's core offered a general fitness program that aimed to connect all-around bodily training to national labor and defense goals, its various levels also provided a way to build a nationally ranked system of competitive athletes.[30] By the 1950s, the "Ready for Labor and Defense" *tiyu* system had become a de facto marker of sports and physical culture in the socialist bloc. Chinese sports leaders had high hopes for adopting this model not only to show reverence for learning from the Soviet Union but also in

---

sent by the Helsinki organizing committee for the upcoming 1952 Olympics, the All-China Sports Federation decided that, although they believed the PRC should participate, the decision hinged on whether or not the Soviet Union would also participate. Chinese Foreign Ministry Archives (CFMA) 113-00097-01: Guanyu woguo shifou canjia shiwujie aolinpike yundonghui (zai Fenlan) de youguan wenjian (Related Documents Concerning Whether or Not Our Nation Participates in the 15th Olympic Games (in Finland)). Most likely this response was made because the Soviet Union, which had not yet officially participated in any Olympic Games, was not yet an IOC member. In late April 1951, Soviet leaders, perhaps because of the IOC's decision to consider allowing "two Germanies" to join, finally decided they would participate in 1952 and sent a telegram to the IOC; in May the IOC voted to recognize their Olympic Committee. Jenifer Parks, "Red Sport, Red Tape: The Olympic Games, the Soviet Sports Bureaucracy, and the Cold War, 1952–1980" (PhD diss., University of North Carolina, 2009), 51–53. In order to remain in solidarity with their "Soviet elder brother" in the face of the IOC, it seems that PRC leaders waited for the outcome of these events. See Shuman, "The Politics of Socialist Athletics in the People's Republic of China, 1949–1966," 84–89.

[29] James Riordan, *Sport in Soviet Society: Development of Sport and Physical Education in Russia and the USSR* (Cambridge: Cambridge University Press, 1977), 128–129.

[30] Xu Yingchao, "Sulian tiyu de jidian jieshao" (Some Introduction to Soviet *tiyu*), *Xin tiyu*, January 1951, 14.

order to join the rest of the Soviet-led socialist bloc on the same playing
field.

Sports competitions with socialist bloc countries – or "friendly" learning experiences, as they were sometimes called – were also considered
vital to bettering China's position in the international socialist movement
as they emphasized the unilateral nature of the Sino-Soviet relationship.
The point of these early exchanges was explicitly to study Soviet sports
models and the training methods of socialist bloc athletes, and to begin to
use sports activities as a way to foster stronger relations with other
countries. Chinese sports leaders also claimed that working with their
Soviet comrades in international sport matters further helped relations
between the countries. This attitude extended to athletes and leaders in
the rest of the Soviet-led world, whom Chinese publications portrayed as
comrades-in-arms seeking to achieve worldwide peace together through
international socialism.

The Soviet-led socialist world of sport in the 1950s was very transnational.
Translations of various materials – sports news, technical handbooks, and
articles about (or written by) famous coaches and athletes – circulated
throughout the Eastern bloc and China. *Xin tiyu* (New Sport) magazine
often translated articles directly from Russian on topics ranging from political theory to mass sport in the Soviet Union and elite athletic achievements
and international success. Articles on technical skills or movements within
specific sports often taught readers through precise descriptions and
depictions. In August 1953, *Xin tiyu* covered the training of elite
Soviet athletes in track and field, accompanied by photographs or
hand drawings illustrating proper technique. One article depicts the
Soviet national record holder for the women's eighty-meter hurdles in
thirteen still shots.[31] A reader could put these skills into practice without
much further guidance. Each issue of the magazine also included
a section called "International Sports News in Brief" that highlighted
recent elite athletic events in the Soviet Union and notable socialist bloc
sports achievements worldwide. This section appeared in nearly every
issue of *Xin tiyu*; some months a reader would be hard-pressed to find
any article in the magazine that did not mention the USSR.

In issues of *Xin tiyu* in the early 1950s, Soviet experts, techniques,
theories, and models saturated the entire realm of sports and physical
culture. Soviet documentaries and books were translated, and an official
directive from the Ministry of Higher Education in April 1953 called for
the recruitment and hiring of Soviet specialists. The Beijing Sports and

---

[31] Ge Wu, "Ye-lin-na.Ge-ji-hao-li ba shi gongchi dilan de jishu" (Elena Gokieli's
Technique in the 80-Meter Hurdles), *Xin tiyu*, August 1953, 24–25.

Physical Culture Research Institute, also established in 1953, hired a Soviet theorist in sports and physical culture, as well as experts in physiology, athletics, football, gymnastics, swimming, anatomy, and hygiene.[32] These experts helped build what would become the nation's central training institute for athletes, coaches, and sports leaders.

Media coverage of athletes and officials from other countries in the socialist bloc reached its apex during this period. Such exceptional athletes as the great Czechoslovakian distance runner Emil Zátopek merited extensive coverage. Zátopek won three gold medals in track and field at the 1952 Helsinki Olympics,[33] setting the Olympic record in the 5,000-meter and 10,000-meter races. He then decided to enter the marathon, having never run one in his life, and beat the reigning British champion while setting a new Olympic record.[34] He was frequently referenced in Chinese articles on running, including two prominent pieces in the January 1953 issue of *Xin tiyu*. One of these included a photograph of him in running gear and a detailed description of his innovative interval training methods.[35] Ironically, a hand drawing of proper running technique accompanying the article does not seem to resemble Zátopek's style at all,[36] which was notorious in the running world for being sloppy and labored.[37]

Zátopek was also held up as a model athlete for readers to follow because of his dedication to the army and devotion to communism. Accompanied by a photo of Zátopek in his military uniform, another article in the same issue of *Xin tiyu* profiled his army background and noted his loyalty.[38] The CCP also considered the PLA an important part of its continued success and it often encouraged youth to join. Many Chinese competitive athletes in the 1950s came from the army,[39] a trend not unusual for socialist bloc

---

[32] Beijing tiyu xueyuan xiaozhi, comp., *Beijing tiyu xueyuan zhi* (Beijing Tiyu Research Institute Records) (Beijing: Beijing tiyu xueyuan xiaozhi bianxiezu, 1994), 176–177.

[33] "Shijie wenming de changpao jianjiang Za-tuo-pei-ke" (World-Famous Long-Distance Runner Zatopek), *Xin tiyu*, January 1953, 18.

[34] Tim Noakes, *Lore of Running*, 4th ed. (Champaign, IL: Human Kinetics, 2003), 382–385.

[35] A. Bu-jia-qie-fu-si-jii, "Za-tuo-pei-ke de changpao lianxifa" (Zátopek's Long-Distance Training Methods), *Xin tiyu*, January 1953, 20–21.

[36] Ibid., 21.

[37] Allison Danzig, "Going the Distance," *New York Times*, July 27, 1952. Danzig wrote, "his little phenomenon of almost super-human endurance and with the most agonizing running style within memory sped 26 miles, 385 yards 6 minutes and 16 seconds faster than an Olympic marathon had ever been traversed before."

[38] Ma-he Ya-luo-mi-er, "Yi ge yisheng xinmu zhong de Za-tuo-pei-ke" (Zátopek in the Eyes of a Doctor), *Xin tiyu*, January 1953, 18–19.

[39] Two athletes from the army who became well known for their international achievements in the mid- to late 1950s were weightlifter Chen Jingkai and female high jumper Zheng

sport. Articles like these on Zátopek thus forged a close link for readers between his athletic duties and obligations to the army, nation, and communist party.

China received official sports delegations at home and sent their own abroad. As I have described in detail elsewhere, smaller events and goodwill tours made up the majority of these exchanges, which aimed simultaneously to exchange sports skills, link athletes and coaches within the socialist bloc, and build on existing political solidarities. Famous teams and athletes from socialist bloc countries, ubiquitous in the Chinese press, made their rounds to China. Most of the gold-medal-winning Soviet gymnastics squad from the Helsinki 1952 Olympics toured China in 1953, an event highlighted in a subsequent Chinese-narrated newsreel showcasing each athlete in action and listing their achievements. A Hungarian football contingent visited in 1954, just a few months before the country sent its "Magical Magyars" to the World Cup final, and toured the country with Chinese "study" teams in tow.[40] Zátopek himself visited China on more than one occasion, including in 1958 when he watched the first official Chinese marathoners surpass his own Olympic marathon time.[41]

Larger sports competitions outside the Olympics also took place in these years. Perhaps the most attended and diverse were those sponsored by the WFYS. Following World War II, the World Federation of Democratic Youth and the International Union of Students founded these mega-events. In the first decade, these events took place every two years in the Soviet-led socialist bloc – Prague 1947, Budapest 1949, Berlin 1951, Bucharest 1953, Warsaw 1955, Moscow 1957 – and included the participation of thousands of athletes. Given the sponsorship and locales, they are generally understood to have been fronts for Soviet interests. They were a common feature of the international socialist landscape, and propaganda surrounding the events touted them as promoting friendship, unity, peace, and similar ideals (Figure 3.1).

Festival organizers strove hard to draw as many people as possible to the two-week events, to make these events high-profile, and to attract media

---

Fengrong. However, even in the early 1950s, the army was the source of athletes for many sports. For example, of fourteen top track and field athletes profiled in a *New Sport* article in November 1953, eight came from the army, three were students, and three were workers. Diao Yi and Li Youkun, "Chuangzao quanguo zuigao jilu de yundongyuanmen" (Athletes Creating the Highest National Records), *Xin tiyu*, November 1953, 10–11.

[40] Amanda Shuman, "Learning from the Soviet Big Brother: The Early Years of Sport in the People's Republic of China," in Robert Edelman and Chris Young, eds., *The Whole World Was Watching: Sport In The Cold War* (Stanford University Press, December 2019).

[41] Bo Dawei, "'Da yundongliang' shi fengshou zhi lu," *Xin tiyu*, November 21, 1958; "Zatopek's Mark Cut," *New York Times*, November 4, 1958.

Figure 3.1 The front of a Soviet postcard from a WFYS event (undated)
Source: personal collection

attention worldwide. The general and somewhat vague political message of
"peace" was often forthright in festival materials. A slogan on the front cover
of a brochure promoting the 1951 festival in Berlin stated in all capitals,
"Youth unite in the struggle for peace against the danger of a new war."[42]
The socialist bloc and Soviet-leaning nations like China often sent large
delegations, and by the 1950s more than 100 countries were represented at
the festivals. Every other year, these mega-events became sites for the
circulations of and interactions between young people not only from the
Eastern bloc and socialist-leaning countries, but also from Western Europe,
North America, Africa, and Asia.[43] Political and academic meetings,

---

[42] International Institute for Social History Amsterdam (IISH), World Festival of Youth
and Students Collection (ARCH01667), folder "III. Berlin," brochure titled "Third
World Festival of Youth and Students for Peace! Berlin 5–19 August 1951."

[43] Of course, not all governments approved, so some people had to make their own travel
arrangements and pay their own way. For example, in the McCarthy era it is unsurprising
that the USA was notorious for making it difficult for people to travel to such events.
Battles between Americans asserting their travel rights also made headlines in the
New York Times when the event was held in Moscow in 1957. It didn't help that some
of these Americans were invited to China and then traveled there afterwards. A quick
Google search of some of those who attended pulls up US congressional record hearings
from the Committee on Un-American Activities on Google books related to their WFYS-
related experience. For a more thorough account of the WFYS as a phenomenon and all

cultural events, sports, and sightseeing were all on the agenda; festival guides and maps in multiple languages were distributed to attendees. And – as indicated by event programs and the high numbers of athletes listed on delegation rosters – the sports events and competitions were a significant component of each festival.[44]

The WFYS gave the PRC's top athletes a way to compete internationally when their Olympic participation increasingly seemed like a pipe dream. PRC involvement in *tiyu* outside the socialist bloc was in a state of flux during these first few years and primarily followed whatever was best for their position vis-à-vis the Soviets. For example, when PRC leaders received an invitation in February 1951 sent by the Helsinki organizing committee for the upcoming 1952 Olympics, the All-China Sports Federation decided that, although they believed that the PRC should participate, the decision hinged on whether or not the Soviet Union would also participate.[45] Once the Soviets had decided to join, however, Chinese leaders followed suit – but they faced their own battle with the IOC, in what became known as the so-called "two-Chinas" issue. IOC rules technically stated that each nation could have only one national olympic committee, but the PRC and the Republic of China (ROC) in Taiwan each claimed to be "China."[46] Just a few days before the opening

the resistance it met, see the plethora of information from numerous archives gathered in Nick Rutter, "Enacting Communism: The World Youth Festival, 1945–1975" (unpublished PhD diss., Yale University, 2013). I should note that the IISH archival files also contain numerous "reports" made by anglophone festival visitors (or spies, perhaps, in some cases) that contain a strong anticommunist/anti-Soviet tone.

[44] By 1955, every festival participant, whether athlete or not, could also earn a sports badge by completing certain sports activities. The sports badge was thus reminiscent of the Soviet-inspired "Ready for Labor and Defense" system discussed earlier in this chapter. For example, a "My Festival Diary" produced for the 1955 event in Warsaw included the section titled "Everybody to the Contests for the Festival Sports Badge." The introductory paragraph professed to participants that winning a badge would "testify to your physical efficiency" and "be one more souvenir from the Festival." The section included a table with three groups of activities in which personal results from sports events (e.g., "60 m. run," "High jump," "Throwing the ball" and so forth) could be penciled in, with specific standards for either a "silver" or "gold" badge. To be awarded a badge, participants had to complete "one standard in each of the three groups of exercises." A list of locations on where to compete for a "Festival Sports Badge" included school stadiums and kindergartens, open every day during the festival from nine in the morning to one in the afternoon. IISH, World Festival of Youth and Students Collection (ARCH01667), folder "V. Warsaw."

[45] Chinese Foreign Ministry Archives (CFMA) 113-00097-01: Guanyu woguo shifou canjia shiwujie aolinpike yundonghui (zai fenlan) de youguan wenjian (Related Documents Concerning Whether or Not Our Nation Participates in the 15th Olympic Games (in Finland)).

[46] Christopher Hill, *Olympic Politics* (New York: Manchester University Press, 1996), 44–45. For the specifics on what happened in these early years, see Shuman, "The Politics of Socialist Athletics," 92–96.

ceremonies at Helsinki, the IOC decided to allow both PRC and ROC delegations to attend as "China."[47] Neither accepted this decision, but when the ROC withdrew in protest, the PRC decided to send a delegation. However, the decision had been made so late that it arrived six days after the start of the Games and only one swimmer (none other than Wu Chuanyu; see below) was able to officially compete. Even after the IOC changed its rules in 1954 to allow territories under the control of a national olympic committee to receive the same recognition as nations, official PRC policy during this period continued to dictate that the PRC would refuse to participate in any event that also recognized the ROC as China.[48] For this reason, the PRC missed out on many events in these years held under the auspices of international federations.[49]

Participation in events like the WFYS thus provided a much more fruitful space for those in the Chinese sports world to forge new connections. Soviet and socialist bloc athletes, among the best in the world, attended these festivals. China had apparently sent a men's basketball team to the Budapest World Student Games in August 1949 (held in conjunction with the WFYS), where the team placed sixth out of nine participants.[50] But two years after the official establishment of the PRC, China sent a slightly larger delegation, which included men's basketball and volleyball teams, to the event in Berlin.[51] The brochure for the 1951 Berlin WFYS boasted the attendance of world-class athletes and boldly stated that the festival was "the only international event where every aspect of the culture and sport of all the peoples of the world finds its highest expression."[52] Outside the Olympic Games – in which it should be remembered that the Soviet Union did not take part until 1952 – this was the premier venue for sports competition. And even after socialist bloc athletes like Soviet gymnast Nina Bocharova and Czechoslovakian Emil Zátopek won gold in Helsinki, they still competed at the WFYS.[53]

---

[47] Morris, *Marrow of the Nation*, 238–239.

[48] Liang Lijuan, *He Zhenliang and China's Olympic Dream* (Beijing: Foreign Languages Press, 2007), 46–47.

[49] The exception, of course, is table tennis. For a detailed explanation of why, see Nicholas Griffin, *Ping-Pong Diplomacy: The Secret History behind the Game That Changed the World* (New York: Scribner, 2014).

[50] *Tiyu nianjian 1949–1962*, 891. All nations, except for France, were firmly in the socialist bloc. In order of finishing place, the participants were: the Soviet Union, Czechoslovakia, Hungary, France, North Korea, China/PRC, Bulgaria, Poland, and Romania.

[51] *Tiyu nianjian 1949–1962*, 34. Approximately 26,000 participants were at the Berlin WFYS.

[52] IISH, "Third World Festival of Youth and Students for Peace! Berlin 5–19 August 1951."

[53] Bocharova and Zátopek are also famous for having later visited China at various times, where they were hailed as model athletes. Elsewhere, using primarily Chinese archival sources, I discuss the visits of star gymnasts from the Soviet Union and top football players from Hungary to China in the early 1950s. See Shuman, "Learning from the

Thus for the new PRC leadership, the appeal of participation in the WFYS included fostering "friendly" relations with new political allies and promoting a positive national image, while also offering the Chinese sports world more opportunities to connect with top athletes and coaches.

Transnational "Returned" Chinese Athletes

Chinese sports leaders, in their efforts to build elite competitive sports programs for this new and growing world of international sport, also scrambled to tap into all potential resources available. One of those resource bases was the overseas Chinese population. Over the course of the 1950s, recruitment efforts to bring ethnically Chinese athletes "back" to China existed in at least several sports. Unlike during the Republican and wartime periods, these athletes were brought to the mainland for training (and, it seems, some received more benefits and resources than other "returned" Chinese at the time).[54] Table tennis is the best-known case – Rong Guotuan, China's first World Champion in 1959, was originally from Hong Kong, as were two prominent coaches.[55] At least one famous woman table tennis player recruited in the late 1950s, Lin Huiqing, was from Indonesia.[56]

One venue in which Chinese sports leaders scouted and recruited such athletes was the World Festivals of Youth and Students. In fact, also at the 1951 WFYS in Berlin were Huang Hongjiu and his teammate Wu Chuanyu, both competing as part of the delegation for the newly independent Indonesian nation and under their Indonesian names of Oei Hong Kioe and Go Tjoan Giok. The team had traveled for forty days from Indonesia,[57] and, according to Huang (Oei), spent about two months in Germany training prior to the event (Figure 3.2). *Neues Deutschland*, mouthpiece of the East German government, published

Soviet Big Brother." (The full citation information is already in footnote 40, hence this is the second instance of the reference and only the short citation is needed.)
[54] This is an issue I am still investigating, based on Glen Peterson's excellent work on the subject of "returned" Chinese and the evidence I have on a few athletes. See Peterson, *Overseas Chinese in the People's Republic of China.*
[55] Griffin, *Ping-Pong Diplomacy*, Chapter 15, "Reconnaisance," describes the process of recruitment.
[56] Liang Yingming, Pinbo yu fengxian: : Yindunixiya guiqiao linhuiqing de pingpang qiu rensheng (Hard Work and Dedication: The Table Tennis Life of Lin Huiqing, a Returned Overseas Chinese from Indonesia) (Beijing: Zhongguo huaqiao chubanshe, 2015). Badminton is another case I am currently exploring.
[57] "Go Tjoan Giok (Indonesien): 'Ich werde unsere Jugend aufrufen, den Freiheitskampf zu verstaerken'," *Neues Deutschland*, August 18, 1951, 6.

Figure 3.2 Huang (left) and Wu (right) with a German coach in East Berlin, 1951
Source: Photograph courtesy of Huang Hongjiu

a greeting in German signed by the Indonesian swimmers using their Indonesian names, which thanked the Free German Youth for a "warm, brotherly welcome" and ended with "Long live peace!" (Figure 3.3).

Wu attracted further media attention when he surprised many with his silver medal win in the 100-meter backstroke and a bronze medal in the 100-meter butterfly.[58] An article in *Neues Deutschland* mentioned these wins and included a photograph of Wu with his handwritten greeting, stating, "Hereby I'm greeting the readers of Neues Deutschland and wishing them good wishes in their fight for an ever lasting Peace! Es lebe Wilhelm Pieck!"[59] The publication of this piece, with its message of peace and support of the German Democratic Republic and (allegedly) delivered by an athlete hailing from a recently decolonized and socialist-leaning nation, was clearly an intentional message from the East German government that political solidarities ran deep.

---

[58] Huang claims that the only reason Wu did not do better in the butterfly is because he did not know the new technique in fashion, the use of a dolphin kick.

[59] "Long live Wilhelm Pieck!" Pieck was the first president of the GDR. "Indonesische Schwimmer verliessen Berlin," *Neues Deutschland*, September 18, 1951.

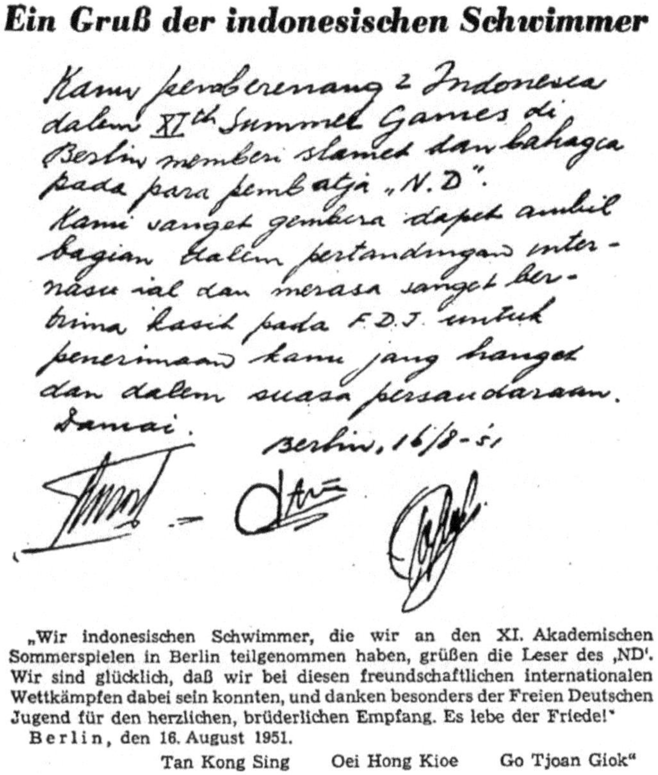

Ein Gruß der indonesischen Schwimmer

Kami pemberenang 2 Indonesia dalem XIth Summer Games di Berlin memberi slamat dan bahagia pada para pembatja „N.D".
Kami sangat gembira dapat ambil bagian dalem pertandingan inter-nasio-ial dan merasa sangat ber-trima kasih pada F.D.J. untuk penerimaan kami jang hangat dan dalem suasana persaudaraan.
Damai.
Berlin, 16/8-51

„Wir indonesischen Schwimmer, die wir an den XI. Akademischen Sommerspielen in Berlin teilgenommen haben, grüßen die Leser des ‚ND'. Wir sind glücklich, daß wir bei diesen freundschaftlichen internationalen Wettkämpfen dabei sein konnten, und danken besonders der Freien Deutschen Jugend für den herzlichen, brüderlichen Empfang. Es lebe der Friede!"
Berlin, den 16. August 1951.
Tan Kong Sing Oei Hong Kioe Go Tjoan Giok"

Figure 3.3 "A greeting from the Indonesian swimmers"
Source: *Neues Deutschland*, August 18, 1951

Wu's second-place win in Berlin also quickly garnered the attention of a new set of Chinese sports leaders. According to Huang Hongjiu, one of these leaders knew that the Indonesian delegation "were not Indonesian" and invited them to visit Beijing immediately. So the delegation made the train trek to China via Poland and Moscow and across Siberia (eleven days on a train, says Huang). After they arrived in Beijing in October 1951, the Indonesians were given the option to join the newly established national swim team in the PRC (Figure 3.4).[60]

[60] According to an online piece by the International Swimming Hall of Fame, which inaugurated Wu Chuanyu in summer 2017, the other two were Chen Gongcheng and a coach named Guo Deguang. See www.ishof.org/wu-chuanyu.html, accessed February 17, 2020.

Figure 3.4 The Indonesian delegation in Beijing, October 1951. In the
back row are Huang Hongjiu (left) and Wu Chuanyu (right)
Source: Photograph courtesy of Huang Hongjiu

According to Huang, it was an easy decision for him and Wu to join the
new PRC team because they loved to swim. The two had grown up together
in Salatiga (Java) and studied the swimming techniques of swimmer-turned-
Hollywood actor Johnny Weissmuller of Tarzan fame. Indonesia did not
have a national team training program – "Johnny Weissmuller was our
coach," joked Huang in his interview with me – and the Indonesian delegation's travel expenses were mostly self-paid through family and private
donations. The official line in the Chinese press was, as it was for many
overseas Chinese who came to the PRC in the early 1950s, that athletes like
Huang and Wu had "returned to the motherland" (*hui dao zuguo*).[61] In
short, and in contrast to the earlier government, the PRC openly claimed
these athletes and willingly funded them. Huang stated that the Indonesian
side was discontent, noting that "my brother sent me a[n Indonesian]
newspaper [that said] Wu Chuanyu, Huang Hongjiu, and Chen

---

[61] Wu Chuanyu, "Wo wei zuguo yingde le yi ke jinzhi jiangzhang" (I Won a Gold Medal for
the Motherland), *Xin tiyu*, October 1953, 26.

Gongcheng is [*sic*] a traitor." Official sources in China have usually claimed (and sometimes still claim) that overseas Chinese "returned" for patriotic reasons, but the way Huang describes it, it just seemed like an opportunity too good to turn down – a professional swimming career suddenly seemed feasible.

Huang, Wu, and the others were sent to the Peking University campus for training. None of them could speak much Chinese when they arrived; Wu communicated through an interpreter using English[62] and, according to Huang, they all took language and politics-related classes at Peking University. Though the lack of Chinese likely made communicating with locals in Beijing difficult, the use of English (and some German) was clearly an asset when dealing with Eastern bloc interpreters, coaches, and athletes.

PRC sports leaders had thus observed and recruited Wu, Huang, and their teammates into the nascent state-sponsored sports system. As previously noted, the PRC was heavily influenced by the Soviet Union, its sports leaders, and its sports model. In stark contrast to the preceding Nationalist government, in which sport was often not state-sponsored and donations or private funds often paid for elite athletes to participate in international competition,[63] the new government clearly professed early interest in investing in a robust state-sponsored sports system that cultivated athletes. It sought out athletes like Wu and Huang specifically to help build up this new system.

Over the next few years, a Chinese national swimming team took shape (Figure 3.5). Although Wu was the only representative of the Chinese delegation to participate officially in the 1952 Helsinki Olympics,[64] Chinese swimmers received training from Hungarian and Soviet coaches in Beijing. Moreover, in June 1953 in the lead-up to the WFYS in Bucharest, Wu was sent to the Soviet Union as part of a larger delegation, where he received

[62] Wu Chuanyu , "Wo wei zuguo yingde le yi ke jinzhi jiangzhang," 26; and Li Lingxiu and Zhou Mingong, "Tiyu zhizi Rong Gaotang" (*Tiyu*'s Son Rong Gaotang), *Tiyu wenhua daokan*, February 2003, 67.

[63] Morris, *Marrow of the Nation*. See, for example, the sections describing China's participation in the 1932 and 1936 Olympic Games in the chapter "Elite Competitive Sport in the 1930s," at 141–184. Among other things, stadiums were paid for by private firms (149) and China's first visit to the Olympics – a story now documented in the film *The One Man Olympics* (2008) – was funded by warlord Zhang Xueliang. Ibid., 169. The exception was for the 1936 Berlin Olympics, in which the Chinese National Amateur Athletic Federation – the affiliate required to choose athletes to send to the Olympics – agreed to pay transportation, room, and board for athletes, though it also allowed "confident competitors able to pay their own way plus five hundred yuan" for training costs. Ibid., 172.

[64] *The Official Report of the Organising Committee for the Games of the the XV Olympiad* (Helsinki: The Organising Committee for the XV Olympiad, 1952), 574, at https://digi tal.la84.org/digital/collection/p17103coll8/id/4746/rec/1, accessed February 17, 2020.

Figure 3.5 Photographs of the Chinese national swim team in 1953. Wu
is sitting in the second row, second from left, and Huang is in the second
row, fourth from right
Source: Photograph courtesy of Huang Hongjiu

several weeks of daily training from the very best Soviet swimming coach at
the time. The hopes were high for Wu; after just eight days of training, the
Chinese side reported, he had already improved his swim times.[65]

The PRC leadership did not have to wait long for its investment to pay off.
China sent a delegation of eighty athletes, including members of the swim
team, to the fourth WFYS in Bucharest in August 1953.[66] Chinese athletes
competed in men's and women's basketball, volleyball, track and field, and
swimming, but the highlight of the trip was when twenty-five-year-old Wu
won the only gold medal for China in the men's 100-meter backstroke.
Following this win, he became a media sensation in China. *Xin tiyu*, which
rarely had the opportunity to highlight the international successes of any
Chinese athlete in these years, included his victory as part of the
"International Sports News Brief" in September 1953.[67] In October, the
magazine included an article that also described his background and

---

[65] Li and Zhou, "Tiyu zhizi Rong Gaotang," 68.
[66] The overall festival attracted approximately 30,000 participants.
[67] "Wo guo huo yi bai gongchi yangyong diyi" (Our Nation Wins First Place in the 100-
Meter Backstroke), *Xin tiyu*, September 1953, 40.

Figure 3.6 Wu Chuanyu, model athlete, arguably the most famous
Chinese athlete of the early 1950s, the "Flying Fish" (*feiyu*)
Source: Front cover of *Xin tiyu*, October 1953

experience,[68] while a huge color photograph of the athlete adorned the front
cover (Figure 3.6).[69] And when the Hungarian football team delegation's
reporter visited Shanghai in early 1954, the Shanghai sports committee set
up an interview for Wu with him.[70] By the time Wu was sent with
a delegation of swimming athletes to Hungary that March, the Foreign
Ministry no longer even listed his birthplace in official documentation as
Indonesia but had changed it to Fujian province (the source of his family
ancestry).[71]

[68] Wu Chuanyu, "Wo wei zuguo yingde le yi ke jinzhi jiangzhang," 26–27.
[69] *Xin tiyu*, October 1953, cover. The other side of the front cover includes several athletes
carrying the flag as part of the athletes' parade.
[70] SMA B126-1-86: Zhaodai Xiongyali zuqiudui lai Hu fangwen gongzuo jianbao: di si hao.
[71] CFMA 118-00278-05: Guanyu Zhongguo qingnian zuqiudui, youyongdui fu Xiongyali
xuexi de shenpan ji ru guojing qianzheng shi, March 15–19, 1954.

Wu, as he became known, also became a Communist Party member, and the first model athlete that Mao himself extolled. "Do you know who Wu Chuanyu is?" Mao asked Wuhan swimmers during a meeting with them some four years later. "Is there anyone now who can do better than him? [You] should learn from Wu Chuanyu and surpass [him]!"[72] Wu also set a precedent for future athletes when his international success won him official roles beyond sport: he was named a representative to the First National People's Congress in September 1954 as the only athlete on the list.[73] Just a month later, at the age of twenty-six, he tragically died in a plane crash while traveling to Hungary to resume training.[74] Sports yearbooks and official publications in China have nevertheless continued to cite Wu's gold medal in Bucharest as "the first time that the five-star flag was hung."[75]

Huang, unlike Wu, saw far less success on the international stage, but he did help forge sports networks and build China's national programs in both swimming and water polo. In the late 1950s, following his own athletic retirement, Huang became a water polo coach at the provincial level in Fujian. The Chinese government has often provided former national-level athletes with sports-related positions following athletic retirement.[76] When the State Sports Commission ramped up its efforts to build competitive sports programs in the mid-1950s, and especially in 1957 in preparation for the 1959 National Games, it constantly lacked qualified personnel.[77] Water polo was a new sport in China at the time, but it was already an extremely popular sport in the socialist bloc with deep political implications, as the infamous "blood in the water" match

---

[72] CCTV International, "'Chuanqi aoyun': jiangshu aoyun chuanqi: Zhongguo de jiao'ao – Wu Chuanyu" (Legends of the Olympic Games: About the Olympic Legend: China's Pride – Wu Chuanyu), December 17, 2007, at http://news.cctv.com/china/20071211/1 07404.shtml, accessed February 17, 2020.

[73] "Zhonghua renmin gongheguo di yi jie quanguo renmin daibiao dahui daibiao mingdan" (First National People's Congress of the PRC Name List), *Renmin ribao*, September 4, 1954. The only other representatives named from the world of *tiyu* were Rong Gaotang, and Ma Yuehan, who were much older sports leaders at the time. See also Li and Zhou, "Tiyu zhizi Rong Gaotang," 67.

[74] "Wo guo youxiu yundongyuan Wu Chuanyu shishi" (The Death of Our Nation's Elite Athlete Wu Chuanyu), *Renmin ribao*, December 25, 1954.

[75] "Da shiji," in *Zhongguo tiyu nianjian 1949–1991*, 6.

[76] This is most obvious when looking at coaches or trainers in almost any sport, although some former athletes have gone on to administrator positions. Well-known examples include table tennis players Rong Guotuan, Zhuang Zedong, and Qiu Zhonghui, as well as former Mao-era volleyball player Yuan Weimin, who went on to coach the women's volleyball team to Olympic gold in the 1984 Los Angeles Olympics. Yuan also later was made vice minister and then head of the State Sports Commission. At the provincial level, this also appears to have been the case; one can choose almost any sport in any province and find a pedigree of former athletes in leading positions.

[77] Shuman, "The Politics of Socialist Athletics," 184.

between Hungary and the Soviet Union at the 1956 Melbourne Olympics attested.[78] It thus seems unsurprising that Huang, a top-notch athlete with international experience (though not well known outside swimming circles), was given a head coaching position for the nascent water polo team in Fujian in 1957.[79] The team fared well over the next few years, including third place at the inaugural National Games in 1959.[80]

Unfortunately, when I interviewed him, Huang preferred not to speak at length about this period of time – perhaps because of personal issues, or perhaps because of his treatment during political campaigns in subsequent years.[81] Huang did not speak of political persecution at any length, but like many overseas Chinese on the mainland during the 1960s, he ran into serious trouble during the Cultural Revolution (although not, apparently, in earlier political campaigns). He spoke about being "sent down" to labor in the early Cultural Revolution, first to a fishing village near the Taiwan Strait until, according to him, authorities worried that he would try to swim across; he was then transferred to a rubber plant inland. He states that he wrote Zhou Enlai five letters about his situation but doubts that his letters ever made it to the premier. Finally, in 1972, he was given the option to leave and join his family in Hong Kong.[82] A few years later he made his way to the Netherlands, where the rest of his family lived and still reside.

And yet, despite these tumultuous events, it is the photographs and memories of the 1950s that he has carried with him throughout the decades. Huang fondly remembers his friend and teammate Wu, and has visited Wu's grave to pay his respects on many occasions (including just a few years ago).[83] During my interview with him, it was also clear

---

[78] There have been numerous news media articles published and two feature-length documentary films produced about this event. For an overview, see Kirsty Reid, "Blood in the Water: Hungary's 1956 Water Polo Gold," *BBC News*, August 20, 2011, at www .bbc.com/news/world-14575260, accessed February 11, 2020.

[79] Fujian sheng difangzhi bianzun weiyuanhui bian, *Zhonghua renmin gongheguo difangzhi Fujian shengzhi tiyu zhi* (Fujian: Renmin chubanshe, 1993), 136.

[80] Ibid., 137.

[81] During our interview, a family member interjected at one point to ask about his "first wife" in the PRC, but he clearly expressed that he did not want to discuss this and I did not press.

[82] Who exactly gave him this option and how is unclear. The policy on overseas Chinese was apparently relaxed at this time and others left as well. According to Glen Peterson, this was related to the impending visit of President Nixon. Peterson, *Overseas Chinese in the People's Republic of China*, 137. Huang insisted it was probably Zhou Enlai who ordered it, which seems plausible, but it is likely also related to the return of Liao Chengzhi, chairman of the Overseas Chinese Affairs Commission, who had been purged in 1967. Fitzgerald, *China and the Overseas Chinese*, 173–179. I have yet to locate any official document from 1972 outlining this policy.

[83] Huang also claims that during the Cultural Revolution the photograph of Wu displayed on the grave "disappeared" temporarily, but that at the direct order of Zhou Enlai it suddenly reappeared within a week.

that the friendships he'd made in the socialist bloc continue to linger with him as positive memories, and that he takes pride in the transnational nature that was this experience. It is thus fitting that one photograph he readily shared with me is that of his "friend Erich Jolig" – a swimming coach who worked in Leipzig. Dated February 15, 1957, on the back of the photograph is a short message to Huang written in a mix of German, Chinese, and English (Figure 3.7).

Conclusion

This chapter has sought to understand the lives and role of transnational "returned" Chinese athletes in 1950s China, in the context of the early PRC government's socialist state-building project. This project aimed to transform the masses into socialist subjects through sports and physical culture, while also developing internationally competitive athletic

(A)   (B)

Figure 3.7 Photograph of Erich Jolig next to a swimming pool (A) with a message on the back (B): "A souvenir for Huang Hongjiu of [*sic*] your Germany friend, Erich Jolig"
Source: courtesy of Huang Hongjiu

programs. A transnational approach is fundamental in understanding this period in early PRC history. Nation-centered histories of the PRC, which have tended to focus on the Olympics, are insufficient in looking at the complexity of a moment in which athletes and other sportspeople frequently moved across the socialist bloc, often for the purpose of exchanging skills, training together, or participating in large-scale, non-Olympic competitions like those at the WFYS . Moreover, as this chapter has specifically demonstrated, nation-centered histories fail to capture the complicated, transnational experiences of ethnically Chinese athletes – recruited from the overseas Chinese population by the PRC government – at a very unique moment in time, to compete for the new socialist state and help build its athletic programs.

Reflecting on Wu Chuanyu's life in hindsight, one can easily see how and why he was claimed by the PRC government as a Chinese athlete and then, following his successes, made into a hero through PRC propaganda. He was a champion swimmer, regardless of national origin or ethnicity; he competed with the very best in the world at the time and he even won. It was his luck that no ethnically Chinese athlete had yet been so successful internationally. In official narratives on Chinese sport, Wu's success at the 1953 WFYS and subsequent fame as a model athlete quickly outweigh any discussion of his background. His election to the National People's Congress seems something of an anomaly given the likelihood that his Chinese may not have been great and it's questionable how much he understood or cared about the politics of the country. (Although he was taking classes at Peking University, he traveled somewhat frequently to compete and his training included both non-Chinese-speaking teammates and coaches.) But we don't know how he felt at the time, and all we have available are the few sources cited in this chapter and the recollections of his teammate and friend, Huang Hongjiu. What we can perhaps conclude, though, is that Wu was actually more than a model *Chinese* athlete: like Huang and others at the time, he was a truly *transnational* athlete.

Moreover, by tracing the lives of "returned" Chinese athletes like Wu and Huang, it is apparent that undergirding China's national project to build a new sports system in the 1950s were the complex motivations of individual athletes – some of whom seem to have professed little to no affinity for "China." Yet these athletes became the very bodies through which the early PRC leadership sought to establish a state-sponsored system and produce the very first representatives of this new socialist state in the international arena. As this chapter has attempted to suggest, the early PRC was thus a fertile time for athletes like Wu and Huang to negotiate their Chineseness and become bona fide PRC athletes. Wu,

Huang, and others helped build programs by gathering knowledge and participating in what at the time were new, transnational sports networks centered on the socialist bloc. Moreover, through these networks, such athletes helped forge important connections for the PRC with its new socialist bloc allies. In this respect, they served as a kind of athlete–diplomat for the new socialist state, helping shore up support for the new leadership and solidify the nation's position within the Soviet-led socialist bloc – in sport, to be sure, but also more broadly.

The early 1950s saw the first instances in which such overseas Chinese athletes were recruited to compete for the new PRC, but not the last. By the late 1950s, PRC sports leaders had recruited top athletes and coaches in table tennis and badminton from Hong Kong and Indonesia – and there are likely also other cases in other sports. The rewards of diversifying and taking a transnational approach in examining these athletes make visible new questions and narratives. For example, elite competitive athletes drawn from the overseas Chinese population received unique benefits and preferential treatment that others did not. Moreover, recruitment seemed to occur on an ad hoc basis and not according to any official timelines. Most of them, including both famous table tennis players like Rong Guotuan and less famous former athletes like Huang, were able to make careers out of their sports skills based on continued government support (until, that is, the early years of the Cultural Revolution). In short, these athletes remained in the sports world after their athletic retirement, thereby providing the backbone of PRC sports leadership in the Mao era – an under-researched issue that this chapter has provided only a glimpse of. This chapter also leads to numerous other questions. What does all this say about the centrality of sport to the building of a new socialist state, or about the extent of the party-state's financial investment to realize a "new" China? To what degree did transnational athletes provide the legwork for the PRC to reach its goals in elite competitive sport? Why, by the 1960s, did the PRC government no longer actively seek out the participation of overseas Chinese sportspeople? And, finally, to open this up more broadly: to what extent did overseas Chinese play a crucial role in these early years in other realms outside sport?

4   Asia's Fourth Rome

Cultural Industries and Cultural Diplomacy
in the International Legitimization of the People's
Republic of China, 1949–1953

Matthew D. Johnson

Making the PRC appear great after 1949 was a technically and organ-
izationally complex problem that required the CCP to mobilize all of
the cultural resources at its disposal. For CCP chairman Mao Zedong,
"greatness" did not only mean looking like the Soviet Union, but also
restoring a sense of national uniqueness and pride. As Mao had stated
immediately prior to the PRC's founding:

Following the arrival of a high tide in economic reconstruction, it is inevitable that
there will be a need to produce a high tide in cultural construction. The era in
which Chinese people are taken to be uncivilized has already passed. We will,
from this point on, arise in the world as a nation [*minzu*] possessing culture to
a high degree.[1]

In Mao's prophetic formulation, culture and civilization were signifiers of
China's grandeur as a country (China) and transnational "nation" (an
ethnic community bound by Chinese culture). To be Chinese in this
double sense was, according to Mao, to be elevated culturally as a result
of the establishment of the PRC – "New China." A key component of the
CCP's post-1949 planning would be ensuring that Mao's prophesy some-
how came to fruition.

For historians, reconstructing the internal challenges of cultural construction would have been difficult in an era when most available sources
also doubled as propaganda for the achievements of the party-state. This
chapter highlights how a range of perspectives available only in the post-
Mao era – diplomatic histories, state document collections, local archives,
the records of the PRC Ministry of Foreign Affairs, and interviews – can
aid us in understanding what "culture" meant to CCP elites and

---

[1] Mao Zedong , "Zhongguo renmin zhanqilai," September 21, 1949, in *Mao Zedong lun
wenhua yishu (zhengqiu yijian ben)*, ed. Wenhua bu zhengce yanjiu shi (author's collection),
106. From speech given at the first plenary session of the Chinese People's Political
Consultative Conference.

functionaries (cadres) during the early years of rule, when China's internal and external social relations were being redefined. Accordingly, the chapter's main focus is on how the PRC's identity as a socialist state led by a communist party was constructed partly in concert with more technically advanced socialist countries such as the Soviet Union and its allies in the Eastern bloc, and how this identity was exported outside China in a way that, paradoxically, was intended to communicate something of the uniqueness and "high degree" of culture that Mao and other CCP leaders associated with their own Chinese heritage.

This inherent tension between internationalism and nationalism within PRC cultural policy was not confined solely to China. Despite the internationalist – we might also say globalist – characteristics of the world communist movement, socialism at the state level was inseparable from legitimizing ideologies of national destiny and from the reversal, through revolution, of the past injustices suffered at the hands of foreign powers. During the 1940s and 1950s, Josef Stalin used the symbol of Russia as a reconstituted universal empire (a "Third Rome") to inspire unity and expansion following World War II.[2] Promoting this image of the Soviet Union as "first among equals" within a broader, quasi-imperial confederation of European states became part of the basis of Stalinist cultural policy.[3] Cultural display was a means of signaling primacy in politics; the Soviet "aesthetic state" melded imagery of both past and present in order to legitimize its material power. There were two intended audiences for these legitimizing acts: those living under the rule of the CPSU, and other countries' leaders and publics, with whom Soviet leaders sought to engage. Here we encounter something of the real meaning of national culture in the context of the early 1950s, both as a kind of spiritual "glue" intended to bind communities together (often for purposes of party-led mobilization), and as a tool of international persuasion through the projection of grandeur and might.

As concerns the more specific case of China, the central argument of this chapter is that, in a manner which paralleled, but did not merely replicate, the global ambitions of the Soviet Union, China's new leaders had clear designs on universalistic claims within Asia. Messianism about China's greatness was an important aspect of Mao's charisma as a leader, and this message was in turn disseminated internationally through

---

[2] Marshall T. Poe, *"Moscow, The Third Rome": The Origins and Transformations of a Pivotal Movement* (Washington, DC: The National Council for Soviet and East Asian Research, 1997), 3–4, 13.

[3] Katerina Clark, *Moscow, the Fourth Rome: Stalinism, Cosmopolitanism, and the Evolution of Soviet Culture, 1931–1941* (Cambridge, MA: Harvard University Press, 2011), 6–11.

repeated reference to the uniqueness and success of China's non-Soviet revolutionary "path." When confronted with the dilemma of how to engage with nonsocialist countries, or those for which revolution was a more distant concern, the CCP's response was instead to engage in more generic forms of cultural diplomacy which highlighted China's achievements as a great and developing nation. Mao and his supporters needed to convince other countries of China's legitimacy as a nation-state to secure their new government in Beijing. International cultural display was a relatively low-cost approach to signaling greatness and earning respect even in settings where relations were not carried out on a basis of socialist "fraternity."

Uncovering the Foundations of Cultural Construction: Context and Method

In terms of its organization, this chapter examines the resulting sequence of steps taken by the CCP to globally communicate China's greatness and legitimacy. Its main focus is the film industry, which played a significant role in the dissemination of information about China's post-1949 reconstruction during the politically turbulent Korean War period.[4] Three of the chapter's sections analyze how cultural production was impacted by Mao's cultural nationalism: in the harnessing of foreign technical aid to create a PRC film industry capable of independently entering world markets, in the building of close technical and cultural relations with communist parties in Korea and Vietnam, and in the broader external representation of China's achievements through international film festivals and film export. The chapter's final section links these efforts to the broader context of cultural diplomacy, through which "new" China's image was incrementally constructed through people-to-people exchange, international meetings, and overseas influence operations.[5]

Drawing on this evidence, the chapter highlights that the CCP's international legitimization efforts through culture simultaneously engaged with

---

[4] Valuable accounts of the Korean War and its diplomatic aftermath include Sergei N. Goncharov, John W. Lewis, and Xue Litai, *Uncertain Partners: Stalin, Mao, and the Korean War* (Stanford: Stanford University Press, 1993); Chen Jian, *China's Road to the Korean War: The Making of the Sino-American Confrontation* (New York: Columbia University Press, 1994); Chen Jian, *Mao's China and the Cold War* (Chapel Hill: University of North Carolina Press, 2001); Simei Qing, *Allies to Enemies: Visions of Modernity, Identity, and U.S.–China Diplomacy, 1945–1960* (Cambridge, MA: Harvard University Press, 2007).

[5] On people-to-people aspects of China's foreign policy, see Anne-Marie Brady, *Making the Foreign Serve China: Managing Foreigners in the People's Republic* (Lanham, MD: Rowman & Littlefield, 2003).

multiple target audiences. This finding reflects the conclusions of contemporaneous observers and diplomatic historians that post-1949 China's relationship with the wider world was defined by several overlapping strategies. One was self-positioning as a model for revolution in Asia and the developing world, underpinned by the nationalistic belief that China should play a special and leading role in the Asian region.[6] A more fundamental goal, particularly until 1951, was seeking territorial reunification and militarily securing peripheral areas, following which point China – following the Soviet Union – began to more visibly explore limited opportunities for "peace" with nonsocialist countries.[7] In China's case, a central objective was internationally recognized statehood, not just membership in the Soviet-dominated community of socialist states.[8] Recent scholarship drawing on Cold War archives has further argued that, from the outset, Mao sought diplomatic independence from the Soviet Union, particularly within Asia.[9] All of these perspectives complement the writings of diplomatic historians in the PRC itself, who have described the 1949–1955 period as one defined by close relations with socialist countries, struggle with the USA, and efforts to establish "normal" relations with countries outside the socialist camp – the latter encompassing relations with newly independent Asian nations and the developing world, and recognition by the United Nations.[10]

More fine-grained findings thus complicate the more caricatured history of the early 1950s as a period in which diplomatic leaning to one side (*yi bian dao*, that is, siding with the Soviet Union against the United States) and following the Soviet model were, in 1954, suddenly replaced by support for nonalignment and peaceful coexistence. Mao was undeniably committed to opposing the "imperialist" forces of the United States and, to a lesser extent, Britain, and France, as evidenced by his analyses of the international

---

[6] A. Doak Barnett, *Communist China and Asia: A Challenge to American Policy* (New York: Council on Foreign Relations, 1960), 65–66.

[7] Ibid., 77–79, 95.

[8] J.D. Armstrong, *Revolutionary Diplomacy: Chinese Foreign Policy and the United Front Doctrine* (Berkeley: University of California Press, 1977), 70–74. See also Zhang Yongjin, *China in International Society since 1949: Alienation and Beyond* (New York: St. Martin's Press, 1998).

[9] Zhihua Zheng and Danhui Li, *After Leaning to One Side: China and Its Allies in the Cold War* (Washington, DC: Woodrow Wilson Center Press, 2011), 3–4. On China's support for Vietnamese communists during the Korean War, see Chen Jian, *Mao's China and the Cold War*; Qiang Zhai, *China and the Vietnam Wars, 1950–1975* (Durham, NC: University of North Carolina Press, 2000). On the cultural dimensions of China's Asian focus, see Michael Szonyi and Hong Liu, "New Approaches to the Study of the Cold War in Asia," in Zheng Yangwen, Hong Liu, and Michael Szonyi, eds., *The Cold War in Asia: The Battle for Hearts and Minds* (Leiden: Brill, 2010), 1–14.

[10] See Xie Yixian et al., *Zhongguo waijiao shi: Zhonghua renmin gongheguo, 1949–1979* (Zhengzhou: He'nan renmin chubanshe, 1988), 8–9; Zhang Lili, *Dangdai Zhongguo waijiao jianshi* (Shanghai: Shanghai renmin chubanshe, 2009), 6.

system.[11] However, from 1949 onward Mao's writings also emphasized the importance of China and the Chinese people re-entering the "world's family of nations," of equality and sovereignty, of relations with capitalist countries, and of national and regional self-determination.[12] War against the United States in Korea was legitimized in terms of what was good for China, for Korea, for the Orient (*Dongfang*), and ultimately for the world.[13] As armistice negotiations began in 1951, Mao reiterated China's commitment to building ties with the peoples of Asia and Europe.[14] Other forms of engagement followed the shift in strategy, with export of goods to nonsocialist countries reaching approximately 33 percent of total foreign-trade value by 1952.[15] Like trade, cultural display and diplomacy also supported Mao's global ambitions, with the 1951–1952 period marked by a "rapid" transition to a "soft and cooperative" line.[16] The resulting reorientation required building international and transnational linkages in ways that were initially unfamiliar to cultural planners schooled in the settings of revolutionary Asia, where China had already adopted a more paternalistic role as an "elder" and experienced socialist country. By 1955, however – the moment of the Afro-Asian Conference held in Bandung, Indonesia – the CCP had begun to position itself as a more genuinely global political force, continuing to draw advice from the Soviet Union while, at the same time, appropriating some of its luster as a civilizational center.

Necessary Dependence, Planned Independence: Building Global Cultural Industries through International Aid and Trade

Soviet technical aid and expert assistance to the PRC's early industry drove forward the transformation into global cultural producer. CCP officials like cultural minister Zhou Yang sought to create a distinctive national style rather than merely replicating elements of Soviet-defined social realism.[17]

---

[11] See Mao Zedong, "Quan shijie fandiguozhuyi chenying de liliang chaoguole diguozhuyi chenying de liliang," December 25, 1947, reprinted in Zhonghua renmin gongheguo waijiao bu, Zhong-Gong zhongyang wenxian yanjiu shi, ed., *Mao Zedong waijiao wenxian* (hereafter *MZDWW*) (Beijing: Zhongyang wenxian chubanshe, 1994), 64–67.

[12] *MZDWW*, 89–91, 113–115, 116–117, 137–138.

[13] Mao Zedong , "Wo jun yingdang he bixu ru Chao can zhan," October 13, 1950, in *MZDWW*, 144.

[14] *MZDWW*, 146–155, *passim*.

[15] Zhang, *China in International Society since 1949*, 28.

[16] Herbert Passin, *China's Cultural Diplomacy* (London: The China Quarterly, 1962), 8.

[17] Zhou Yang, "Zai quanguo di yi jie dianying juzuo huiyi shang de guanyu xuexi shehuizhuyi xianshizhuyi wenti de baogao (jielu)," March 11, 1953, reprinted in Wu Di, ed., *Zhongguo dianying yanjiu ziliao, shang juan* (hereafter *ZDYZ*) (Beijing: Wenhua yishu chubanshe, 2006), 329–344.

102   *Matthew D. Johnson*

Structures and channels for propaganda resembled those of the Soviet Union, particularly during the 1950s.[18] However, the CCP had also developed an independent approach to propaganda during the First United Front (1923–1927) period and after. Post-1949, the Soviet Union returned as an important and more experienced partner in creating films suitable for international exhibition.

Among the first Sino-Soviet productions were the documentary films *Victory of the Chinese People* (*Zhongguo renmin de shengli*, 1950) and *Liberated China* (*Jiefangle de Zhongguo*, 1950). Filmmakers working in areas recently occupied by the PLA re-created vivid scenes depicting the economic benefits of "liberation," the capture and punishment of oppressors, and popular enthusiasm for CCP rule. The CCP Central Committee Propaganda Department dispatched personnel directly to war zones to ensure that the project was completed. As part of the propaganda system, the Xinhua News Agency was responsible for fulfilling detailed requests from the center to provide footage of war-damaged factories restored to productivity, rebuilt railroads and bridges, land reform, the liberation of minority areas, the erection of monuments to revolutionary martyrs, and public trials of "imperialist" elements within society.[19] Upon release, the films were used as domestic and international propaganda to legitimize the new PRC government.

Victory of the Chinese People and *Liberated China* were not only meant to convey, in grandiose terms, the CCP's achievements in rebuilding China's economy and society. As films, their quality was also indicative of the CCP's ability to deliver technically and aesthetically complex products using the cultural industries now under its control. Soviet advisers and technicians played important roles in this process, supervising camera work, directing the filming of the National Inauguration (*kaiguo dadian*) ceremony held on October 1, 1949, editing footage, and creating colorized prints. Chinese filmmakers also assisted in the production of Soviet-made films introducing the PRC to Soviet bloc audiences, including *A Day in Shanghai* (*Shanghai de yi ri* in Chinese sources) and a planned feature concerning nineteenth-century explorer Nikolai Mikhailovich Przhevalesky (1839–1888), who had traveled to Tibet.[20]

---

[18] Julian Chang, "The Mechanics of State Propaganda: The People's Republic of China and the Soviet Union in the 1950s," in Timothy Cheek and Tony Saich, eds., *New Perspectives on State Socialism in China* (Armonk, NY: M.E. Sharpe, 1997), 76–124.
[19] Huadong ju xuanzhuan bu, "Zhonggong zhongyang xuanchuan bu guanyu xiezhu paishe Zhongguo jiefang zhanzheng yingpian deng wenti de zhishi," December 24, 1949, Shanghai shi dang'anguan (hereafter SHMA), A22-2-18.
[20] Yang Senyao, "Shanghai de wenhua yishu jiaoliu," in Zhong-Gong Shanghai shiwei dangshi yanjiu shi, ed., *Fengyu licheng, 1949–1978* (Shanghai: Shanghai shudian chubanshe, 2005), 285; Beijing dianying zhipianchang xingzheng chu, ed., *Yjiuwuling nian*

In addition to Soviet assistance, studios also drew on other international resources for purposes of propaganda filmmaking. Equipment and film stock were imported. Cameras, projectors, and replacement parts were often still of American, German, Japanese, and Soviet manufacture.[21] The China Film Equipment Company (Zhongguo dianying qicai gongsi), established in July 1951, imported equipment from Czechoslovakia, Poland, and the Soviet Union that would allow PRC filmmakers to reach the standards established by more technologically advanced industries.[22] Three main studios existed in the early 1950s: Northeast (later renamed Changchun), Beijing (which produced newsreels and documentaries), and Shanghai. Northeast was originally constructed by the Japanese–Manchurian government before capture by CCP forces during the Third Civil War (1945–1949); even during the 1950s, Japanese technicians continued to supervise aspects of production as well as the processing of film stock.[23] Nearby Ha'erbin was also home to a 35 mm film projector factory of Russian origin, which in 1950 was transferred to Chinese ownership by the Soviet company Sovexportfilm.[24]

Technical assistance and equipment from socialist countries, particularly Czechoslovakia and the Soviet Union, were essential to getting the PRC's film industry up and running following more than a decade of internal conflict beginning in 1937 with the War of Resistance to Japan. Studio construction and reconstruction required imported inputs; the early history of China's post-1949 film system was in large part a history of material aid.[25] Soviet assistance was critical in routing additional equipment obtained from Great Britain, Japan, West Germany, and the United States toward China; Hong Kong represented another key

gongzuo zongjie ji yijiuwuyi nian gongzuo fangzhen yu renwu (Beijing: Beijing dianying zhipianchang xingzheng chu, 1951), 32–33. The film, directed by Sergei Yutkevich, "when ... finished in 1951, was not distributed in China. No official reason was offered, but it was clear that the discovery by a European of China's art and antiquity was not a fit subject for China's modern audience and national feelings." See Jay Leyda, *Electric Shadows: An Account of Film and the Film Audience in China* (Cambridge, MA: The MIT Press, 1972), 189–190.

21 Interview, December 2004; Beijing dianying zhipianchang xinwen chu, ed., *Xinwen dianying gongzuo zongjie hui huikan* (Beijing: Beijing dianying zhipianchang xinwen chu, 1950), 193.

22 Tian Jingqing, *Beijing dianying ye shiji (1949–1990)* (Beijing: Zhongguo dianying chubanshe, 1999), 32; Gou Yusheng, "Luo Jingyu," in Zhongguo dianyingjia xiehui, dianying shi yanjiu bu, ed., *Zhongguo dianyingjia liezhuan, di er ji* (Beijing: Zhongguo dianying chubanshe, 1982), 216–222.

23 Yang Haizhou et al., eds., *Zhongguo dianying wuzi chanye xitong lishi biannian ji (1928–1994)* (Beijing: Zhongguo dianying chubanshe, 1998), 41–42.

24 Tian, *Beijing dianying ye shiji (1949–1990)*, 53.

25 Yang et al., *Zhongguo dianying wuzi chanye xitong lishi biannian ji (1928–1994)*, 44; Xu Qianlin, *Zhongguo dianying jishu fazhan jianshi* (Beijing: Zhongguo dianying chubanshe, 2005), 56–58.

conduit for trade with the nonsocialist world in film stock, equipment parts, and other necessities.[26]

Such assistance and trade were critical because of the large-scale propaganda effort that war and state consolidation required. During the first year of the PRC's existence, culture and education were placed under central control, while planning began for the elimination of old cultural forms. News was centralized and standardized, and the CCP sought to build a united front internally while eliminating enemies. The Korean War brought a new dimension of co-ordinated psychological mobilization to the fore, with the CCP Central Committee issuing a directive on October 26, 1950, to begin instilling "faith in victory" and the destruction of a "fear America" mentality on a national scale.[27] By 1951, three major propaganda campaigns were already underway: the Resist America/Aid Korea campaign, the land reform campaign, and the Campaign to Suppress Counterrevolutionaries.[28] Planning and regularization of propaganda were high on the CCP's agenda, with the first national meeting on propaganda work convened that May.[29] Chief propaganda official Hu Qiaomu stated that propagandists should above all remain focused on the "patriotic movement."[30] The resolution that emerged from the meeting emphasized improving and expanding the domestic propaganda system.[31]

Despite calls from CCP leaders to the cultural bureaucracy to galvanize popular support through patriotic mobilization, actual film production was uneven. Between 1950 and 1951, PRC studios produced twenty-six feature films, twenty documentaries (two in color), and sixty-two newsreels.[32] Between 1952 and 1953, nineteen feature films and sixteen documentaries were produced. Internal paralysis was one

---

[26] Interview, July 2006; Yang et al., *Zhongguo dianying wuzi chanye xitong lishi biannian ji (1928–1994)*, 44.

[27] "Zhonggong zhongyang guanyu zai quanguo jinxing shishi xuanchuan de zhishi," October 26, 1950, in Zhonggong zhongyang wenxian yanjiushi, ed., *Jianguo yilai zhongyao wenxian xuanbian (di yi ce)* (Beijing: Zhongyang wenxian chubanshe, 1992), 436–440.

[28] Di si ci wendai hui choubei zu qicao zu, Wenhua bu wenxue yishu yanjiuyuan lilun zhengce yanjiushi, *Liushi nian wenyi dashiji, 1919–1979* (n.l.: Weiding gao bu de fanyin, 1979), 131.

[29] "Zhongguo Gongchandang di yi ci quanguo xuanchuan gongzuo huiyi," in Zhongyang xuanchuan bu bangongting, ed., *Dang de xuanchuan gongzuo huiyi gaikuang he wenxian* (Beijing: Zhongguo zhongyang dangxiao chubanshe, 1994), 1–5.

[30] Ibid., 19.

[31] Di yi ci quanguo xuanchuan gongzuo huiyi guanyu jiaqiang dang de xuanchuan jiaoyu gongzuo de jueyi, in ibid., 28–33.

[32] Chin Tak-Kai, *A Study on Chinese Communist Propaganda, It [sic] Policy and Operations (Zhongguo xuanchuang zhengce yu yuntong)* (Hong Kong: Jindaishi yanjiusuo, 1954), 80–81.

reason. Filmmakers aspired to Soviet standards but in acting, scriptwriting, camera work, and other key areas the main source of experience was cultural work in the former CCP base areas or private commercial studios of Shanghai and Hong Kong.[33] Lack of ideological and aesthetic cohesion was reflected in the backgrounds of filmmakers themselves. Within Beijing alone, according to one former insider, personnel were drawn from private and "Western" Shanghai, CCP-controlled northeast China, former Japanese-propaganda studios in Manchuria and Beijing, and the pre-1949 Guomindang (GMD) Central Propaganda Section (Zhongyang xuanchuan gu).[34] Mechanization lagged behind international standards; developing and processing film by hand was the norm until 1952.[35]

Film production provided one example of how material and personnel limitations impacted cultural agendas on the ground. Yet the industry was also characterized by emerging forms of organization and a sense of purpose. CCP-controlled artistic and literary organizations had been formed immediately in 1949.[36] Ideological criticism and inquests impacted studios in 1950; that same year, cultural workers were mobilized en masse to serve the propaganda needs of the Korean War.[37] Thought reform, or "rectification," in the cultural sector was relaunched in November 1951.[38] Amidst this imposition of political discipline, filmmakers continued study American journals such as the *Motion Picture Journal*, the *Hollywood Reporter*, *Film Daily*, and *Cinema* in order to make films that could compete with Hollywood.[39] American films captured during the Korean War were stored in Film Bureau archives for use by CCP propagandists, their circulation restricted to high-level and creative cadres.[40] Politically reliable filmmakers were instructed to mine successful Hollywood features, such as *The Sound of Music*, for technical insights; these films became reference points for budgeting according to international standards.[41] When Film Bureau adviser Vasily Zhuravlyov arrived in Beijing from the Soviet Union in 1954, he found that his Chinese counterparts were interested in technical aspects

---

[33] Yuanzhi bianji weiyuanhui, ed., *Beijing dianying xueyuan zhi, 1950–1995* (Beijing: Beijing dianying xueyuan chubanshe, 2000), 4; interview, May 2005.
[34] Interview, May 2005.
[35] Interview, July 2006; Shanghai shi dianying ju bangong shi, "Shi nian yilai Shanghai dianying shiye de juda fazhan he bianhua (chubu ziliao)," September 25, 1959, SHMA B177-1-220.
[36] *Liushinian wenyi dashiji, 1919–1979*, 123–125.   [37] Ibid., 127, 129.
[38] Ibid., 136; "Zhonggong zhongyang guanyu zai wenxue yishu jie kaizhan zhengfeng xuexi yundong de zhishi," November 26, 1951, in *Jianguo yilai de wenxian xuanbian (di er ce)*, 461–467.
[39] Zhongyang renmin zhengfu wenhua bu dianying ju to Beijing shi renmin zhengfu xinwen chuban chu, July 28, 1951, BJMA 8-2-589.
[40] Interview, December 2004.   [41] Ibid.

of production but not in merely "aping" Soviet features.[42] As Zhuravlyov also recorded, leading CCP cultural official Zhou Yang instead placed considerable stress on developing a national film style and successfully entering the "world market for cinema."[43] A Beijing filmmaker from the period further recalled that "the attitude was to take the best from all over the world," including both Moscow and Hollywood.[44]

Expanding Cultural Engagement with Communist Asia

Film industry reconstruction and positioning of China as a contributor to world cinematic culture were made possible through a combination of Eastern bloc and Soviet aid, and domestic adaptation of a variety of external models and influences. In terms of storytelling and aesthetic influence, commercial success vied with political ideology as an indicator of which films to emulate. Hollywood, though externally disparaged, was nonetheless closely studied. While filmmakers working within the CCP propaganda and culture system expanded their experience and perfected their craft, they also transferred their knowledge to other communist movements within Asia. Within a few short years, films made in the PRC were being regularly used for external communication and propaganda aimed at the outside world.

Liu Shaoqi, who by the early 1950s was likely second only to Mao within the CCP, had clarified the direction of PRC foreign policy in a speech given at the World Federation of Trade Unions in 1949. China would focus on supporting labor movements and national liberation movements within Asia.[45] Additional emphasis would be given to armed struggle based on the "path of the Chinese people" from colonialism to liberation. The CCP would not hurry to establish relations outside the Soviet bloc. At a subsequent December 1949 speech given to the Trade Union Conference of Asian and Australasian Countries, Liu again stated that the goal of China's foreign policy would be armed struggle against imperialism and the Asian bourgeoisie.[46] Internally, Liu also articulated an independent revolutionary role for China within Asia. Addressing attendees at the first national propaganda work conference held in May 1951, Liu claimed that the Chinese ethnicity (*minzu*) had always possessed "culture and theory," and that levels of Marxism within China were already very high.[47] In order for China's anti-imperialist

---

[42] V. Zhuravlyov, "Mission in China (Memoirs of a Movie Director)," *Far Eastern Affairs* 2 (1987): 79. My thanks to Paul G. Pickowicz for providing a copy of this valuable source.
[43] Ibid.   [44] Interview, April 2005; interview, May 2005.
[45] Barnett, *Communist China and Asia*, 80.   [46] Ibid.
[47] Liu Shaoqi, "Dang de xuanchuan zhan shang de renwu," May 23, 1951, *Dang de xuanchuan gongzuo huiyi gaikuang he wenxian*, 6.

model to spread outward ("victory will not only be won in China"), other countries in the Orient (*dongfang*) would also be "made to believe [*xinfu*] Marxist Leninism."

To supplement military and political aid to Asian communist movements, China also began to export cultural aid. Compared with many other decolonizing countries, the CCP had inherited a sizable stock of studio facilities and equipment as a result of having "taken over" (*jieguan*) former Japan- and GMD-built cultural industries. By the Korean War's end, this material base had been augmented with newer studios, film-processing equipment, and factories for the large-scale domestic manufacture of cameras and projectors.[48] Better resources allowed the CCP to provide filmmaking support to regional allies. Communist parties in North Korea and Vietnam received technical missions of Chinese filmmakers, as well as PRC-produced film equipment, during the early 1950s.[49]

The relationship between the PRC and North Korea was commercial as well as political. Korea served as a market for films produced in the PRC, including those made by the Kunlun, Wenhua, Guotai, and Datong private studios, which were merged with the state-owned sector in 1952.[50]

Co-operation was anchored, however, by China's aid to the North Korean propaganda effort. Filmmakers from the Korea State Film Studio (Chaoxian guoli yinghua zhizuosuo in Chinese sources) traveled to Beijing during the early 1950s to help out with sound-recording facilities and other production equipment.[51] China and North Korea exchanged raw motion picture footage of the Korean War for propaganda purposes, and pooled resources in order to coproduce documentary and educational films highlighting the achievements of each country for both internal and external audiences.[52]

More PRC filmmakers, actors, and other cultural workers were deployed to Korea as the war intensified. Director Shi Dongshan and actress Yu Lan visited soldiers on behalf of the Chinese People's Protect World Peace and Oppose American Invasion Committee (Zhongguo renmin baowei shijie heping fandui Meiguo qinlüe weiyuanhui).[53]

---

[48] Shanghai shi dianying ju bangong shi, "Shanghai dianying jishu he jijie gongye de fazhan qingkuang," September 28, 1959, SHMA B177-1-324; "1954 nian wenjiao weisheng gongzuo de baogao (cao'an)," n.d. [1954–1955], BJMA 11-2-50; *Zhongguo dianying jishu*, 56–57.
[49] See, for example, Yang et al., *Zhongguo dianying wuzi chanye xitong lishi biannian ji (1928–1994)*, 56.
[50] Hu Chang, *Xin Zhongguo dianying de yaolan* (Changchun: Jilin wenshi chubanshe, 1986), 113.
[51] *Yijiuwuling nian gongzuo zongjie*, 7, 32, 34.   [52] Ibid., 19.
[53] Disici wendai hui choubei zu qicao zu, Wenhua bu wenxue yishu yanjiu yuan lilun zhengce yanjiu ce, eds., *Liushi nian wenyi dashiji, 1919–1979* (n.p., 1979), 131, 148.

Camera operators and photographers risked their lives to capture images of military victories, report on the alleged bombing of civilians by American aircraft, and draw international attention to the destruction caused by enemy forces.[54] Projectionists also visited North Korea as part of goodwill mission (*weiwen tuan*) cultural activities, which included film screenings for Chinese and allied troops along with live appearances by celebrities. Some of the films were also viewed by POWs who, as noted by film scholar Jay Leyda, did not entirely reject the "Chinese-produced movies."[55]

Cultural co-operation between the CCP and other communist movements in Asia was a form of diplomacy that established China's position as senior partner in state building and external propaganda. Filmmakers from North Korea used Northeast Film Studio facilities to produce seven feature films, twelve documentaries, and forty-eight newsreels.[56] One particularly noteworthy instance of collaboration was the documentary *Oppose Germ Warfare* (*Fandui xijun zhan*, 1952), which claimed to provide visual evidence of American use of biological weapons in Korea and northeast China.[57] Architects, technicians, and filmmakers from China also participated in the construction of a new film studio in North Korea, completed in November 1953. Coproduction and aid links also connected China with the Communist Party of Vietnam. PRC filmmakers assisted Vietnamese counterparts with the production of documentary films such as *Liberated Hanoi* (*Jiefangle de Henei* in Chinese sources), and assisted with the filmed recording of meetings between Chinese and Vietnamese leaders.[58]

Making China's Culture Visible to the World

Cultural relations with North Korea (Democratic Republic of Korea – DPRK) and North Vietnam (Democratic Republic of Vietnam – DRV) reflected three aspects of diplomacy during the early 1950s: support for communist-led "national liberation struggles" in Asia, defense of China's borders, and expansion of the international reach of propaganda work.[59]

---

[54] Interview, January 2005; interview, February 2005.
[55] Leyda, *Electric Shadows*, 202.   [56] Hu, *Xin Zhongguo dianying de yaolan*, 140.
[57] See Zhongyang dianying ju Beijing dianying zhipianchang, ed., *Fandui xijun zhan* (Beijing: Renmin meishu chubanshe, 1953); Shan Wanli, *Zhongguo jilu dianying shi* (Beijing: Zhongguo dianying chubanshe, 2005), 128.
[58] Interview, January 2005.
[59] Peter van Ness, *Revolution and Chinese Foreign Policy: Peking's Support for Wars of National Liberation* (Berkeley: University of California Press, 1970), 11; "Zhonggong zhongyang guanyu jianquan ge ji xuanchuan jigou de jiaqiang he jiaqiang dang de xuanchuan jiaoyu gongzuo de zhishi," February 25, 1951, *Jianguo yilai zhongyao wenxian xuanbian (di er ce)*,

Leaning toward the Soviet Union and countries of socialist Europe were evident in patterns of diplomatic and cultural exchange as well. However, the more rigid position of "uniting with communist states" was tempered by probing efforts to see China's statehood recognized more broadly among the international community.

The Northeast Film Studio (formerly the Manchuria Motion Picture Corporation) and Northeast Film Management Company together represented China's first important hub for motion picture import and export.[60] The former represented the CCP's most advanced film production facility until the mid-1950s and was partly staffed by Japanese technicians who had stayed in China to work with the new government.[61] Domestically, the Northeast Film Studio was held up as a model CCP-managed cultural industry.[62] Early feature films produced there, such as *Daughters of China* (*Zhonghua nü'er*, 1949), *Light Spreads Everywhere* (*Guangmang wanzhang*, 1949), *Zhao Yiman* (1950), and *The White-Haired Girl* (*Baimao nü*, 1950), were shown at home and exported to the Soviet Union, Czechoslovakia, Poland, Hungary, Bulgaria, Malaya, and Indonesia in 1950. Within the Eastern bloc, *Daughters of China* and *Zhao Yiman* earned China official recognition for filmmaking at Czechoslovakia's Karlovy Vary International Film Festival, where both films were awarded prizes.[63]

Earning international film prizes was an important form of cultural display that fulfilled nationalist aspirations to enter the "world market" for cinema. The awards also served to build up China's prestige among international audiences. China's Beijing Film Studio News Department (Beijing dianying zhipianchang xinwen chu) complemented Northeast Film Studio films by producing documentary-style perspectives on realities unfolding within China through titles such as *One Million Heroes Cross Jiangnan* (*Baiwan xiongshi xia Jiangnan*), *Opening and Transforming the Great Southeast* (*Da Xi'nan kaige*), *The Red Flag Flutters in the West Wind* (*Hongqi manjuan xifeng*), and *Stepping on the Road to Life* (*Tashang sheng lu*).[64] These films were also shown at the Karlovy Vary International Film Festival as external propaganda for the achievements of the CCP's revolution. Two Sino-Soviet coproductions undertaken in Beijing,

75–79. The CCP Central Committee directive called for the establishment of a new international propaganda office (*guoji xuanchuan chu*).
[60] Hu, *Xin Zhongguo dianying de yaolan*, 41.   [61] Ibid., 113.
[62] See, for example, Yang Jing, *Dongbei fangwen lu* (Beijing: Sanlian shudian, 1950), 263–266.
[63] Zhongguo dianyingjia xiehui dianying shi wenhua bu, ed., *Zhongguo renmin gongheguo dianying shiye sanshiwu nian, 1949–1984* (Beijing: Zhongguo dianying chubanshe, 1986), 350.
[64] *Xinwen dianying gongzuo zongjie hui huikan*, 3–43.

Victory of the Chinese People and *Liberated China*, won the Soviet Union's Stalin Prize in 1951, which celebrated achievements in socialist culture and arts.[65]

As a reflection of cultural policy and, ultimately, foreign policy, films made during the early 1950s conveyed messages about China's unique role and experience. Documentaries *Victory of the Chinese People* and *Liberated China* were praised in the domestic film press for their extensive scenes depicting China's "ages-old history" (*youjie de lishi*).[66] The unique civilizational achievements of "the Chinese people" were as important to the narrative framing of such films as was China's close relationship with the Soviet "big brother." During the Korean War, documentaries like *The Chinese People's Goodwill Mission to North Korea* (*Zhongguo renmin fu Chao weiwen tuan*, 1952) emphasized PRC contributions to the war effort and provided visual evidence for the high regard in which Koreans held their Chinese allies.

Positioning China at the center of a web of overlapping friendship and amities provided a legitimate national identity for the CCP-ruled PRC at a time when the country was enmeshed in international conflicts (Korea, Vietnam, Taiwan, Tibet) and was still unrecognized by the United Nations or by numerous other foreign governments. International recognition through culture, and the external portrayal of China as a civilized and modernizing country, were held up by domestic newspapers as evidence that China's people were winning accolades for their "bravery" and "heroism" under the CCP's leadership.[67] Over time, China's international visibility through cinematic propaganda increased. Films produced during the early 1950s were regularly exported and shown in "fraternal" socialist countries such as the Soviet Union, Czechoslovakia, Poland, Hungary, Romania, Bulgaria, East Germany, Albania, North Korea, Mongolia, and Vietnam.[68] However, they also reached Indonesia, Burma, India, Pakistan, Sweden, Denmark, Finland, Austria, Australia, Ceylon, the United States, Italy, Japan, the Philippines, Iran, Turkey, Chile, Brazil, Israel, Mexico, Iceland, and Colombia. As one contemporaneous

---

[65] *Yijiuwuling nian gongzuo zongjie hui huikan*, 3.

[66] *Yingxi xindi* (Shanghai), 1950, nos. 2, 3, 7.

[67] "Wo guo dianying de guoji shang de rongyu," *Dagong ribao*, October 13, 1951; "Zhongguo renmin dianying wei shijie heping shiye fendou de guangrong chengjiu," *Dongbei ribao*, October 26,1951; "Deguo dianying gongzuozhe dui Zhongguo xin dianying de ganguan," *Dazhong dianying*, September 1952, reprinted in Wenhua bu dangshi ziliao zhengji gongzuo weiyuan hui, Duiwai wenhua lianluo ju dangshi ziliao zhengji gongzuo lingdao xiaozu, ed., *Dangdai Zhong–wai wenhua jiaoliu shiliao, di yi ji* (hereafter *DZWJS*) (Beijing: Wenhua yishu chubanshe, 1990).

[68] "Wushi duo guojia fangyingle wo guo yingpian," *Renmin ribao*, January 21, 1953, in *DZWJS*, 499–500; "Shijie ge guo renmin re'ai xin Zhongguo dianying," *Dazhong dianying* 18 (1954), in *DZWJS*, 504–511.

American observer noted, China "participated vigorously in international film festivals, and ... made efforts to stimulate the circulation of ... films abroad."[69] Film reception was constrained by several factors, which pointed to the limitations of China's cultural diplomacy. Exhibition was limited or forbidden in some countries for political reasons, as when *Liberated China* was rejected from the Festival de Cannes in 1951, allegedly at American urging.[70] Depictions of China's ancient culture could still be read as markers of contemporary difference or backwardness. At the Sixth Karlovy Vary International Film Festival opening ceremonies, representatives from China and North Korea were congratulated by Czechoslovakia's propaganda minister for the "lengthy histories of advanced culture" possessed by these two "ancient states of the Far East."[71] However, these same events also placed great emphasis on the technological superiority of the Soviet Union as a standard to which other socialist countries should aspire. Yet outside Europe and the Eastern bloc, China was potentially seen as a symbol of modernity and progress, as in 1952, when the exhibition of Chinese films and products at the India International Film Festival and International Industries Fair was noted as attracting "continuing crowds."[72]

The Early 1950s: A Transitional Era in Cultural Diplomacy

As suggested by the shift toward a wider range of international venues for film exhibition, 1951 marked a turning point in the PRC's relationship with countries beyond the socialist camp. The change in orientation was reflected at multiple organizational levels. Regional research and policy advisory clusters, such as the Ministry of Foreign Affairs Policy Committee Southeast Asia Group (Waijiao bu zhengce weiyuanhui nanya zu), began to appear within the central state bureaucracy. In June 1951, the Overseas Chinese Affairs Committee (Huaqiao shiwu weiyuanhui) convened its first Overseas Chinese Expanded Conference.[73] New mechanisms for people-to

---

[69] W. Phillips Davison, *International Political Communication* (New York: Frederick A. Praeger, 1965), 200.
[70] "Russia Asked to Withdraw Film," *New York Times*, April 19, 1951, 49; "Soviet Film Is Barred: Cannes Festival Objects to the Showing of 'Liberated China'," *New York Times*, April 20, 1951, 24; "Russia Protests Fete Film Ban," *New York Times*, April 22, 1954, 74.
[71] "Zhongguo dianying daibiao tuan zai dahui fabiao de shumian baogao," in Zhongguo dianying daibiao tuan, ed., *Guanyu diliujie guoji dianyingjie de baogao* (Beijing: Xin dianying zazhishe, 1951), 59.
[72] "Bombay Is Center for Red Activity: Exhibits of Communist Lands at Industry Fair and Other Efforts Impress Indians," *New York Times*, January 18, 1952, 7.
[73] Chin, *A Study on Chinese Communist Propaganda*, 138.

-people contact, such as the India–China Friendship Association, were developed and expanded.[74] Japanese students were permitted to study (illegally, in the eyes of Japan's government), and the appearance of Australian cadres linked to the World Federation of Trade Unions Eastern Liaison Bureau, located in Beijing, also suggested widening ties with communist political circles.

The shift appears to have taken place at roughly the same time as the beginning of Korean War armistice negotiations, when incremental change to the Soviet Union's "two-camps" approach to international relations became observable as well. Festivals of Soviet films in India and a Soviet cultural offensive in Western Europe also began in 1951.[75] Convening of the International Economic Conference in Moscow that year led to more trade contracts with noncommunist countries in 1952.[76] The end of China's invasion of Tibet created further space for amity. Mao's comments at a reception held for the ambassador of India, reprinted in the *People's Daily* on January 26, 1951, sounded a new note by describing China, India, and the Soviet Union as "peace-loving countries" whose people should "unite and strive for peace" in Asia and the world.[77] Subsequently, *People's Daily* analysis of voting patterns among United Nations member countries referenced "Arab–Asian" nations rather than maintaining a two-camps distinction between socialism and imperialism.[78]

Cultural exchange began to expand as a result. In 1950, the Ministry of Foreign Affairs (MFA) had regarded exchange mainly as a feature of countries within the Soviet-controlled bloc and Asia: Romania, Poland, Czechoslovakia, Hungary, Bulgaria, Vietnam, Albania, North Korea, and Mongolia.[79] Prior to the Korean War, the Ministry of Culture had also made tentative inquiries to the MFA concerning whether cultural and academic exchange would be permitted with all countries recognizing the PRC – a list that included Norway, Sweden, Finland, Denmark, Ceylon, England, Israel, and Pakistan.[80] By 1952, "hundreds" of Indian visitors had traveled to China, leading to the arrival of an official Indian cultural

[74] Passin, *China's Cultural Diplomacy*, 8.
[75] Frederick C. Barghoorn, *The Soviet Cultural Offensive: The Role of Cultural Diplomacy in Soviet Foreign Policy* (Princeton: Princeton University Press, 1960), 196.
[76] Barnett, *Communist China and Asia*, 95.
[77] J.D. Armstrong, *Revolutionary Diplomacy: Chinese Foreign Policy and the United Front Doctrine* (Berkeley: University of California Press, 1977), 70–74.
[78] Ibid.
[79] "Waijiao bu guanyu wo yu waiguo wenhua jiaoliu shi zhi Wenhua bu fu han," March 6, 1950, MFA 118–00054-08(1).
[80] "Wenhua bu guanyu wo yu guowai wenhua jiaoliu shi zhi Waijiao bu han," March 1, 1950, MFA 118–00054-07 (1).

delegation in 1953.[81] French cultural missions and youth and intellectual travel also began in 1952.[82] The Peace Conference of the Asian and Pacific Regions (Yazhou ji Taipingyang quyu heping huiyi), convened that August, brought delegates from thirty-seven countries to view China first-hand. At the end of the conference, participants approved a declaration promising to increase future cultural exchange. In 1951, the CCP issued an invitation to Chilean poet Pablo Neruda to visit Beijing for the second anniversary of the PRC following Neruda's tour of Russia; warming rela-tions between the two countries would result in the establishment of the Chilean–Chinese Cultural Institute in Santiago, Chile, one year later.[83] In April 1953, Finland and Sweden also sent cultural representatives to China.[84]

Likewise, delegations from China traveled more broadly and frequently beginning in 1951. The initial focus was the socialist camp: a national youth cultural group (Zhongguo qingnian wenyi gongzuo tuan) traveled to East Germany (German Democratic Republic – GDR) and other Eastern European countries, musicians performed abroad in May, cultural repre-sentatives were dispatched to the Soviet Union in October.[85] A cultural troupe organized by the Communist Youth League also reached India and Burma in 1951.[86] Overseas cultural propaganda planning undertaken by the MFA and the Cultural Liaison Bureau (Wenlian ju) included further plans for dispatch of an acrobatics troupe to Northwestern Europe; economic exhibitions across Europe and in India, Myanmar, and Pakistan; and add-itional exhibitions in Southeast Asia on art crafts (*gongyi pin*) and changes in conditions affecting women.[87] In 1952, Sweden and China established a joint association for the promotion of cultural relations (*wenhua guanxi cujin xiehui*), covering culture, the arts, literature, folk studies, and educa-tion, as well as "social and political issues, national movements, commerce, and industry."[88] In late April 1953, a group of PRC delegates, including an economist, a philologist, and an interpreter, attended the first Continental Cultural Conference held in Santiago, Chile, in late April 1953.[89]

---

[81] Passin, *China's Cultural Diplomacy*, 8.   [82] Ibid.

[83] Lin Chou, *The Diplomatic War between Bejing and Taipei in Chile* (Maryland Series in Contemporary Asian Studies 3, University of Maryland School of Law, 2001), 15–17.

[84] *Liushi nian wenyi dashiji, 1919–1979*, 146.   [85] Ibid., 133–135.

[86] Xie Yixian et al., *Zhongguo waijiao shi: Zhonghua renmin gongheguo shiqi, 1949–1979* (He'nan renmin chubanshe, 1988), 143; See also "Yijiuwu'er niandu zhuwai shiguan wenhua xuanchuan gongzuo jihua di er ci huiyi jilu," June 4, 1952, MFA 110–00179-01(1).

[87] MFA 110–00179-01(1).

[88] "Ruidian yu Zhonghua renmin gongheguo wenhua guanxi cujin xiehui huizhang," November 18, 1952, MFA 110–00108-01(1).

[89] Lin, "The Diplomatic War between Bejing and Taipei in Chile," 15–17.

The breadth of areas covered by "culture" in such agreements suggests that in some instances, culture was simply a cover for establishing dialogue concerning any number of issues. However, as in the case of the film industry, there is also evidence to suggest that the CCP used cultural relations to promote a vision of China as a unique and civilized nation in terms that transcended socialist high modernism (even while remaining embedded within its categories). In October 1952, the People's Literature Press (Renmin wenxue chubanshe) began republishing notable "ancient classics," such as the *Water Margin*, *Romance of the Three Kingdoms*, and *Journey to the West*.[90] A magazine, *Chinese Literature* (*Zhongguo wenxue*), was simultaneously established in Japan. As in the Soviet Union, China's leaders also sought to project an image of their country as a cosmopolitan and aesthetically sophisticated society. Literary events were organized to commemorate the work and lives of foreign writers from countries including Britain, Japan, Russia, and (later) the United States. The forerunner of the journal *World Literature* (*Shijie wenxue*) was founded in 1953 to curate and analyze literary work produced outside China.[91]

Overseas cultural and propaganda work also had a clandestine side. Strengthening of external cultural liaison work was principally the domain of the Ministry of Culture and, at a higher level, the State Council.[92] However, within Asia, the CCP Politburo Overseas Work Department (Zhongyang zhengzhiju haiwai gongzuo bu) and Overseas Regional Work Office (Haiwai diqu gongzuo chu), as well as the PRC's network of overseas consulates and embassies, played a decisive role in managing overseas Chinese affairs, including through the office's Cultural Work Committee.[93] Friendship and peace committees, democratic societies, trade promotion, and student associations all linked back to the CCP Politburo system and the Overseas Chinese Affairs Committee.[94] Pro-CCP newspapers were established in Indonesia and Malaya. Other liaison and exchange activities focused on India, Japan, and Burma. The Ministry of Culture also engaged in surreptitious propaganda export through sales representatives such as the Hong Kong Southern Film Company (Xianggang nanfang yingye gongsi), which was the PRC's main conduit to private film companies and theaters in Southeast Asia.[95] One underappreciated benefit of overseas film export was an accumulation of foreign currency. When officials within the Ministry of

---

[90] *Liushi nian wenyi dashiji, 1919–1979*, 140.   [91] Ibid., 146.

[92] See "Zhongyan wenhua bu dang zu guanyu muqian wenhua yishu gongzuo zhuangkuang he jinhou gaijin yijian de baogao," September 10, 1953, in *Jianguo yilai zhongyao wenxian xuanbian (di wu ce)*, 21–37.

[93] Chin, *A Study on Chinese Communist Propaganda*, 135–136.   [94] Ibid., 138.

[95] "Wenhua bu guanyu han shang wei Aomen tigong yingpiang chukou jiehui banfa de gonghan," April 1952, MFA 118–00414-03(1).

Culture observed in April 1952 that censorship had become lax in Macao, they consulted with the MFA on the possibility of using a theater already acquired by the Southern Film Company to screen new features produced in China as means of bringing in additional revenue through box office earnings.[96]

Consequences: China's Global Cultural Network

Whether global audiences were convinced of China's greatness as a result of the buildup of cultural industries, dissemination of international propaganda through cultural export and exchange, and amplification of China's voice through cultural diplomacy and other media is an open-ended question. The mere fact of legitimizing efforts does not tell us whether legitimacy was the result. What can be learned is that in addition to China's more obvious participation in patterns of exchange within the socialist camp, the scope of cultural activity was broader and potentially more Asia-focused than might be suggested by narrower readings of internationalism in practice.[97] The vision of a "third way" toward national independence that was neither capitalist nor communist was particularly influential in decolonizing Asia, and China's leaders attempted to position themselves, through culture, as bearers of unique national and Asian values.[98] Indeed, even at the very outset of the Cold War, Soviet leaders Josef Stalin and Nikita Khrushchev had exhibited signs of concern over China's potential influence throughout Asia and other geopolitically contested regions, including the Middle East.[99] For the CCP, the culmination of this early 1950s wave of new relations with Asian states was symbolized by state premier Zhou Enlai's visible role at the Asian–African Conference held in April 1955 in Bandung, Indonesia,

[96] Ibid.
[97] On the recent rediscovery of "socialist internationalism," see, for example, Patryk Babiracki and Austin Jersild, eds., *Socialist Internationalism in the Cold War: Exploring the Second World* (New York: Palgrave MacMillan, 2016). Concerning a more China-centered example of "international in practice," Timothy Cheek notes simply and accurately that other cosmopolitan conversations such as vernacular cosmopolitanism and Chinese universalism have been "overshadowed" by Maoism. See Timothy Cheek, "Chinese Socialism as Vernacular Cosmopolitanism," *Frontiers of History in China* 9, no. 1 (2014): 102–124. See also Tina Mai Chen, "International Film Circuits and Global Imaginaries in the People's Republic of China, 1949–1957," *Journal of Chinese Cinemas* 3, no. 2 (2009): 149–161.
[98] On Asian alternatives to dominant Cold War ideologies, see, for example, Mark T. Berger, *The Battle for Asia: From Decolonization to Globalization* (London: RoutledgeCurzon, 2004); Odd Arne Westad, *The Global Cold War: Third World Interventions and the Making of Our Times* (Cambridge: Cambridge University Press, 2005).
[99] Westad, *The Global Cold War*, 66–70.

at which delegates pledged their commitment to principles of world peace, international co-operation, and nonalignment.[100] Zhou's April 19, 1955, speech to the conference also included telling references to the significant "contributions to humanity" made by African and Asian civilizations – "brilliant and magnificent ancient cultures," as he described them.[101]

This chapter has suggested, however, that even the view of China as more "Asian" in diplomatic orientation is not entirely accurate as a revision of current paradigms. Direct trade between the PRC and Western Europe (as opposed to trade via Hong Kong, which had continued in more limited form throughout the war years) also returned in 1955.[102] Domestic upheaval, cultural interpenetration, expansionism, and internal security concerns emerging against a backdrop of modernization and nation building characterized global politics to such a degree that some archival researchers have begun to speak of a "postwar world" – a global condition transcending the Cold War logic of blocs and rival alliance systems.[103] By the end of the Korean War, patterns of cultural exchange, like trade relations, had diversified and proliferated. A crucial vector of influence was the mass media, which gained even greater ubiquity during the Korean War when it was increasingly used for purposes of state building, international propaganda, and psychological warfare.[104] In pragmatic terms, the integration of film *into* diplomacy represented another innovation of the era, as evidenced by high-ranking CCP ambassador Zhang Wentian cabling foreign-intelligence chief Li Kenong on April 6, 1954, to report,

When Vice Minister of the Soviet Union Kuznetsov received me on the 3rd, he expressed the hope that our delegation at Geneva would make better efforts to carry out additional propaganda work and coordinate diplomatic activities for the

---

[100] On Zhou's role at Bandung, see Zhonggong zhongyang wenxian yanjiu shi, ed., *Zhou Enlai nianpu, 1949–1976 (shang juan)* (Beijing: Zhongguo wenxian chubanshe, 1997), 464–472.

[101] The timeline here thus differs from other accounts which locate the genesis of China's "alternative" conception of socialism in the early 1960s – in other words, at the time of the split between the PRC and the Soviet Union. On cultural and ideological relations between China and the developing world generally, see Robert J. Alexander, *International Maoism in the Developing World* (Westport, CT: Praeger, 1999). On Zhou's speech, see *Zhou Enlai nianpu*, 465.

[102] Alexander Eckstein, *Communist China's Economic Growth and Foreign Trade: Implications for U.S. Policy* (New York: McGraw-Hill, 1966), 97–101.

[103] See, for example, Masuda Hajimu, *Cold War Crucible: The Korean Conflict and the Postwar World* (Cambridge, MA: Harvard University Press, 2015).

[104] On the growth of postwar communications networks generally, see Philip M. Taylor, *Global Communications, International Affairs and the Media since 1945* (London: Routledge, 1997).

purpose of expanding the influence of New China. Such work could include showing movies, organizing speeches, small-size exhibitions, and cultural performances. The Premier instructs that you should immediately consider work on this.[105]

By the mid-1950s, the PRC's nascent international cultural infrastructure stretched from Geneva to Jakarta, underpinned by cultural industries and politically directed exchange networks at home.[106] Mao's promise to make the world see China as civilized first required that the world be made to see; as influence expanded, recognition of China's greatness would surely follow. While events like the Taiwan Strait crisis and the Vietnam War made it clear that the first guarantee of the CCP's security was the use of force close to home, construction of concentric circles of cultural display, and exchange stretching beyond Asia into Europe, Africa, and the Americas, provided some measure of reassurance that China was beginning to escape the Soviet Union's shadow and was, once again, a unique and sovereign national state in its own right.

---

[105] "Cable from Zhang Wentian to Li Kenong, 'Concerning the Soviet Suggestion on Propaganda Work at Geneva'," April 6, 1954, PRC FMA 206–00004-04, trans. Chen Zhihong, Wilson Center Digital Archive, at https://digitalarchive.wilsoncenter.org/document/110596.

[106] Notes on China's post-Geneva preparations for propaganda work at the Asian–African Conference are summarized in "Summary of the Informal Discussion on Information Material Work during China's Preparation for the Asian–African Conference," January 17, 1955, PRC FMA 207–00020-01, obtained by Amitav Acharya and translated by Yang Shanhou, Wilson Center Digital Archive, at https://digitalarchive.wilsoncenter.org/document/114635.

Part II

Domestic Governance

Inheriting Empire, Revolutionizing Society

Introduction to Part II

Like all revolutionary movements that succeed in taking power, the CCP was faced with immense challenges in 1949. The more obvious and immediate of these challenges were external: how to take power, quash lingering resistance, restore social order, resettle refugees, and begin the process of restoring a war-ravaged economy. The last of these involved conundrums that the Guomindang had failed miserably at: taming hyperinflation, reopening factories, and ensuring that cities that could not feed themselves had sufficient grain. The internal challenges facing the CCP were no less severe, if not quite as visible; how the CCP was to transform itself from what was, in the words of Kenneth Jowitt, a "party of a new type – a combat party" that had quite literally been engaged in actual combat in the course of a lengthy civil war into a civilian party-state, albeit a still revolutionary one with a mission to fundamentally remake society into a revolutionarily pure one.[1] The objective circumstances that the CCP had to work with were at best difficult: thin coverage of an enormous and varied territory, primitive communications, and an indifferent-to-hostile population in much of central and southern China. Amid all this, the young PRC had to achieve internal coherence as a government led by the CCP, establish control over often unruly populations in distant locations, and begin the process of implementing revolutionary programs despite a very limited resource base.

In different ways, each of these chapters calls attention not only to *what* was done in terms of domestic governance (establishing control, implementing revolutionary programs), but also to *how* it was done in the "happy" early to mid-1950s when support for the new government was high. The Strauss chapter posits that "New China" was consolidated through a shifting mix of modalities: the bureaucratic and the campaign.

---

[1] Kenneth Jowitt, *New World Disorder: The Leninist Extinction* (Berkeley: University of California Press, 1992), 253.

Focusing on Sunan, the wealthy region in and around Shanghai south of the Yangzi river, the bureaucratic modality was geared to the establishment and "strengthening" of formal state organizations, rendered internally coherent through hierarchy, rule orientation, precedent-based decision making, and a radical simplification of complex realities through processes of depersonalization and classification of relevant units (people, incomes, housing) through standardized categories. The campaign modality, in contrast, aimed at just the opposite: rather than breaking units down into standardized categories, the campaign condensed and intensified policy through an extraordinary push to mobilize emotions and overcome enemies, both real (counterrevolutionaries, landlords) and metaphorical (disease, "wasteland" swamps, backward political views, illiteracy). While both bureaucracy and campaign modalities can be traced back to the late imperial period, by 1949 a variant of the campaign modality that relied on popular support and whipped up crowds baying against defined class enemies had become especially important as a signature repertoire of the revolutionary CCP under Mao. While, in theory, bureaucratic and campaign modalities are in tension with each other, in the early 1950s bureaucratic and campaign modalities were largely mutually supporting. The bureaucratic instruments of hierarchy, co-ordination, and classification were necessary to implement campaigns; in the early 1950s, campaigns, in turn, invigorated bureaucracy by mobilizing commitments, generating public support from broad publics, and rapidly overcoming social resistance, thus projecting state power further into rural areas than would have otherwise been possible.

Although the drama and excitement of mass mobilizational campaigns in the dramaturgy of the revolutionary state capture popular imagination both inside and outside China, it is the core components of the bureaucratic modality – hierarchy, standardized categories, the presumption of obedience within the bureaucratic organization and on the part of populations subject to orders by the state's bureaucratic organization, and ultimately the integration of the state from central to very local levels – that are demonstrated repeatedly in each of these chapters. Each of these chapters in different ways details ways in which the meat and potatoes of bureaucratic integration either did not fit at all with social realities, were implemented to resolve completely different problems, worked at cross-purposes with other directives, or simply quashed locally lived experiences in favor of central control, even when they were in alignment with the state's claimed goals. Some of these problems originated in how particular categories or repertoires that evolved in one region of the country were mechanically applied everywhere else for the sake of internal coherence. Strauss concentrates on two major overlapping campaigns in Sunan in the early 1950s, the Campaign to Suppress Counterrevolutionaries and land reform. Here she demonstrates that the backstage preparation of collecting materials, assigning class categories, and implementing policies according to Marxist-derived class categories simply didn't work well. The received categories of landlord, rich peasant, middle peasant, and poor and hired peasant for rural locations, and counterrevolutionary, local bully, leader of counterrevolutionary sect, and traitor for urban areas, simply did not align with Sunan's commercial economy, labor flows, or social realities. In rural areas, there weren't enough proper landlords to go around to be struggled against. The individuals who were supposed to be hated according to their class categories often weren't. And, conversely, directives that middle peasants should not be objects of struggle sessions often collided with other rules to single out for struggle only those who were most hated by the masses. In rural and small-town Sunan, those most hated were typically those who had collaborated with the Japanese occupation, and, embarrassingly for the CCP cadres who had to administer these campaigns, these ex-collaborators were often middle peasants.

Similarly, Ruan's exploration of "peasant" status in Shanghai and other cities in the early to mid-1950s makes it clear that the state classified hundreds of thousands of Shanghainese as "peasants" to "return to the countryside for production." This decision was not based on the suitability of these urbanites to engage in agricultural production or rural life, but for other reasons: the CCP's deep anxiety and mistrust of cities as unproductive sites of decadence, and the practical need to relieve pressure on local services. In Ruan's account, CCP authorities separated urbanites into two broad categories: unproductive "consumers" who needed to be downsized and productive "producers" who were deemed worthy of nurturing with support. One way to rid the city of its excess mouths to feed was to (re)classify all manner of undesirable urban "consumers" as peasants, thus justifying their dispersal "back" to the countryside. In this way, the hundreds of thousands of drifters, the unemployed, landlords who had fled the countryside, the poor, and "refugees" were assigned new, and vastly inferior, statuses that typically did not reflect their actual occupations or life experiences. "Refugees" had often been in the city for years and were employed. "Drifters" and "the poor" who were assigned peasant status might have had parents who had migrated from the countryside but had never lived in rural areas themselves, much less engaged in farm work. The counties and townships that could reasonably be determined as the natal locations were reluctant to accept, and therefore assume responsibility for, so many thousands when land allocations had already been made. Where they were made at all, land allocations to these incomers were insufficient, while those who were returned to small towns were given neither land nor jobs. By the time an interim solution was found in "opening up wasteland for production" in the hinterland of Jiangxi, the Shanghai labor bureau had given up any pretense that it was resettling "refugees" and indicated as much in its report on the subject that it was dispersing around 300,000 people to Jiangxi to relieve unemployment. Unsurprisingly, many of those relocated to the countryside found ways to return to Shanghai, only to undergo further cycles of dispersal, and ultimately it was only the establishment of collectives that could not refuse assignees that rendered the assignment of peasant status a reality.

In contrast to the Strauss and Ruan chapters that consider the ways in which centrally mandated standardized categories were accepted and implemented by local municipal governments, Murray and Serrano's piece goes straight to the question of central control over the periphery. In the early 1950s, Hainan was as remote a part of China as one could find: a subtropical island historically administered from Guangdong, itself a peripheral, if commercially important, region of China's far south. Prior to 1949, Hainan was riven with ethnic tensions, plagued by lawlessness and militarization, and weakly governed from the mainland. It was also, most unusually, the site of a homegrown guerilla communist movement that not only operated almost completely independently of the central CCP for over two decades but attracted an unusually large percentage of tough female fighters. The Communist movement on Hainan was in most ways a living example of what the CCP valorized: self-reliant, hardscrabble, and full of poor women of unimpeachably good class backgrounds who had found their own way to fight for liberation. But this is not what the CCP did when the southbound cadres of the PLA took over Hainan. Instead, the administration from the central CCP considered the homegrown movement, with its surprisingly high component of female fighters, to be unruly and obstructionist and went about imposing its own, highly gendered, norms on the island through a brutal campaign of "anti-localism" in which women fighters were disbanded and told to go home, marry, and have families. When faced with a choice between working with and valorizing a local experience in which the sympathetic local leading cadre actually did have "close links with the people" on the one hand, and imposing centrally determined order, control, and standardization of patriarchal gendered norms on the other, the initial wave of administrators from the center opted for the latter rather than the former. Half a generation later, the experience of the women fighters of Hainan would be valorized in a classic revolutionary opera, *The Red Detachment of Women*. Despite its name and association with the far left in the Cultural Revolution, the opera wrote out much of the actual experience of the women fighters, with a central role for a fictional male cadre who reasserted male leadership and authority. The actual Hainanese cadre who sympathized with the local women fighters was, in the name of overcoming localism, removed from the island to a faraway position. It is likely that Hainan, as a district of Guangdong, fell afoul of centrally dispatched cadres for the same reasons as its home province did. Ezra Vogel's classic work on Guangzhou reveals the complex story about how the (Cantonese) cadre was himself ousted brutally in the name of anti-localism when he objected to the centrally determined categories for land reform and attempted to implement land reform in a way that took into account the strong lineages and links to overseas communities that were a feature of Guangdong landholdings.[2] As the province went, so too did the island of Hainan. The CCP's claims to be sensitive to local conditions and valorize close links to the people were repeatedly breached when these ideals clashed with the importance of Party discipline and state reintegration, which necessitated the acceptance of hierarchy, even when the rules, policies, and standardized categories handed down from the center made little sense. These chapters all hint at, but don't elaborate on, another aspect of the PRC that is seldom discussed for the 1950s before the Anti-Rightist campaign: the sheer waste that the government was prepared to inflict on its citizens in the name of strengthening the state and carrying out the revolution. Millions lost their lives or were publicly humiliated in struggle sessions in the Campaign to Suppress Counterrevolutionaries and in land reform, often because of the capricious assignment of class labels and bureaucratic incentives to meet quotas from above. Hundreds of thousands in Shanghai, and likely many hundreds of thousands more, were told that they were peasants even when they demonstrably were no such thing, and, on the basis of this bureaucratic simplification, were thrown out of the urban settings in which they had made their lives in order to solve a bureaucratic problem of insufficient urban resources. And of course, the real, lived experience of the female fighters who had spent over twenty years fighting a guerilla war in the wilds of Hainan was first summarily dismissed, and then, years later, sanitized for the consumption of an imagined socialist audience. One can only speculate what happened to the tough women who were suddenly told to refeminize themselves according to dominant gender norms. Thus, for all the importance of the campaign modality as an important repertoire of policy implementation, it was the bureaucratic modality that administered both campaign and everyday hierarchy. And while the

---

[2] Ezra Vogel, *Canton under Communism: Programs and Politics in a Provincial Capital 1949–1968* (Cambridge, MA: Harvard University Press, 1969), esp. Chapter 3 on land reform.

visible, theatrical mass campaigns capture the imagination and are remembered even now as times of excitement and drama, it was perhaps the everyday bureaucratic administration of hardened categories and the imposition of centrally determined policies that had the greater impact on people.

5 Modalities of State Building
Bureaucracy, Campaign, and Performance in Sunan, 1950–1953[*]

Julia C. Strauss

This chapter revisits and extends some of the arguments made in a much longer, explicitly comparative, monograph that focuses on a large question: how did two such ideologically diametrically opposed single-party regimes as the revolutionary People's Republic of China (PRC) and the conservative Republic of China/Taiwan managed to impose themselves over territories in which they came in as armies of occupation, build state institutions in their preferred images, and emerge with such well-consolidated states within only a few short years? Here I focus on the young PRC in Sunan. Regime consolidation is, of course, an ambiguous term, but when gauged by the criteria of (1) the establishment of internal security and social order, (2) the extension of state power to very local levels of society, (3) the development of sufficient capacity to implement core state policies, and (4) the ability to elicit the behavioral acquiescence, if not the active support, of key sectors of society, then the PRC in Sunan was by any standard unusually rapid and successful cases of regime consolidation. The PLA vanquished the Guomindang National Army much more quickly than anyone had imagined would be the case in 1949, and was immediately confronted with the problem of imposing its political authority far more *extensively* than had been any twentieth-century regime since the Qing, and far more *intensively* than had ever before been the case, extending central state power down to the level of the village. We know now that "New China" under the CCP managed to establish internal security, close off exit options and harden borders, extend state power to very local levels of society, implement core policies, fundamentally remake the countryside, and garner at least acquiescence if not active support from core constituencies of its population with

---

[*] This chapter draws from and extends the core arguments of Julia C. Strauss, *State Formation in China and Taiwan: Bureaucracy, Campaign, and Performance* (Cambridge: Cambridge University Press, 2020).

remarkable speed and effectiveness. Even more astonishingly, it managed to do so over an extensive and diverse territory, much of which it came to as a thinly stretched army of occupation. What is now often forgotten is how none of these fundamental tasks of regime consolidation was foreordained. The year 1949 presented a daunting policy environment of weak domestic institutions, thinly spread cadres, lack of popular support in much of the country, and sharp regional security tensions.

Sunan – the southern Jiangsu counties of the lower Yangzi region, centered on Shanghai, with its great cities, navigable waterways, long growing season, and port of Shanghai – had long been the economic heartland of China, and in the first half of the twentieth century it had also became its industrial center. Any Chinese central government with aspirations to "wealth and power" by definition had to incorporate and access the vast resources of the region. But the ecology, economy, and society of the lower Yangzi were utterly different than the harsh rural environment in which the CCP had expanded, consolidated its base, and fielded the peasant armies that had overcome the Guomindang in the late 1940s. How the CCP would translate its ethos, goals, and repertoires from impoverished rural north China to wealthy, commercialized Sunan was put on hold for the first year it was in power, when its overriding goals were to establish the new state, bring down hyperinflation, ensure the subsistence of cities unable to feed themselves, register populations, and restart production. These immediate priorities led the young People's Republic to be as initially accommodating as possible to all but the most unreconstructed of enemies, defined as those who had worked for Guomindang intelligence and security (*tewu*) organizations. It was not terribly surprising that this early inclusiveness did not last: the CCP had long been committed to the revolutionary transformation of state and society. How it could do so given its relatively small numbers and its weak social roots outside its old base areas in north China was an open question. In order to implement the transformational policies to which it aspired, the young PRC needed both much-augmented capacity and much-diminished social resistance. And it needed these things very, very quickly.

I suggest that the way in which the young PRC so rapidly increased state capacity while reducing social resistance was intimately bound up with its two signature modalities of state building: (1) the bureaucratic and (2) the campaign. Both encompassed logics of state organization and policy implementation that reached back into the "deep history" of the late imperial Chinese state, now augmented by the combination of Party, state, and military fusion that characterized the CCP under Republican-era insecurity and militarization. I argue that in the early 1950s bureaucracy and campaign were co-produced in varied and often subtle ways that were mutually supporting and frequently co-constitutive. This pattern replicated the patterns by which the CCP expanded in north China over the course of its long civil war with the Guomindang.[1] Over the longer run of the Mao-era PRC, however, the inherent tensions between bureaucratic and campaign modalities of policy making came to define fundamental contradictions in the revolution itself. The fusion of campaign and bureaucracy that was so effective in the early stages of the revolution (taking power, mobilizing against identifiable "enemies" to push through revolutionary policies in the face of potential social recalcitrance) worked much less well when the obvious enemies of the revolution (landlords, exploiters, merchants, and "feudal" intellectuals) had been vanquished and rural and urban citizens were nearly all absorbed into work units dominated by the CCP.

Modalities of State Building I: Radical Simplification through Bureaucracy

Scholars of China have long acknowledged its state's longevity, its history of civil service by open competitive examination, its struggle-laden transformation to the "modern" in the twentieth century, the nomenklatura system of appointment it adopted from the Soviet model in the PRC, and the way it did or did not work in different sectors or at different spatial scales.[2] Despite the frequency with which the state is invoked as integral to most subjects on post-1949 China, after Franz Schurmann's seminal work *Ideology and Organization in Communist China* (1966, 1969), very few have systematically explored the concept of the state's bureaucratic organizations, and what this has meant, both normatively and practically, in a mid-twentieth-century Chinese context.

---

[1] See Joseph Esherick, "Revolution in a Feudal Fortress: Yangjiagou, Mizhi County, Shaanxi, 1937–1948," *Modern China* 24, no. 4 (October 1998): 339–377; and Philip C. C. Huang, "Rural Class Struggle in the Chinese Revolution: Representational and Objective Realities from the Land Reform to the Cultural Revolution," in *Symposium: Rethinking the Chinese Revolution. Paradigmatic Issues in Chinese Studies, IV, Modern China* 21, no. 1 (January 1995): 105–143, for the ways in which organizational hierarchies, discipline, categories, and quotas were enforced during pre-1949 land reform campaigns in north China.

[2] The literature here is vast, but a very preliminary bibliography would include Benjamin A. Elman, *Civil Examinations and Meritocracy in Late Imperial China* (Cambridge, MA: Harvard University Press, 2013); John P. Burns, *The CCP's Nomenklatura System: A Documentary Study of Party Control of Leadership Selection, 1979–1984* (Armonk, NY : Sharpe, 1989); Vivienne Shue, *The Reach of the State: Sketches of the Chinese Body Politic* (Stanford: Stanford University Press, 1988); Frederick Teiwes, *Politics and Purges in China* (New York: Routledge, 1993). Kimberley Ens Manning and Felix Wemheuer, eds., *Eating Bitterness: New Perspectives on China's Great Leap Forward and Famine* (Vancouver: University of British Columbia Press, 2011) illustrates beautifully how central policies played out very differently in different locations.

This is not surprising. The translations in Chinese for "bureaucracy" and "bureaucratic" (*guanliao*), and "bureaucratism" (*guanliaozhuyi*), convey a particularly noxious set of connotations: official arrogance, remoteness, and lack of responsiveness or accountability. Mao detested "bureaucracy" and went to extreme lengths to create and maintain a Yan'an-era revolutionary "mass line" that demanded "close links with the people" to pre-empt the emergence of "bureaucratism" in the revolution. But whether it is called "bureaucracy" or, as it is in the nomenclature of the CCP, "state organs," no state can exist *without* formal, hierarchical administrative organizations with claims over policy domains that can make real the state's centralizing claims over territory. The state's administrative organizations provide the skeleton without which even self-maintenance is impossible: at a minimum they must extract resources, maintain centrality, establish internal order, and provide for external defense. Depending on the values and core agendas of the state's political elites, they also implement a wide range of other potential policies.

But what are the essential properties of these state administrative organizations? How do they function? And how do they come into existence? It is precisely this set of questions that is addressed by what I call "bureaucratic modalities of state building." Following Weber, I define the "bureaucratic" as the properties inherent to "state institutions": formal organizations, hierarchical lines of authority that garner the compliance of lower levels in the hierarchy, and impersonal rule making.[3] By definition, a bureaucratic organization is one that is organized hierarchically. Decisions reached at higher levels must be incumbent and binding on lower levels in the hierarchy to ensure internal coherence. Bureaucratic modes of policy implementation function by rule making over relevant classes of things, situations, or circumstances.[4] And their first ordering principle – the one that ensures coherence and state strength – is predicated on obedience and discipline: that lower levels in the hierarchy will accept the rules (and the standard classifications engendered by those rules) and execute the orders decided on at higher levels in the hierarchy.

In order to implement policy, though, the state must first "make legible" the societies and economies within which it operates.[5] This process of "making legible" occurs through bureaucratic logics that *radically simplify*

---

[3] For the classic statement of Weber's conception of bureaucracy, see Max Weber, *From Max Weber: Essays in Sociology*, ed. H. H. Gerth and C. H. Mills (London: Routledge, 1948), 196–203.

[4] This is known in public administration circles as the "politics/administration dichotomy" but is often elided as "the policy/administration dichotomy." It has a lengthy lineage from Woodrow Wilson's seminal article "The Study of Administration," *Political Science Quarterly* 2, no. 2 (1887), 197–222.

[5] James C. Scott. , *Seeing Like a State: How Certain Schemes to Improve the Human Condition Have Failed* (New Haven: Yale University Press, 1999).

complex realities through *rules of depersonalization.* The bureaucratic modality classifies and records data that are segmented into standardized categories that break down wholes (individual people, ecosystems, transport systems, diseases) into constituent units (incomes, square footage of housing, miles of railroad track or tarmac, numbers of vaccines administered or moving violations recorded, hectares of forest logged). In this way, units can be counted and recorded, and information passed up through the organizational hierarchy so that policy decisions can be made and passed back down the administrative hierarchy for implementation. In a bureaucratic modality, each standard classification, and how each should be treated, will in principle merit the application of the same rule for as long as the rules are not changed.

The kinds of standardized classification, monitoring, and record keeping so integral to a bureaucratic modality and so necessary for the state to be able to implement preferred policies presuppose the existence of a coherent and responsive state organization with a fair amount of capacity. This trifecta of desirable attributes – coherence, responsiveness, and capacity – was in uncertain evidence in the years before and after 1949. The young PRC was committed to strengthening the state, and even as it consciously avoided the term *gualiao* ("bureaucratic") it often stressed a fundamentally bureaucratic set of logics in so doing. Newly formed Party and state organizations in Shanghai in the early 1950s issued regular exhortations to "strengthen organization" and "strengthen (state) organs" (*jiaqiang zuzhi, jiaqiang jiguan*). "Strengthening organization" was accomplished through expanding the capacity of state organizations to collect and record information according to standardized units of measure, to report this information in a timely way, and to implement and report on policies decided by higher levels of the organization and radically expand systems of accounting and statistics.[6] "Strengthening" also stressed discipline, hierarchy, and timeliness in reporting in a system in which most of what the higher levels of the state "saw" was what lower-level officials reported of their own activities. Personnel sufficiently trained in meat and potatoes of the bureaucratic modality – statistics and accounting to standardize, simplify, and exert a modicum of control through counting, recording, and checking on local implementation – were in perennially short supply. The need to "strengthen statistical/accounting work" (*jiaqiang tongji/kuaiji gongzuo*) was acute well into the 1950s. Shorn of the language of Weberian bureaucracy, the CCP nonetheless subscribed to many of its key precepts: institutionalized hierarchy, inequality, standardization, rule making, and

---

[6] Anurabh Ghosh, *Making It Count: Statistics and Statecraft in the Early People's Republic of China* (Princeton: Princeton University Press, 2020).

record keeping an inescapable part of regime consolidation and state building in the immediate aftermath of 1949 in New China.

Modalities of State Building II: Radical Simplification through Campaign

Yundong is typically translated into English as "campaign" – a term with multiple meanings that have accreted over time. It makes its first appearance at roughly the time of the English civil wars of the mid-seventeenth century when it referred to short, often seasonally defined, periods of army field operations. A century later, "campaign" included military-*like* activities pursued for short and distinct periods involving a struggle or organized attempt to achieve a definite result. By the early nineteenth century, "campaign" expanded further to encompass collective action (e.g., rent reduction campaigns in Ireland) and elections.[7] In Chinese, *yundong* also had a fairly narrow set of original meanings: the movement of objects (as in physics), and the quickening of blood flow through the intestines (as in Chinese medicine). By the end of the second decade of the twentieth century, *yundong* came to be used for the social movements that protested weak and ineffective governments: after 1925 it was often entangled with leftist organization and agitation. Although Mao's "Reflections on the Peasant Movement in Hunan" was written in 1927, it took another two decades for *yundong* to be transformed into what it would become: a process that was as much directed, planned, and staged from above by the vanguard party as it was a social movement from below. In the generation before 1949, the expansion of *yundong* closely paralleled the rise of the party-state, moving from the realm of physical activity and sports, to social movements, to something fairly close to the notion of campaign that is most commonly used in Chinese now: the state's extraordinary mobilization of people and resources to implement a specific program to accomplish particular goals in a defined period of time.

The scholarship on the Mao-era PRC makes much of the mass mobilizational *yundong* it launched on a nearly annual basis.[8] Indeed, the broad-brush outline of successive national campaigns after 1949 serves as a shorthand for the history of revolutionary China itself during these

---

[7] See *Compact Edition of the Oxford English Dictionary* (Oxford, 1991), 324, s.v. "campaign."
[8] For early works of scholarship that focused on campaigns in the People's Republic of China, see James R. Townsend, *Political Participation in Communist China* (Berkeley: University of California Press, 1969), esp. Chapter 7, "Political Life in Communist China"; and Charles Cell, *Revolution at Work: Mobilization Campaigns in China* (New York: Academic Press, 1977), which proposes a schematic for campaigns of different types.

years.[9] This chapter posits a more capacious definition of campaign: that a campaign is an *extraordinary* and *temporary* mobilization of human and material resources for the rapid accomplishment of a specific goal (or set of goals). By this definition, it is clear that the Chinese state from the Qing to the present day has regularly resorted to campaigns as a method of policy implementation. The significance of campaigns for China's state making and policy implementation goes well beyond the big, splashy mass mobilizational campaigns that so punctuated the Mao years.[10]

Irrespective of goals, type, or time period, a campaign modality of policy implementation is characterized by the following three attributes: (1) the mobilization of state administrative organizations ("the bureaucracy") for the intensification of focus around implementing a particular program, (2) fixed and typically short duration, and (3) a big and well-publicized push to accomplish clearly defined targets and goals. Like the bureaucratic modality of policy implementation, the campaign modality *radically simplifies* complex realities. But it does so in an utterly different way. Rather than break down complex and interconnected phenomena into constituent and standardizable parts amenable to rules, the campaign simplifies through (1) fusion, (2) compression, and (3) emotionally charged narrative. In this way, the complex and multifaceted is merged into an organic whole, the time allotted for implementation is drastically reduced, and the emotional commitments of the implementers and the public are amplified through the invocation of morality tales.

Campaigns invariably require as a first step the extraordinary intensification of focus and mobilization of resources within the state, and it is here that the campaign's intersection with the consolidating Chinese

---

[9] Merle Goldman, "The Party and Intellectuals: Phase Two," in Roderick MacFaraquhar and John K. Fairbank, eds., *The Cambridge History of the People's Republic of China*, vol. 1 (Cambridge: Cambridge University Press, 1987), 432–477.

[10] On campaigns in the Qing, see Pierre-Étienne Will, R. Bin Wong, James Lee, Jean Oi, and Peter Perdue, *Nourish the People: The State Civilian Granary System in China, 1650–1850* (Ann Arbor: Center for Chinese Studies, University of Michigan, 1991); on Republican China see Arif Dirlik, "The Ideological Foundations of the New Life Movement: A Study in Counterrevolution," *Journal of Asian Studies* 34, no. 4 (August 1975): 945–980; Wennan Liu, "Redefining the Legal and Moral Roles of the State in Everyday Life: The New Life Movement in China in the mid-1930s," *Cross-current: East Asian History and Culture Review* 2, no. 2 (November 2013): 335–365; Chieko Nakajima, "Health and Hygiene in Mass Mobilization: Hygiene Campaigns in Shanghai, 1920–1945," *Twentieth-Century China* 34, no. 1 (2008): 42–72. On post-Mao China, see Melanie Manion, *Corruption by Design: Building Clean Government in Mainland China and Hong Kong* (Cambridge, MA: Harvard University Press, 2004), esp. Chapter 5; M. Scot Tanner, *Strike Hard: Anti-crime Campaigns and Chinese Criminal Justice, 1979–85* (Ithaca: Cornell University Press, 1999); Ralph A. Thaxton Jr., *Force and Contention in Contemporary China: Memory and Resistance in the Long Shadow of the Catastrophic Past* (Cambridge: 2016).

state's other modality of bureaucratic implementation is both co-constitutive and full of potential tension. The campaign typically focuses on readily graspable objectives, justifies its policies toward the objectives in straightforward morally based stories, and claims that a rapid push to achieve the objectives will solve a larger outstanding social, political, or economic problem. In contrast to bureaucracy, which is organized around the regular, the standardizable, and the predictable in its procedural and precedent-oriented manner of implementation, a campaign is *by definition* extraordinary, often sidestepping or overriding the procedural and rule-bound in its efforts to realize quick results. When state institutions are nascent, well-run campaigns may aid their expansion and consolidation by mobilizing internal commitments and clearing away social resistance. At the same time, campaigns exist in ambiguous tension with bureaucracy and law, which are predicated on the consistent application of rules and categories. Campaigns need the organizational capacity and coherence that bureaucratic hierarchies provide, but their modality of implementation – extraordinary mobilization, sharp focus, compressed time scale, and sidestepping of rules – is the opposite of the bureaucratic, which stresses the regular, the rule-bound, the precedent-oriented, and hierarchical discipline. Campaigns cannot completely undercut the formal institutions of the state, whose normal workings reify hierarchy and precedent-based rule making because they need bureaucratically organized institutions to carry them out, but, without strict limits, their very modality of implementation runs the risk of so doing.

Supporting Modalities of Policy Implementation with Performance; or, the How Is as Important as the What

Questions of performance permeate both bureaucratic and campaign modalities of state building. "Performance," like "campaign," encompasses very different meanings. This is particularly so in academia, where different disciplines use the term in overlapping but distinctive ways. "Performance" is a "speech act that brings something into being" (J. L. Austin), overlaps with "theatricality" (Schechner), complements meaning-making and ritual (Goffman, Collins, Turner) or social movements (Tilly), and is embrocated in the theatricality of the state itself (Geertz, Berezin).[11] While the disciplines and levels of social theory

---

[11] The literatures here are vast, but a partial bibliography would include John L. Austin, *How to Do Things with Words*, 2nd ed. (Oxford: Oxford University Press, 1976); Richard Schechner, *The Future of Ritual: Writings on Culture and Performance* (London: Routledge, 1995); Erving Goffman, *Interaction Ritual: Essays on Face-to-Face Behavior* (New York: Anchor Books, 1967); Randall Collins, *Interaction Ritual Chains* (Princeton:

engaged by these literatures differ, there is broad agreement that the content of political performance is made through culturally coded symbols, and commonly understood narratives and practices communicated through the content and the delivery of speech, dress, and manner of performance. In the early years of the PRC, the combination of regional insecurity, and the need to build effective state institutions quickly in the face of indifference or wariness of the local population, led the CCP in Sunan not only to establish order and implement signature policies, but also to place particular stress on valued performative registers in both campaign and bureaucratic modalities to communicate the party-state's identity and expectations to the population. In short, *how* policy was communicated and performed was as important as *what* policies were decided on and implemented. Campaigns that played out in public space were obviously theatrical, seeking to engage the emotions (support, righteous indignation, a sense of opportunity) while displaying regime norms to the population. Less obviously, the bureaucratic modality could also be performative. Here the person of the state cadre and the manner of his or her articulation of state policy were particularly important. The state cadre was, in theory, to refrain from being a remote figure who ventured out only to demand requisitions, rather s/he was to be a visible and approachable presence who served the people. In New China, cadres were not to be invariably male figures in their fifties or sixties, but whenever possible young, energetic, engaged, and, in certain spheres such as "women work" and public hygiene, even female. Unlike Guomindang officials, cadres were not dressed in foreign clothes, speaking a substantively different language by either using a dialect so different or technocratic jargon so thick that direct communication was impossible; rather, cadres were expected to wear plain clothing and communicate in revolutionary language that was unflowery and direct. Official representatives were to approach

Princeton University Press, 2004); Victor Turner's many works, the most important of which are perhaps *The Ritual Process: Structure and Anti-structure* (Ithaca: Cornell University Press, 1969), and "Social Dramas and Stories about Them," *Critical Inquiry* 7, no. 1 (Autumn 1980): 141–168; Charles Tilly, *Contentious Performances* (New York: Columbia University Press, 2008); Charles Tilly, *Regimes and Repertoires* (Chicago: The University of Chicago Press, 2006), Clifford Geertz, *Negara: The Theatre State in 19th Century Bali* (Princeton: Princeton University Press, 1981); Mabel Berezin, "The Festival State: Celebration and Commemoration in Fascist Italy," *Journal of Modern European History* 3, no. 1 (2006): 60–74; Jeffrey Alexander, *The Performance of Politics: Obama's Victory and the Democratic Struggle for Power* (Oxford and New York: Oxford University Press, 2010); and Joseph Esherick and Jeffrey Wasserstrom, "Acting Out Democracy: Political Theatre in Modern China," *Journal of Asian Studies* 49, no. 4 (November 1990): 835–865.

field sites by bicycle or on foot rather than by black Mercedes with smoked windows. New rules (orders, directives, regulations) were now communicated by loudspeaker blaring in a singsong official voice; newsprint reproduced the state's new vocabulary. All these actions so inherent to the everyday rule-orientation of state administration were equally part of the dramaturgy of state power.

Building the Revolutionary State in Sunan: The Campaign to Suppress Counterrevolutionaries and Land Reform, 1950–1951

After coming into the wealthy cities of lower Jiangnan in the spring of 1949 with the troop discipline that effected an orderly takeover, the CCP spent its first year in power explicitly signaling its moderation and inclusiveness toward all but the most recalcitrant – those who had worked in the outgoing Guomindang's security organizations. Countrywide, the new government's initial priorities were to reassure the population, get production and basic services going again, bring hyperinflation under control, and feed hungry urban areas that could not supply themselves. Nowhere was this moderation and inclusiveness more in evidence than in the careful way that wealthy Sunan – so essential for any Chinese government – was incorporated. This moderation and inclusiveness under the rubric of progressive "New Democracy" only lasted for about twelve months. Under the twin pressures of external regional insecurity with the outbreak of the war in Korea in the early summer of 1950 and the CCP's own internally motivated determination to implement a revolutionary set of programs, roughly a year after coming to power the government launched three nearly simultaneous major countrywide campaigns: the Campaign to Resist America/Aid Korea (autumn 1950), the Campaign to Suppress Counterrevolutionaries (launched on October 10, 1950, but reaching its peak in Sunan in spring 1951), and the Campaign for Land Reform (with preparation and test sites in the autumn of 1950, but in Sunan also climaxing in the spring of 1951). The Resist America/Aid Korea campaign was a set of public demonstrations to rally patriotic opinion behind the new government, and convince urban populations, many of them previously pro-American, that America was the new enemy. Because it was aimed at rallying patriotic support against an *external* enemy, the Resist America/Aid Korea campaign was intensely public, but both short-term and limited in scope. The campaigns to suppress counterrevolutionaries and for land reform, on the other hand, were explicitly geared to identifying and extirpating newly identified *internal* enemies.

While both campaigns were squarely set on wiping out groups now deemed to be beyond the possibility of inclusion in revolutionary society, the Campaign to Suppress Counterrevolutionaries, bloody as it was, was less transformational than land reform, which aimed to both rid the polity of landlords *and* push through a comprehensive transfer of wealth in the countryside. Nevertheless, in Sunan the two campaigns were conducted at the same time, followed similar trajectories, and overlapped significantly in their actual targets, which ended up including large percentages of "evil bullies" (*e'ba*) – a loose category of rural and semirural socially undesirable power holders. In the peri-urban area around Shanghai and in Sunan's county towns, the two campaigns merged to such an extent that they were mutually indistinguishable in the spring "high tide" of 1951. In addition, both campaigns were characterized by similar trajectories and problems: (1) the need to generate the extraordinary mobilization of the regime's new government organizations in applying and communicating new categories to the population, (2) definition and stigmatization of a minority, and (3) results that required local cadres able to tack back and forth between the bureaucratic and rule-bound and the mobilization of the masses in a highly public dramatic show in the form of the public accusation/struggle meeting (*kongsu hui/douzheng hui*).

Because local cadres were tasked with running these campaigns on their own initiative with exclusively local resources, higher levels of the party-state relied on signals sent to lower-level cadres through circulars, reports, guidelines and regulations, study sessions, training sessions, and the occasional work team sent down to check and provide guidance, mobilizing the commitment of local cadres was a precondition for success. Initially in Sunan, both campaigns were tough sells, with significant foot-dragging from local cadres. There were two reasons for this reluctance: (1) the previous year had been one of explicit inclusion and moderation, and local cadres wondered with some frequency why such a radical shift to uncompromising violence was necessary, and (2) the state's new categories of enemy frequently made little to no sense.

In Shanghai state cadres were initially reluctant to "vigorously" pursue putative counterrevolutionaries, holding a "generally 'merciful view' [*renci guannian*], which supposed that 'education could solve all problems.'" Others insisted that their own offices didn't harbor any counterrevolutionaries, or even grumbled that a major campaign to suppress counterrevolutionaries was "like cracking a nut with a sledgehammer" (*xiaoti dazuo*).[12] When Luo Ruiqing, minister of security, toured the cities

---

[12] SMA (Shanghai Municipal Archives) A22/2/50, "Shifu jiguan ganbu buchong tianbiaozhong de xuanchuanjiaoyu gongzuo zongjie" (General Report on the Dissemination and

of central and south China in February of 1951 to check on the progress of the campaign, he was shocked by the local authorities' cautious attitude, reluctance to forge links with the masses, and insufficiently strong implementation.[13] While central authorities conceded that Nanjing, the recent Guomindang capital, had smashed a satisfyingly large number of counterrevolutionary networks, they held that Nanjing's regular judicial procedures were far too slow and its sentencing inappropriately lenient, with only two counterrevolutionaries given a death sentence for the entirety of 1949–1950. On these grounds Nanjing was publicly held up as a particularly egregious example of "excessive lenience" (*kuanda wubian*) that needed rectification.[14]

At least Sunan had a quantifiably large number of urban counterrevolutionaries to "smash." Such was not the case for land reform. Whatever else the Communist underground in Sunan may have been able to effect, generating mass rural enthusiasm for land reform had long been problematic.[15] Well into 1950, local cadres wondered why peaceful division of land (*heping fendi*) was not possible, and nearly constantly reported to their superiors that there was little a priori hatred for landlords, as most landlords were smallholders who only rented out a portion of their holdings. Many of the rural young were upwardly mobile and only engaged in agriculture part-time. Most aspired to becoming factory workers (and many migrated, at least part-time, to where the factories were). Absentee landlords were extremely common, and economic and social relations were "very complicated." Some cadres went as far as to warn against imposing methods of "pure class struggle" (*danchun douzheng*) that were inapplicable at best and counterproductive at worst. In the outlaw-riven marshes just east of Shanghai proper, landlords were "of many types, simultaneously engaged with industry or other kinds of work, and class resentment over land use, when it existed, was directed at 'outsiders,' often refugees, who were squatting on local land."[16] The regime presumed that there was a large reservoir of poor-peasant discontent and hatred of landlords to be tapped, but in Sunan, where rural conditions were utterly different from those in the north China

Education Work on the Municipal Government Cadre's Supplementary Forms), July 3, 1951.

[13] Luo Ruiqing, "Guanyu Wuhan, Shanghai deng chengshi zhenfan gongzuo dekaocha baogao" (Investigation Report on the Suppression of Counterrevolutionaries in Wuhan, Shanghai and Other Cities), March 20, 1951, in *Lun renmin gong'an gongzuo*, 55–58.

[14] "Zhongyang gong'an bu guanyu quanguo gong'an huiyi de baogao," October 26, 1950, in *Jianguo yilai zhongyao wenxian xuanbian*, vol. 1, 442, p. 190.

[15] See Chang Liu, "Making Revolution in Jiangnan: The Communists in the Yangzi Delta Countryside, 1927–1945," *Modern China* 29, no. 1 (January 2003): 3–37.

[16] SMA A71-2-82, "Yangjing qu tugai gongzuo zongjie baogao (1)," November 16, 1951.

countryside in which land reform campaigns had been implemented with such success, this core assumption simply did not hold.[17] Ultimately it was the *political* imposition of will from above that broke through the foot-dragging, natural caution, and scruples of local cadres. In Shanghai in November 1950 a regional conference on land reform was convened that put local cadres on notice that implementing land reform in a vigorous manner was now necessary. Similarly, in February 1951 Luo Ruiqing toured the big cities of the Yangzi river valley, and levied especially harsh criticism of Nanjing for being too cautious in its prosecution of counterrevolutionaries. Prior to these signals, local cadres feared, for some reason, that they would be blamed for mistakenly shedding blood. After the Luo Ruiqing tour and the Shanghai Conference on Land Reform, they feared that they would be blamed for insufficient vigor in prosecuting enemies of the revolution. It is little wonder that "sharp strikes" and rapid shifts to the left ensued.

The Co-production of Bureaucracy and Campaign

Those running the Campaign to Suppress Counterrevolutionaries and land reform had to identify who was (and was not) a counterrevolutionary or landlord, and this involved an enormous – and frequently enormously bureaucratic – set of tasks. Take, for example, the determination of counterrevolutionary status. A counterrevolutionary could be labeled as such based on his (very infrequently was it her) formal position in a *tewu* security organization or high office in the outgoing Guomindang government, or by undesirable forms of behavior such as being an evil bully (*e'ba*), a traitor (*hanjian*), or a leader of a counterrevolutionary sect (*fandong huimen tou*). Since it was much easier to assign counterrevolutionary status due to having held office in the Guomindang (confirming paper trails typically existed) than it was to assess counterrevolutionary status by ongoing undesirable behavior, the campaign involved a pre-campaign drive throughout Sunan in the winter of 1950–1951 to encourage the former to come forward and register with the state by promising lenience to those who complied. This preparatory sub-campaign was almost exclusively bureaucratic in goal (registration) and implementation (gathering and filing paperwork). In retrospect, it is clear that this

---

[17] Of course, in north China the CCP's standard categories of "landlords," followed by rich, middle, and poor peasants, then hired laborers, often didn't make a great deal of sense either; frequently there weren't enough bona fide landlords to go around. But in north China there seems to have been substantial land hunger and willingness to engage in violence that was typically absent in Sunan. See Huang, "Rural Class Struggle in the Chinese Revolution"; and Esherick, "Revolution in a Feudal Fortress."

registration drive prepared the evidentiary basis for the "sharp strikes" and full-scale social mobilization later in the spring of 1951. But at the time what was to come was not obvious at all. This kind of lenience had been offered by the regime from its earliest days in power, and the winter registration drive might well have been understood as nothing more than a tidying-up administrative exercise.

Consider the case of Nanjing, later held up as a negative example of going far too easily on counterrevolutionaries. On January 20, 1951, the Nanjing Military Administration Committee published an edict that required all *tewu* counterrevolutionaries to register with their documentary proofs. To manage this workload, Nanjing underwent an extraordinary, but temporary, expansion of its public-security registration capacity. It set up fourteen temporary district registration stations, and all state organizations, schools, and enterprises were ordered to establish registration stations or registration small groups. Within three days 1,516 had registered; by the end of the fifth day, 4,298; and at the end of March, a city of roughly 850,000 had registered a total of 18,611 *tewu* counterrevolutionaries. This registration sub-campaign well illustrates some of the dynamics by which bureaucratic and campaign modalities were co-constitutive in early regime consolidation: the sudden expansion of bureaucratic state capacity necessary to implement the campaign was temporary, but the information gathered was permanent, providing a substantial reservoir of self-acknowledged counterrevolutionaries that could be drawn upon later.[18]

As had been the case in north China, the land reform campaign involved an enormous amount of preparatory activity that was rule-oriented and classification-driven. Here the investigations and report writing were even more intensive, as the campaign extended to every village in rural Sunan. Land reform also required lengthy periods of study and discussion, and extensive inquiries into local land tenure and wealth holding. This was followed by the division of classes to permanently assign a status to each rural family of landlord, petty landlord, wealthy peasant, middle peasant (subdivided into upper, middle, and lower), and poor and hired peasants. The first and most fundamental distinction in this classification scheme was whether a given household was part of an "exploiting class" who survived on the basis of someone else's labor, or a "laboring class" who survived on the basis of their own labor.

In order to identify their likely targets, the Campaign to Suppress Counterrevolutionaries and land reform both had as a first phase

---

[18] Nanjing Gong'an Zhi, 192–193.

a preparatory period of intense investigation (which could only be carried out in accordance with fixed criteria) and registration (which required forms, standardized categories, and accessible systems for storage and retrieval of data). The early stages of these campaigns intensified a bureaucratic modality of policy implementation through identification of individuals or households according to regular rules and the local implementation of policies and rules determined by higher levels in the hierarchy. The deployment of extraordinary political will and resources, particularly in the land reform campaign in Sunan, also *expanded* the state's reach as it mobilized the commitment of cadres.

Implementing such a large-scale campaign to reach so deeply into rural society meant that in Sunan the preparations for land reform campaigns required training very large numbers of people, often young, to go down to the most grassroots level of the countryside to augment the local administrative capacity that was already present. In the Shanghai suburbs alone, 460 lecturers and teachers from local universities and middle schools were trained and sent down to the countryside. There they were joined by 4,616 activists who were largely from poor peasant backgrounds. Over one-fifth of these (1,042 of 4,616, or 20.57 percent) were eventually regularized as permanent cadres. In late 1950, the Sunan Party Village Work Committee planned to train an eventual further 11,333 cadres to provide guidance and support for the three land reform districts of Suzhou, Changshu, and Songjiang.[19] Along with the permanent classification of the rural population on the basis of new class distinctions, one of the more important by-products of the land reform campaign in Sunan was the identification and training of large numbers of committed loyalists, a substantial minority of whom would remain in the villages to which they had been dispatched, where they established a stronger rural core of CCP cadres to guide later rural campaigns.[20]

---

[19] JPA (Jiangsu Provincial Archive) 3006-3-360, "Benhui [zhonggong sunanzu dangwei nongcun gongzuoweiyuanhui] Sunan ganbu xunlian tongjibiao" (Chinese Communist Sunan Group Party Village Work Committee Sunan Cadre Training Statistics), n.d, 1950.

[20] SMA B14/1/80, "Shanghai shi jiaoqu xunlian ganbu shu peiyang jijifenzi qingkuang" (The Situation for Shanghai Municipal Outer District Cadre Training and the Cultivation of Activists), and "Sheng tudi gaige qianhou xiangcun jiceng ganbu bianhua qingkuang tongjibiao" (Statistical Form on Changes in Village-Level Local Cadres before and after Land Reform), both 13 of internally numbered file, dated December 31, 1951; SMA B14/1/6 "Jiaoshi canjia tudi gaige di'yi xiaozu mingdan ji duiyuan tongjibiao" (Instructors Participating in Land Reform: The First Small Group Name List and Statistics), 1951.

The How Is as Important as the What: The Performative and the Theatrical

The Campaign to Suppress Counterrevolutionaries and land reform drew on precisely the same repertoires in Sunan. The culmination of both campaigns, the high tide (*gaochao*), was enacted through a form of participatory theatre for the "masses." The "script" of mass revolutionary campaign first articulated in full form in north China was handed down to Sunan cadres to enact. Instructions from above were very clear: the Campaign to Suppress Counterrevolutionaries and land reform absolutely *required* the fear and anger of cathartic mass emotion, and the graphically public corporeal destruction of the "old" (feudal, corrupt) as a form of cleansing and public identification with the "new" (modern, clean, and bright). The mass accusation/struggle session aimed to gather as much as possible of the adult population as a unitary participant spectator audience in one place, where the specific device of "speaking bitterness" (*suku*) was acted out by pre-coached victims, selected well in advance of the proceedings for their capacity to stir up the sympathy of the crowd. Even though there was an enormous amount of behind-the-scenes preparation for mass accusation sessions, the events themselves needed to *appear* to be spontaneous, directly participatory, and unmediated by intermediate organizations and visible procedures. The show had many functions: to educate the public, to stiffen the resolve of cadres, to give activists a chance to establish their credentials, and to publicly expunge the impure. In this febrile environment, the individual merged with the others in the audience, and this newly forged public collective was given a literal voice with a culminating roar of catharsis that erased the boundaries between state, society, and individual. In the public accusation/struggle meeting, the CCP transferred to Sunan a repertoire with a form (public gathering), process (the emotional high of the "stirred-up" masses), and content (hatred toward defined class enemies) that had served it so well in making revolution in the very different society and economy of north China. The party-state in Sunan remained deeply attached to the *gaochao*, the way in which it instructed the wider population in the normative values, and the momentary, but nonetheless real, way in which it brought about a merging of popular and state will.

In these public dramas, local voices were articulated through direct participatory action unmediated by clear rules and procedures. In fact, clarity about rules and procedures was seen to be the antithesis of a proper "high tide." CCP guidelines dictated that the peak of the campaign's "high tide" be the visible result of appropriately mobilized "stirred-up" masses. Local cadres were expected to demonstrate that, over the course of the campaign, the masses' consciousness had been raised through the *gaochao*; in turn, the *gaochao* was only effective insofar as revolutionary consciousness was demonstrated through the collective voicing of mass hatred for counterrevolutionary and landlord evildoers and exploiters. This mass venting implicitly rallied around the new government in colluding in the state's bloody violence against defined enemies. But in neither the Campaign to Suppress Counterrevolutionaries nor land reform were these public accusation/struggle meetings the spontaneous events that they might have appeared to be to the participant audiences of the time.

Local cadres planned carefully for these public spectacles. They chose the sites of the accusation meeting and set up raised platforms to serve as informal stages. They identified and coached activists and sympathetic accusers. They decided on which accusers would come forward in what order, and gave accusers rough scripts that comprised which accusations ought to be made in what order. In this way, they ensured that the crowd was first warmed up by less serious accusations before the most graphic cases of blood debt released the highest level of sympathetic emotion toward the end of the proceedings. In the Shanghai outer-district village of Meituo, such was the emphasis on preparation for the big public struggle meeting that there were no less than *three* meetings of the relevant rural cadres to "unify understanding, move forward mobilization, and strengthen policy education." Cadres were also expected to form a full plan for the accusation meeting, "fully grasp and review" the materials of the struggle targets, and organize the logistics. They were counseled to commence accusation meetings no earlier than 4:00 p.m. but conclude before 6:00 p.m., in order to avoid hunger, boredom, and wandering attention from the masses. They were also directed to ensure that those who were from the district were seated first and closest to the stage, while observers from outside the district were to be allowed in somewhat later. Such was the obsession with planning and control that local cadres in Meituo even went so far as to run full dress rehearsals several days before the main event, complete with selected individuals from "the masses" to sit in the audience. Since the two accused – a landlord by the name of Cai Heng, and an "evil bully" by the name of Sun Jize, had already been arrested and were in detention, local cadres thought that this early run-through was a good way to smooth out organizational issues, pre-educate the public, and stiffen the resolve of activists. The Meituo cadres did concede that the masses who attended this rehearsal wondered aloud why the later more public accusation meeting attended by thousands was necessary. What Cai Heng and Sun Jize thought of having to play the part of accused villain more than once can only be imagined.[21]

As the denouement of these campaigns in Sunan followed scripts and stage directions handed down from higher levels, there was considerable pressure to replicate the organizational forms, the dramatic content, and the resounding transformation of the masses that the leaders of the CCP had used to such great effect in north China. Peasants were organized into peasant associations, youth associations, and women's associations on the north China model, but there is little evidence that these duly constituted mass organizations contributed much to the high drama of public mass accusation sessions in Sunan. Instructions to local cadres insisted that the process of accusation had to be dramatically embodied as a confrontation of archetypes: the now chastened and physically diminished evildoer, the righteous victim, the exhortation of an indignant crowd now merged into a collective whole in support of the traumatized victims, and, just offstage, the state that was putting on the production.

While cadres were expected to obsessively prepare for mass accusation meetings ahead of the proceedings, the actual "high tide" (*gaochao*) of the event was in principle in the hands of the masses. Cadres were directed to leave key moments of decision to the now "stirred-up" crowd. Instruction booklets counselled that formulaic slogans be avoided, and urged that the sight of the targets onstage coalesce into appropriate slogans of "noise and color" (*yousheng youse*). In the mass accusation meeting in Meituo, this formula was followed quite closely when the stirred-up crowd directly incited the public beating of "evil bully" Sun Jize. Instructions stipulated that the collective voice of the masses be heeded. When the crowd shouted, "bow your head," the accused was to bow his head; when it followed up with "drop to your knees," he was supposed to drop to his knees. If the crowd agitated for the accused to be beaten, the leading cadres in charge were to acquiesce in the demands of the masses. At the peak of the "high tide," when the crowd was called on to decide the fate of the accused, if the masses called for immediate public revenge to be taken, the authorities were either to permit the accused to be beaten to death *in situ* or to lead the accused off the stage to be publicly executed forthwith. In those instances when the crowd wished to show mercy after the accuser spoke bitterness and the accused recognized his guilt, the target could then be turned over to the regular processes of the people's courts (i.e., back to a more bureaucratic modality of policy implementation).[22]

---

[21] SMA A71-2-76-30, "Zhonggong Shanghai Shi Meituo xiang zongzhi weiyuan hui, guanyu erci douzheng hui de jieshao cailiao" (CCP Shanghai Municipality Meituo Village Combined Committee, Introductory Materials on Two Struggle Meetings), 1951.

[22] Ibid.

Higher-level cadres also insisted that the public accusation sessions include the wronged engaging in direct "face-to-face" (*mian dui mian*) accusation of the target. The evildoer was required to "publicly acknowledge" his previous crimes (*chengzui*) before the masses as "without this kind of public acknowledgment of crimes the entire [process] is fake."[23] Individual contrition, and by extension the accused's recognition of the state's new categories of the pure and the depraved, good classes and bad classes, was felt to be necessary for proper resolution of the onstage drama. If the accused did not express penitence, ask for forgiveness, and symbolically accede to the state's new order, then the mass accusation session was deemed to have been unsatisfying and incomplete. In the rare instances for which there are detailed accounts of those who refused to acknowledge their crimes (and by extension the authority of the state), such as Sun Jize, mentioned above, the cadre who wrote up the final report was palpably indignant that Sun "died without recognizing his mistakes," thus denying the validity and legitimacy of New China.[24]

Records from Qingpu County, Shanghai County, and the Shanghai *jiaoqu* confirm that large numbers of mass struggle sessions were convened and that those "targets" predetermined to be most evil and hated were promptly led off to the execution ground. The degree to which "the masses" happily played their part in these public dramas is, however, uncertain. Some evidence suggests that crowds could and did get so riled up that they engaged in extraordinarily violent behavior. Records from Shanghai County reveal that nearly a third (224 of 779) of recorded "accusation targets" (*douzheng duixiang*) "were strung up and beaten as they were struggled against" (*douzheng zhong bei diaoda*) in mass accusation meetings (see Figure 5.1). What are we to make of this high number? Were these crowds given free rein to express what was already latent, or were they actively egged on by local cadres? Were those who did the stringing up and beating a minority, and if so, what was the reaction of the majority who witnessed these events? Was this staged violence, ostensibly popular and spontaneous, instigated by activists and tolerated by local cadres, or were local cadres themselves the instigators? Were most of the people who witnessed the spectacle genuinely "stirred up" or did they have sneaking sympathy for the accused? And, given that land reform was supposed to target landlords, how many of the specific "targets" who were

---

[23] JPA 3006-3-271, Sunan Tugai Weiyuanhui Mishuchu, "Guanyu fadong qunzhong wenti de baogao," 1951, italics added.
[24] SMA A71-2-76-30. "Zhonggong Shanghai shi Meituo xiang zongzhi weiyuan hui, guanyu erci douzheng hui de jieshao cailiao."

Figure 5.1 A mass accusation session
Source: *Jiefang Ribao* (Shanghai), April 11, 1951

strung up and beaten were landlords at all, given how few bona fide landlords there were to go around in in the lower Yangzi region?[25]

Given the bureaucratic incentives for local cadres to report dutifully that the public accusation meeting had been a success, that the crowd's consciousness had been raised, and that the accused had admitted his mistakes amid a resounding "high tide" of collective emotional hatred for state enemies and support for the state's righteousness, it is not surprising that there are only hints of anything else in the archival record. There are, however, scattered accounts that hint that while some were eager to participate in violence, others were either simple spectators or were quietly disapproving of the proceedings. Mass audiences could and sometimes did adopt a "plague-on-both-your-houses" attitude. In one struggle meeting in Taicang County, Liangbei Village, two people from the crowd rushed the stage, taking over the proceedings.[26] After the struggle meeting, many in the audience could be heard grumbling that "those

---

[25] QDA (Qingpu District Archives) 1/1/38, "Douzheng cishu tongjibiao" (Statistics on Numbers of Struggles), 2–3, 1951; MDA 13/1/37, "Shanghai xian jiesu tugai gongzuo douzheng qingkuang tongjibiao" (Statistics on Shanghai County Struggle Sessions at the Conclusion of Land Reform), November 18, 1951. These statistics also reveal that less than half of the "struggle targets" in Shanghai County were landlords of any description.

[26] This instance of rushing the stage would have been more than enough for the cadre in charge to have been smacked down with a stern reprimand from superiors, who

conducting the struggle were all bad people." In Gaodu's Qiqiao Village, things did not go to plan at all: rather than coming off with contrition on the part of landlords and a convincing reaffirmation of public support for the regime, evidently, the struggle meeting's audience opined that "both the recipients and the actors [of the struggle session] were all bad – [this is just a show of] bad people beating up other bad people."[27]

At present, many of the available qualitative records on land reform *kongsu hui* in Sunan are either so formulaic ("the crowd was stirred up"), or so heavily focused on anecdote to make a negative point ("the masses were *not* stirred up") that it is impossible to gauge how typical or atypical the anecdote in question might be. We so far lack the detailed and lengthy eyewitness accounts of the kind that parallel those that we have for north China from William Hinton and the Crooks, that convey whether the kind of violence unleashed in public accusation meetings was genuinely popular, bringing about freely flowing tears and spontaneous accusations. But given how different conditions were in rural Sunan and north China, it isn't terribly surprising that local cadres' internal reports occasionally pointed to cadre and/or mass failure to understand their parts in this new form of the state's moral drama.

On occasion, even the most dispossessed – the "poor and hired" peasants without land of their own, remained "unstirred." In Zhenru's Luchangqiao and Changtou Villages, even the poorest held throughout the entire campaign that subjecting landlords to house arrest and then publicly struggling against them was the business of local cadres as representatives of the state and had nothing to do with them personally. Despite the best efforts of local cadres to conduct propaganda and raise consciousness, most middle peasants remained "asleep" and refused to be stirred up at all.[28] In a separate (non)event in Luchangqiao, a poor peasant named Qian Ahyou was reckoned to have particularly suffered at the hands of the local landlord. For whatever reasons, Qian remained (in the view of the local cadre who wrote the eventual report) incomprehensibly reluctant to appear at struggle sessions and play his part in the proceedings. Qian preferred to lie low and avoid the entire business for some three to four days and finally had to be (directly) "accompanied to the meeting by the village cadre."[29] (Although there is no further

cautioned against allowing new, unproven accusations to be brought forth spontaneously from the crowd.

[27] JPA 3006-3-271, "Guanyu fadong qunzhong douzheng cailiao zhailü," April 1951.

[28] SMA A71-2-84, "Zhenru qu Diantai xiang Luchangqiao cun Changtou cun tugai jianchazhong de qingkuang baogao" (Investigative Report on Land Reform in Zhenru District, Diantai Village, Luchangqiao and Changtou Hamlets), August 11, 1951.

[29] Ibid.

information about this case, one can guess that the village cadre prevailed upon Qian to conform.) Regular reports from Shanghai County, the *jiaoqu*, and Sunan, in general, are replete with stock complaints about the "backward political consciousness of the masses." When specific examples of this sort of mass "backwardness" are cited, they include the cynical view that Chiang Kai-shek's return was right around the corner, and that the process of land reform had nothing to do with *them*, as it was something that cadres were imposing from above and from outside. On occasion, even those whom the CCP assumed ought to fall within the categories most likely to be vociferous in support of struggle against the old order remained frustratingly unmoved to participate.

A critical report on the difficulties of stirring up the masses compiled by the Sunan Land Reform Investigation Unit in April 1951 is full of detailed, if anecdotal, evidence that confirms that in many locales cadres had to overcome a great deal of natural reluctance on the part of the "masses" to be "stirred" to physical violence. In one case in Jiading County, Mawei District, Beiguan Village, cadres clearly incited the masses to demand physical violence when the performance onstage apparently went off script. A local cadre placed in the crowd shouted out for the accuser onstage to "go ahead and hit him!" At this juncture,

From the stage (where the accused and a peasant who was "speaking bitterness" towards the accused), the district cadre (who was directing the proceedings) instructed the man who was "speaking bitterness," "if the masses say 'hit him' then you have to go ahead and hit him." But the man in his appointed role to "speak bitterness" demurred for quite a while with the repeated insistence that "I've never hit anyone before, and I will not hit him."

As the crowd continued to call for the accuser to use physical force, the man on the stage eventually hit the accused twice. The crowd continued to bay for more violence, and in the end the accuser landed some seven or eight blows on the accused. In this case, there were three elements that incited an accuser who was clearly reluctant to engage in physical violence: the triggering call of the local cadre in the audience, the formal authority of the district cadre on the stage, and mass hysteria from the crowd.[30]

In other localities, things did not play out in this way. There were occasions when local cadres took on a role quite opposite of that of inciter to violence. Local cadres could and did dampen down the physical violence of accusatory theatre by keeping tight control over the proceedings, or even discreetly postponing the show until tempers had cooled. In

[30] JPA 3006-3-271. "Guanyu fadong qunzhong douzheng de cailiao zhailü," April 1951.

Kunshan's Yebi Village, the local cadre opened the public accusation session with the warning to the crowd that "*he* was the one passing judgment, and that anyone who went ahead and 'strung up and beat' an accused target would have to take responsibility for so doing." In another instance involving a particularly despised "little tiger" (*xiaohu*), the local cadre refused to let the prisoner go to his appointed struggle session, on the ground that if the prisoner had to face the public, he would surely be beaten to death.[31]

The qualitative evidence that is at present available is profoundly ambiguous on what is the most important question of all: how public accusation meetings were received and understood by the most important audience for the show – the crowds that were called to vicariously partici-pate in this publicly performed drama as spectators and chorus. Some accounts suggest that the show of mass accusation sessions followed the script and the outcomes desired by higher levels in the CCP: representing popular will, whipping the crowd into a frenzy of popular support for the regime's dispatch of class enemies. Local reports typically include statis-tics that suggest that most of the rural population "participated" (*canjia*) in land reform accusation sessions, but in this context "participation" meant showing up and being counted. Formulaic reports conclude that "the masses were stirred up" and that justice was done, with resounding affirmation for the state's violence against class enemies. Some of the qualitative evidence supports the notion that as local cadres lurched radically leftward after November 1950, they and local activists incited the "masses" to publicly denounce and commit violence against those targets deemed hateful exploiters, with mixed results. Other accounts point to the limits that local cadres could (and did) put on the degree of uncontrolled violence that they would permit on their watches.

The CCP in 1950–1951 demanded that the drama of the mass accus-ation meetings developed under wartime conditions of rural north China be fractally replicated in the very different urban and rural environments of central and southern China. Higher levels of the party-state made it clear that they expected the proceedings to culminate in the drama of "stirred-up" masses accusing evil counterrevolutionaries and landlords, reaffirming collective unity with the state and its violence against defined enemies. Sometimes the show went well; sometimes it did not. Urban Sunan was full of individuals who had until very recently worked along-side those now cast as evil counterrevolutionaries. Rural Sunan was a region in which the dividing line between exploited and exploiters was blurred, landlords were weak, social and economic mobility was high, and

---

[31] Ibid.

in many places local people appeared to have thought that their own local landlords weren't such bad sorts at all.

A series of questions regarding mass accusation sessions during the campaigns for land reform and the suppression of counterrevolutionaries awaits further research. Even though these public displays of state violence against targeted enemies were staged by the state and acted out by a small number of designated activists and specially handpicked victims, we still do not have the kind of evidence that systematically supports the state's claims of indignantly stirred-up masses. Were the majority in the audience scared, bored, or enthusiastic in their condemnation? The fragmentary accounts that we have for Sunan at present suggest that in some cases the state did put on a convincing show, in others the majority felt fear and pity for the accused, and in still others most felt that the entire undertaking had nothing to do with them. Given the demands placed on local cadres that public accusation meetings be put on in a certain way and demonstrate key markers of success (an aroused crowd that shouted the right slogans, face-to-face accusations, and the penitent accused acknowledging prior crimes and errors onstage), cadre reports on the struggle meetings typically invoked a standard reporting formula: the masses were stirred up and raised their revolutionary consciousness, the evil received their just punishment, and everyone supported the righteousness of the revolutionary's state's actions. In Sunan, not only was the party-state's insistence on a reckoning with those defined as enemies of the state highly public; also the form itself demanded that the individual, the crowd itself, and the regime come together in a (temporary) revolutionary unity. The large venues (usually outdoors) for the stage, the simplified emotional narratives of prior suffering, and the now shackled representatives of evil personified bowing before the combined power of the state and the masses were all integral components to generate the unified collective fury of the masses with the judgment of the state.

In this way the public performance of the "high tide" (*gaochao*) pulled against a bureaucratic modality of policy implementation based on the principles of hierarchy, precedent, procedure, and process, even though it was "bureaucracy" that made it possible to put on the show. Indeed, the very *point* of the mass accusation meeting high tide was to steamroller over normal procedures and processes with a raw emotional power that fused the state and the imagined collective public. Even if these mass struggle sessions were in fact heavily stage-managed events, and the spontaneity of the accusations levied was more apparent than real, it is not at all clear at this early stage in regime consolidation that the "masses" understood that the outcome of public struggle sessions was foreordained and that their designated role was that of the chorus: to be stirred to emotion, to cheer and clap on cue, and to collectively reaffirm the moral righteousness of the regime in stamping out vicious enemies.

The very form of the mass struggle meeting was as much a heuristic device for educating the participants in the audience about the new regime's norms and rhetoric as it was a means for dispatching individuals deemed to be enemies of the state. (Since the relevant counterrevolution-aries, landlords, and bullies had already been identified and incarcerated, speedy and secret execution or imprisonment would likely have done the job just as well.) The state claimed to represent, reproduce, and make public the legitimate position and opinions of "the masses"; the masses, in turn, learned what was expected of them in collective action in new forms of political participation unmediated by organizations or procedures. Further, the very public and staged nature of the mass struggle session provided a visible point of rupture with the "old" – it not only rid society of enemies, but did so in a way to communicate to the largest possible number of ordinary people that the new government meant business about transforming the evils of the old society. Public accusation sessions also implicitly bloodied the hands of all of those who shouted in support of the regime's violence. When the show went well, local participation and representation were articulated through a publicly affirmed unity and merging of crowd and state. Mass representation was not channeled through either regular procedures or a formal organization such as the peasant association. Rather, it was fused to the state in a dramatic, but temporary, emotional high that provided a widely understood moment of no return – after which nothing would ever be quite the same again.

Conclusion

In the early to mid-1950s, state-making elites in Sunan subscribed to the view that campaign and bureaucratic modalities of state making were mutually supporting: campaigns were deployed precisely to establish and strengthen the bureaucratic institutions of the state by mobilizing the commitments of cadres and overcoming social resistance. Conversely, campaigns required functional and loyal cadres able and willing to engage the regular bureaucratic institutions of the state such as hierarchy, infor-mation flows, orders, and procedures to go through old documents and write new ones, organize the visits of superiors or work teams, and so on. When they worked well, campaigns energized bureaucracy, but also presupposed the existence of a functioning bureaucracy. In such a large polity with such thinly spread loyal cadres, transformational policies of the kind that the CCP wished to implement in the early 1950s could perhaps only be realized through campaigns inaugurated by the central government that were implemented at local levels, and the administrative capacity to do otherwise did not exist. The optimistic assumption that campaign and bureaucratic modalities of policy implementation – the basic "stuff" which comprised state activity – were coproduced and mutually reinforcing was largely accurate during these early years of regime consolidation.

Given the early success of these twinned modalities in the early 1950s, it is worth reflecting on why the mutual reinforcement and coproduction of bureaucratic and campaign modalities in the early 1950s gave way to sharpened tension and contradiction between the two. The answers to this question can only be provisional, but it is likely that the CCP's inability and unwillingness to adapt its mobilizational repertoires to the different social and economic environments of central and south China were at the heart of these later difficulties. For the CCP, mass mobilization, striking at the representatives of isolated enemy classes and achieving a genuine, if temporary, public groundswell of support for the Party's revolutionary violence, was not simply a technique of revolution to be altered or discarded in the light of new circumstances, but was instead fused with the CCP's understanding of revolution and indistinguishable from the CCP's success in achieving, much earlier than expected, a heroic victory and the extension of its presence in the newly occupied areas of central and south China after mid-1949. Once this public performance of revolutionary fervor and public legitimation was an integral component of the campaign, it would prove ever less possible to jettison, even under the vastly changed circumstances of the mid-1950s, when accusation/struggle sessions were increasingly conducted within the confines of the work unit, in which everyone was hyperaware of the degree to which struggle sessions were shows put on by power holders. Campaigns that designated enemies and targets worked much less well when the putative "enemies" looked, spoke, and acted more or less like everyone else. Once the usual suspects had been rounded up and dispatched, succeeding waves of struggle against counterrevolutionaries, black classes, or other identified deviants could only turn inward in ever more destructive waves, while campaigns geared to one aspect of production or construction almost of necessity would throw regular procedures and rules into abeyance. In the long run, the elements of campaign mobilization that proved to be so important to revolutionary success in taking power and establishing the power of the revolutionary state were exactly those that under the changed circumstances of post-regime consolidation would prove to be so destructive.

6 The Wilds of Revolution
Anti-localism and Hainanese Women in the Early People's Republic of China

Jeremy A. Murray and Alexander J. Serrano

Introduction, Background, and Sources

The passage of the New Marriage Law on May 1, 1950, less than a year after the founding of the People's Republic of China (PRC), reflected the high priority of women's rights under the new government. It outlawed concubinage, arranged marriage, bride selling, and other vestiges of patriarchal cultural and social practices. The May 1950 passage of the law exactly coincided with the final day in the successful Communist campaign for the southern island of Hainan, a Nationalist holdout that was defeated by a combined force of Hainan's Communist guerrillas and mainland Communist forces who crossed the narrow Qiongzhou Strait. Due to Nationalist (1927–1950) and Japanese (1939–1945) blockades of Hainan Communist forces, the mainlanders had only been in sporadic contact with the island's guerrilla forces, and when they came ashore they were immediately struck by the high participation of women in Hainan's guerrilla forces.

The women fighters of Hainan might reasonably have been featured nationally and globally as a model of China's revolutionary new society. But instead, newly arrived mainland administrators considered the female cadres and soldiers of Hainan particularly obstructive to early governance of the island. Furthermore, when Hainan's women fighters finally were granted the national spotlight, in the various dramatic productions of *The Red Detachment of Women*, it would be in a distorted narrative that introduced fictional, mainland, male characters to discipline and lead the women.

In the early 1950s, as the PRC consolidated its new regime, political work under the broad umbrella of "anti-localism" (*fan difang zhuyi*) targeted local leaders and policies that favored – or were alleged to favor – local interests at the expense of national priorities. These priorities included foremost land reform (*tugai*) and military training/preparedness (*lianbing*). Hainan was among the last large areas to be taken over in the

153

spring of 1950, and it was expected to implement these policies on an accelerated schedule. The island itself lies off the southern coast of the Guangdong Province, with an area of about 13,650 square miles (35,354 square kilometers), only about 300 square miles smaller than its neighbor to the east, Taiwan. Due to its remote location and Nationalist and Japanese blockades, the local Communist leadership of Hainan had spent long periods of their twenty-three-year revolution out of contact with Party leadership on the mainland, sometimes opposing major central directives.[1]

Most notable and recent among the Hainan Communist leadership's divergence from mainland Party Central directives had been the local leaders' decision not to abandon the island and withdraw their fighting forces in 1946. Two mainland orders were issued in close succession: one to "retreat north" (*beiche*) to Shandong Province, and the other to "retreat south" (*nanche*) to Indochina/Vietnam. The Hainan leadership replied that such retreats were tactically impossible without massive loss of life since they did not trust the Nationalist forces under the militarist Chen Jitang (1890–1954) to grant them safe passage from their guerrilla bases. In their replies, the Hainan Communist leadership under Feng Baiju (1903–1973) added that the orders were also not practical because the Hainan Column's many gains would be handed back to the Nationalists, Communist supporters would be in danger, and the value of having local forces in the anticipated campaign to take the island would be lost.[2] This last point would be prescient since other smaller islands (Dengbu and Jinmen) would be fiercely held by the Nationalists, with the notable difference that they did not have Communist guerrilla forces operating there. The Hainan Communist leadership which had determined not to follow this 1946 order was still in power at the time of the final Communist takeover in the spring of 1950.[3]

Hainan island was part of Guangdong Province in 1950 and had been directly administered by the mainland for much of its history. Incorporated into the mainland Chinese Han dynasty in the second century BCE, the island consistently presented challenges to governors and magistrates, based on its remoteness and insularity, the resistance of

---

[1] Xing Yikong, Peng Chunglin, and Qian Yue, *Feng Baiju jiangjun zhuan* (Biography of General Feng Baiju) (Beijing: Zhonggong dangshi chubanshe, 1998), 325–344.

[2] Zhonggong Hainan shengwei dangshi yanjiu shi (Office of the Chinese Communist Party Hainan Provincial Committee Party History Research Office), ed., *Zhongguo gongchandang Hainan lishi* (Chinese Communist Party Hainan History) (Beijing: Zhonggong dangshi chubanshe, 2007), 432–439.

[3] Qiongya wuzhuang douzheng shi ban'gongshi (Office of the History of Hainan's Armed Struggle), ed., *Qiongya zongdui shi* (History of the Hainan Column) (Guangzhou: Guangdong renmin chubanshe, 1986), 209–217.

its indigenous Li population, its deep ties to neighboring states in Southeast Asia, and administrative concerns about separatism.[4] Suppression campaigns against the Li were a regular occurrence in Hainan's relationship with mainland regimes. As the island's coasts were settled by Han Chinese from the mainland, the Li were forced into Hainan's mountainous interior.[5]

The island's negligence in the mainland political worldview is captured in Sun Yat-sen's (1866–1925) willingness at one point to mortgage the island to the Japanese empire to help fund his revolution to unite the mainland.[6] Hainan was then governed by a succession of militarists who professed loyalty to Sun's successor, Generalissimo Chiang Kai-shek (1887–1975), but who in fact had a rocky relationship with Chiang. The full-scale Japanese invasion of China that began in July of 1937 pushed Chiang's government far to the west to the wartime capital of Chongqing (Chung-king). From early 1939 until the end of World War II in 1945, Hainan was occupied and governed by the Japanese Navy, and in 1945 Nationalist rule under Chen Jitang resumed.[7]

The Japanese authorities had shown special interest in deepening ties with the indigenous Li in an effort to divide the Hainanese population against itself, and also because Hainan's iron deposits were inside Li territory.[8] But while the Japanese were successful in extracting iron from Hainan using Li enslaved labor, the more significant Li alliance that developed in this period was with the Communist revolutionaries who fought both the scattered Nationalist forces and the Japanese. The Hainanese Communist movement survived from 1926 to 1950 in some form, sometimes numbering only a few dozen fighters, and in other periods having thousands of regular soldiers and holding large base areas. The local character of the revolution involved alliances with the Li, strong connections to Indochina/Vietnam and other Southeast Asian states, and a pragmatic guerrilla focus on survival.[9]

---

[4] Edward H. Schafer, *Shore of Pearls: Hainan Island in Early Times* (Berkeley: University of California Press, 1970).
[5] Anne Csete, "Ethnicity, Conflict, and the State in the Early to Mid-Qing: The Hainan Highlands, 1644–1800," in P. K. Crossley, H. F. Siu, and D. Sutton, eds., *Empire at the Margins: Culture, Ethnicity, and Frontier in Early Modern China* (Berkeley: University of California Press, 2006), 229–252.
[6] Jeremy A. Murray, *China's Lonely Revolution: The Local Communist Movement of Hainan Island, 1926–1956* (Albany: State University of New York Press, 2017), 52–53.
[7] Richard T. Phillips, "The Japanese Occupation of Hainan," *Modern Asian Studies* 14, no. 1 (1980): 93–109.
[8] Kunio Odaka, *Economic Organization of the Li Tribes of Hainan Island* (New Haven: Yale, Southeast Asia Studies, 1950; originally published in Japanese in 1942).
[9] Murray, *China's Lonely Revolution*.

In the early PRC, Hainan was shaken by the anti-localism campaigns, especially by the impact on Hainanese women soldiers. The anti-localism campaigns came to target not only perceived favoritism and nepotism among local leadership, but also those aspects of local revolutionary movements that distinguished them from the emergent national norms and narratives of the revolution. In Hainan, this included the prominent role of women fighters. Local narratives of revolution, local heroes, local characteristics, and local flavor were subject to scrutiny insofar as they might compete with the Mao-centered teleology of victory, with its particular landmarks, flashpoints, and triumphs.

The popular essayist Xin Lijian recently pondered why Mao Zedong (1893–1976), in his view, "hated localism" even more than he hated his nemesis Chiang Kai-shek and the Nationalists. His provocative answer was that, even from the early 1930s, Mao was "always an outsider cadre" (*conglai dou shi wailai ganbu*), and this led him to be suspicious and jealous of the local connections of comrades who worked within their home regions.[10] Historian Gregor Benton explores how a crucial arm of the Chinese Communist fighting force was essentially sacrificed on the altar of public opinion in January of 1941. In that incident, Mao's dithering and possibly willful negligence allowed the Communist New Fourth Army to be engulfed and massacred by Nationalist forces.[11] Benton's work, along with others', like Stephen Averill's, emphasizes the localized struggles that built on social and political networks, particular to each region. In granular detail, they locate the success of the diverse communist movements in their flexibility, creativity, and pragmatism, and indeed the local character of their surrounding region.[12]

In the early PRC and through the 1960s, anti-localism campaigns hemmed in not only localist policies, but also local revolutionary identity, and revolutionary stories. The high proportion of women fighters in the Hainan Communist revolution comprised one of its important distinguishing local features. As such, both the female leadership and their revolutionary legacy were overlooked and later actively suppressed in

---

[10] Xin Lijian, "Mao Zedong weishenme tonghen difang zhuyi?" (Why Did Mao Hate Localism?), reproduced in *Difang wenge shi jiaoliu wang* (Cultural Revolution Local History Exchange Network), online database, April 1, 2018, at http://difangwenge.org /simple/?t16724.html.

[11] Gregor Benton, *New Fourth Army: Communist Resistance along the Yangtze and the Huai, 1938–1942* (Berkeley: University of California Press, 1999). This work was a sequel to Benton's earlier *Mountain Fires: The Red Army's Three-Year War in South China, 1934–1938* (Berkeley: University of California Press, 1992).

[12] Stephen C. Averill (with Joseph W. Esherick and Elizabeth J. Perry), *Revolution in the Highlands: China's Jinggangshan Base Area* (Lanham, MD: Rowman and Littlefield, 2006).

favor of a narrative that featured male mainlanders liberating backward Hainan.[13]

As in nearly all historical contexts, war in this era was culturally inscribed as a masculine sphere, and women, when considered in the context of war, were seen as the wards and victims of violence. In *Women Warriors and Wartime Spies of China*, Louise Edwards provides examples of women whose lives do not fit into these conventions, like the Communist fighters of Hainan. Edwards finds – and this chapter also aims to emphasize – that in such cases of lives lived outside such norms and dominant narratives, reality can be distorted to fit into a more familiar or traditional story.[14]

In his study of women within Communist forces during the War of Resistance to Japan (World War II), David Goodman examines the context of three counties in southeastern Shanxi Province, in northern China. Goodman's analysis provides a basis and an impetus for this work, and it includes aspects that are echoed here, and some that confirm his suggestion of profound variation in terms of the causes and results of women's participation in the revolution across the vast Chinese map and localized contexts. While he notes the importance of various factors such as the class backgrounds of women taking part in the revolution, Goodman emphasizes the primary role of specific local conditions in shaping women's participation in Chinese Communist revolutionary movements. Moving beyond the specific context of Yan'an, the relatively secure and unique power center of the Communist revolution in this period, Goodman finds that when Communist leaders began their work beyond Yan'an and beyond China's cities, the "inevitable result was that the development of organization and policies was highly localized, and influenced greatly by local conditions."[15] This attention to specific contexts reflects a longer trend that has followed increasing access to Chinese archives beginning in the 1980s.

---

[13] "Zhonggong Hainan quwei guanyu zai tugai yundong zhong zhuyi jiaqiang funü gongzuo de jueding" (Resolution of the Chinese Communist Party Hainan District Committee on Paying Attention to Strengthening Women's Work in the Land Reform Movement), March 8, 1951, reprinted in Hainansheng shizhi gongzuo ban'gongshi, Hainansheng dang'anju (History Work Office of Hainan Province, Hainan Provincial Archives), ed., *Hainan tudi gaige yundong ziliao xuanbian (1951–1953)* (Selected Materials from the Hainan Land Reform Movement (1951–1953)) (Haikou: Hainansheng Wenhua Guangdian chubanshe, 2002), 16–18.

[14] Louise Edwards, *Women Warriors and Wartime Spies of China* (Cambridge: Cambridge University Press, 2016), 201–203.

[15] David S.G. Goodman, "Revolutionary Women and Women in the Revolution: The Chinese Communist Party and Women in the War of Resistance to Japan, 1937–1945," *China Quarterly*, no. 164 (December 2000): 918.

In her survey of academic writing on women in Chinese history and social sciences between 1970 and 2004, Gail Hershatter wrote,

One could say that the initial question animating much early feminist scholarship on twentieth-century China – was the revolution good or bad for women? – no longer compels attention. It has been replaced by inquiries that are more localized (where?), more segmented (which women?), and more attentive to the multiple contradictory levels of state activity and the unintended but often powerful consequences of state policies.[16]

Considering the female military and political personnel on Hainan before and after the Communist takeover, the question whether the Communist revolution was "good or bad" is complicated by the sources. The role of women in Hainan's Communist revolution was essential, with numbers ranging between 15 and 30 percent of military personnel throughout the duration of the revolutionary period (1927–1950).[17] The drama *The Red Detachment of Women* has been so completely adopted as an iconic national Chinese drama that it eclipses the Hainan historical narrative of women fighters, not to mention the entire island. This pattern conforms to the one illuminated by Louise Edwards, as noted above. In the historical record beyond the brief 1930–1931 existence of the actual military unit made famous in a bowdlerized drama, the women fighting in the Hainan Communist forces are surprisingly scarce in histories and contemporary documents.[18]

This study relies on a collection of sources that include official Chinese Communist Party (CCP) directives; Hainan provincial gazetteers or government reference volumes on a number of topics published after 1949; biographies of prominent Hainan figures of the revolution; speeches, songs, and other communications from the revolutionary period; scholarly writings in Chinese and English; and a series of collected histories known as *Qiongdao Xinghuo* (Hainan Island Spark), which is similar in format and mission to the massive national oral-history project known as *Wenshi Ziliao* (Literary and Historical Materials). While the collection of materials for *Wenshi Ziliao* volumes began in 1959, the first volume in the Hainanese collection, *Qiongdao Xinghuo*, was published in

---

[16] Gail Hershatter, "State of the Field: Women in China's Long Twentieth Century," *Journal of Asian Studies* 63, no. 4 (November 2004): 993–994.

[17] Qiongya wuzhuang douzheng shi ban'gongshi (1986), 309; Ye Shuming, "1952 nian, Hainan fan difang zhuyi" (Hainan Anti-Localism, 1952), in *Difang wenge shi jiaoliu wang* (Cultural Revolution Local History Exchange Network), online database, September 9, 2010, at http://difangwenge.org/read.php?tid=5028&page=e.

[18] Qiongdao xinghuo bianjibu (Hainan Spark Editorial Department), ed., *Qiongdao Xinghuo (5), Qiongya funü geming douzheng zhuanji* (Hainan Spark (5), Hainan Women's Revolutionary Struggle Volume) (Guangzhou: Qiongdao xinghuo bianjibu chuban, 1981), 1–4.

1980. The contents of these volumes are partly influenced by the post-Mao climate of relative political openness, and also by the informal campaign for the island's long-desired provincial status, which would gain momentum in the 1980s and culminate with provincial status for Hainan, separate from Guangdong Province, in 1988. The Hainan collection was published as *neibu faxing* or "for internal distribution," a broad term that encompasses a spectrum of different classification levels.[19]

The Hainan provincial gazetteers (*shengzhi*) were produced to catalog the revolution and the rule of the PRC, and they reiterate and emphasize a Marxist feminist line, through which the women of Hainan were liberated from the "feudal" past and their individual liberal freedoms are subsumed within the larger revolutionary goals and victories. In certain ways, and for some women, this would later culminate in the GLF of the late 1950s, in which women were meant to be liberated from household work through the establishment of collective dining halls and the implementation of child care in newly organized communes. Political scientist Kimberley Ens Manning found an uneven experience of this liberation for women depending on whether they were close to power structures or remote from them.[20] Manning considers the village power structures during the GLF, and how proximity to village elites shaped women's experience of this period.[21]

While there are scant and only oblique mentions of difficulties for Hainanese women in the early PRC noted in the official provincial gazetteers, a more complex picture emerges from the other sources noted above. In a 2010 essay, the prolific historian of Guangdong and southern China Ye Shuming pointed to the active ways in which the struggles of women soldiers demobilized on Hainan were muted in the public record and they were told to return home, marry, and start families.[22]

---

[19] Eugene W. Wu, "Library Resources for Contemporary China Studies," in D. L. Shambaugh, ed., *American Studies of Contemporary China* (London: Routledge, 1994), 272; This *Qiongdao Xinghuo* series was made fully available to me as an admitted foreign scholar in library and archival settings on Hainan in 2008.

[20] Kimberley Ens Manning, "Marxist Maternalism, Memory, and the Mobilization of Women in the Great Leap Forward," *China Review* 5, no. 1 (Spring 2005): 83–110. "Marxist maternalism," Manning notes, was interpreted in China in such a way that the CCP leadership deemed fit for current conditions, including the explicit endorsement of traditional marriage and motherhood roles for women, which were at odds with earlier Marxist writers like Friederich Engels, who anticipated the dissolution of the traditional family.

[21] Neil J. Diamant, *Revolutionizing the Family: Politics, Love, and Divorce in Urban and Rural China* (Berkeley: University of California Press, 2000).

[22] Ye, "1952 nian, Hainan fan difang zhuyi."

Women in Hainan's Revolution

There are various explanations for the relatively large ratio of women serving in the Hainan Communist movement. Precise numbers of women in the military are difficult to track during the revolutionary period, but the most common figures cited by authoritative sources range between 15 and 30 percent of the Hainan Communist military. In explaining this phenomenon, historians note the high rate of men leaving the island for long periods, either as fishermen, as conscripted soldiers on the Chinese mainland, or to find work in neighboring Southeast Asia.[23]

Feng Baiju, the most prominent revolutionary leader in this period, noted the independence of the women who joined the Communist revolution and alluded to their miserable treatment by their husbands. Feng remembered in 1968,

There were women who were better soldiers than the men. If a husband tried to stop his wife from joining the movement, we killed him. Some women would take matters into their own hands, and if a husband resisted them joining the movement, they might take a knife and kill him in his sleep.[24]

This evocative image of the vengeance of the downtrodden woman was not unique to Hainan, but the scale of women leaving their parents or husbands to join the revolution in Hainan was indeed remarkable. Hainanese men being away from home for extended periods, for work on the Southeast Asian mainland or for fishing work, certainly was a crucial factor as well. Momentum also became a factor according to contemporary accounts that cite women having heard, through Communist propaganda and word of mouth, about women fighting alongside men in the revolution.[25]

Li Xiaolin, expert in the history and recent situation of women serving in the Chinese military, notes that from 1949 to 1993, female participation in the People's Liberation Army (PLA) ranged between only 4.5 and 8 percent.[26] Li also notes that a high proportion of these women were from elite backgrounds, and served as noncombat officers as opposed to enlisted women.[27] This national trend is also at odds with the Hainan

---

[23] *Qiongdao Xinghuo (5)*, 1–4.

[24] Feng Baijiu, "Guanyu wo canjia geming guocheng de lishi qingkuang" (The History of My Participation in the Revolutionary Process), in *Feng Baiju yanjiu shiliao* (Feng Baiju Research Materials) (Guangzhou: Guangdong renmin chubanshe, 1988), 421.

[25] Ibid.; *Qiongdao Xinghuo (5)* (1981), 1–4.

[26] Li Xiaolin, "Chinese Women Soldiers: A History of 5000 Years," *Social Education* 58, no. 2 (1994): 67–71.

[27] Li Xiaolin, "Chinese Women in the People's Liberation Army: Professionals or Quasi-professionals," *Armed Forces and Society* 20, no. 1 (Fall 1993): 74.

context, where women who participated in the Communist movement were not disproportionately from elite backgrounds.

From the first days of the Civil War, women had already begun to take part in the armed struggle of the Hainan revolutionary movement. The visibility of women leaders increased recruitment of women fighters. One such leader in the early Hainan Communist movement was Chen Yuchan (1899–1927), who was killed in the aftermath of the Nationalist massacres and executions that launched the Civil War in April of 1927. Chen was a talented student who joined the CCP while studying in Guangzhou in 1924, returned to Hainan in 1927, and was captured and killed after forming and leading several women's organizations.[28] Another prominent woman in the early Hainan Communist movement was Liu Qiuju (1899–1949), who played an important military leadership role until her death on the eve of the Communist takeover. Unlike Chen, Liu was not a student, and when her husband died of illness soon after their marriage, she joined a Communist peasant association and quickly became its leader. These two examples illustrate an important shift in the Communist revolution on Hainan. While Chen brought radical ideas and Party organization from outside to the villages of northern Hainan, Liu was trained in the militias and Party schools established in her village, where she learned to read and write. Liu represented the shift toward a Hainan revolution that was not brought to the island by central Party directives but grew out of the island itself.[29]

Chen and Liu are just two among many women who were leaders in the early Communist revolution on Hainan. There is also, of course, the real historical unit that inspired the Cultural Revolution drama *The Red Detachment of Women*, most famously a modern ballet, but also produced as a nonmusical film and a Beijing opera. Within the scope of the actual Hainan revolution, *Red Detachment* represented a temporary women's unit of 103 soldiers, commanded by women. The unit only lasted about a year before being disbanded, and its surviving members were then integrated into other fighting units. These integrated fighting units became the norm on Hainan for the remainder of the revolutionary period.[30] The surviving members of the real-life "Red Detachment"

---

[28] Hainansheng difangzhi ban'gongshi (Hainan Provincial Gazetteer Office), ed., *Hainan shengzhi: Haiyang zhi/Geming genjudi zhi* (Oceans Volume/Revolutionary Base Area Volume) (Haikou: Nanhai chuban gongsi, 2006), 295.

[29] Ou Yingqin and Zhu Ruchong, "Hainan funü de guanghui bangyang – Liu Qiuju" (A Glorious Example of a Hainan Woman – Liu Qiuju), in *Qiongdao Xinghuo (5)*, 9–10.

[30] Zhou Shike et al., "Zhongguo gongnong hongjun Qiongya duli ershi nüzi jun tewulian" (Chinese Workers and Peasants Red Army Hainan Independent Second Division Women's Special Service Company), in *Qiongdao Xinghuo (5)*, 1–9.

being reintegrated into military units of both sexes was a move away from traditional "women's work" and toward a more thoroughgoing equality. The brief existence of the "Red Detachment" saw it tasked not only with fighting duties, but also with noncombat roles like education, propaganda, and espionage. Once the unit was disbanded, its surviving members joined integrated units and continued in combat roles.[31]

In a collection of historical documents and other writings on the Hainan revolutionary movement, political scientist Chen Chuanxiong summarized the key distinguishing features (*tese*) of Hainan's Communist revolution:

1 early attention and consistent adherence to strategic thinking in armed struggle;
2 being faced with a strong enemy, narrow room for maneuver, a lack of outside aid, and remoteness from the central geographical environment;
3 operational policy of independence and flexibility;
4 the mobilization of women for warfare, obtaining support from overseas Chinese, uniting with ethnic minorities to carry out a broad national people's war.[32]

Chen's list of Hainan's distinguishing features is a mixture of prescience and pragmatism. The first item implies anticipation of Maoist guerrilla struggle and rural militarization. In explaining the second and third items, Chen indicates why decisions by the Hainan Communist leadership were correct even though they sometimes seemed to flout orders from the central Party command on the mainland. The final crucial item is the most explicit in pointing to a context that was culturally and socially distinct from mainland China.

Chen cites this diverse revolutionary coalition as part of a "broad national people's war" (*guangfan de quanminzuxing de renmin zhanzheng*), or an all-inclusive struggle.[33] While they were an important part of Hainan's revolution, overseas Chinese and ethnic minorities came under scrutiny and suspicion in the early PRC. The prominent role of women, however, should not have presented a political problem in the early years of Communist rule, and indeed was a potential propaganda coup for world revolution and sexual equality.

The Hainan provincial gazetteer (*shengzhi*) published in 2006, which covers the revolutionary base areas (*geming genjudi*), includes the lyrics for

---

[31] Zhonggong Hainan shengwei dangshi yanjiu shi, *Zhongguo gongchandang Hainan lishi*, 167–169.
[32] Chen Chuanxiong, *Qiongya geming yanjiu wenji* (Hainan Revolution Research Collected Works) (Urumqi: Xinjiang renmin chubanshe, 2003), 139–148.
[33] Ibid., 147.

three songs that were popular throughout the revolution.[34] The three songs reflect the increasing centrality of women within the Hainan revolutionary movement, from being completely ignored, to being acknowledged in a supporting role, to taking on a crucial, and in some ways defining, position within the Hainan Communist movement.

The first song is short ("Build the Soviet Base Area" ("Jianli suweiai")), and gives no mention of women, but it also gives no specific mention of Hainan's revolution being distinct from the Chinese or the world revolution. This song was also sung in other regions of China:

> Come! Come! Come!
> Worker and peasant soldiers, arise,
> Fight the Nationalist reactionaries,
> Build the soviet base areas,
> Let us all swiftly arise!

In the second song ("Support the Red Army, Fight the Jackals and Wolves" ("Zhiyuan Hongjun da chailang"), the locale of Hainan could be guessed at (mountain bases, rice paddies), but is not specific, and the role of women is included, but in a way that is supportive of an implied male fighting force:

> Deep in the mountains, singing loudly,
> Women in the soviet area are busy cutting wood.
> You cut the wood, come to me to burn the charcoal,
> Send it to the Red Army, to cast a knife, a gun.
> Shoulder your burden, I'll carry my basket,
> As we talk and laugh.
>
> In the fields, singing loudly,
> Rice fields turn as golden waves,
> You came to me threshing with your sickle,
> To give the Red Army their fill of rations,
> Shoulder your burden, I'll shoulder my burden,
> Support the Red Army, fight the jackals and wolves.

In the third of the three songs, the Hainan setting is clear, and the role of women is in the title and at the heart of the song. "Today's Women Are True Elf-Spirits" ("Dangjin nüzi zhen jingling") is a longer and a more detailed song, with some similar imagery but more clearly touting Hainan and the women fighting in the revolution there:

> The mountains are treeless, bald,
> The riverbeds are cracked,

---

[34] All three of the song lyrics are reprinted in Hainansheng difangzhi ban'gongshi, *Hainan shengzhi: Haiyang zhi/Geming genjudi zhi*, 198–199.

The cage of a thousand years will be smashed,
The Communist Party is the leader.
Women revolutionaries, with a martial spirit,
Holding sword and gun, are busy training;
The Workers' and Peasants' Red Army has female generals,
Today's women are true elf-spirits [*jingling*].

Marx initiated the revolution,
And guides the course to be respected;
On Hainan, the red flag waves high,
The working women fight on expeditions.

Vines wrap around trees, and trees support vines,
Hearts forged with the Party's revolution;
Defending Red Hainan Island,
Charge, capture, become the vanguard.

By the spring of 1950, when the Communist takeover of Hainan was complete, women had become an essential part of the revolution. Songs like "Today's Women" enshrined this sentiment and gave voice to the fighting spirit of Hainan. This explicit celebration of high female military participation made it both statistically and also culturally relevant. It had become a point of pride for Hainan.[35]

While gender equality was the stated policy in the early PRC, and the Marriage Law was the first prominent piece of legislation, in practice there were ongoing questions as to the Party leadership's commitment to true equality. Just eight years earlier in 1942, Ding Ling (1904–1986), one of the leading voices of women in the Chinese Communist revolution, had embarrassed some leaders of the Party, including Mao Zedong, for their perpetuation of misogyny in their personal behavior. Ding had risked all with her March 8, 1942 essay, in which she sharply rebuked the leadership, and by implication Mao himself, who had recently cast off his third wife to take a younger actress as his new bride in Yan'an.[36] Ding was accused of "narrow feminism," and she was pressured to retract her statements. She was again targeted in the mid-1950s for "bourgeois idealism" and the baffling charge of conspiracy to form an anti-Party group.[37] The case of Ding reflects the shifting and sometimes arbitrary revolutionary itinerary of the CCP in terms of gender relations.

---

[35] Duo Zhong, "Jiaofei nü yingxiong Su Laigui" (The Woman Bandit Hero Su Laigui), in *Qiongdao Xinghuo (5)*, 161.

[36] Ding Ling, "Thoughts on 8 March (Women's Day)," reprinted at https://libcom.org/library/thoughts-8-march-women%E2%80%99s-day.

[37] Andrew G. Walder, *China under Mao: A Revolution Derailed* (Cambridge, MA: Harvard University Press, 2015), 28, 134.

The Wilds of Revolution

A 2010 volume gathered accounts of the "southbound cadres" (*nanxia ganbu*) who made their way from northern to southern China from 1948 through the early years of the PRC. Some of the accounts betray a missionary's ecstasy:

Thousands of cadres and fighters formed a column, starting in Shandong and Shanxi. From the blood-red, and snow-white, and black earth, they bid farewell to their wives and children, and set forth across the mountains, across the Yellow River and the Yangzi. Looking back, we can say this: "Going south" laid the foundation for the regime of New China; "going south" is a part of the solidification of history … Most of them did not leave behind a penny for their descendants, but they left behind a valuable spirit of dedication, they left a monument to history, and they will live forever![38]

The sacrifice of the southbound cadres and their mission "solidified history" in the early PRC. The unnamed and untamed southern regions in this heroic framing are the *terra nullius* at least in revolutionary terms. The cultural parallels between industrious northerners and lazy Hainanese persists to this day in popular culture, and it informed the biases of the southbound cadres. The Communist conquest of China, concluding in Hainan, in some ways followed a pattern of history. Chinese dynasties were usually conquered from north to south, with the imposition of a new heavenly mandate. The vastness of the Chinese territory and its enormous cultural and linguistic diversity meant that these conquests from north to south sometimes felt like the imposition of a foreign hegemony on southerners like the Hainanese. In 1950, the new ruling ideology and mandate were initially welcomed by a popular local revolutionary movement, and the Communist leadership on Hainan celebrated its arrival and shared in the victory.[39]

But in spite of some leadership continuity in the early governance of the island, almost immediately there were certain ways in which this new mainland regime reinforced longer trends in the ways that mainlanders had related to the people of Hainan. The island had long been considered an economic liability at best by previous Chinese regimes. At worst, it was a den of piracy and banditry, and a death sentence for officials banished there for some transgression that might include the Confucian moral duty of loyal remonstrance, as in the case of luminaries like Su Shi (Su Dongpo, 1037–1101). Officials sent to the island to govern it were

---

[38] Ye Ding, ed., *Nanxia! Nanxia! Xin Zhongguo de jijiehao* (Go South! Go South! The Rallying Cry of New China) (Wuhan: Wuhan chubanshe, 2010), p. i.
[39] Zhonggong Hainan shengwei dangshi yanjiu shi, *Zhongguo gongchandang Hainan lishi*, 565–571.

faced with seemingly constant uprisings of the ethnic Li people of the island's mountainous interior, and piracy that transcended borders and frontiers.[40] The southbound cadres arriving from the mainland surely were aware of stereotypes about the island's exotic backwardness.

By the summer of 1952, Feng Baiju was still serving in the island's leadership and had heard complaints from many of his former guerrilla, militia, and regular-army comrades about difficulties they were having returning to civilian life. Many had been relieved of duties and overlooked for promotions by senior mainland officers, some under the cloud of accusations of insufficient revolutionary zeal or patriotism.[41] These reports about treatment under the new regime would embroil Feng in a national campaign over the next five years to eradicate perceived local interests and individuals that threatened Beijing's revolutionary goals. Feng had been the unquestioned political and military leader of the Communist movement on Hainan throughout most of its twenty-three-year fight for existence (1927–1950), and then had been appointed director of the Hainan Administration Office by the Guangdong Provincial Administration. As his revolutionary comrades came to ask him for help or to complain about mistreatment, it was clear that, in their eyes, Feng was still the leading authority on Hainan. But his position was weakened that summer and he would continue to suffer setbacks over the coming years due to the anti-localism campaign.

The crackdown on "localist" leaders would reverberate for decades, since top national leaders were deeply involved in the process, including a young and energetic Zhao Ziyang. Zhao had helped to target leaders perceived as being too soft in the implementation of national land reform policies. He would go on to become premier, and Ye Jianying and Xi Zhongxun were just two more of the prominent national figures involved both in the anti-localism campaign and in the historical debate exonerating its targets in later years.[42] "Localist" leaders were accused of putting local or regional interests over national priorities, including Feng, Gao Gang, Rao Shushi, Gu Dacun, Fang Fang, and others.

Feng was especially close to the revolutionaries and resistance fighters of Hainan. The Communist movement on the island had experienced many changes, many devastating defeats, and shifts in alliances and tactics. While the territory it controlled varied widely throughout this period, the movement's very survival was its greatest achievement, and its celebratory slogan

---

[40] Schafer, *Shore of Pearls*.

[41] Wu Zhi and He Lang, *Feng Baiju zhuan* (Biography of Feng Baiju) (Beijing: Dangdai chubanshe, 1996), 762–765.

[42] Chan Sui-Jeung, *East River Column: Hong Kong Guerrillas in the Second World War and After* (Hong Kong: Hong Kong University Press, 2009), 157–158.

in 1950 was "For twenty-three years, the red flag never fell" (*ershisan nian hongqi bu dao*). The 1950s saw the demobilization of revolutionary fighters and military personnel, with many experiencing difficulties adjusting to life after the war. In the summer of 1952, Feng heard complaints from comrades whom he knew well and had known through decades of struggle; however, the cultural tensions with the southbound cadres on Hainan further compounded the transition process.

In many accounts of this process, including biographies of Feng Baiju, women were being told by southbound cadres to return to a homely existence of marriage and child-rearing. But after a twenty-three-year struggle, some of these women knew nothing other than a life of military conflict, and they had no homes to return to (*wujia kegui*), and the orders of these mainland cadres were impossible for them to obey. According to political scientist Ezra Vogel's account of the southbound cadres in his early study of communism in Guangzhou (Canton),

the rank and file of the Southbound Work Team consisted mostly of young activist intellectuals recruited from the northern universities and briefly trained in earlier liberated areas for their work as cadres as the south was taken over. Despite their heterogeneity, the Southbound Work Team members had at least two things in common: they came from a higher-class intellectual background, and they came from the north and were all fluent in Mandarin.[43]

In some documents from the early PRC, it seems that the Hainanese women with long revolutionary experience were considered a liability to the new state-building efforts. One directive from March 8, 1951, provides guidance and background for southbound cadres in their dealings with revolutionary women veteran cadres on Hainan. Published on International Women's Day, the directive provides instruction on how to deal with the women of Hainan, how to implement the new Marriage Law, and how to help to end abuse and inequality. But in the final portion of the directive, the southbound cadres are instructed to take special care in dealing with the Hainanese women cadres:

Pay attention to cultivating and improving the ability and theoretical level of women cadres. Hainan women cadres generally have struggled for a long time. They are determined and passionate about the revolution, but their cultural level and theoretical level are low. Therefore, in the early stages of liberation of the whole island, as they entered the cities, some women cadres were pessimistic and negative, thinking that they had poor ability, low culture, and no future, while others indulged in hedonistic thoughts, demanding demobilization, being with

---

[43] Ezra F. Vogel, *Canton under Communism: Programs and Politics in a Provincial Capital, 1949–1968* (New York: Harper and Row, 1971; first published 1969), 52.

their loved ones, and disobeying the organization's allocation and work needs. This was a very serious and widespread occurrence.[44]

Anti-localism did not begin and did not end with the "anti-localism campaigns" of the PRC. Policies like the "rule of avoidance" had long existed in imperial China, by which imperially appointed magistrates, governors, and other officials were not permitted to serve in their home county or home province, or in the county or province neighboring their home region. In Confucian philosophy, and even in pre-Confucian cultural practices, connection to one's family, ancestral home, and home region are of paramount importance. While this is certainly not unique in Chinese culture, these family and regional ties are especially strong and reified in long-standing rituals and texts. In her study of Chinese migrations, Diana Lary wrote, "Confucian maxims on the joys of home were ingrained in official teachings and pronouncements; the ancestral cult, which insisted that people stay close to their families and the graves of their ancestors, was underlined. '*Fumu zai, bu* yuan-you' [As long as the father and mother are alive, do not go far away]."[45] Magistrates quickly learned that the strength of these ties could also be turned against central authority, whether that authority was a greenhorn official from another province or the imperial army. The force of local identity on Hainan, and the mythologies that grew around it, could be a potential threat to establishing mainland orthodoxy, as in the case of the Communist conquest.

A mainland narrative of the revolutionary victory on Hainan quickly emerged in which the role of local revolutionaries was diminished and the inexorable force and will of the mainland armies was amplified as a kind of historical inevitability coming across the water: a "people's flotilla."[46] In many historical accounts of Hainan's revolution, the mainland forces are referred to as the "great army" (*dajun*), and the Hainan Column (*Qiongya zongdui*) receives only a passing acknowledgment. This negligence is misleading. In battles as late as November of 1949, the Nationalist forces had held islands much more difficult to defend than Hainan. These

---

[44] "Zhonggong Hainan quwei guanyu zai tugai yundong zhong zhuyi jiaqiang funüü gong-zuo de jueding," in *Zhongguo gongchandang Hainan lishi* (Chinese Communist Party Hainan History) (Beijing: Zhonggong dangshi chubanshe, 2007; first published 1951), 16–18.

[45] Diana Lary, *Chinese Migrations: The Movement of People, Goods, and Ideas over Four Millenia* (Lanham, MD: Rowman and Littlefield, 2012), 67.

[46] Liu Zhenhua, *Hainan jiefang* (Liberating Hainan) (Shenyang: Liaoning renmin chu-banshe, 1998), 81; Han X., "Hainandao saotao zhan" (The Hainan Island Mop-Up Campaign), from *Xinghuo liaoyuan* (A Single Spark Can Start a Prairie Fire), translated and reprinted in the appendix of R. R. Probst, "The Communist Conquest of Hainan" (PhD diss., George Washington University, 1982), 228.

battles included Jinmen (Kinmen or Quemoy) and Dengbu, where the Nationalist forces inflicted heavy casualties and have even prevented the Communist takeover of Jinmen through the time of this writing. But one key difference on these two islands was a lack of a substantial Communist force behind enemy lines that could co-ordinate with a landing force.[47]

Feng Baiju was a seasoned revolutionary and a dedicated Communist leader, and he understood the priorities of national strength and solidarity. His speeches in the early days of Communist rule on Hainan repeatedly noted that, "without the great army, Hainan could not have been liberated."[48] Feng's popularity endures on Hainan, and in 1950 it was at a new high-water mark. But this popularity and support became a liability in the early transition from revolution to rule. His role in fielding and forwarding complaints from demobilized soldiers and overlooked cadres in this period was perceived as "anti-Party" and "localist" and would earn him demotion and reassignment to mainland Zhejiang.

The Patriarchal Postwar Period

After considering the distinguishing features of the Hainan context, there is also the question of women in the military around China in this period, women in societies around the postwar world, and women in the military and/or in combat up to the present day. These frames of comparison provide some context to the place of women in the Hainan Communist revolution and in the years that followed. In spite of the rhetoric of sexual equality, political planning that included equal participation by women was not easily accomplished. As Vogel notes in his study of the early PRC from a southern perspective, "Aside from students, the women of China, most of whom were tied down with domestic chores, were obviously the largest untapped reservoir of potential labor power." Even in 1958, things still moved slowly in terms of mobilizing women:

In late spring in [Chengzhou] in [Henan] and [Chengdu] in [Sichuan], housewives had been organized into small workshops while a small number of them looked after the children, the sick, and the aged and did the cooking. For a moment it looked as if this vision of urban communes would be followed in all of China but suddenly, possibly because of the opposition of powerful party leaders who feared disruption of the urban economy, the program for mobilizing urban women stopped before it blossomed in [Guangzhou] and most of the nation."[49]

---

[47] Wu and He, *Feng Baiju zhuan*, 709–722.
[48] Feng Baiju, "Zai qinggong dahui shang de jianghua" (Speech at the Celebration) (June 9, 1950), reprinted in *Feng Baiju yanjiu shiliao*, 202–207.
[49] Vogel, *Canton under Communism*, 244.

In another study by Li Xiaolin, this one on the *longue durée* history of women soldiers in China, she writes about both the prominent role of women in the early PRC military and the contentious place of women veterans in society after demobilization. This seems to reflect the reality of many women on Hainan island in this period:

After the communist victory in 1949, the PLA became primarily a force for counterinsurgency, for postwar reconstruction of the societal infrastructure, and for the mobilization of the peasantry for land reform. Much of the military cadre was demobilized and assumed civilian administrative positions. In 1951, despite an engagement of Chinese combat troops in the Korean War, 150,000 women cadres (8 percent of the total cadre corps) were assigned to civilian positions. Chinese women soldiers did go to war during the Korean War as cultural workers, nurses, doctors, and telephone operators. These PLA women were ostracized as were most Chinese POWs when they returned home.[50]

Li further notes that, in the early PRC, the regime "minimized the role of women in the military" in the wake of the Korean War, and their national numbers declined from 14.5 percent to below 10 percent. Li notes that, by the 1990s, under 5 percent of China's military personnel were women, and scholars of the Chinese military still noted similar numbers as recently as 2016.[51] In terms of local cultural factors shaping women's participation in the military in Hainan, it is also worth noting the larger regional history.

The broader cultural context of Southeast Asia, and Hainan's place within this macroregion, have interested scholars in cultural, economic, and geostrategic terms, especially as the South China Sea has become a flashpoint in potential global conflict. Hainan fits into the region in terms of the especially high representation of women within fighting forces. For example, the Vietnamese Communist fighting forces also saw relatively high female participation.[52]

In a recent volume of essays, *Women Warriors in Southeast Asia*, the authors consider the long history of women who fought in conflicts throughout the region, including both maritime and mainland Southeast Asia, which places Hainan more or less in the geographical

---

[50] Li, "Chinese Women Soldiers," 67–71.

[51] Ibid. Also see Elsa Kania, "Holding Up Half the Sky? The Evolution of Women's Roles in the PLA (Part 1)," and Elsa Kania and Kenneth Allen, "Holding Up Half the Sky? The Evolution of Women's Roles in the PLA (Part 2)," both in *China Brief* (the Jamestown Foundation), 16, 15–16 (October 4 and October 26, 2016), at https://jamestown.org/p rogram/holding-half-sky-part-1-evolution-womens-roles-pla, https://jamestown.org/pro gram/holding-half-sky-part-2-evolution-womens-roles-pla.

[52] Karen Gottschang Turner and Phan Thanh Hao, *Even the Women Must Fight: Memories of War from North Vietnam* (New York: Wiley, 1998). See also Su Phung, "Women of the Vietnam War: Fighting for the Revolution" (unpublished master's thesis, History Department, California State University–Fullerton, 2013).

northern-central area of the region.[53] This interdisciplinary set of essays considers long-term anthropological contexts and modern revolutionary geopolitics to frame a space in which women warriors have been ignored and excluded in histories of conflict in spite of their prominent role. Violence toward women in wartime has long been deployed as a method of terrorizing a population. While not detracting from this subject, as Louise Edwards notes in *Women Warriors and Wartime Spies of China*, it is also important to expand our understanding of the role of women in wartime to include more than exclusive victimhood. Political scientist Elisabeth Prügl also urges careful consideration of the ways in which sexual violence and victimization of women have been framed as a special context of war:

Framing conflict-related sexual violence as strategic and thus different from such violence outside armed conflict problematically obscures that "peace" typically is built on a patriarchal bargain. The new visibility of sexual violence may therefore lead us to begin to question the distinction between war and peace and recognize the pervasive harm done to populations gendered "other" in the wars that constitute their everyday lives.[54]

Sociologist Myra Marx Ferree examined the ways in which the rapidly shifting political and social context of the fall of East Germany (the German Democratic Republic) affected the status and roles of women in various organizations. In her interviews of women who experienced this transition, she captured the striking idea that "the time of chaos was the best," and that the most tumultuous phase "was a period when anything was possible."[55] Ferree tracks several phases of this transition, and her interview subjects suggest that during the more chaotic period, there were more opportunities for feminist activism and organization.

Considering periods of flux and chaos as opportunities for gains, and the return of social and political stability potentially bringing a return of familiar, oppressive, patriarchal norms, can also describe the revolutionary and then post-revolutionary phases on Hainan. Sociologists and historians have also tracked the wartime and postwar popular imagery surrounding gender roles, not only in the military but throughout society. Media studies scholar Maria Cristina Santana captures this in her study of women's work roles in World War II, followed by the return of men to many of these roles in the

---

[53] Vina A. Lanzona and Frederik Rettig, eds., *Women Warriors in Southeast Asia* (Abingdon: Routledge, 2020).
[54] Elisabeth Prügl, "Sexual Violence: A New Weapon of War," *Globe: The Graduate Institute Review* 23 (Spring 2019), at https://graduateinstitute.ch/communications/news/sexual-violence-new-weapon-war.
[55] Myra Marx Ferree, "'The Time of Chaos Was the Best': Feminist Mobilization and Demobilization in East Germany," *Gender and Society* 8, no. 4 (December 1994), 606.

postwar era. The gains made by women who were newly normalized in many spheres of the workplace would pave the way for continued gains, but the immediate postwar period saw a deliberate reversion to more traditional roles reinforced in policy and expressed in cultural conservatism.[56]

In China, while women's experiences varied greatly across different underground communist movements, the 1950s saw an effort to propagate a kind of "Marxist maternalism," as Manning notes. This meant that the kind of radical sexual equality experienced by some local groups during the revolution and the war with Japan, such as the fighters of Hainan, would be supplanted by a social model that stressed motherhood and economic and social roles based on physiological differences. The formative experience of military service led women revolutionaries in Hainan and in other regional struggles to naturally postpone motherhood, and develop a "strong aversion to any association with woman-work" and even women's organizing within the Party apparatus, which was considered a "dead-end job" for women cadres.[57] From its earliest organizations on Hainan in 1926, women had insisted on radical equality.[58]

This postwar reversion on Hainan to more traditionally patriarchal gender roles involved the demobilization of an extraordinarily high proportion of local Communist fighters who were women. Historian Wang Zheng finds that several developments in popular-culture depictions of women soldiers coincided in the early 1960s. In February 1961, CCP chairman Mao Zedong wrote a short poem called "Militia Women: Inscription on a Photograph" ("Wei nübing tizhao").

> How bright and brave they look, shouldering five-foot rifles
> On the parade ground lit up by the first gleams of day.
> China's daughters have high-aspiring minds,
> They love their battle array, not silks and satins.[59]

Wang also notes that some 1961 covers of the journal *Youth of China* included women militia fighters.[60] In the same year, leading PRC filmmaker Xie Jin directed the first prominent version of the *The Red*

[56] Maria Christin Santana, "From Empowerment to Domesticity: The Case of Rosie the Riveter and the WWII Campaign," *Frontiers in Sociology* 23 (December 2016), at www.frontiersin.org/articles/10.3389/fsoc.2016.00016/full.
[57] Kimberley Ens Manning, "The Gendered Politics of Women's Work: Rethinking Radicalism in the Great Leap Forward," *Modern China* 32, no. 3 (July 2006): 357–358.
[58] Hainansheng difangzhi ban'gongshi, *Hainan shengzhi: Haiyang zhi/Geming genjudi zhi*, 186.
[59] Mao Zedong, "Militia Women: Inscription on a Photograph" (February 1961), in *Mao Tse-tung Poems* (Beijing: Foreign Languages Press, 1976), 38; and republished at www.marxists.org/reference/archive/mao/selected-works/poems/poems28.htm.
[60] Wang Zheng, "Creating a Socialist Feminist Cultural Front: *Women of China* (1949–1966)," *China Quarterly* 204 (December 2010): 846–847.

Detachment of Women drama as a nonmusical film, and it won top national awards. But as Wang notes about the *Youth of China* covers, the women fighters are portrayed with men depicted centrally and in command.[61] In the Xie Jin film, an invented male commander teaches the women and is dramatically martyred in the final moments. By the early 1960s, while women were depicted more prominently in popular military roles, it was consistently under the command and guidance of men.

Several sources note that Premier Zhou Enlai was told about the fighting women of Hainan in March of 1953 and replied, "They are a model for world revolution! A movie should be made about them!"[62] But by the time a major nonmusical feature film was finally made in 1961, followed by a model ballet and Beijing opera, the facts had been altered to reinforce the narrative of mainland Maoist revolution, and of male dominance. In all of these versions, the details are essentially the same in their normative distortion of the history of women fighters on Hainan, and, perhaps, in the Chinese revolution overall.

The character of Hong Changqing, the male Party representative or commissar (*dang daibiao*) in *Red Detachment* is a fascinating construction. There was no Hong Changqing. He was conjured by male authors who felt that a story about an all-woman fighting unit would not make for good drama.[63] This choice to add a fictional male authority figure represents the clear delineations around women warriors even in the Cultural Revolution, ostensibly a moment of radical gender equality. Throughout the drama, Hong repeatedly disciplines the female protagonist Wu Qionghua (sometimes Qinghua). He saves her from her brutal master, welcomes her to the Communist revolutionary base area, gives her a pistol, but then takes it away when she proves too undisciplined to handle it properly. She ultimately earns the weapon back, and Hong Changqing ultimately dies a martyr, tied to a tree and burned alive. His gendered discipline becomes immortal, sublimated throughout the final moments of the drama and the reverent women are instructed by his didactic sacrifice.[64] In one final twist that represents the intersection of region and gender in the revision and erasure of Hainanese military women's agency, it is revealed in the lyrics of the operatic version of *Red Detachment* that the fictional Hong is in fact

[61] Ibid., 847.
[62] Liu Zhenhua, *Hainan zhi zhan* (The Battle for Hainan) (Shenyang: Liaoning renmin chubanshe, 2015), 81–82. Also see Zhu Y., *Fengyu licheng* (The Course of History (lit. "the course of wind and rain")) (Haikou: Hainan chubanshe, 2005), 468.
[63] Zhu, *Fengyu licheng*, 468.
[64] China Ballet Troupe, ed., *Red Detachment of Women: A Modern Revolutionary Ballet* (Peking: Foreign Languages Press, 1972; first published 1970).

a *mainlander*, sent to Hainan to lead the revolution there.[65] And so in this conjured epilogue to the anti-localism campaign, the invented character of Hong embodies both the mainland *and* the patriarchal norms that were amplified in the retelling of the history of the woman warriors of Hainan's revolution.[66]

Today, as in countless countries, women in China play an essential role in the military, though their traditionally gendered roles in publicity campaigns, along with the question of women in combat and in the military in general, continue to be matters of some controversy.[67] In Hainan, the tradition of high participation of women in the military continues.[68]

---

[65] Feng Zhixiao, dir., *Hongse niangzi jun* (Red Detachment of Women) (Beijing opera film, Chinese People's Liberation Army, August 1 production, 1972).

[66] Jeremy A. Murray, "Taming the Southern Frontiers through Song and Dance: Chauvinisms (Male and Han) in *The Red Detachment of Women*," in Paul Gladston, Beccy Kennedy-Schtyk, and Ming Turner, eds., *Visual Culture Wars at the Borders of Contemporary China: Art, Design, Film, New Media and the Prospects of "Post-West" Contemporaneity* (London: Palgrave MacMillan, 2021), 179–200.

[67] See Kania, "Holding Up Half the Sky?"; and Kania and Allen, "Holding Up Half the Sky?"; Huang Zheping, "China's Female Soldiers Fly Fighter Jets, but Its State Media Would Rather Focus on Their Dancing Skills," *Quartz*, June 24, 2017, at https://qz.com/1036701/ chinas-female-pla-soldiers-are-flying-fighter-jets-but-its-state-media-would-rather-focus -their-dancing-skills; C. Ge, "Can of Worms: Pictures of Elite Chinese Female Soldiers Eating Creepy-Crawlies in Training Reignites Debate about Women's Role in Military," *South China Morning Post*, April 20, 2016, at www.scmp.com/news/china/society/article/19 37371/can-worms-pictures-elite-chinese-female-soldiers-eating-creepy.

[68] "Hainan: '00-hou' nübing zai budui lilian chengnian huisa qingchun hanshui" (The Post-2000 Generation of Women Soldiers Sweat through Adult Army Training), *Toutiao ribao* (Headline Daily), December 12, 2018, at https://kknews.cc/zh-cn/mili tary/ejo3bqr.html; Li Lei, "Wo sheng kaizhan nübing yu zheng duixiang tige fujian" ("Our Province Carries Out Physical Examination of Prospective Enlisted Female Soldiers) *Xinhua/Hainan ribao*, August 15, 2019, at www.hq.xinhuanet.com/news/201 9-08/15/c_1124877300.htm.

7 Reconstruction and Solidification

The Restructuring of "Peasant" Status in the 1950s
Dispersal of Shanghai's Urban Population

Ruan Qinghua

In modern times, the development paths of the major nations of the world
have shown that industrialization and modernization will necessarily bring
about urbanization, and with it the transformation of agricultural populations into industrial workers and urban populations as they move into
cities. But after the establishment of the People's Republic of China
(PRC), the People's Government instead began large-scale mobilization
of urban populations away from Shanghai and other large and medium-
sized cities, either returning people to their homes in the countryside or
moving them to other rural villages to undertake the work of agricultural
production. In doing so, they transformed these city residents back into
peasants, realizing the "ruralfication" of the urban population. Why, at the
very outset of establishing its government, would the Communist Party of
China (CPC) – which set as its purposes the saving of a nation in peril and
the establishment of an industrialized, modern state – start down a path of
dispersing urban populations and resettling them in the countryside, a path
so at odds with Western nations' industrialization and development? In the
extant literature on the initial industrialization and urbanization in the
PRC, the issue of urban population is not discussed.[1] In research related
to the dispersal of urban populations from large cities like Shanghai, most
studies focus on isolated incidents and do not situate them in the industrialization and urbanization of New China.[2] This chapter mainly explores

---

[1] Hu Angang, "China's Seventy Years of Industrialization: From Lagging Behind to
Leading," *Journal of the Central Institute of Socialism* 5 (2019); Yan Ying and He Aiguo,
"New China's Seventy Years of Industrialization," *Fujian Tribune* 7 (2019); Zeng Chun,
"The Dawn of China's Rejuvenation: Explorations in China's Initial Industrialization,"
China Industry and Information Technology, October 2019.
[2] Zhang Kaimin, *Shanghai rekou qianyi yanjiu* (Research on Shanghai Population
Migration) (Shanghai: Shanghai Social Sciences Press, 1989); Chen Li, "Research on
the Policies of Reduction of Workers in the Early 60s and Mobilization of Urban
Population to Go Down to the Countryside," *Contemporary China History Studies* 6
(1996); Li Ruojian, "The Peak and Decline of Urbanization and During the Great
Leap Forward," *Population and Economics* 5 (1999), Xie Lingli, *Sixty Years of Population
Development in Shanghai, Shanghai renkou fazhan 60 nian* (Shanghai: Shanghai People's

the issue of the relocation of Shanghai's urban populations through publicly available materials and files collected in the Shanghai Municipal
Archives. It is argued that before and after the establishment of the PRC,
the CCP defined cities as "production bases" and also saw "old cities" as
"centers of consumption," which not only were full of politically unreliable
people, but also had many people who depended on the service industry
and "backwards industries" to make a living, as well as many unemployed
vagrants and parasitic populations. It was for this reason that the CCP and
the People's Government found many ways to disperse "nonproductive
populations" from the city and resettle them in the countryside, thereby
reducing pressure on urban supply chains and ensuring that cities could be
transformed into industrial production bases.

Shanghai's "Consumer Population"

The CCP believed that Shanghai was a consumer city, so there was a large
consumer population that needed to be evacuated to other places in order
to transform the city into a production base. In March 1949, the Public
Report of the Second Plenary Session of the Seventh Central Committee
of the Communist Party of China stated that the CCP, "as of now, begins
a new period moving from the city to the countryside, in which the city
leads the countryside."[3] Mao Zedong clearly stated during the plenum,
"Beginning on the first day we take over management of the cities, our
eyes must be set on the restoration and development of this city's production," which is the Party's "central task." "Only by restoring and developing urban production and transforming a city of consumption into one
of production can the People's regime be consolidated."[4] From this point
on, "turning cities of consumption into cities of production" became the
CCP's basic governing policy for cities,[5] as well as the guiding thought for

---

Press, 2010). He Yongtai, "Analysis of the Reduced Staff Policy in Shanghai during the
Early 1960s," *Journal of East China Normal University* (Philosophy and Social Sciences),
September 2010; Qiu Guosheng : "Staff Reduction in the City–Countryside Conflict and
Its Resolution in Early 1960s Shanghai," *Historical Research in Anhui* 6 (2011).
Zhang Kun, "Shanghai's Mobilization of Personnel to Relocate Elsewhere and Control
of Urban Scale from 1949–1976," *Contemporary China History Studies* 3 (2015).

[3] "The Public Report of the Second Plenary Session of the Seventh Central Committee of the
Communist Party of China" (March 23, 1949), National Archives Administration of China,
Zhonggong zhongyang wenjian xuanji di shiba ce (Selected Files of the Central Committee of
Communist Party of China), vol. 18 (Central Party School Press, 1992), 195.

[4] Mao Zedong, "Report to the Second Plenary Session of the Seventh Central Committee
of the Communist Party of China," March 5, 1949, in Mao Zedong xuanji di si ce
(Selected Works of Mao Zedong, vol. 4) (People's Publishing House, 1967), 1366.

[5] "Turning Cities of Consumption into Cities of Production," *People's Daily*, March 17,
1949.

newly liberated city management and transformation, becoming "the general policy for the People's city work."[6] Shanghai was, in the eyes of the CCP, the most representative "city of consumption," with a large "consumer population." The population of Shanghai around May of 1949 was about 5.4 million,[7] of which over half was "consumer population." At the time, the term "consumer population" mainly referred to the almost 250,000 "old personnel" (Guomindang regime employees or those with close relations to them) received by the Shanghai Military Control Committee,[8] close to 200,000 students of all kinds,[9] 250,000 unemployed workers, about a million store workers, 650,000 people in poverty, 170,000 vagrants, and 100,000 runaway landlords and rich peasants and their families in the early years of the PRC.[10] There were also many who were family members of the "producer population," so the "consumer population" made up much more than half of the city's total population.

By April of 1955, the population of Shanghai had increased to 6.99 million, with the basic population, which included personnel "working in industry, construction, and fields with national significance such as higher education, railways, shipping by air and sea, as well as the ports," accounted for only 1.18 million, or 16.99 percent of the city's total population. The service population, meaning personnel "working in commerce, administrative enterprises, and culture, education, and sanitation departments," accounted for about 1.19 million people, or 17.14 percent of the city's total population. The rural production population was over 200,000, making up 2.49 percent, and the population of other "non-employed persons," such as children, students, the elderly, and the general population of those not working, those who had lost their employment, and the temporary population, totaled over 4.4 million, or 62.93 percent of the total population.[11]

---

[6] "Jinan Municipal Industry and Commerce Forum Discusses How to Establish a City of Production," *People's Daily*, May 24, 1949.

[7] Shanghai gaikuang (Shanghai: A General Summary) recorded Shanghai's population as 5.45 million as of November 1948. Shanghai Municipal Archives, *Shanghai jiefang shang ce* (The Liberation of Shanghai, vol. 1) (China Archive Press, 2009), 3. Another estimate is 5.4 million as of March 1949. Zou Yiren, Jiu Shanghai renkou bianqian de yanjiu (A Study of Population Change in Old Shanghai) (Shanghai: Shanghai People's Press, 1980), 91.

[8] Hao Xianzhong, "Shanghai's Reception and Settling of Old Shanghai Personnel before and after the Establishment of New China in 1949," *CCP History Studies* 1 (2004).

[9] Chen Yi, "Working Report on the Shanghai Military Control Committee and People's Government for the Two-Month Period of June and July," *People's Daily*, August 13, 1949.

[10] "How Many Impoverished People Are There in Shanghai?" *Wen hui bao*, August 8, 1949.

[11] "Municipal Party Committee Directives on Strengthening the City's Residence Permit Management and Multi-stage Population Reduction (Draft)" (July 1, 1955), Shanghai Archives Hall (Shanghaishi Dang an guan), B 2-2-10.

For the CCP and the People's Government in Shanghai, it was necessary to significantly disperse and reduce Shanghai's "consumer population" in order to realize the goal of "the transformation of Shanghai from a city of consumption into a city of production." In reality, the dispersal of Shanghai's urban population and control of the total urban population were always the basic governing goals of the Shanghai People's Government after the PRC's establishment.

However, where should the population be dispersed? And how should they be resettled? These two issues in particular required the new regime's consideration. They could not simply shift their problems to a neighbor: they needed to reduce Shanghai's population but, more importantly, also ensure that they could resettle permanently elsewhere. But Shanghai was actually facing economic depression, severe inflation, high unemployment rates, and a strapped financial situation. The city lacked sufficient financial resources to resettle the vast population that awaited dispersal. Therefore the Shanghai Military Control Committee, the Municipal Party Committee, and the municipal government took every opportunity to reduce the pressure by dispersing different groups in different ways, and under different auspices. The most important way they did this was to emphasize their original "peasant" status: whether they had moved to the city three or five years ago or had already been away from the countryside for decades, as long as they or their parents' generation had come from a village, they were designated "peasants." Once they had been labeled "peasants," the People's Government could justify their dispersal and removal, thereby increasing the effectiveness of urban population dispersal, as well as its legitimacy. By designating these people "peasants," they could more easily designate their destinations as well, by having them "return" to "their" villages.

Removal of "Natural-Disaster Victims" to Their Places of Origin and the Dispersal of the Urban Population

In the name of mobilizing refugees and disaster victims to return to their hometowns, an evacuation of many urban poor people out of Shanghai, next to the truly affected disaster victims and refugees, had taken place to achieve the goal of reducing the urban population. This is a notable feature of the first phase of Shanghai's population evacuation. On May 28, 1949, the Shanghai People's Government was established, and immediately set about the task of providing emergency relief to, and dispersing, the refugees who were mostly concentrated in Huxi, the western part of Shanghai. By June 8, after only ten days, they had relocated 200,000 people to the countryside.[12] But the Shanghai Military Control Committee and the municipal government believed that there were at least 1.8 million refugees in Shanghai, and that even greater dispersal measures were necessary.[13] On June 23, the Military Control Committee "called on charity organizations and groups to assist the government as much as they can in the removal of refugees who are unable to return to the countryside."[14] On June 25, the Military Control Committee called together the representatives of all suburbs to a joint conference to "deliberate together on the concrete implementation methods for the moving of refugees back to the countryside for production."[15] Relevant departments in the municipal government and the Military Control Committee further formulated the refugee dispersal plan, setting the mobilization of refugees to return to the countryside from the end of June into July as a central goal and requiring that dispersal of a million of Shanghai's refugees be successfully completed by the end of July. Due to the fact that Shanghai's "refugees" mainly came from neighboring provinces, the plan required that all areas of east China send representatives to Shanghai to assist in the dispersal, especially requiring the Shandong provincial government, the Northern Jiangsu Administrative Office, the Northern Anhui Administrative Office, and others to form an organization especially for the purpose of handling these cases in a uniform way, to better realize their reception after dispersal from Shanghai.[16] On July 24, the CCP East China Bureau also released directives requiring "the dispersal of Shanghai refugees back to the countryside for production."[17]

From the end of May to the beginning of August, Shanghai removed 300,000 refugees from the city in total.[18] The Military Control Committee subsequently drew up an even more ambitious plan to disperse an

[12] Xiong Yuezhi, Shanghai tongshi di shisan juan (The General History of Shanghai, vol. 13) (Shanghai: Shanghai People's Press, 1999), 15.

[13] Shanghai Archives Hall, Dongyuan nanmin huanxiang shengchan gongzuo jihua cao'an (Draft of Working Plan to Move Refugees Back to the Countryside for Production), Shanghai Archives Hall B 168-1-681.

[14] "To Decrease Population Burden, Military Control Committee Removes Refugees Back to the Countryside for Production," *Jiefang Daily*, June 24, 1949.

[15] "City Suburb Representative Discusses Methods of Returning Refugees to the Countryside Yesterday," *Jiefang Daily*, June 26, 1949.

[16] Dongyuan nanmin huanxiang shengchan gongzuo jihua cao'an (Draft of Working Plan to Move Refugees Back to the Countryside for Production), Shanghai Archives Hall B 168-1-681.

[17] CCP East China Bureau, "Directives on Shanghai Dispersal of Refugees Back to the Countryside for Production," *Jiefang Daily*, August 5, 1949; "Concrete Methods for CPC East China Bureau Directives, Shanghai Dispersal of Refugees Back to the Countryside for Production," *People's Daily*, August 8, 1949. Also see Shanghai Archives Hall B 168-1-680.

[18] Chen Yi, "Report on the Work of the Shanghai Military Control Committee and People's Government for the Two-Month Period of June and July," *Jiefang Daily*, August 7, 1949.

additional 2 million people during the winter and spring of 1949–1950.[19] The municipal government established the Shanghai Municipal Dispersal of Refugees Back to the Countryside for Production and Relief Committee, the "Dispersal Committee" (Shuweihui), especially for this purpose, on August 27, 1949, establishing district dispersal committees under the auspices of receiving committees, as well as dispersal work stations, in every district.[20] Prior to this, under the leadership of the District Takeover Committees, many grassroots work units of major "refugee" districts had established a "refugee return mobilization committee" (*baojia*) for the mobilization of refugees to return to the countryside.[21] Meanwhile, the Dispersal Committee also began to work with the Emergency Joint Relief Committee, or "Emergency Relief Committee" (Linjiuhui), organized by the "Shanghai Civil Charity Association" (Shanghai minjian cishan tuanti lianhehui), using the six central working stations previously established by the Emergency Relief Committee. Some cadres were also transferred in to form three work teams dispatched to the Xuhui, Yangshupu, and Zhabei districts to conduct key-point investigations. Dispersal workstations were then set up in twenty city districts, with the receiving committee commissioner serving as the station head and the former Emergency Relief Committee central working station chief as the station deputy.[22] So far, Shanghai had established refugee dispersal leading organs, forming a refugee dispersal network that covered the entire city.

Through more than a month of intense propaganda mobilization, by the end of August, Shanghai had dispersed another approximately 100,000 "refugees" back to the countryside.[23] Yet fewer and fewer refugees were willing to go back to the countryside. From September to the end of December in 1949, Shanghai dispersed 30,000 or more people, falling far short of a million, let alone the goal of 2 million set in the plan.[24]

The rapid growth of Shanghai's population in the modern era was basically due to the explosive growth of the refugee population during the war.[25] After the war ended, some refugees would leave Shanghai, but many would

[19] "Shanghai Military Control Committee Draws Up Plan to Disperse Two Million People Back to the Countryside for Production," *People's Daily*, August 13, 1949.

[20] "Municipal Government Materials on the Dispersal of Refuges Back to the Countryside for Production" (September 1949), Shanghai Archives Hall, B 1-2-281.

[21] "First Group of Refugees from Jing'an Temple Return to the Countryside with Tickets Waived," *Jiefang Daily*, July 28, 1949.

[22] Shanghai Dispersal Committee, "General Report on the Two-Month Period of September and October," November 17, 1949, Shanghai Archives Hall, B 1-2-3565.

[23] "Summary of the Work of the Dispersal of Refugees to the Countryside for Production" (end of December 1949), Shanghai Archives Hall, B 168-1-683.

[24] Ibid.

[25] Zou Yiren, *Jiu Shanghai renkou bianqian de yanjiu* (A Study of Population Change in Old Shanghai) (Shanghai: Shanghai People's Press, 1980), 3–5.

become long-term residents of the city. However, in the eyes of the municipal government authorities, the large number of refugees who poured into
Shanghai during that short period of time put all kinds of pressure on the
city. Therefore, the dispersal of refugees was a measure often used by the
Shanghai municipal government of that period. In early 1942, after Japan
occupied the Foreign Concessions, the Japanese Shanghai puppet municipal government began to disperse 600,000 refugees back to the countryside
within a short period of time.[26] In 1946, the Guomindang regime returned
to Shanghai and also funded the return of refugees to the countryside, once
even planning to send refugees to Jiangxi Province to develop land for
agricultural cultivation.[27] However, the work of dispersing and sending
away refugees was not smooth, and forceful measures were often needed.
In 1949, on the eve of Shanghai's liberation, the Guomindang government's
Shanghai–Wusong Garrison Command was ordering the dispersal of refugees, and had even mobilized the army and declared martial law, threatening, "All persons without identity papers or civil service credentials may only
leave voluntarily today, otherwise soldiers will be dispatched to remove
you." Also, "Those who refuse to be escorted outside this territory will be
dealt with at once under martial law."[28] Clearly, the mobilization of the
dispersal of refugees from Shanghai has never been an easy task.

This was in no small part because, in the early days of liberation, the
"refugees" Shanghai sought to disperse were not necessarily refugees of war
or natural disaster, without homes or livelihoods, needing to return home
urgently. The CCP's East China Bureau directed the major eastern
Chinese coastal cities, including Shanghai, to disperse not only refugees
and victims of natural disasters, but also some urban residents, and the
purpose of this dispersal was very clear: "decreasing the burdens on
cities."[29] The Shanghai Military Control Committee required the dispersal
of "unemployed workers, unemployed shopkeepers, and their families,

---

[26] Tao Juyin, *Gudao jianwen – Kangzhan shiqi de Shanghai* (Events on an Isolated Island:
Shanghai in Wartime) (Shanghai: Shanghai People's Press, 1979), 119.

[27] Qiu Guosheng, *Chengshihua jincheng zhong Shanghaishi wailai renkou guanli de lishi yanjin
(1840–2000)* (The Historical Progress of Shanghai's Non-native Population
Management during the Process of Urbanization (1840–2000)) (Beijing: China Social
Sciences Press, 2010), 88–89; Ruan Qinghua, "'Protecting Private Property' or
'Stabilizing People's Livelihood'? An Analysis of Shanghai Municipal Government's
Dilemma in the 'Incident of Corpse Deposit' during the Civil War Period," *Journal of
East China Normal University* (Philosophy and Social Sciences) 4 (2011).

[28] "Joint Bulletin from the Shanghai Municipal Government and Shanghai–Wusong
Garrison Command" (April 27, 1949), Shanghai Archives Hall, Q 1-10-335, cited in
Qiu Guosheng, Chengshihua jincheng zhong Shanghaishi wailai renkou guanli de lishi
yanjin, 89.

[29] CCP East China Bureau, "Directives on Shanghai Dispersal of Refugees Back to the
Countryside for Production" (August 5, 1949), Shanghai Archives Hall, B 168-1-680.

totaling 1 million people; 650,000 impoverished people, 170,000 jobless drifters, and 100,000 runaway landlords."[30] These were clearly not all "refugees," but they were dispersed from the Shanghai area as refugees. The Military Control Commission and municipal government needed to use the excuse of dispersing "refugees" to mobilize a "mass movement," so that they could achieve their goal of clearing out the city and reducing the consumer population.[31] After the end of the war, the victors assisting refugees to return to their homes had natural legitimacy, so it was both a necessary part of the work of clearing out the occupied area and a way to win the gratitude of actual refugees. Under the banner of dispersing "refugees," it was also possible to fully leverage all sorts of humanitarian organizations and resources to assist the government in completing this work. Furthermore, since these people had fled difficult situations and still faced troubles in their current locations, dispersing "refugees" was right and logical, drawing support and assistance from those considered local city residents. Therefore, those who came to the Shanghai area to escape difficulties and those who lived on the streets were refugees; unemployed workers mobilized by the All-China Federation of Trade Unions to return to their homes in the countryside were also refugees; drifters and those who "through education" were willing to return to the countryside were also refugees; and those "nonworking" persons whom the courts or public-security organs had "sentenced to return to the countryside or participate in production and transformation in villages," as long as they were willing to go, were also considered "refugees." Even personnel and workers of the former government, sent by various organs to the countryside, could be considered among those "refugees" returning to the countryside.[32] This is all to say that, as long as one was willing to leave Shanghai, one could be dealt with as part of the movement to disperse "refugees." Even unemployed drifters could be directly sent home without going through the process of being taken in and reformed, but those who did not return to the countryside could be dealt with by the legal and public-security organs and ultimately forced to leave Shanghai in the end anyway.

However, in the second half of 1949, the areas that were the primary destinations for Shanghai's population dispersal, including northern Jiangsu, northern Anhui, and Shandong, were hit by serious flooding,

[30] "Shanghai Military Control Committee Draws Up Plan to Disperse Two Million People Back to the Countryside for Production," *People's Daily*, August 13, 1949, 2.

[31] CCP East China Bureau, "Directives on Shanghai Dispersal of Refugees Back to the Countryside for Production" (August 5, 1949), Shanghai Archives Hall, B 168-1-680.

[32] "Decision by Committee on Shanghai's Dispersal of Refugees Back to the Countryside for Production Relief on Standards for Transport Tickets and Provisions Given during Dispersal and Removal," Shanghai Archives Hall, B 1-2-3565.

with affected persons numbering in the tens of millions. A large number of the "refugees" that Shanghai had previously sent there flowed back into Shanghai as disaster refugees once again, and meanwhile more disaster victims fled to Shanghai to escape famine. The CCP's Ministry of Internal Affairs clearly required all areas to temporarily halt population dispersal work, saying that as for "those disaster refugees who have already fled to various regions, it is not permitted force them to go back to their places of origin, and it is required to immediately mobilize the masses of your regions to provide mutual support and aid voluntarily."[33] Shanghai had no choice but to temporarily halt the dispersal of refugees and establish locations where people displaced by natural disasters and living on the streets could be admitted and sheltered from the winter cold. However, after Shanghai was bombed by Guomindang airplanes in February of 1950, the municipal government took the opportunity to continue to implement their policy of dispersing disaster refugees. This time, though, they emphasized that "refugees" and "natural-disaster victims" would be dispersed together, and at the same time they would continue to disperse other urban populations. Following this, the work continued off and on indefinitely in Shanghai. This was in spite of the East China Military and Administrative Committee requiring that "natural-disaster victims from all regions who have come to Shanghai and have some means of supporting themselves and have already participated in production, those not relying on local government relief," not be sent back home. Although Shanghai emphasized that those who were sent back to the countryside were all "actual victims of natural disaster,"[34] in truth there were still many who had lived for years in Shanghai, and some who had even found work and had their own places of residence, who were sent back to the countryside as "natural-disaster victims."

Mobilizing "Peasants" to Return to the Countryside for Production

Evacuation of the urban population out of Shanghai in the name of mobilizing farmers to return to their hometowns, in order to achieve the goal of reducing the urban population, is a significant feature of the second stage of Shanghai's population evacuation. From the beginning of the modern era, peasants in areas surrounding Shanghai had the

---

[33] "Shanghai Municipal People's Government Order" (end of December 1949), Shanghai Archives Hall, B 169-1-680.
[34] Shanghai Relief Branch Committee, "Report Submitted on Issues Related to the Work of Accommodation and Removal of Natural-Disaster Victims" (April 2, 1951), Shanghai Archives Hall, B 1-2-492.

habit of using their time off from agricultural work to travel to Shanghai to make extra money. They would take on odd jobs to make some extra income while reducing the consumption of food stores at home, returning home for spring plowing and production. This increase in seasonal population from outside Shanghai did not end in 1949, and especially following the implementation of the state grain monopoly in rural areas in 1953, nearby peasants came to Shanghai to make a living in even greater numbers, undoubtedly increasing pressure on the grain supply chains in Shanghai. In 1955, the Municipal Party Committee and government decided to implement rationed distribution of grain,[35] and needed a clear count of the city's population, as well as to reduce the number of peasants coming to make a living in the city. Therefore, in April 1955, Shanghai began to mobilize the seasonal populations who came via boat to return to their homes for production, and by July 1, the Municipal Party Committee formally released directives to "shrink Shanghai," requiring that measures be taken to "strictly limit influx and actively encourage outflux," thus dispersing from the city between 500,000 and 1 million people, among them from 400,000 to 600,000 via mobilization and removal to their places of origin, in the second half of 1955 and the first half of 1956.[36] On July 2, the General Affairs Office of the Municipal Party Committee released the "Plan to Mobilize City and Countryside Residents from Elsewhere to Return to Their Place of Origin for Production," requiring that "all those in this city from other cities or the countryside without proper and stable professions, and whose places of origin have the conditions for production and life, must be strongly mobilized to return to their places of origin in waves."[37] The mobilization work was carried out with the co-operation of all departments, each doing their part.

The Municipal Civil Affairs Bureau was in charge of mobilizing "peasants" to return to the countryside. On July 15, it published its "Plan for Mobilizing Peasants to Return to the Countryside for Production Work," requiring that "all those whose places of origin have the means of production (such as land and labor) or means for living (such as a support system or relatives to support one in one's place of origin via remittances), and

---

[35] Tang Shuiqing, Shanghai liangshi jihua gongying yu shimin shenghuo (1953–1956) (Planned Supply of Shanghai Grain and City Resident Life (1953–1956)) (Beijing: Shanghai Lexicographical Publishing House, 2008), 150.

[36] "The Municipal Party Committee's Directives on Enhancing the City's Household Residence Permit Management and Reducing Population in a Multi-staged Manner (Draft)" (July 1, 1955), Shanghai Archives Hall, B 2-2-10.

[37] Shanghai Municipal Party Committee Office, "Preliminary Plan for Mobilizing Residents from Other Cities and Countryside Areas to Return to Their Places of Origin for Production Work (Draft)" (July 2, 1955), Shanghai Archives Hall, B 2-2-10.

those peasants who must or may return, must all be strongly mobilized to return to the countryside for production."[38] The specific categories included the following: (1) those awaiting employment or without proper or stable employment in the city; (2) workers in government organs, the military, enterprises, and schools, as well as the families, nannies, and servants of residents; (3) temporary workers in industrial factories; (4) workers let go from jobs in struggling industries who originally came from rural villages.

From April 1955 to June 1956, Shanghai dispersed a total of 637,255 people though mobilizing "peasants to return to the countryside for production."[39] Of those dispersed to the countryside, 15.6 percent had arrived in Shanghai prior to 1945, and over 30 percent had arrived before 1949.[40] Some of these "peasants" dispersed to the countryside had even lived in Shanghai for decades, but were still sent back as peasants.[41] Of these 637,255 "peasants" who had been sent back to the countryside, 450,613, or 70.7 percent, had long-term household registration permits for Shanghai, while 34,646, or 5.4 percent, had temporary household registration permits. Only 10,740 people clearly lacked household registration permits, accounting for just 1.7 percent, while the household registration permit situation was unclear for 141,256 of them.[42]

As an important measure by which the urban population was dispersed and pressure on the city decreased, "mobilizing peasants to return to the countryside for production" was employed many times in Shanghai thereafter. In March 1957, the Shanghai Municipal People's Committee required "the beginning of work to mobilize peasants to return to the countryside for production," and planned to mobilize "natural-disaster victims and residents of other cities and rural areas who blindly flowed into this city"; the families of cadres, employees, military, and police residents; the masses who came back to the city to find employment and

---

[38] "CPC Shanghai Municipal Party Committee Releases Shanghai Civil Affairs Bureau Party Organization 'Plan for Mobilizing Peasants to Return to the Countryside for Production Work'" (July 21, 1955), Shanghai Archives Hall, A 45-1-1-105.

[39] The above data come from different dates of the Shanghai Statistics on Persons Returned to the Countryside for Production, Shanghai Archives Hall, B 25-1-15, B 168-1-866-1.

[40] Shanghai Statistics on Persons Returned to the Countryside for Production (April 1955–June 1956), Shanghai Archives Hall, B 25-1-15, B 168-1-866-1.

[41] "Report by Zhang Zhiqiang to the Civil Affairs Bureau Party Organization, Also Reported to the Provincial Party Committee and Political and Legal Affairs Party Organization" (September 1955), "Report by the Jiangsu Provincial Civil Affairs Bureau Party Small Group to the Political and Legal Affairs Party Organization and Provincial Party Committee" (September 10, 1955), Jiangsu Provincial Archives, Su 3085 – long-term – 115.

[42] Shanghai Statistics on Persons Returned to the Countryside for Production (April 1955–June 1956), Shanghai Archives Hall, B 25-1-15, B 168-1-866-1.

escape famine; and employees transferred to this city from elsewhere to return to their places of origin and participate in agricultural production.[43] In 1959, Shanghai once again set about "mobilizing agricultural labor to return to the countryside for production," mobilizing and removing 253,000 people to do so in the period of over two months from March 19 to June 10. The report especially explains that "among these personnel are approximately 62,000 people from elsewhere who blindly flowed into this city," which is to say that more than 190,000 had been living in Shanghai for some time, and that they had also been mobilized to leave the Shanghai area and return to the countryside, once again entering agricultural production.[44] It could be said that throughout the 1950s, Shanghai was continuously mobilizing "peasants" to return to the countryside for production and relocating those who had long been in Shanghai back to their hometowns to work in agricultural production once again.

Despite their status as peasants who "returned to the countryside for production," the actual conditions for production in their destinations were terrible. According to an investigation by Jiangsu Province, from 1955 to 1956, of those mobilized by Shanghai to return to the countryside, at least 10–15 percent were "homeless," and "their homes lack both land and houses." Half of the lands of "peasants returned to the countryside" were less than the average field size of the local masses, and, among these, many were "not large enough to sustain life."[45] Land was even scarcer for those personnel returning to small towns or villages: over 56 percent of them had no land at all, and the small towns and villages could not provide or arrange work for them.[46]

In 1955 and the following years, although many people who had lived for quite a while in Shanghai were sent away from the city as part of the "movement to mobilize peasants to return to the countryside for production," they were always identified as "peasants." Although they had lived

---

[43] Shanghai People's Committee, "Plan to Begin the Work of Mobilizing Rural Residents to Return to the Countryside for Agricultural Production" (March 10, 1957), Shanghai Archives Hall, B 127-1-83.

[44] Investigative Small Group on Halting the Blind Flow of the Agricultural Labor Force into This City, "Work Summary Report on Mobilizing Agricultural Labor Force to Return to the Countryside for Production" (June 27, 1959), Shanghai Archives Hall, A 11-1-34-32.

[45] "Report by the CPC Jiangsu Provincial Civil Affairs Bureau Party Organization to the Political and Legal Affairs Party Organization and Provincial Party Committee" (September 10, 1955), Jiangsu Provincial Archives, Su 3085 – long-term – 115.

[46] "Comprehensive Statistics on the Main Conditions of the Return of Peasants to the Countryside from Shanghai during July and August of 1955 in the Four Special Districts, Eight Counties, and 19 Townships in Yangzhou, Yancheng, Suzhou, and Zhenjiang, Jiangsu Province," Jiangsu Provincial Archives, Su 3085 – long-term – 115.

in Shanghai for a long time, the majority had gained Shanghai resident status, and they lacked houses and land in the countryside, yet they were still considered "peasants" and dispersed back to the countryside. In 1955, Tianjin also conducted large-scale mobilization of "peasants to return to the countryside," moving over 150,000 people from the city to locations elsewhere during that year, and in actual practice also dispersed many who had long lived in Tianjin and worked there for many years, transforming them back into "peasants."[47] In truth, the dispersal of all kinds of "excess population" to villages to undertake agricultural production, and the transformation of those populations into "peasants," were measures utilized by many large cities after the establishment of the People's Republic of China.

Evacuate the Urban Population to Reclaim Wasteland in the Countryside

The evacuation of a large number of urban poor and workers in the so-called backward industries to reclaim wasteland in rural areas, and transform them into farmers engaged in agricultural production, was another important means for Shanghai's urban migration and resettlement. In early July 1955, the Municipal Party Committee directives on "shrinking Shanghai" also proposed "relocating the labor force that was originally engaged in agricultural production or might transition into agricultural production from this city to other provinces to develop land for agricultural production."[48] Jiangxi became the primary choice for Shanghai's large-scale movement of people to open up land for agricultural production, and in late August the Shanghai Municipal Party Committee decided to send 90,000 households, or about 300,000 people, to the province to open up land for production.[49]

Under the unified leadership of the Municipal People's Committee Population Office, Shanghai mobilized all types of personnel through "organizational integration" (*tiao kuai jiehe*) and co-operation through "division of labor" (*baogan fengong*) to move to Jiangxi to open up land for agriculture. The nine groups initially designated as targets for mobilization were young people, unregistered unemployed workers,

---

[47] Lai Xinxia and Chen Weimin, Tianjin de renkou bianqian (Changes in Tianjin's Population) (Tianjin: Tianjin Ancient Books Publishing House, 2005), 155.

[48] "The Municipal Party Committee's Directives on Enhancing the City's Household Residence Permit Management and Reducing Population in a Multi-staged Manner (Draft)" (July 1, 1955), Shanghai Archives Hall, B 2-2-10.

[49] Shanghai Labor Bureau, "Notice on Fact-Finding Work on the Organization of Unemployed Personnel for Relocation to Open Up Land for Agriculture" (August 29, 1955), Shanghai Archives Hall, B 127-1-1429.

out-of-work students (primary- and middle-school graduates), mobile peddlers, unneeded rickshaw workers, registered unemployed personnel, wharf workers not included in the staffing structure, established peddlers and personnel employed in the service industry, and unneeded personnel who lived and worked on boats.[50] These could primarily be grouped into three major categories: students and young people who could not go on to higher education or find employment, unemployed workers, and some personnel in industries which the bureau believed should be dissolved.

In October 1955, Shanghai began to send people to a test site for opening up land for agriculture, and by January 1956, 4,712 households had been sent to Jiangxi, including 7,498 members of the Shanghai workforce and totaling 12,961 people including their family members.[51] In early 1956, the Municipal Party Committee decided to organize those without an occupation and unemployed personnel, totaling 61,000 households of 231,500 people, to relocate to Jiangxi to open up land for agriculture.[52] This number grew to more than 80,000 households, totaling about 300,000 people, in March.[53] In February 1952, Shanghai began large-scale relocation to Jiangxi for the purpose of opening up land for agriculture, and by the end of April, 4,332 households, numbering 20,162 people with family members included, had been relocated.[54] But this was the end of the movement. Including the test site period relocations, Shanghai relocated a total of 33,123 people, only achieving a tenth of what it had initially planned. Rickshaw drivers and three-wheeled-cart workers made up 9,129 of these,[55] while maritime boat workers made up 3,862,[56] as well as 279 households of over

---

[50] Preliminary Comments on the Mobilization of Voluntary Work to Open Up Land for Agriculture" (November 7, 1955), Shanghai Archives Hall, B 168-1-863.

[51] The Municipal Party Committee initially designated 6,000 laborers, totaling 10,000 people including family members, for a test site opening up land for agricultural development. "Preliminary Summary of Test Site Work by This City's Masses in Jiangxi to Open Up Land for Agriculture (Draft)" (February 1956), Shanghai Archives Hall, B 168-1-863.

[52] "Plan for This City to Shrink Population in 1956 (Draft)" (early 1956), Shanghai Archives Hall, B 25-1-2.

[53] "Budget Report by the Shanghai People's Committee on This City's Funds for Relocation of People to Jiangxi to Open Up Land for Agriculture in 1956" (March 1956), Shanghai Archives Hall, B 25-2-17-1.

[54] "Relocation of People to Open Up Land for Agriculture Work Summary (Draft)" (January 1957), Shanghai Archives Hall, B 168-1-872-1.

[55] Shanghai Transportation Bureau Rickshaw and Three-Wheeled Cart Management Office, "Brief Summary of Mobilization of Rickshaw and Three-Wheeled-Cart Drivers to Go to Jiangxi and Participate in Opening Up Land for Agriculture in March and April of 1956" (late April 1956), Shanghai Archives Hall, B 25-2-9-73.

[56] "Maritime District People's Committee Brief Report on Civil Affairs Work" (June 4, 1956), Shanghai Archives Hall, B 59-2-78-168, cited in T ian Xin, "The Game of

800 people from the Shanghai Transportation Company.[57] Most of the rest were unemployed workers and other workers from "eliminated industries," as well as some young people who had been unable to find jobs. These people were initially "working-class" members of all professions, but in the "shrinking Shanghai" of 1955, with the policies that "those with lands return to the countryside, and those without open up land for agriculture," "all without work return to the countryside" was the order of the day anyway.[58] Furthermore, work personnel also warned them that "it is better to leave sooner than later, and better to leave now than soon, the quicker the better."[59] Against this backdrop, those "peasants" whose parents' generation had left the village, or who had personally been away from the countryside for many years, were sent to Jiangxi to open up land for agriculture and agricultural production and once again became "peasants."

Those "peasants" who had been in the Shanghai area for many years already found it difficult to work in agricultural production and adapt to life in villages, so they quickly "flowed back" to Shanghai. During the test site phase of opening agricultural land in 1955, there were already people escaping back to Shanghai from Jiangxi, and after 1956 even more fled back to the city. By 1959, of the more than 30,000 Shanghai residents who had been sent to Jiangxi to open up land for agriculture, more than 20,000 had "flowed back" to Shanghai at some time or another. But most of these personnel "flowing back" to Shanghai were mobilized a second or even a third time to return to Jiangxi to open up land for agriculture or were sent to their original places of origin to undertake the work of agricultural production, with a small fraction of them going to places such as Gansu and Anhui. Others who were totally unwilling to return to Jiangxi to open up land for agriculture were settled in the villages in Shanghai's suburbs to participate in the work of agricultural production.[60]

Interests in Power, Society, and Place in the Removal and Settlement of Shanghai's Maritime District Residents in the 1950s" (master's thesis, East China Normal University, May 2013), 39.

[57] "Short Summary of Shanghai Transportation Company Park Organization Transportation of Masses to Open Up Land for Agriculture" (April 1956), Shanghai Archives Hall, B 152-2-921.

[58] "The State of This City's Work to Mobilize Peasants to Return to the Countryside" (August 1955), Shanghai Archives Hall, B 2-2-10.

[59] "Summary of Relocation of People to Open Up Land for Agriculture (Draft)" (January 1957), Shanghai Archives Hall, B 168-1-872-1.

[60] Shanghai Civil Affairs Bureau Party Organization, Shanghai Transportation Bureau Party Organization, and Shanghai Labor Bureau Party Organization, "Report on Handling the Backflow of Land Reclaimers from Jiangxi" (September 21, 1959), Shanghai Archives Hall, B 168-1-104.

Conclusion: The Reconstruction and Solidification of "Peasant" Status

The population evacuated from the city would be resettled to the countryside to engage in agricultural production and fixed in the countryside through collectivization and the household registration system, turning an urban population into a rural population again, and ultimately achieving the goal of reducing the population of large cities.

How can urban residents who have already lived for a long time in the city be transformed once more into peasants? How can they be made to accept their peasant status and settle in a village, rather than re-entering the city? And how can those removed from the city be resettled? These were the most important questions that required resolution in Shanghai's relocation of urban populations elsewhere. The CCP and People's Government gave land to some "refugees" dispersed from the city back to the countryside through New Area Land Reform, which of course resulted in their transformation into "peasants." Some of the "natural-disaster victims" dispersed back to the countryside following the land reforms were assigned a small amount of the public land retained during the land reforms in their places of origin, while some received some land that local governments had taken from other peasants to settle Shanghai's dispersed population. These people, because they now had land, also automatically gained peasant status along with it.

In the "shrinking Shanghai" of 1955, there was no land for the vast majority of those who were dispersed back to the countryside from Shanghai. Local governments in Jiangsu Province and elsewhere took as their main principle "policy measures to actively stabilize matters and the spirit of carrying things out to the end, to ensure all needs of peasants returning to the countryside are met and that they may undertake agricultural production with an easy heart."[61] However, even the best of

---

[61] "Jiangsu CPC Provincial Party Committee Authorized Report to the Political and Legal Affairs Party Organization on Settlement of Peasants Dispersed by Shanghai Back to the Countryside" (August 16, 1955); "Plan for the Receiving and Settling of Shanghai's Peasants Taking Part in Agricultural Production (Draft)" (August 12, 1955), Jiangsu Provincial Archives, Su 3085 – long-term – 115. In order to speed up progress in mobilization, some work units and organizations provided financial assistance to dispersed personnel. The Shanghai Rickshaw and Three-Wheeled-Cart Management Office provided each worker returning to the countryside with an average of thirty yuan, and from June to December of 1955 the office dispersed a total of 15,000 people, providing 375,000 yuan in total. Shanghai Municipal People's Committee Transportation and Shipping Office, "Shanghai Transportation Bureau Report on the Socialist Transformation of Rickshaws and Three-Wheeled Carts"(1955), Shanghai Archives Hall, B 7-2-217, cited in Shen Feifei, Jianguo chuqi Shanghai renliche hangye yanjiu (1949–1956) (Research on the Shanghai Rickshaw Industry in the Early Years of the PRC (1949–1956)) (master's thesis, Shanghai Normal University, April 2012), 48.

intentions cannot produce something from nothing, and after the land reforms, Jiangsu, Anhui, Zhejiang, and other areas all faced severe hardships during Shanghai's period of "returning peasants to the countryside." In October of 1955, the CCP Central Committee issued its "Decision on the Agricultural Co-operation Issue," endorsing a faster pace of transition to agricultural co-operation and rapidly pushing the agricultural socialist transformation to its peak. Across the country, the vast majority of peasants in all areas joined "semi-socialist co-operatives" (*chujishe*) or "fully socialist co-operatives" (*gaojishe*). The establishment of a large number of fully socialist co-operatives made it possible for Jiangsu and other provinces to resettle personnel returning to the countryside, and most personnel returning to the countryside were assigned places in co-operatives, even the blind, orphans, widows, and the elderly all joined in eating from the same "big pot" of socialism.[62] Although some repeatedly "flowed back" to Shanghai, on the whole they were all once again mobilized to return to the countryside, and ultimately most of the personnel Shanghai dispersed to the countryside became peasants in fact as well as in name.

Of those who were relocated to Jiangxi from Shanghai in 1955 as "masses opening up land for agriculture," besides some who returned to Shanghai or relocated to other provinces, most rode the wave of the agricultural collectivization movement, joining local agricultural production co-operatives in Jiangxi and establishing themselves as peasants. The Shanghai Youth Volunteer Land Reclamation Team, a major project of the city's Communist Youth League (CYL) Committee, was personally designated a "communist youth co-operative" (*gongqingshe*) by Hu Yaobang in late 1955, and thereafter enjoyed a golden reputation in China's youth movement. Following this, the Jiangxi Provincial Party Committee, the Shanghai Communist Youth League Committee, and Jiangxi De'an County Party Committee provided a great amount of assistance for the development and existence of the Communist Youth Co-operative. In March of 1958, they established the state-run De'an CYL Comprehensive Agricultural Reclamation Site, and Shanghai's young land reclaimers became workers with steady incomes in a state-run agricultural production site.[63] Those from Shanghai who stayed in

---

[62] Jiangsu Provincial Civil Affairs Office Report, "Notice on the Settlement of Shanghai's Peasants Dispersed Back to the Countryside" (September 14, 1955), Jiangsu Provincial Archives, Su 3085 – long-term – 115.

[63] Communist Youth League Shanghai Municipal Party Committee, "Comments on the Current State and Future Work of Shanghai's Youth Volunteers Opening Up Land for Agriculture in De'an County, Jiangxi" (May 30, 1956), Shanghai Archives Hall, B 25-2-11; Min Xiaoyi, "A Brief Account of the Shanghai Youth Volunteer Land Reclamation

these agricultural production sites finally became agricultural workers from Jiangxi, realizing the transformation and reconstruction of their status.

As the CCP established its government in the early days, in order to stabilize the cities it received and subsequently relocated a large number of people to take part in opening up land for agricultural cultivation who were from groups deemed politically unreliable, including natural-disaster victims, disbanded soldiers, rich peasants or landlords on the run, unemployed vagrants, and prostitutes.[64] At the same time, in order to transform Shanghai from a "center of consumption" into a "base of production," it also continuously conducted large-scale dispersal of the city's "consumer population." Through the "refarmerization" of some of the city's population, the state was able to reduce the supply of grain, oil, and other provisions in the city; reduce the city's salary-related expenses; and in general be as frugal as possible with its financial resources and conserve them for use in the state's industrialization process. This "urban restriction" seems on the surface to be a path totally at odds with urban-ization, but in fact it was a strong measure employed by the CCP to push forward its urbanization, especially heavy urbanization, given its lack of resources and insufficient funds.

Team and Their Activities in the 1950s," *Academic Journal Shanghai Youth College of Management* 1 (2006).

[64] Ruan Qinghua, *Shanghai youmin gaizao yanjiu (1949–1958)* (Reforming Vagrants in Shanghai (1949–1958)) (Shanghai: Shanghai Lexicographical Publishing House, 2009), 141–142.

Part III

Legitimacy and Local Agencies

Introduction to Part III

In the third part of this volume, we would like to demonstrate that everyday realities in 1950s China could vary from the bigger revolutionary picture drawn by the Party for New China.

One important challenge in the consolidation phase of Chinese socialism was to create a strong unitary state, with its full complement of bureaucratic rules and hierarchical discipline. More important, however, was the Party's "close links with the masses" through the exercise of the mass line (from the people to the people). Having come to power in the first place based on its putative strong links with the masses, the party-state believed that the revolutionary consciousness among the people could be raised, the norms and principles of the revolution internalized, and participation in the revolution broadened if close links to the people were forged and maintained. There is ample evidence that the revolutionary party-state cared deeply about not only remaking society and the state but also engaging this remaking in ways that created and retained "close links to the masses." Such "close links" presumed that "the masses" would be receptive and responsive to the revolutionary message.

However, the Party's ideal of socialist unity was often challenged by the realities of everyday life in 1950s China that could vary from the unified socialist ideal. Rather, it was shaped by a wide range of local conditions, identities, and realities of the lives of the people. This part demonstrates that although many people in China proudly considered themselves socialist during the 1950s, the realities of ordinary daily life were not necessarily dominated by Marxist ideals.[1]

Zhang Jishun's chapter discusses the contradictions that could have occurred between the vision of revolutionary culture of the Chinese Communist Party and the individual difficulties within the processes of revolutionary transformations in 1950s China. She describes the multiple frustrations experienced by a revolutionary cultural worker in

---

[1] Covell F. Meyskens, "Rethinking the Political Economy of Development in Mao's China," *Positions: Asia Critique* 29, no. 4 (2021): 809–834.

the film industry, who repeatedly ran up against the relative recalcitrance of film stars as well as changes in Party line that went unreasonably soft on film stars who sidestepped being remade in a convincing manner.

This part also makes clear how complex China's revolutionary transformations were. For example, when we turn to Zhang Jishun's movie stars who transitioned from the old regime to the new, it may well be that they claimed to have reformed their hearts as they lined up for new roles and eventual membership in the Chinese Communist Party, but by what set of criteria could higher-ups truly know anything that subjective? Party cadre Li Ming witnessed the behavior of the film stars up close and personal and had good reason to doubt that the movie stars in question were doing much other than conforming to the revolution at a surface level. While she was overruled by higher-ups at the time, Li Ming's anxieties were grounded in a set of questions that would, over the long run, haunt the Party until the passing of Mao: if the legitimacy of the revolution and the CCP has to be ultimately internalized in individuals, how can one tell if it has been? How much revolution is enough revolution? What if individuals are only adapting the forms of the revolution – its new vocabularies and institutions – to pursue agendas that are, after all, self-interested rather than selfless, and not genuinely remaking themselves? And who was the final arbiter of such subjective questions?

Aminda Smith's and Jing Wenyu's chapters demonstrate how the party-state sought to create institutional forms of responsiveness to "the masses." First was by opening channels of communication through letters and visits (*xinfang*) – or direct forms of petition. Direct petitioning had featured in late imperial China and through the investigation and settling of claims against putatively abusive Party bosses, and while the blizzard of letters and visits that complained about everything from local cadre abuse of power to the state of the public toilets was such that backlogs and lack of response were inevitable, the promise of responsiveness as a proper part of the mass line and the revolution remained. In other circumstances, interested parties availed themselves of the form of letters and visits to pursue private complaints, using new forms and new vocabularies to make claims on the revolutionary state. Furthermore, Smith demonstrates how communal life could differ from the bigger revolutionary picture of the Party – people's daily and personal problems such as public hygiene, education, and working conditions very often were much more important for them than their enthusiasm for socialist unity.

Jing Wenyu's chapter shows another aspect of the realities of 1950s China: the newly established campaign-style governance not only led to mass mobilization and legitimacy building, but also created local spaces to exploit the new socialist system's weaknesses. At the local level, it also offered cadres new opportunities to abuse their position for personal factional gain. In this respect, Jing demonstrates how resentful villagers were more than astute in accessing the legal institutions of the state through formal, if also questionable, charges of rape and illegal landlord reconfiscation of land to pursue local cadres who had either used their preferential access to benefit themselves and their families or flouted long-held norms about village subsistence through the vigorous pursuit of GLF policies. Whether it was a committed cadre attempting to garner genuinely revolutionary responsiveness from the only modestly reformed film stars she was attempting to inculcate, or everyday people using a channel opened up by the mass line to make demands on the state, or disgruntled villagers resorting to the formal mechanism of legal investigation of unpopular cadres, both the party-state and the population over which it held formal authority were engaged in a dance for responsiveness. The Party was determined to inscribe the revolution and its values onto the hearts and minds of individuals: individuals wished to protect themselves and/or pursue their own interests under the new rubric of the revolution and "New China." In Xi's China, the CCP needs to revive sources of legitimacy. In that sense, we can observe a political rectification for cadres. They must demonstrate morality and integrity in order to improve the CCP's level of popular support.[2] If we draw a comparison between realities in 1950s China and today, we'll see that the challenge to stamp out spaces to exploit the socialist system has not diminished.

What this part makes clear is that in such different realms as the Shanghai film industry, grumbles about the state of public toilets, and investigations into local cadre abuses, individuals had substantial latitude for agency as they adapted to new revolutionary vocabularies, new revolutionary norms, and new revolutionary institutions. Thus old-school film stars quickly learned "how to write self-criticisms, historical autobiographies, and essays of criticism, and the correct formats for taking a political stance" (Zhang). The "rhetoric of the mass line established letters and visits as a legitimate site for making claims on the state and encouraged ordinary people to use it" (Smith).

---

[2] See Aleksandra Kubat, "Morality as Legitimacy under Xi Jinping: The Political Functionality of Traditional Culture for the Chinese Communist Party," *Journal of Current Chinese Affairs* 47, no. 3 (2018): 47–86.

8   Anxiety in the Revolutionary Turn
Shanghai Film Personnel in the 1950s

Zhang Jishun

Introduction

After the establishment of CCP mainstream ideology in Yan'an, the colonial commercial metropolis was often rejected, while a metropolitan mass culture and cultured urbanites often became the targets of criticism. Mao Zedong, in his speeches at the Yan'an Forum on Literature and Art (hereafter the Yan'an Forum) used the term "garrets of Shanghai" to describe such cultured urbanites' natural home,[1] warning that they must, through a long period of transformation, eliminate "the petty bourgeois kingdom in their innermost souls" before they would be able to truly solve the "core issue of serving the workers, peasants, and soldiers."[2] The Yan'an Forum presented the goals and the vision of CCP revolutionary culture and described the decommercialization of urban culture and the creation of people of a new culture, which would become two intimately related parts of the revolutionary agenda after the CCP assumed power. The film industry was the first priority, and it not only was subsumed into the Party-controlled planning system, but also saw the "revolutioniza-tion" of film stars, as individuals and representatives, which was tightly bound up with the plan for creating the nation and its socialist culture.

This chapter focuses on the story of one individual, the actress Li Ming,[3] who started out as a military arts soldier in the New Fourth Army, in order to examine the different ways in which revolutionary actors at the Shanghai Film Studio and film stars from the prerevolu-tionary era participated in the transformation to a revolutionary culture in

---

[1] Most residences in Shanghai had *tingzijian* (garrets or pergolas), and were narrow, with low square footage. Because the housing market in Shanghai was tight, these were usually rented out at low rates and were often the homes of the cultured.

[2] Mao Zedong, "Talks at the Yan'an Forum on Literature and Art," May 2, 1942, in *Mao Zedong xuanji: Di san juan* (Selected Works of Mao Zedong, vol. 3) (Beijing: People's Publishing House, 1991), 857.

[3] Li Ming was born in November 1923 in Taizhou, Jiangsu Province. In 1940, she joined the New Fourth Army's Northern Jiangsu Command Headquarters Field Service, which was later transformed into a military arts troupe. In November 1949, she joined the Shanghai Film Studio as an actress, retiring in 1987 and passing away in Shanghai in 2011.

the 1950s. As a newcomer to film, with the dual identity of actress and Party cadre, Li Ming was often unable to reconcile her revolutionary ideals with her new career. Challenges to her identity as a Party cadre came not only from the older generation of film stars but even more so from the Party to which she was so loyal. Li Ming's experiences provide a new way to understand the revolutionary agenda through an examination of the Party, the celebrities, and the complex relationship among them from the perspective of one of "the Party's own."

The fates of those in film during the Mao era have received considerable attention in English-language scholarship, but the focus has largely been on artists from the previous privately operated era and their tragic ends. The main objects of analysis and exploration have been their works in film – studies have taken their film texts as a kind of cultural representation to reveal the complex political operations and social transformations behind them, as in Paul Pickowicz's research on the "complicit" Zheng Junli and on the sacrificial lamb Shi Hui,[4] or as in Wang Zhuoyi's key case study of *Song Jingshi*,[5] which analyzes how private-sector artists participated in the various conflicts and compromises on the behind-the-scenes agenda.[6] In the picture presented in the film text, the daily politics of the film studio are still a fuzzy zone, and grassroots Party members and cadres are abstract "Party agents." My focus, in contrast, is not on the film personnel as they appear in the film texts, but rather as they existed in the power structure and the landscape of "everyday politics." Instead of using the film text as an analytical tool, I return to research on revolutionary history through individual materials and official files. In this way, this chapter constitutes research on micro-politics during the transformation of urban culture in the 1950s as well as an exploration into the history of mentalities in the changing revolutionary culture.

Personal family materials are among the important historical sources used for this study. As the daughter-in-law of Li Ming, an entirely chance opportunity led me to discover a trove of "secrets" that Li Ming had not divulged to her family during her lifetime, including confessions and accusations from the Cultural Revolution period as well as copies from individual dossiers. These materials substantiated or made sense of some

---

[4] Paul G. Pickowicz, "Zheng Junli, Complicity and the Cultural History of Socialist China, 1949–1976," *China Quarterly* 188 (December 2006): 1048–1069; Paul Pickowicz, "Acting Like Revolutionaries: Shi Hui, the Wenhua Studio, and Private-Sector Filmmaking, 1949–1952," in *China on Film, A Century of Exploration, Confrontation, and Controversy* (Lanham, MD: Rowman & Littlefield, 2012), 157–212.
[5] *Song Jingshi*, dir. Zheng Junli, 1955.
[6] Wang Zhuoyi, "From the Life of Wu Xun to the Career of Song Jingshi: Crisis and Adaptation of the Private Studio Film-Making Legacy, 1951–1956," *Journal of Chinese Cinemas* 5, no. 1 (2011): 13–29.

of the important details in her self-published collected works.[7] Official files and published works, such as the autobiography of Zhao Dan, are also among the essential sources used in this study. I spoke multiple times with family members of several individuals who worked at the Shanghai Film Studio about their memories and understandings of their parents, and relatives of that generation encouraged me to see things from different points of view. I strove to maintain both distance and empathy with all kinds of sources and records in order to bring together the historical facts and logic in my analysis.

Entrants

As the CCP military occupied the city, the plan to establish "absolutely dominant" state-run film production studios under the leadership of the Party was enacted. One important measure in this plan was to bring in a group of revolutionary literature and art workers from all the field armies and the liberated regions in order to destroy the monopoly of the older generation of filmmakers and to establish a new order in the film industry.

In May 1949, the Third Field Army of the People's Liberation Army took over control of Shanghai, and Li Ming entered the city with the army just as the Shanghai Film Studio was recruiting new talent. As "wartime literature and arts soldiers," Li Ming and her husband Tian Ran were both selected as actors.[8] In the early 1950s, cadres from the East China Military Region and the liberated regions were successively reassigned to the studio, forming a "team of revolutionary film personnel" at the Shanghai Film Studio. From this team, a new community was formed constituting the first group of filmmakers, including actor Bai Yang and director Tang Xiaodan, who were from the previous era but had been selected by the state-run studio.

As a newcomer to film, Li Ming was extremely lucky. In one of the first films in which she appeared with the Shanghai Film Studio, *Tuanjie qilai dao mingtian* (Unite Together toward Tomorrow),[9] she played a dancer who worked in a textile factory, while Bai Yang played the lead actress. Having joined the army at the age of seventeen and entered the Party at the age of nineteen, Li Ming had a political advantage that gave her important revolutionary capital in her status as an actress. The Party

---

[7] Li Ming, *Jinsheng wuhui: Li Ming shiwen ji* (No Regrets in This Life: Collected Poetry and Writings of Li Ming) (Shanghai: self-published, 2004).

[8] Tian Ran (1920–2011) joined the New Fourth Army Military Arts Troupe in 1941 and the Shanghai Film Studio in early 1950, where he worked as an actor, assistant director, and director.

[9] *Tuanjie qilai dao mingtian*, dir. Zhao Ming, 1951.

group of the Shanghai Film Studio had always placed grassroots, frontline "Party authority" in the hands of such revolutionary filmmakers, putting them in charge of all kinds of internal Party jobs. Starting in 1952, Li Ming thus served as Party branch secretary for almost all of the films for which she was part of the production group, whether she had the lead or appeared in a nameless role.[10]

However, both the established personnel and the new entrants in the studio were all extremely sensitive to how the leadership of the Party would be carried out at the grassroots level. Even though "director-centered" filmmaking was severely criticized during the Anti-Rightist campaign, at the production site it remained unclear whether, metaphorically speaking, the Party commanded the gun – as Mao Zedong had famously declared – or the gun commanded the Party.

The shooting of a 1953 narrative film reflecting on life on the frontier gave Li Ming her first taste of being "Party branch secretary." Although she did not appear on-screen very much, after being appointed Party branch secretary for the production crew she led the troupe of several dozen to the Tibetan plateau in Qinghai province to shoot on location. After living there for a time, several of the old-guard film personnel could not stand it any longer and began "fighting to return to Shanghai." Li Ming used her experience from working on base, first "individually doing thought work" to persuade them, and then, when that failed, "holding a public criticism session." Although this settled matters, those who were the objects of criticism were very unhappy and they therefore developed an enduring dislike of her.[11]

There are many such recollections. Li Ming had complex feelings about serving as both an actress and a Party branch secretary. She once wrote,

At the deepest level, I don't want to do the work of a Party branch secretary.
    It's difficult to do, and you can't please people no matter how hard you try. It'd be better just to do creative work, to have fun, and to become famous. But when the Party committee assigned me this task, I also felt it was expressing confidence in my political abilities. I couldn't refuse to take on the responsibility, and in a small way it's nice to be the boss.[12]

Despite these mixed feelings, the conflicted Li Ming still had a strong "organizational awareness," and quite proactively she reported to her

[10] Li Ming, "CCP Party Member Registration Form (draft)," May 1, 1985, in Li Ming's personal collection.
[11] Li Ming, *Jinsheng wuhui*, 27.
[12] Li Ming, "Explanation of Crimes during the Seventeen Years of Maintaining the Black Line in Literary and Art Work," December 6, 1968, in Li Ming's files (returned to Li Ming after the Cultural Revolution).

superiors on the various doings of her production group and acting troupe, keeping a particularly watchful eye on the film stars from the previous era. Much of this is recorded in her Cultural Revolution confessions.[13] Not all of Li Ming's "little reports" drew the attention of the studio leaders, but she still clung to the belief that it was her duty as a revolutionary actress and as an expression of her loyalty to the Party, such that the strongest impression she left on later generations at the Shanghai Film Studio was that "Auntie Li Ming was very revolutionary" and "very leftist." In her later years, she admitted, "I had been in the army since I was a child and I listened to the Party. I admired Chairman Mao in a religious way, blindly following him and following the leftist line just as closely."[14]

Political Competition in the New Work Environment

From the establishment of the Shanghai Film Studio to just before the Hundred Flowers movement, the studio produced thirty-four narrative films over a period of five years. Based on records that state that 541 creative artistic personnel were employed in the studio in 1956, this comes out to 0.06 films per person, a shockingly low production rate.[15] With the Party managing and controlling all stages of the entire film production process, not only was the production period extended but it also became difficult to predict the future of a film. This was especially true given Mao Zedong's personal criticism of the film *Wu Xun zhuan* (The Life of Wu Xun) in September 1951 and the nationwide literature and arts rectification campaign in 1952.[16] The leftist Shanghai film personnel became caught up in a political maelstrom, facing difficulties of having "no films to shoot." The issue of how to shoot "films of the workers, peasants, and soldiers" as required by "The Speeches" presented new difficulties on top of existing ones.

It was the artists who formerly worked for the privately run studios who felt the danger most keenly. They urgently sought to work for state-run studios and change their "second-class-citizen status."[17] In early 1953, after they were incorporated into the Shanghai Film Studio, though they received the personnel status of "state cadres" and enjoyed the corresponding "state

---

[13] Ibid.   [14] Li Ming, *Jinsheng wuhui*, 167.
[15] *Shanghai dianying zhipian chang gongzi gaige shishi jihua* (Salary Reform Implementation Plan of the Shanghai Film Studio (Draft)), 1956, in Shanghai Municipal Archives (SMA), B 177-1-88.
[16] *Wu Xun zhuan*, dir. Sun Yu, 1951.
[17] Xia Yan to Zhou Yang, August 25, 1952, personal collection.

salary" benefits, their political status had not changed.[18] Zhao Dan, the major film star who played Wu Xun, once lamented,

> When I went out, people who had seen me on-screen would point and poke at me behind my back, saying, "Look at Wu Xun!" In the studio's internal small group, some individuals proposed investigating my history, which put me in an even more difficult position, so I said, "Once the matter becomes political, it can't be undone. When your political life is over, your artistic life dies along with it!"[19]

The lack of opportunities to shoot films and the difficulties of meeting the "worker, peasant, and soldier" standard also reflected the importance of one's "political life." Stars worked hard to adapt to the new everyday political life in which the name of the game was "Studying hard every day, and only then will you get paid." They studied how to write self-criticisms, historical autobiographies, and essays of criticism, and the correct formats for taking a political stance. Even film reviews were full of political terms rather than of persuasive evaluations.[20] The most idealistic action at the time was to request to join the Communist Party. By 1955, over forty of the old-guard film personnel had put forward applications to join the Party.[21]

Although Li Ming had a sense of political superiority, as a new female actress nearing her thirties it was cruelly true that there were few opportunities for her – her revolutionary advantage did not weigh heavily in such decisions. In 1954, Li Ming encountered a setback when she was dropped from playing the female lead in *Dujiang zhencha ji* (Reconnaissance across the Yangzi River),[22] missing out on her first chance to play a leading role. But, luckily, in 1955 she performed the role of Fanyi in Cao Yu's famous play *Leiyu* (Thunderstorm) when it was put on by the Shanghai Film Actors' Theater Company. Recovering from her initial setback, Li Ming went on to star, or appear, in six successive films, specializing in portraying Communist Party members. The key figure in Li Ming's escape from danger was a man who himself was experiencing adversity: Zhao Dan, who at the time was directing. Li Ming was totally won over by this talented film star, and she would forever remember his support and confidence in her.[23] Personal experience

---

[18] SMA, B 177-1-88.
[19] Zhao Dan , "Confessions of Crimes after Liberation," June 13, 1973, in *Zhao Dan zishu* (Autobiography of Zhao Dan), ed. Li Hui (Zhengzhou: Elephant Press, 2003), 169.
[20] Tang Xiaodan's diary, January 10 and March 14, 1950, in *Chenmo shi jin: Tang Xiaodan riji* (Silence Is Golden: Tang Xiaodan's Diary), comp. Lan Weijie (Beijing: Commercial Press, 2016), 5, 14.
[21] Lin Lin (Party secretary of the Shanghai Film Studio Committee), "Draft of Speech Given at the Intellectual Work Conference of the Shanghai Municipal Party Committee," February 24, 1956, in SMA, A 22-1-275.
[22] *Dujiang zhencha ji*, dir. Tang Xiaodan, 1954.   [23] Li Ming, *Jinsheng wuhui*, 178, 194.

taught her that the Shanghai Film Studio would not be able to produce good films without the help of those stars from the previous era.

However, at the workplace and in everyday life, Li Ming was not at all complimentary of her celebrity colleagues. She did not approve of their "old-celebrity" style or their messy personal lives, and she did not understand why, despite the large socialist faction at the Shanghai Film Studio, things still proceeded in "the old film studio way whereby the big stars called all the shots," and even studio leaders were very cautious and tiptoed around these all-powerful actors.[24]

Li Ming was not the only person to feel this way. At the Shanghai Film Studio, everyone had opinions about how the Party organization had "no rule over the studio." Everyone thought that prior to 1953, ideological reform work had actually been "somewhat rough," and afterwards the studio was mainly "right-leaning and conservative, and it had abandoned the Party leadership."[25] But "all-powerful actors" were also the targets of many Party members. Some even complained that the "united front" had become a shield that they used to deflect criticism, and they could even go over the heads of the Party organization "in a flash 'uniting' with the mayor or the bureau head."[26]

Li Ming in particular could not imagine that a star could become "the Party's own person" without a painful transformation. In her opinion, those people did not meet the standards of Communist Party members. In the seventeen years before the Cultural Revolution, she did not introduce a single member of the old guard to join the Party.[27] "Closed-doorism" was extremely widespread among Party members at the Shanghai Film Studio, and the film personnel who sought to enter the Party were cut off at the first pass. On numerous times, deputy minister of culture Xia Yan demanded that the studio Party secretary actively resolve the issue of the most famous actors, such as Bai Yang, joining the Party, but many Party members said, "The development of Party members must be done in accordance with Party standards."[28] As a result, as of 1955, only four members of the old guard had joined the CCP.[29] Party members openly announced that this was a sign of strict adherence to Party

---

[24] Ibid., 27.
[25] Shanghai Film Studio, "Investigative Report on the State of Intellectuals," in "Compilation of the Shanghai Municipal Party Committee's Investigative Reports on Intellectuals," December 6, 1955, in SMA, A 22-1-282.
[26] Ibid.
[27] Li Ming, "On the Revisionist Party-Building Line (Shanghai Film Studio Actors) Troupe" (confession materials), January 1, 1970 (returned to Li Ming after the Cultural Revolution).
[28] SMA, A 22-1-282.   [29] SMA, A 22-1-275.

principles and maintenance of the purity of the organization. However, they could not predict how swiftly the Party was about to change.

Fortune and Fate

Starting in the second half of 1955, the CCP's more relaxed policy toward intellectuals and the Hundred Flowers movement were rolled out, and the Shanghai film industry began to recover. Film production became more active, and opportunities for celebrities to appear on the silver screen grew as well. For example, the film star Shangguan Yunzhu, who specialized in playing the role of a big-city girl, successfully transitioned into playing a head nurse in a film about a CCP unit fighting against the Japanese Army.[30] Zhao Dan of *Wu Xun zhuan* played the lead in two back-to-back films within a year. At the beginning of 1956, over ten directors and actors from the Shanghai Film Studio made it onto the "National List of Notable Artists," and as "First-Level Intellectuals" they received the best political and everyday treatment.[31]

There was also a sudden change of fortunes on the issue of celebrities joining the Party. In March 1955, a CCP document entitled "Actively Accept High-Level Intellectuals to Join the Party" was distributed,[32] and according to the unified approach in the work of the central Party intellectuals, "closed-door-ism" and "sectarianism" within the Party were henceforth considered incorrect tendencies that required thorough inspection and correction. The Shanghai Film Studio began to accept Party members more quickly, and several famous directors and actors joined the Party. A new protocol for joining the Party was implemented from above, and the admission of famous artists into the Party was determined directly by the Shanghai Municipal Party Committee. The Party secretary of the studio would make the introduction, and acceptance by grassroots Party members was only a formality. Opposition and doubts were often invalid, and they were often criticized.

---

[30] Female lead in the film *Nandao fengyun* (Storm on the Southern Island) (Bai Chen, 1956).

[31] "National List of Notable Experts in the Cultural and Educational System under the Central Administration," original undated, in SMA A22-1-286; Intellectual Issues Office of the Shanghai Municipal Committee, "Explanation of the Standards for High-Level Intellectuals," "List of Shanghai High-Level Intellectuals and the First Batch of Artists," February 23, 1956, in SMA, A22-1-285.

[32] CCP Party Central Committee, "Telegram in Reply to the Shanghai Bureau on the Issue of the Acceptance of High-Level Intellectuals into the Party," March 31, 1955, in CCP Central Committee Party Literature Research Center, ed., *Jianguo yilai zhongyao wenxian xuanbian, di liu ce* (Selected Important Documents from after the Founding of the Nation, vol. 6) (Beijing: Central Party Literature Press, 1993), 137.

Like many Party members, Li Ming felt helpless and depressed about these matters. She once wrote,

When stars join the Party, they become "all-powerful," and Party members don't even have the right to know what's going on. Take Bai Yang, for example – although studio leaders knew she didn't often come to the studio, she remained apart from the masses, and she had a bad influence on Party members and the masses, they still put pressure on Party members to accept her. The municipal Party committee has already said, "You must all abandon sectarianism. If you don't help them, the municipal Party committee will."

One higher-level Party secretary and studio leader personally held a branch meeting to introduce her, and before and during the meeting, he praised her for historically following the leftist movement in film and refusing to act in bad productions. Although the Party branch meeting accepted Bai Yang into the Party, she was still often away and very seldom participated in organizational life. Li Ming once raised this issue to the studio Party secretary, and she was required, in turn, to do persuasion work among the masses. Most Party members opposed her, saying that she was a united-front personage in the Party.[33]

The most authoritative power behind the change in the stars' fates came from Mao Zedong. Beginning in 1956, Mao met many Shanghai Film Studio stars, with Shangguan Yunzhu attracting special attention. Her image as a Party member on the silver screen could not erase the ceaseless scandals in her private life, especially the title of a "member of a corrupt family" that she had received during the "Three Antis" campaign of 1952, when her husband was falsely accused of being corrupt. Although she quickly divorced her husband, her previous extramarital affairs were exposed, and she was subject to severe criticism from the organization. According to the internal political line, she was a "backward element."[34]

In early 1956, Mao Zedong invited several famous people from Shanghai to dine and talk, and unexpectedly Shangguan Yunzhu was among them. This news spread quickly through the studio and many people congratulated her, but there were also many detractors. This was not only true of prejudiced Party members – even a few of the old-guard film stars raised objections to the studio leaders: "Why should they arrange for such a backwards element to meet the Great Leader?"[35] The studio Party committee felt this was a thorny issue, but reported to the municipal Party committee, "Our studio has not repented its

---

[33] Li Ming, "On the Revisionist Party-Building Line (Shanghai Film Studio Actors) Troupe."
[34] SMA, A 22-1-275.   [35] Ibid.

sectarian tendencies because of Chairman Mao's personal work with Shangguan Yunzhu; on the contrary, such tendencies have spread unchecked." We must struggle against such this kind of "incorrect tendency," "taking Shangguan Yunzhu as a typical example, educating our entire party and all of our cadres through our efforts with and education of her."[36] Shangguan Yunzhu's fate had totally turned around, as she was transformed overnight from a "backwards element" into a "model for education."

In March 1957, even more important news came from Beijing. Zhao Dan and actors Shi Hui and Wu Yin, as well as director Wu Yonggang, had just been invited as non-Party members to participate in the CCP State Propaganda Work Conference. In the evening of March 8, during a literature and arts discussion that took place in Zhongnanhai, Mao Zedong encouraged the film industry to catch up with Japan in terms of the number of narrative films put out annually, saying, "Putting out three times as many would be best." Zhao Dan then heard Mao Zedong directly calling out his name:

Zhao Dan! Sun Yu didn't do a good job of arranging things, huh? You've worked with him. Once things are arranged, things will be better. The film you worked on together, *Wu Xun zhuan*, was criticized, but that's nothing. If a film isn't written well, just write another, and sooner or later you'll finish the task.[37]

With this encouragement from the Great Leader, *Wu Xun* no longer hung from his neck like an albatross, and joining the Party, which had been his wish for a long time, looked like it might come to pass. During the propaganda work conference, Shi Ximin, who led the group from Shanghai and was director of propaganda in the municipal Party committee, had been continuously pointing out Zhao Dan's faults at critical moments, creating distance between himself and the other three.[38] One month after his return from Beijing, Zhao Dan was accepted as a probationary Party member in the Party organization of the Shanghai Film Studio.

From then on, "received by Chairman Mao" became a red line in the politics of the Shanghai Film Studio Party Committee. During the Anti-Rightist campaign, the branch of the China Democratic League at the Shanghai Film Studio had nine members who were listed as rightists,

---

[36] Ibid.
[37] CCP Central Committee Party Literature Research Center, *Mao Zedong nianpu 1949–1976, di san juan* (Chronicle of Mao Zedong 1949–1976, vol. 3) (Beijing: Central Party Literature Press, 2013), 102.
[38] Zhao Dan , "Addition to My Confessions of Crimes after Liberation – The Anti-Rightist Campaign in 1957," August 11, 1969, in *Zhao Dan zishu*, 190–192.

while fellow league members director Ying Yunwei and Shangguan Yunzhu, having been received by Mao Zedong, managed to escape the fallout. Although Shangguan Yunzhu had been internally labeled a rightist, she ultimately got off as an individual who had "serious rightist thought errors." In April 1959, Mao Zedong once again personally invited Shangguan Yunzhu to dine, with Jiang Qing accompanying them.[39] She was received by Mao seven times in total, a rarity even among the stars at the Shanghai Film Studio.

The Difficulties of Leaving

During the Anti-Rightist campaign, over forty film personnel were labeled rightists, with several well-known film stars among them. The most unfortunate was Shi Hui, who, after being struggled against, ended his life by jumping into the sea. The stars who escaped such a fate all left the studio for the countryside to better understand the feelings of the workers and peasants through experience, and to transform themselves. Their public expressions of their political stances became increasingly radical, and they expressed a desire to "completely endorse the Anti-Rightist campaign," and some even thought that "we have been too lenient with the rightists."[40] Li Ming's stance fluctuated somewhat. On the one hand she continued to report on "anti-Party speech" to the Party committee,[41] and on the other hand she spoke out on behalf of several actors, explaining that they were mainly "complaining" of having "no films to shoot" and their speech was not serious enough to count as "anti-Party" or "anti-socialist".[42]

During the GLF, Li Ming had even more trouble bridging the gap between the left and the right. Spurred on by the Great Leader's call to produce "300 films a year," the film industry was under pressure to report incredible progress in production, and Li Ming did not want to be left behind. She dove into the shooting of art-house documentaries, both writing and starring in *Tieshu kaihua* (The Iron Tree Blooms),[43] which depicted a female worker's great technological innovations. Like others of this genre, this film had virtually no audience, and in 1962 the Ministry of Culture ordered that it no longer be screened, giving the reason that such

---

[39] Personal communication with Shangguan Yunzhu's son, Ran Wei, April 8, 2019.
[40] Organized by the Propaganda Department Office of the Shanghai Municipal Party Committee, "Reflections Following the Forum on Literature and Art Held by Premier Zhou in This City," January 2, 1958, in SMA, A 22-2-554.
[41] Li Ming, "On the Revisionist Party-Building Line (Shanghai Film Studio Actors) Troupe."
[42] Li Ming, *Jinsheng wuhui*, 26.   [43] *Tieshu kaihua*, dir. Gao Heng, 1958.

films "have wrong tendencies such as excessive propaganda, communist wind, and a lack of scientific spirit based on real conditions."[44] In addition, a number of recently released and well-received films were suddenly criticized by the Ministry of Culture. These included films in which Li Ming had acted, such as *Qing chang yi shen* (Lasting Love and Deep Friendship) and *Fenghuang zhi ge* (Song of the Phoenix) as well as her husband's directorial debut, the comedy *Xingfu* (Happiness).[45] What especially troubled Li Ming was that *Fenghuang zhi ge* was the story of a *tongyangxi*, a girl raised to be the wife of a son in another family in the "old society," but who grew up to become a female cadre in the "new society." Even this was labeled a problem film. The criticism from Zhou Enlai that was spread within the studio was that this film "did not reflect the requirements of the times, with peasant landlords and rich peasants who were still so savage even after the corporatization of agriculture. The film was thought to represent anti-feudalist individualism."[46]

In early 1959, among over 270 personnel, Li Ming and her husband Tian Ran were named by the organization to assist in the establishment of film production studios in other provinces, and they were relocated to Fujian. This was a time during the Great Leap Forward when different areas throughout the country were caught up in a mad push to establish narrative-film studios. In March, just after Li Ming and her entire family had settled in Fuzhou, the Ministry of Culture ordered that all studios currently being built "take decisive measures to properly step away from the project."[47] In November, with the approval of the Propaganda Department of the Shanghai Municipal Committee, Shanghai Film Studio began recalling creative personnel who in waves had been assisting operations in Fujian.[48] In May 1961, Li Ming and her husband officially returned to the Shanghai Film Studio. During the time they had worked in Fujian, Li Ming had been the subject of criticism from the organization

---

[44] Ministry of Culture, "Notice on Halting the Distribution of Films That Violate the Spirit of Current Policies," September 8, 1962, in Wu Di, ed., *Zhongguo dianying yanjiu ziliao, 1949–1979 (zhong)* (Chinese Cinema Research Materials, 1949–1979 (vol. 2)) (Beijing: Culture and Art Publishing House, 2006), 412–413.

[45] *Qing chang yi shen*, dir. Xu Changlin, 1957. *Fenghuang zhi ge*, dir. Zhao Ming, 1957. *Xingfu*, dir. Tao Ran and Fu Chaowu, 1957.

[46] Zhou Enlai, "Minutes of Talks at the Symposium of Directors of Film Studios," April 18, 1958, Ministry of Chang Chun Film Studio, in Wu Di, *Zhongguo dianying yanjiu ziliao, 1949–1979 (zhong)*, 185.

[47] Ministry of Culture, "Report to the Central Government regarding the Guidelines for the Construction of Film Studios in Various Regions," March 27, 1959, Ministry of Culture Files, in Wu Di, *Zhongguo dianying yanjiu ziliao, 1949–1979 (zhong)*, 260.

[48] Municipal Film Bureau to the Propaganda Department of the Municipal Party Committee, "About How Our Bureau Supported Fujian Personnel to Deal with Problems," November 7, 1959, in SMA, A 22-1-448.

and the masses for some of her "rightist-leaning" remarks, such as, "Is the rush to build film studios everywhere an instance of overexcitement?" and "Has moving toward communism been raised too early?"[49] These remarks were not corrected until her return to the Shanghai Film Studio.

Left, right, start, stop – amidst this wavering turmoil, Li Ming said goodbye to the Shanghai Film Studio of the 1950s. By this time, most of the actors from the liberated regions had taken up different work or had left in succession. There were few actresses who had begun as revolutionary literature and arts soldiers and had remained at the Shanghai Film Studio.

Conclusion

From her arrival to her exit, Li Ming's initial ten years in the film industry were suffused with revolutionary dilemmas. As one of "the Party's own," Li Ming consciously kept a distance from her film star colleagues. She was suspicious of them to the point of doubting their expressions of loyalty to the Party. Although she accepted that film could not be separated from the creations of the old film stars, and that they could be used by the Party, they were, at best, "targets of the united front" and could not become "the Party's own." As a Party cadre, Li Ming faithfully carried out the tasks assigned to her by the organization, but she also found it difficult to reconcile her dual roles as actress and cadre, a challenge that left her with many complaints. Most importantly, she could not determine what the Party truly wanted from her – be a revolutionary actress or a Party member?

As a newcomer, Li Ming had no way of predicting that the New China cultural transformation plan, which had been kick-started and anticipated by the film industry, had only just begun, or that the value of the revolution was far greater than the meaning of construction, so this was only the beginning of a long series of revolutionary dilemmas that she would face.

The early 1960s, when Li Ming returned to the Shanghai Film Studio, was a golden period for the old film stars. In the big movie theaters across the country, giant photographs of twenty-two "People's Actors of the New China" were displayed, and the seven from the Shanghai Film Studio were all stars from the previous era. This, however, was but a short-lived moment. From the end of 1963 to 1964, Mao Zedong began a comprehensive attack on literature and art, and the rectification

---

[49] Li Ming, "Explanation of Crimes during the Seventeen Years of Maintaining the Black Line in Literary and Art Work."

campaign in these spheres became ever more feverish. The "honeymoon period" for the Party and the stars was over.

As the film stars were pushed closer and closer to the abyss that was the Cultural Revolution, the darkest hour in Li Ming's revolutionary life was about to begin. Not long after the beginning of the Cultural Revolution, Li Ming's experience was not much different from that of the celebrities, except that she did not go to jail and she was accused of a different "crime" – labeled a "traitor to the Party." This is another shocking story, but it remains rooted in the Party, the adored leader, and the Communist revolution to which this Communist Party member had remained faithful all her life.

9   Letters from the People

The Masses and the Mass Line in 1950s China

Aminda M. Smith

In February 1954, a letter sent from the city of Kaifeng and addressed to "Chairman Mao Zedong" arrived at the Party Central offices in Beijing. The letter writer, Wang P, reported that he had written to his city government several times but had "never received a satisfactory response" to a problem that was "truly threatening the health of the people in the Xinmenguan neighborhood." There was no public bathroom near Xinmenguan, explained Wang, who noted that as a result some people were collecting urine and excrement in receptacles and then emptying those receptacles into the street. Others were making the long walk to the nearest restroom, but as that facility was serving the residents in its own neighborhood *and* the residents of Xinmenguan, there was "always a line," and "quarrels were common." Furthermore, Wang wrote, "cleaning and repair teams can't keep up, and the bathroom is always dirty, with broken lights." Wang implored the head of state, "Dearest Chairman, won't you come here yourself, or send someone else, to investigate and ensure that the Kaifeng Municipal Government serves the people" by "fixing this unsafe and unhygienic situation?"[1]

Wang P probably knew that people had been taking their concerns directly to the highest Chinese authorities for hundreds, maybe thousands, of years.[2] There is a great deal of scholarly work tracing the origins and development of China's "petition system" and its important role in mediating disputes, monitoring public sentiment, and serving as a "safety valve" for dissent and social unrest.[3] The long cultural (and practical) history of

---

[1] Original letter consulted in Huang X's personal collection. As some of the documents referenced in this chapter contain sensitive material, I have changed and/or abbreviated names and sometimes altered identifying personal and place information if doing so did not affect the analysis. I have not changed the names of people whose stories, as referenced here, were also publicized in the PRC (such as Zhang Shunyou).

[2] Qiang Fang, *Chinese Complaint Systems: Natural Resistance* (New York: Routledge, 2013).

[3] Kevin O'Brien and Li Lianjiang, *Rightful Resistance in Rural China* (Cambridge: Cambridge University Press, 2006); Kevin O'Brien, "Rightful Resistance," *World Politics* 49, no. 1 (October 1996): 31–55; Li Lianjiang, "Political Trust and Petitioning in the Chinese Countryside," *Comparative Politics* 40, no. 2 (January 2008): 209–226; Qin

petitioning in China has led most anglophone scholars to portray it as a somewhat transhistorical phenomenon, which endured after the establishment of the People's Republic of China (PRC) and therefore marks a continuity between the Chinese Communist Party (CCP) and their many predecessors.[4] Some Chinese scholars concur that the contemporary institution is the PRC version of a long-standing tradition, but they often argue that within the CCP's system of "letters and visits" were revolutionary innovations which meant that the new system was only very tangentially connected to previous practices.[5] While the latter view certainly overstates the discontinuity, the former view may not sufficiently capture the deep ways in which Maoist political culture reshaped what it meant to be a member of the people in the People's Republic.

Although the PRC term *xinfang* is often rendered, somewhat reductively, as "petition," its more literal translation, "letters and visits" (*xin* and *fang*) better reflects the CCP's claim that their conversations with the masses would be more expansive and egalitarian than those of any earlier regime. Pre-PRC institutions tended to reserve petitioning (often by decree) for reporting official corruption, appealing injustices, and/or airing grievances that had great social or legal import. Of course, people had long used capital appeals and other avenues to take all manner of concerns to the state, but the diversity of individual petitions notwithstanding, the CCP devoted rhetorical and practical resources to increasing both the volume and the scope of correspondence.[6] The Shanxi provincial government, for example, instructed subordinates, "Make your reception office bustle like a market, where people come to have heart-to-heart chats whether or not they have specific issues to raise."[7] Anything the people might say, according to this official rhetoric, could potentially be of great political significance. As the head of the central government's North China Bureau, Liu Lantao, wrote in the Party's national newspaper, the *People's Daily*, "The most minute of the People's matters are the foundation of the People's major matters."[8] Liu's words reiterated the CCP's widely publicized claim that ordinary people had

Shao, "Bridge under Water: The Dilemma of the Chinese Petition System," China Research Center, online at chinacenter.net.

[4] Carl Minzer, "Xinfang: An Alternative to Formal Chinese Legal Institutions," *Stanford Journal of International Law* 42 (2006).

[5] For a good discussion of the differing opinions, among both anglophone and sinophone scholars, see Wang Bingyi, "Xinfang zhidu dianji: Mao Zedong yu xinfang zhidu (1949–1976)," *Zhengzhi yu falu pinglun*, January 2011: 149–157.

[6] On the diversity of earlier petitions, see Jonathan Ocko, "I'll Take It All the Way to Beijing: Capital Appeals in the Qing," *Journal of Asian Studies* 47, no. 2 (May 1988): 291–315.

[7] Shanxi Provincial People's Government, "Guanyu renzhen guanche chuli qunzhong lai xin jueding de zhishi," June 30, 1951, *Shanxi zhengbao*, August 1951, 117–118.

[8] Liu Lantao, "Zhonggong zhongyang huabei ju di san shuji Liu Lantao zai chuli Zhang Shunyou shijian huiyi shang de jianghua," *Renmin ribao*, May 30, 1952.

the right and the opportunity to approach the state about personal and local concerns and that such concerns were an integral part of political discourse. This discourse was idealized, but it had very practical implications. As the CCP transitioned from a band of guerilla rebels to the governors of the official Chinese state, leaders feared losing the grassroots connections that had not only helped them win hearts and minds but also allowed them to tap into a reservoir of much-needed intelligence. Urging people to share all of their thoughts with the state offered the potential for a surveillance network that reached right into ordinary people's private lives. Indeed, the ability to allow sufficient popular participation to retain support, while at the same time maintaining tight control and surveillance down to the individual, were two of the promises offered by Mao Zedong's "mass line" (*qunzhong luxian*).

The mass line was the cornerstone and perhaps the most famous articulation of early CCP governance theories. It posited that all truth, all theory, and all correct policy had to originate in the ideas held by "ordinary laboring people."[9] A hallmark of what made Maoist "people's democracy" different from its liberal predecessors, the mass line was once lauded by scholars and activists as a model for fomenting revolutionary social and political change.[10] Academics and other observers have since come to take a more reserved, sometimes cynical, position. The mass line now appears regularly in the literature as a strategic method for winning support, quelling resistance, and carrying out surveillance, all of which, according to this view, served the Party more than it did the people. Thus, while recent scholarship identifies the mass line as a key to CCP success, it also tends to cast the idealistic rhetoric of mass participation and leadership accountability as somewhat disingenuous.[11]

This chapter explores the CCP's work with letters and visits as one of the instruments that Party leaders themselves used to observe and gauge the nature and success of their mass-line work.[12] Xi Zhongxun (veteran revolutionary and father of current Party chairman Xi Jinping) once proclaimed, "Handling letters and visits from the people is 'keeping in

---

[9] Mark Selden, *The Yenan Way in Revolutionary China* (Cambridge, MA: Harvard University Press, 1971), 212; Stuart Schram, *The Political Thought of Mao Zedong* (Cambridge: Cambridge University Press, 1989), 9, 45.

[10] John Service, "The Growth of the New Fourth Army: An Example of the Popular Democratic Appeal of the Chinese Communists," reproduced in Joseph Esherick, ed., *Lost Chance in China: The World War II Dispatches of John S. Service* (New York: Random House, 1974); Selden, *The Yenan Way*.

[11] For a review of recent literature, see Patricia M. Thornton, "Retrofitting the Steel Cage: From Mobilizing the Masses to Surveying the Public," in Sebastian Heilmann and Elizabeth J. Perry, eds., *Mao's Invisible Hand: The Political Foundations of Adaptive Governance in China* (Cambridge, MA: Harvard University Press, 2011), 237–268.

[12] Wang Bingyi, "Xinfang zhidu dianji," 153–154.

close touch' with the masses, serving the people, heart and soul, and implementing the mass line."[13] Documents from this endeavor certainly show that the people's views were not consistently represented in political discourse and that mass-line rhetoric did sometimes aid Party Central in its more authoritarian endeavors. However, the history of letters and visits also reveals that the early PRC state was never able to fully realize the potential of this particular surveillance tool. At the same time, the central importance of mass-line discourse gave both rhetorical and practical power to ordinary people, in ways that had marked effects on state and society. Precisely because it was idealized, the rhetoric of the mass line established letters and visits as a legitimate site for making claims on the state and encouraged ordinary people to use it.

Discarded Letters, Negligent Cadres, and the Mass Line

This chapter draws on government records about letters-and-visits work, found in district- and municipal-level archives and purchased from secondhand document dealers.[14] Some of these sources are original texts, produced by local units (such as village Party branches and street-level police stations); others are copies of documents produced by municipal, regional, or central authorities. Some are duplicates of documents also held in state archives, others were once held in government archives but were discarded, still others appear to have been discarded by the state unit that produced them. Although this chapter focuses on the state's administrative records, my collections also include hundreds of individual letters as well as copies and summaries of letters contained in archives and published propaganda. Some of these letters came to me in individual envelopes, addressed to state units. In some cases, there is no way to know whether they were ever received. In other cases, the letters bear serial numbers, official stamps, and even reports added by the receiving units. Some of the original letters are parts of larger collections, preserved by receiving units or submitted to superiors.

How many such letters would I need before I considered them representative? Whatever that number might be, I am certain I will not reach it. It is possible, however, to identify more general trends and themes by

---

[13] Xi Zhongxun, "Yi shi wei jian, kai chuang xinfang gongzuo xin jumian," in Diao Jiecheng, *Renmin xinfang shilue* (Beijing: Beijing jingji xueyuan chubanshe, 1996), 2.

[14] For more on the document trade in China, see Jeremy Brown, "Finding and Using Grassroots Historical Sources from the Mao Era," *Dissertation Reviews*, 5 December 2010. As Brown and others note, while there has been much scholarly debate about the value and proper uses of garbage sources, leading experts on PRC history and politics, with extensive archival experience, regularly use these sources and do not dispute their authenticity.

placing individual letters back into the context provided by the state's administrative documents.[15] Wang P's complaint about Kaifeng's bathrooms, for example, seems to be quite representative, as local units across the country tallied significant numbers of letters about toilets. Praise for model workers who fixed and cleaned bathrooms was also a common theme in CCP propaganda.[16]

Wang's letter might also be typical in that it appears to have been written voluntarily, even with passion. In this way, letters and visits had a special place among the concrete practices associated with the mass line. As CCP legal theorist Wang Bingyi argued, the Party valued "letters and visits from the people as information that the masses sent and delivered on their own initiative."[17] To be sure, officials encouraged people to share their feedback with the state, but participation was still expected to be voluntary. There were cases where cadres organized or instructed people to write letters with specific content, but such instances were rare, relative to the volume of letters. More importantly, superiors early on ordered subordinates to stop orchestrating mass letter campaigns, as the volume of incoming correspondence was already overwhelming.[18] Mao once learned that his office had received more than 9,000 "best-wishes" letters, written by individuals, but at the behest of local Party units. In the margins of the related report he wrote, "Organizing the masses to write batches of salutary letters is bad. Don't do this in the future."[19] Thus, unlike political study sessions, mass campaigns, or other more top-down efforts to get people to take part in political affairs, letters and visits could be, and often were, much more genuine initiations from "the masses."

The masses-initiated nature of letters and visits was one reason why Party officials became increasingly concerned about the handling of correspondence after the establishment of the PRC in 1949. Party mythology celebrates the pre-takeover years as a time when the Party leaders,

[15] There has been a robust discussion in Soviet history on letters to the state and their role in governance, citizenship, and the possibilities they offer for accessing public opinion. For example, Sheila Fitzpatrick, "Supplicants and Citizens: Public Letter-Writing in Soviet Russia in the 1930s," *Slavic Review* 55, no. 1 (Spring 1996): 78–105; C. J Storella and A. K. Sokolov, eds. *The Voice of the People: Letters from the Soviet Village, 1918–1932* (New Haven: Yale University Press, 2013).

[16] See, for example, "Xibei jun qu de yi ge weisheng gongzuo mofan tuan," *Renmin ribao*, 31 August 1952; "Nei meng caoyuan shang de aiguo weisheng gongzuo," *Renmin ribao*, 13 September 1952.

[17] Wang Bingyi, "Xinfang zhidu dianji," 155.

[18] Zhonggong zhongyang bangong ting mishu shi, "Guanyu chuli qunzhong laixin de baogao," April 30, 1951, in Zhonggong zhongyang wenxian yanjiushi, ed., *Jianguo yilai zhongyang wenxian xuanbian*, vol. 2 (Beijing: Zhongyang wenxian chubanshe, 1993), 268–9.

[19] Zhonggong zhongyang bangong ting mishu shi, "Guanyu chuli qunzhong laixin de baogao."

in rural base areas, had close relationships with ordinary people, regularly listened to those people, and attempted to serve their needs. That this vision is romanticized does not diminish the very real successes that the CCP had in allowing sufficient, support-generating popular participation while also preserving tight central control and exercising broad surveillance powers. In the early 1950s, when the area under Communist jurisdiction increased by 200 percent and leaders were increasingly sequestered in their Beijing compound, officials heightened their attention to letters and visits, arguing that handling correspondence correctly was crucial to maintaining that otherwise untenable relationship with the people, which was a precondition for the successful implementation of the mass line.

Emblematized by the shorthand phrase "from the masses, back to the masses," the *line* in question was ideally a circular route. Mao famously likened the role of the Party to that of a processing plant: cadres should observe and listen attentively to the people, apply Marxist/Leninist/ Maoist theory to reject incorrect ideas and understand the full scope of the correct ones, and then propagate those truths in a "concentrated and systematic" form, while still ensuring that people could recognize them as their own.[20] The process should then repeat, picking up knowledge and creating better practice with each loop, in "a never-ending upward spiral" of revolutionary development.[21] As Wang Bingyi explained, letters and visits provided an opportunity for that full mass-line cycle: letters and visits

are a direct reflection of the ideas held by the masses of the people; the information they send and deliver is both the basis for the Party and the state's policy decisions and an excellent opportunity to publicize the explanations of our polices; it is also an important site for testing the effective implementation of polices.[22]

Crucially, however, a complete recursive cycle (the masses express an idea, the Party theorizes it and propagates the theory until the masses accept it as their own) did not need to occur for an activity to constitute part of the implementation of the mass line. We might make a useful distinction here between *the mass line*, as an ideal vision of governance, in its totality, and *mass-line work*, as any aspect of the concrete practices through which the Party conversed with the people. As Yu Jianrong has shown, "the mass line was the *modus operandi* [*yunxing fangshi*] of the

---

[20] Schram, *The Political Thought of Mao Zedong*, 315–317.
[21] On the mass line as an endless ascending spiral, see Cao Dahua, "New Knowledge, New Consciousness: Writing on Practice for the New Phase," *CCP News*, 17 August 2017, at http://theory.people.com.cn/n1/2017/0817/c40531-29475608.html.
[22] Wang Bingyi, "Xinfang zhidu dianji," 155.

letters-and-visits system."[23] Thus the individual tasks that were part of the process (reading a letter, writing a report, replying to a letter writer, and so on) could each, on their own, be categorized as the work that furthered the mass line.

In both internal cadre-training materials and publicized propaganda, central leaders dictated and modeled ideal practice. In 1951, Mao issued a famous memo, copied to virtually every Party and state unit across the country:

> We must pay serious attention to the people's correspondence, properly handling letters from the people and satisfying all of the masses' legitimate demands. We should see this task as one of the methods for strengthening the close ties between the Communist Party and the people. We should not take a bureaucratist attitude by treating this lightly or brushing it aside.[24]

In fact, tales of Chairman Mao and his own letters comprise a not-insignificant portion of the mytho-historical anecdotes about his concern for the masses. As the state-run Xinhua News Agency reminded netizens, in a post so widely shared it's now ubiquitous, "Mao Zedong was committed to really listening to the people's voices, and he took letters from the people very seriously. He regularly tore open and read the letters he received and tried his utmost to reply." According to "incomplete statistics," in 1950, during the first ten days of May, Mao reportedly answered almost eighty letters, including eighteen in a single day.[25]

Impressive as his reply rate might have been, Mao couldn't have made a dent in the letters he received. During the first three months of 1951, for example, the secretariat at Party Central received 19,660 letters sent from members of the masses and addressed to the chairman.[26] As those letters arrived, the central secretariat was responsible for following the official policies, regularly revised and promulgated: they assigned each letter a case number, recorded a brief summary of its content, investigated the matter, and either drafted a reply or transferred the letter to a relevant unit. That unit was then expected to follow the same procedures and report back to Party Central about their handling of each case, as well as

---

[23] Yu Jianrong, "Geming lunli yu xinfang zhidu xiandai zhuanxing de kunjing," *Xueshu jiaoliu* 272, no. 11 (November 2016): 42.

[24] Mao Zedong, "Zhuanfa zhonggong bangongting mishushi guanyu chuli qunzhong laixin de baogao de piyu," 16 May 1951, in *Jianguo yilai Mao Zedong wengao*, vol. 2 (Beijing: Zhongyang wenxian chubanshe, 1987), 310.

[25] Xinhua News Agency, "Mao Zedong yi tian hui 18 feng qunzhong laixin shi mian jingzi," 19 September 2011, at http://news.xinhuanet.com/lianzheng/2011-09/19/c_122055415 .htm, accessed March 2016.

[26] Wu Chao, "Xin Zhongguo xinfang zhidu de chuangjian he fazhan (1949–1957)," *Dang de wenxian* 4 (2012): 95.

about other letters they had received directly.[27] They were to use similar procedures in dealing with visits. Over time, official documents began to employ the abbreviation "letters and visits" or *xinfang*, but during the 1950s the state was much more likely to use the longer phrase "letters and visits from the people" and its variants.

As Wang P's bathroom complaint suggests, most people did not begin by writing directly to Mao or other top leaders; they turned instead to village- or neighborhood-level Party cadres, officers at local police stations, or staff in district-level government offices. In Beijing, for example, the Qianmen District People's Government received 432 letters and visits during the second half of 1952. Of the letters and visitors, 206 had come directly to the Qianmen office, whereas 226 cases had been transferred by the central government and other units, including newspaper editorial offices, which sent 117 letters.[28] Unfortunately, the compiler of the report noted, they had experienced some "problems with foot-dragging," and thus some of those letters had piled up, unanswered, for quite a while, leading to "dissatisfaction among the masses."[29]

Wang P expressed just such dissatisfaction when he wrote to Mao complaining about unresponsive local cadres, and he was not alone. Reports from the 1950s regularly noted that letters were unopened, hidden, and even burned in some cases. And when staff did read letters, they "just handled those that were easy to handle," wrote a cadre from Shaanxi, adding,

But then they drag their feet on the more complicated ones. Even when they have letters that aren't that complicated, they get busy with other work and just sit on the letters for long periods without doing anything to handle them, to the point that they sometimes just completely forget about them.[30]

In July 1951, the Beijing Municipal Government admitted that, like their subordinates, they too had problems with foot-dragging and backlogs. As an example, they cited Beijing resident Chen C, who wrote to Deputy CCP Chairman Liu Shaoqi, to ask for help finding work. Liu's office transferred the letter to the Beijing Municipal Government with instructions to investigate and help Chen find employment if appropriate. "We sent people to arrange a meeting, but they didn't find the person in question," wrote a municipal cadre. "Then they shelved it for five

[27] See, for example, "Zhengwuyuan guanyu renmin lai xin he jianjian renmin gongzuo de jueding," June 7, 1951, in Zhong gong zhong yang wen xian yan jiu shi, *Jianguo yilai zhongyao wenxian xuanbian* (Beijing: Zhongyang wenxian chubanshe, Xinhua shudian faxing, 1992).
[28] "Qianmen qu zhengfu 1952 niandu renmin laixin laifang gongzuo baogao," Beijing Municipal Archives, 39-1-154.
[29] Ibid.
[30] "Guoyi xian renmin zhengfu chuli qunzhong laixin ji jiejian renmin qunzhong gongzuo de baogao," December 5, 1951, *Shaanxi zhengbao* 12 (1951), 16–17.

months. Only when Party Central pressed us, did we again send cadres to find the person and resolve the situation."[31]

In July 1952, Beijing's Xuanwu District Government confessed that nearly everyone in their unit "had failed to take letters from the masses seriously enough on an ideological level." The central problem, the report asserted, was that cadres thought that "handling letters from the masses was small stuff, that it was simply helping individual members of the masses solve problems, and that it didn't have much of an effect." As an example of the kinds of problem this attitude created, the report cited Wang G, who had written to accuse her husband of abusing her and evading taxes: "Cadres simply transferred the letter to the tax bureau and didn't press it. During the Five Antis, Wang wrote again, this time to the mayor, saying that the government had not handled this for her." When the municipal government pressed the Xuanwu unit on Wang's letter, "we discovered that our system was not being implemented correctly, we had foot-dragging and backlogs. Mundane problems were often taking two weeks to be handled. Some cadres would receive letters and not register them or handle them and not keep any record."[32]

Even citizens answering the call to suppress counterrevolutionaries could find themselves rebuffed when they visited government offices. In March 1952, a twenty-nine-year-old cart driver from Shanxi apparently marched into the offices of the Central Committee's North China Bureau. He introduced himself as Zhang Shunyou and then began to rant,

I've been all over Suiyuan, Chahar, and Shanxi and visited 27 offices. It took five months. This not only delayed production, but I also used up all of my savings, sold my clothes, my blankets, my pipe, and more. When I was out of money, I went behind my parents' backs and sold our household's grain to cover my travel costs. Altogether, I spent more than 240,000 yuan.[33]

Zhang then accused government personnel of making his ordeal even worse by mistreating and verbally abusing him along the way. At one point, he claimed, Public Security officers actually arrested *him*, when in fact Zhang was the one attempting to report a criminal. In response to the "People's Government call to enthusiastically report counterrevolutionaries," Zhang had been trying to officially accuse his boss as a fugitive landlord and murderer.[34]

---

[31] Beijing shi renmin zhangfu, "Guanyu 1951 nian shangbannian chuli renmin laixin he jiejian renmin de baogao," July 1951, Beijing Municipal Archives 2-3-69.

[32] Xuanwu qu renmin zhengfu, "Guanyu chuli renmin qunzhong laixin de zongjie baogao," December 1952, Beijing Municipal Archives, 2-3-69.

[33] Zhang Shunyou and Li Hengying, "Wo jianju fangeming fenzi shi zaoyu le zhongzhong zunan," *Renmin ribao*, 30 May 1952, 3.

[34] Ibid.

Narratives of citizens, such as Zhang Shunyou, terrorizing each other with political accusations dominate our understandings of the Mao era. That vision is reflected, for example, in a memorable scene from the documentary *China: A Century of Revolution*, in which the narrator remarks that PRC citizens were encouraged to "inform on their neighbors," and viewers see a woman dropping a note into a locked box labeled "accusations" (*jianju*), a kind of correspondence that was explicitly included in the "letters and visits" category.[35] But the related documentation suggests that while the CCP's efforts to make and maintain grassroots information networks promised unprecedented surveillance powers, this promise was *not* realized in the 1950s; on the contrary, the state was repeatedly frustrated by its inability to receive key information, which superiors blamed in large part on problems with the vast bureaucracy of undertrained, overworked, unruly, and obstinate cadres.

This was especially clear in the "Zhang Shunyou affair." In 1951, Zhang was in Inner Mongolia working for a small-scale grain merchant named Song Yude. That year, the CCP launched the Campaign to Suppress Counterrevolutionaries. According to Zhang's account, upon hearing this news, Song suddenly declared that he was moving his operation to another province and changing his name. "I began to suspect," Zhang recalled, "that Song Yude was not a good fellow, and I thought I should report him." Sometime later, Zhang claimed, he also learned that villagers from Song Yude's hometown had accused him as a despotic landlord who had murdered a villager. Zhang took this information to the Datong People's Government. He told government personnel that he wanted to report Song as a fugitive landlord, who had murdered a member of the masses, changed his name to avoid detection, and attempted to evade the campaign to suppress counterrevolutionaries. But cadres sent Zhang away, ostensibly because he had not acquired the appropriate letter of introduction. These were the events that launched Zhang Shunyou's several-months-long trek to visit government units in three provinces before eventually storming into the Beijing offices of the North China Bureau.[36] The ensuing investigation concluded that Song was indeed guilty. He was executed as a counterrevolutionary in 1952.[37] We know Zhang Shunyou's story because North China Bureau chief and Central Committee member Liu Lantao saw it as a model case for the

[35] *China: A Century of Revolution: The Mao Years, 1949–1976*, dir. Sue Williams, Winstar, 2004.
[36] Zhang Shunyou and Li Hengying, "Wo jianju fangeming fenzi shi zaoyu le zhongzhong zunan."
[37] Liu Yajuan, "Zhang Shunyou Shijian: Yige dianxing de shudianxing ge an," *Zhongyang yanjiuyuan jindai shi yanjiusuo jikan* 84 (2014): 187.

Party's ongoing efforts to rectify "cadre errors." Zhang's case was included in a textbook and used in party-state units nationwide during the Three Antis rectification movement, which took aim at three broad categories of cadre misdeeds: bureaucratism, commandism, and violations of law and order. Several of the other cases in the primer were also about cadre error related to letters and visits, and many units reported positive outcomes after study sessions. A report from Beijing's Xuanwu District Government, for example, read, "We had been bureaucratist in our work. Thus, we organized a 'Study the Zhang Shunyou Affair' campaign, and since then, we have remedied the cadres' mistaken mind-set of not taking seriously letters from the masses. They have recognized its importance."[38]

But despite that and other expressions of optimism, problems continued and reports throughout the 1950s admitted that many letters went unanswered, and many visitors were ignored.[39] The fact that some cases were handled while others were simply filed away and even thrown away confirms what recent grassroots histories of the PRC have shown: experience at the local level was uneven and extremely difficult to generalize.[40] The CCP might have wanted to institute a Big Brother-style surveillance state, and the PRC was surely experienced as one by some people. But other people experienced no such tyranny because accusations about them, mailed to the state or dropped in letter boxes, were never opened. And a striking number of visitors to state and Party units were sent away unheard. Throughout the 1950s, if you were seeking help from the state, you might have found cadres frustrating and unresponsive or helpful and kind. If your neighbor informed on you and that letter happened to be handled, you might have experienced the terror of an unexpected arrest and possibly an unjust incarceration, but if an office worker at wit's end shoved that letter into a desk drawer, you might have gone on without so much as an inkling that you had ever been accused at all.

Furthermore, letters-and-visits records suggest that, while there were exceptions, individuals were not generally arrested or even formally criticized based on citizen accusations alone. In the Qianmen reports, for example, cadres dismissed several accusations because "we investigated

---

[38] Xuanwu qu renmin zhengfu, "Guanyu chuli renmin qunzhong laixin de zongjie baogao," December 1952, Beijing Municipal Archives, 2-3-69.

[39] Zhonggong Beijing shiwei bangongting guanyu chuli renmin laixin laifang gongzuo zhong cunzai de jige wenti ji gaijin yijian baogao," May 1956, Beijing Municipal Archives, 1-6-1161.

[40] Jeremy Brown and Matthew Johnson, *Maoism at the Grassroots: Everyday Life in China's Era of High Socialism* (Cambridge, MA: Harvard University Press, 2015).

but the accusation turned out to have no basis in fact."⁴¹ In his work on
industrial accidents and sabotage, Jeremy Brown similarly demonstrates
that cadres were fairly circumspect in handling accusations. Workers and
site supervisors did sometimes allege counterrevolutionary sabotage, but
Brown finds little evidence that such accusations typically shaped the
handling of the cases. Rather, he shows, investigators usually worked to
get all the facts, and the accused were frequently acquitted of political
charges and simply found liable (or not) for accidental mistakes.⁴² And
sometimes incompetence at lower levels meant that even true accusations
could go unprosecuted. In the case of Zhang Shunyou, Song Yude's
execution might have been a terrifying public spectacle, but it took far
more than a note in a letter box to bring about that outcome.

Zhang Shunyou, the Wan Family, and Narratives of State Unresponsiveness

Would-be petitioners Wang P and Zhang Shunyou were just two of the
thousands who took their cases to the central authorities in the 1950s.
Such stories abound in archives and in fiction, film, and journalism.
Zhang Shunyou's narrative in particular is similar to that of the famous
petitioner He Biqiu, or Qiu Ju as she was named in Zhang Yimou's film
adaptation of *The Wan Family Lawsuit*.⁴³ The story follows a young wife
who tirelessly pursues justice on behalf of her husband, because a village
leader kicked him in the groin during a minor altercation. Like Zhang
Shunyou, this petitioner also becomes increasingly frustrated as she visits
office after office. The title of the novella is especially significant as Wan is
both a common surname and a character that means 10,000. "The
resulting meaning," as Xudong Zhang notes, "is 'a myriad of lawsuits',"
evoking all the many Wans, Zhangs, and so on who ceaselessly demanded
that the state serve the people.⁴⁴

Such stories certainly appear as indictments of the PRC state. Even by
the CCP's own standards, as Wang Bingyi notes, letters and visits were "a
convenient, practical tool for testing the mass line," a "significant measure
of whether or not the Party and state are implementing the mass line."⁴⁵

---

⁴¹ "Qianmen qu zhengfu 1952 niandu renmin laixin laifang gongzuo baogao," Beijing
Municipal Archives, 39-1-154.
⁴² Jeremy Brown, unpublished paper presented at the Chan Workshop in New PRC
History, Los Angeles, February 2015.
⁴³ *The Story of Qiu Ju*, dir. Zhang Yimou, 1993; Chen Yuanbin, *Wan jia susong: Chen
Yuanbin fazhi ticai xiaoshuo ji* (Beijing: Falu chubanshe, 1992).
⁴⁴ Xudong Zhang, *Postsocialism and Cultural Politics: China in the Last Decade of the Twentieth
Century* (Durham NC: Duke University Press, 2008), 291.
⁴⁵ Wang Bingyi, "Xinfang zhidu dianji," 155.

Central authorities clearly referenced that yardstick, regularly citing examples of mishandled letters in their accusations that cadres were "separating themselves from the masses." Thus narratives of state unresponsiveness were also a key part of the CCP's own discussions about whether and how they were implementing the mass line and maintaining close ties to the people. As Dan Chen notes, scholars regularly invoke the analogy of the "safety valve" to illustrate how CCP political practices "allow space for feedback and challenges" but in ways that "contribute to authoritarian resilience by relieving public frustration, reducing the propensity to contentious politics, and in some cases enabling the government to collect information on potential opposition groups or emerging problems."[46]

Letters and visits allowed people to express their opinions and ask for assistance, and also allowed higher authorities to blame bumbling subordinates if the people's concerns went unaddressed. As early as April 1951, subordinates were already pushing back, arguing that they were not mishandling correspondence but that ordinary citizens had the impression that their chances were better with higher officials, perhaps because of older cultural (and maybe even somewhat universal) tropes about the good ruler versus the corrupt local official. When Party Central criticized Beijing's Qianmen District Government, for instance, cadres groused about how their superiors had learned of their mistakes in the first place: "The masses have the mind-set that if you go to the higher authorities or to the newspapers, you'll get a more satisfactory response."[47]

In fact, this sentiment – that if "higher-ups" only knew the true situation, they would rectify problems immediately – regularly recurs in fictional, journalistic, and historical sources alike.[48] This served those "higher-ups" well. As Jeffrey Kinkley explained, the state was enthusiastic about Zhang Yimou's film *Qiu Ju da guansi* because, while some government personnel were officious and incompetent, in the end the state served the masses.[49] The cases of Zhang Shunyou and his fellow petitioners were widely reported, in internal administrative documentation and in publicized propaganda, because they carried a similar message.

As these stories were retold in the *People's Daily* and elsewhere, they suggested that links in the mass line were broken but that the larger system was still intact. Letter writers and "higher-ups" both created

---

[46] Dan Chen, "Review Essay: The Safety Valve Analogy in Chinese Politics," *Journal of East Asian Studies* 16, no. 2 (July 2016): 281.

[47] "Qianmen qu zhengfu 1952 niandu renmin laixin laifang gongzuo baogao," Beijing Municipal Archives, 39-1-154.

[48] Most recently, in the documentary of Zhao Liang, dir., *Shangfang* (Petition), 2009 and Yan Lianke, *Sishu* (The Four Books) (Hong Kong: Mingpao chubanshe, 2010).

[49] Jeffrey Kinkley, *Chinese Justice, the Fiction: Law and Literature in Modern China* (Stanford: Stanford University Press, 2000).

narratives in which higher-ranking members of the Communist Party were committed to the mass line and to protecting the people's interests but were thwarted by rank-and-file cadres who oppressed the people and flouted the mass line. Political scientists have noted the ways in which contemporary petitioners appropriate this kind of discourse. Kevin O'Brien put it nicely: "Acting in the name of loyalty to the revolution and its founder they 'search for the real Communist party' and level charges against 'commandist' and grasping cadres who 'oppress the masses' and are not 'authentic communists.'"[50]

That the state was so well served by the rhetoric of the mass line, including its complementary discourse of cadre error, has led a number of scholars to suggest that the democratic side of democratic centralism was overstated. There was once vigorous debate about the extent to which mass-line rhetoric translated into real practice. In what is probably the best-known exchange, between Mark Selden and Chen Yungfa, Chen criticized Selden's 1971 monograph *The Yenan Way* for its overly sunny portrayal of CCP governance, which Chen alleged overstated the democratic elements of the mass line. In Chen's 1986 study, he found that the Party was actually riddled with corruption and regularly relied on brute force and intimidation when dealing with the masses.[51] In his 1995 response, Selden argued that the democratic spirit of the mass line was still an important part of early Communist successes, but he conceded that Party leadership was more authoritarian and that democratic practices were less common than he had originally assumed. Some have even taken the conclusions of the Chen–Selden debate a step further and suggested that the mass was little more than a propagandistic veneer for governance that was far more authoritarian in practice.

In fact, however, calling the mass line a veneer for authoritarianism is a bit like calling the head of a coin a veneer for its tail. The mass line was always quite explicitly articulated as both democratic and dictatorial. Chen, Selden, and Stuart Schram have all highlighted the way the mass line was crafted to mitigate tensions between the need to preserve the centralized power of a self-identified "dictatorship" and to maintain support for the state by allowing sufficient popular participation.[52] The rhetoric of cadre error helped the mass line do just that: while errant cadres were clearly a factual reality which plagued the state, they were also a key discursive construction which allowed the mass line to do what it

---

[50] O'Brien, "Rightful Resistance," 40.
[51] Chen Yungfa, *Making Revolution: The Communist Movement in Eastern and Central China, 1937–1945* (Berkeley: California University Press, 1986).
[52] Ibid., 520; Schram, *The Political Thought of Mao Zedong*, 97–98; Selden, *China in Revolution*, 243.

was formulated to do – mitigate the tensions inherent in democratic centralism.[53]

The Two Faces of the Mass Line

The history of letters and other reports from ordinary people highlight the dual character of the mass line, which has also been well substantiated by political scientists, who have argued that mass-line rhetoric and practice were key factors enabling CCP success, as useful tactics for gaining popular support and gathering useful intelligence.[54] Patricia Thornton has shown that while the mass line served the state and did not usually benefit the masses, it was nevertheless "a double-edged sword."[55] On the one hand, as both Thornton and Li Lifeng have demonstrated, the Party successfully used "mass-line methods to identify and cultivate both poor peasants and local activists" who could help Party cadres "to effectively uncover and reframe preexisting grievances as class-based contradictions."[56] Thornton explains that reinterpreting social tensions, "in terms set by the Party center," as "deep-rooted class-based conflicts," justified "the intercession and continuing oversight of the Party." And "listening closely to the masses" allowed officials to monitor and respond to popular opinion as well as to gain valuable intelligence information – sending cadres to engage in mass-line work also gave the CCP the opportunity to surveil Chinese society down to the individual, grassroots level and was thus partly responsible for the Party's ability to quell resistance and institute tight centralized control.[57]

On the other hand, "however, in the decades following the revolution, the Party's own success at grassroots organizing" installed "the revolutionary masses" in all manner of "Party or state-sponsored mass organizations," which "were curiously apt at the articulation and pursuit of collective interests not in keeping with the 'mass line' defined by the center."[58] The

---

[53] Elsewhere I elaborate on the reality and the discourse of cadre error as key elements in CCP governance. Aminda Smith, "Long Live the Mass Line: Errant Cadres and Post-disillusionment PRC History," *Positions: Asia Critique* 29, no. 4 (2021): 783–807.

[54] Liu Yu, "From the Mass Line to the Mao Cult: The Production of Legitimate Leadership in Revolutionary China" (PhD diss., Columbia University, 2006).

[55] Thornton, "Retrofitting the Steel Cage," 238.

[56] Quoted in ibid., citing Li Lifeng, "Tugai Zhong de suku: yi shong minzhong dongyuan jishu de weiguan fenxi," *Nanjing daxue xuebao*, no. 5 (2007), 97–109.

[57] As Michael Schoenhals has shown, in addition to receiving reports from ordinary citizens, the new PRC state aggressively recruited and trained a grassroots network of intelligence agents whose explicit charge was to "spy *for* the people" by spying *on* the people in their homes, factories, schools, and even public bathrooms. Michael Schoenhals, *Spying for the People: Mao's Secret Agents, 1949–1967* (Cambridge: Cambridge University Press, 2012).

[58] Thornton, "Retrofitting the Steel Cage," 238.

documents associated with letters-and-visits work highlight that double-edged nature of mass-line work, which did enable real, if limited, participation on the part of ordinary people, sometimes in ways that were at odds with state goals, but not always. The state did regularly further its own aims and overrule complainants, though people also periodically subverted state goals. It is important to note, however, that in many cases "the masses" and the state worked in concert with one another; even in ideal models of mass-line governance, popular participation could go hand in hand with brutality, large-scale incarcerations, and even mass executions.

There is plenty of evidence to suggest that citizen informants sometimes willingly abetted the Chinese Communist government in its dictatorial goals. Daniel Leese recounts a memorable example in which a man commenting on the state of an actual cabbage was accused of calling Mao Zedong a rotten cabbage. The accusation landed the falsely accused in a labor camp for twelve years.[59] But questions about the truth or veracity of individual claims notwithstanding, it is important to note that Leese's case suggests that the state violated the mass line only in not thoroughly verifying the initial accusation. In cases where they did so, even a long prison sentence could theoretically be consistent with the mass line, which was always explicitly both authoritarian and democratic.

As it appears in propaganda and cadre-training materials, the message in the Zhang Shunyou affair was that the mass line was genuinely implemented, in the end, and that the outcome was an execution. Party propaganda often insisted that executions and incarcerations were entirely consistent with the mass line because "the masses demand we suppress counterrevolutionaries," and Zhang Shunyou's case might suggest that this claim was sometimes true.[60] Song Yude's execution certainly exposes what Mark Selden called "the dark side of mobilizational politics," but that outcome also troubles any assumption that the "dictatorship of the masses" was not at least partially supported by some members of those masses.[61] All accounts, including his own, suggest that Zhang Shunyou did participate in governance, at least by a mass-line definition. We might dispute that definition and question the mass line as a theory with any real democratic elements, but that is very different from claiming that the theory was simply a veneer or a tactic which served primarily the state. And while some people may have used mass-line rhetoric to their own benefit, subverting state aims in the process, for Zhang Shunyou his desire and that of the state's seemed to

---

[59] Daniel Leese, "Revising Political Verdicts in Post-Mao China: The Case of Beijing's Fengtai District," in Brown and Johnson, *Maoism at the Grassroots*, 115.
[60] Liu Yajuan, "Zhang Shunyou Shijian," 189.   [61] Selden, *China in Revolution*, 243.

work in concert with one another. And significantly, as Liu Yajuan discovered, Zhang also appears to have felt that this collaboration later made him the target of unwanted state attention.[62]

In most cases, however, the masses and the state worked together in ways that were less suggestive of dictatorship. A majority of the letters sent to the Qianmen government between 1949 and 1958 were petitions for material aid, demands for infrastructure improvements, or requests for help with personal problems. Most were similar to issues that citizens in other countries might also take up in a letter to their local representative. During mass mobilization efforts, like the campaign to suppress counterrevolutionaries, more overtly political reports increased, but even then, many of the so-called "accusations" were still similar to complaints one might make at the Better Business Bureau. The same was true, to a certain extent, of letters sent to Public Security units during the same period. In an October 1952 report from the Beijing PSB, for example, accusations against counterrevolutionaries comprised 15 percent of the letters received, including four anonymous letters alleging that a man living in one city *hutong* was a fugitive landlord from Hebei, who had worked for the Guomindang and was concealing his assets. But the majority of cases were about more mundane crimes. There were reports of kids vandalizing a wall. There were several complaints about accidental and intentional property damage to homes and businesses. There were requests that the police help mediate disputes. Even accusations against "criminal capitalists" were often about businesses that overcharged for services or products.[63]

In one work report, Qianmen District government cadres noted that they had received 432 letters and visits during the second half of 1952. They categorized the cases as in Table 9.1.[64]

The more specific content of the individual letters was diverse. There were several complaints, as always, about dirty bathrooms, as well as unhygienic restaurants and other similar problems. One letter complained about a shoemaker who was charging for high-quality leather but using leather of low quality. One husband and father visited to ask for social relief to help support his wife and six children. A woman with a disabled child wrote to ask the government to institutionalize her son. A local resident reported the circulation of a "pornographic musical recording" and asked the government to confiscate it. There were a few accusations of adultery and some requests that the government arrest particular "counterrevolutionaries." There were

[62] For Zhang's own views, see Liu Yajuan, "Zhang Shunyou Shijian," 189–191.
[63] Beijing Municipal Public Security Bureau, "Beijing shi gongan renmin laixin gongzuo baogao," March 14, 1952, Beijing Municipal Archives, 40-2-152.
[64] "Qianmen qu zhengfu 1952 niandu renmin laixin laifang gongzuo baogao," Beijing Municipal Archives, 39-1-154.

Table 9.1

Reports on illegal business operators	62 cases
Reports on spies, tyrants, and concealing property	6 cases
Reports on cadres or street-level representatives with bad work habits	10 cases
Requests for work or social relief	75 cases
Requests for admission into schools or training programs	8 cases
Suggestions about city construction, city appearance, and public hygiene	108 cases
Notes of thanks to the government	2 cases
Requests for fixing/improving roads, houses, buildings, and other structures	24 cases
Requests for housing	7 cases
Requests for mediation in wage, marriage, housing, and family disputes	86 cases
Other	44 cases

numerous complaints about cadres, nurses, and shop clerks with "bad attitudes." According to the cadres, by December of that year, they had successfully responded to 412 of the 432 letters.[65]

Conclusion

Despite their "foot-dragging and backlogs," local authorities reported
that they were able to resolve many of the problems brought to them by
the masses, and while some of those problems were requests for arrests
and even executions, the vast majority of them were more like Wang P's
lavatory complaint than they were like Zhang Shunyou's political accusation. Taken together, the letters citizens wrote suggest that many people
were more concerned about the state of the bathrooms than about the
state of the nation. If most people were most worried about the quality of
their daily lives, as suggested by letter tallies, then the PRC state was
probably able to satisfy many of them. Chen X, who lived in Beijing's
Qianmen District during the 1950s, told me (in 2016) that she went to
both street-level cadres and the local police station from time to time
when she needed something. She'd never been to the district government,
she noted, because cadres at the lower levels "would take care of things."
I asked her if cadres were bureaucratic or rude, and she replied, "Well,
people are busy and not everyone has a great attitude all the time, but
we're all neighborhood people, so if you talk things over, there's usually
no problem in the end."[66] Of course, Chen's memories are no more the
last word than is a 1952 quote from another Qianmen local, Shen X. Shen
was quoted, in a district government report, as saying, "The People's

[65] Ibid.   [66] Informal conversation with Chen X, March 2016.

government really is the People's own government. If something isn't right, you just talk to the cadres and they make it right. The Party and the government really serve the People."[67] Whether or not Shen ever made such a remark, the sheer number of letters that people sent to the state suggests that people understood that they had the right to approach their government for help about everything from bathrooms to serious crimes. And the detailed reports that cadres compiled further suggested that they were often able to resolve the cases. But if local governments could not or would not help, many people took their cases to a higher authority. Some of those petitioners may have seen themselves as participating in a transhistorical Chinese tradition, and some were probably also moved by the new Communist state's mass-line rhetoric, at least insofar as it encouraged them to believe that even the smallest and most mundane of their personal matters might also matter to the state. The majority of the letters I have read were addressed to the government on the understanding and with the confidence that it was reasonable to ask the state to intervene on a citizen's behalf; they did not read like interactions between terrorized people and a state they feared.

Indeed, even the incarcerations and executions, which are certainly evidence of state-sponsored terror, also occurred in response to popular participation in some cases. The records on letters and visits also suggest, however, that as common as incarcerations, executions, and terror may have been, they did not characterize the daily experiences of everyone, or even almost everyone. It was not the case, as Frank Dikötter and others have claimed, that the 1950s were characterized, first and foremost, by terror.[68] Terror was very real, but it was very unevenly experienced. Many people's most pressing concerns were poor sanitation, rude service professionals, unresponsive (but not terrifying) cadres and police, infidelity and other kinds of family crisis, and, most of all, making ends meet. And for issues of these kinds, the mass line did seem to operate. We may think of Mao's populist promises in macro-political terms, but Maoism was also manifestly about the quotidian and was, at least sometimes, genuinely and successfully implemented on that material level. And mass-line work, as made visible in letters and visits from the people, was one crucial way in which everyday Maoism was experienced and realized both by agents of the state and ordinary PRC citizens.

---

[67] "Qianmen qu zhengfu 1952 niandu renmin laixin laifang gongzuo baogao."
[68] Frank Dikötter, *The Tragedy of Liberation: A History of the Chinese Revolution, 1945–1957* (London: Bloomsbury, 2013), xi.

10 Cadres, Grain, and Rural Conflicts

A Study of Criminal Cases in a Village during the Great Leap Forward

Jing Wenyu

A decade into its rule, the government of the People's Republic of China embarked on a new, dramatic, and disastrous national project. Designed to forge an industrialized country in one short, sharp campaign, the Great Leap Forward (hereinafter GLF, 1958–1961) brought widespread hunger to China's countryside as the central authorities, eager to meet their ambitious modernization goals, requisitioned substantial quantities of grain from agricultural producers in the villages. Alongside these quotas came a heightened politicization that impacted every domain of rural society, as the Party sought to effect a radical transformation of the rural world through vigorous, campaign-style enforcement. These efforts continued even in the face of famine. In late 1959 and early 1960, as the death toll rose, the central government doubled down, reviving the 1957 Socialist Education Movement (SEM) to counter rural "rightist opportunists" opposed to the GLF. Only in the second half of 1960, when the threat of mass starvation in rural China had been joined by the prospect of imminent depletion of grain reserves in the major urban centers, did the authorities change course and implement a moderation of the GLF.[1] In the countryside, this moderation was marked by the opening of the so-called "Anti-Five Winds" campaign,[2] which sought to redress the worst excesses of the previous two years.

The extensive academic literature on the GLF explores a range of issues, including the causes of the disaster, the extent and severity of the famine, and the strategies and practices of resistance adopted by rural residents as the catastrophe unfolded.[3] Micro-historical approaches have

---

[1] Felix Wemheuer, *Famine Politics in Maoist China and the Soviet Union* (New Haven: Yale University Press, 2014), 115–153.

[2] Referring to bureaucracy, coercion, blind command, boasting, and communism, five categories of error supposedly fallen into by local cadres since the opening of the Great Leap.

[3] For example, Wangling Gao, *Zhongguo nongmin fanxingwei yanjiu (1950–1980)* (Counteraction by Chinese Peasants (1950–1980)) (Hong Kong: The Chinese University Press, 2013); Felix Wemheuer and Kimberley Manning, eds., *Eating Bitterness: New Perspectives on China's Great Leap Forward and Famine* (Vancouver: University of British

proved particularly fruitful, offering new insights into the dynamics of mass starvation and the responses of those struggling to survive in the countryside.[4] The present chapter attempts to move these efforts in a fresh direction, providing a grassroots perspective on the GLF through the lens of the local judicial system during the famine and the subsequent recovery. Drawing on local archival records and on-the-ground interviews, I examine two criminal cases in a Shandong village in early 1960, highlighting how, in the hyper-politicized context of the GLF, factional struggles among rural elites took on a dangerous new significance. At this moment of extreme material shortage, competing groups used all the tools at their disposal, including state-sanctioned legal mechanisms, to gain the upper hand over their opponents. This exploration of judicial practice at the local level encourages us to refocus on an aspect of the GLF that, given the scale of its human consequences, it can be easy to neglect; that is, its character as a political event. The Great Leap, like the many movements that had preceded it in the 1950s, was a campaign, a moment when the everyday life of millions took on a new and intense political aspect. It is to this quality – and the paths and possibilities that it created at the local level – that I hope to turn our attention.

Xu Village lies in western Shandong, close to the Yellow River and the provincial border with Henan. On the eve of the GLF, it was a close-knit community formed from two lineages: the Xus, who constituted two-thirds of the population, and the Zhaos, who made up the remainder. Relations between the two lineages were friendly and co-operative. The Xus, the more powerful lineage, were said to have settled in the village around the mid-sixteenth century, during the reign of the Jiajing Emperor (r. 1522–1566). Membership of the lineage was divided between an "elder" branch, itself composed of four subbranches, and a smaller secondary branch. As the largest grouping in the community, the elder branch had long dominated the key leadership positions in their namesake village.

The gazetteer for L County, in which Xu Village is situated, records that the Chinese Communist Party (CCP) first arrived in the area in 1934.[5] The Party drove through land reform in 1946 and 1947, shortly before winning final control of the county from the Nationalist

---

Columbia Press, 2011); Wemheuer, *Famine Politics*; Jisheng Yang, *Tombstone: The Great Chinese Famine, 1958–1962* (New York: Farrar, Straus and Giroux, 2012).

[4] See Ralph A. Thaxton Jr., *Catastrophe and Contention in Rural China: Mao's Great Leap Forward Famine and the Origins of Righteous Resistance in Da Fo Village* (Cambridge: Cambridge University Press, 2010).

[5] Throughout this chapter, names of places and people are anonymized or pseudonymized to protect the privacy of those involved, as well as the staff who provided access to the archive files.

Guomindang in August 1948. The administrative restructuring that accompanied communization in 1958 saw Xu Village combine with four other local settlements to form Li Production Brigade. This brigade encompassed around 2,000 people, divided between thirteen production teams. The approximately 400 residents of Xu Village comprised two of these teams – the fifth, which covered the parts of the village east of the main road, and the sixth, which lay to its west. In light of what follows, it is worth noting that one feature of the reorganization of village life in the late 1950s was a change in gendered division of labor. During the GLF, women in Xu Village were mobilized to participate more substantially in agricultural production and the public sphere. Yet this did not necessarily lead to increased political authority: instead, with the majority of working-age men reassigned to construction projects outside the village, a handful of male cadres were able to dominate affairs within its borders.

In early 1960, the revival of the SEM saw the downfall of two of these cadres, Xu Quan, a production team leader, and Li Xin, the production brigade secretary. Between them, these two men had exercised significant control over the course of the GLF in Xu Village. Now, their opponents in the Xu lineage made a series of incendiary allegations against them, leading to their removal from office, prosecution, and long-term imprisonment.

Whatever the truth of the charges against Xu and Li, the nature of which will be explored in detail below, it seems clear that the specific allegations were less significant to their removal than was the general sense that they had abused and misused their power. For the forces arrayed against them, the two men's departure created an opportunity to moderate the GLF months ahead of the official rectification campaign later in the year. In Xu Village, contrary to the authorities' intentions, the SEM became not a means to intensify the GLF, but a chance to undermine it by a factional seizure of local power. This sudden reversal of fortunes illustrates the centrality of campaign-style politics to rural life in the early People's Republic of China (PRC). The top-down imposition of one campaign, the GLF, sparked the disastrous famine, and it was local agency in the manipulation of another campaign, the SEM, that began the process of recovery long before the official go-ahead was given.

The files of evidence against Li and Xu paint an abundantly detailed picture of the agents and local conflicts at work in their fall from grace. Interrogation records combine with witness testimony, usually referred to as "exposure materials" (*jiefa cailiao*), in two archival files which form the basis of this chapter: for Li Xin, a 166-page dossier detailing his investigation for rape, and for Xu Quan, a document of 114 pages outlining his apparent "reseizure" of property confiscated during land reform, the crime of "reversing the reckoning" (*daosuan*).[6] As well as evidential documents – "exposure materials" collected by a judicial cadre on a visit to Xu Village from 29 to 31 January 1960, plus police and court interrogation records[7] – the two files include key legal instruments such as arrest reports, indictments, and verdicts (dating from February and April 1960), plus documentation relating to a court review of the men's convictions (October 1962).[8] The exposure materials in particular paint Li and Xu as deeply corrupt men, suggesting that their actions exacerbated conflicts in the village and that these ultimately led to a rebellion of the Xu lineage.

Below, we will explore the two criminal cases, identifying the way in which they were apparently constructed by local forces among the village elite, who shared an abiding opposition to Li and Xu. A close reading of the exposure materials will lead us to consider the conflicts at work in the village as the SEM got underway and suggest how the cases came together in its wake.

The Case of Li Xin: Power and Sex in the GLF

On January 25, 1960, three days before the Chinese Lunar New Year, three women appeared in the office of the commune committee, some miles from Xu Village, claiming that they had been raped by their brigade secretary, Li Xin. A legal cadre was soon dispatched to the village to investigate. The investigation, completed in just two days on January 30 and 31, gathered thirty-five "exposure materials" pointing to a range of wrongdoings by the alleged perpetrator. Soon afterwards, thirty-nine-year-old Li was arrested by the L County Public Security Bureau. He promptly confessed his guilt under interrogation. At his trial on April 29, Li Xin was sentenced to twenty years' imprisonment for four counts of rape, one attempted rape, sheltering a "class enemy" (Xu Quan) and engaging in adultery with Xu's wife, Zhang Fan.

Li Xin's conviction in spring 1960 was a sudden twist in a previously positive tale. Officially classed as a "poor peasant" on the basis of his family's socioeconomic status, Li had received only a year of schooling, but the picture that emerges from the files is of a highly competent individual.[9] He

---

[6] These documents, respectively titled "Li Xin Rape Case, 1960" and "Xu Quan Property Reseizure Case, 1960," are numbers, 53-3-830 and 53-3-1520 in the L County Archive.

[7] Undated, but probably created between March and April 1960.

[8] Below, documents from the archival files are referenced based on their content, so testimony on Li Xin's case provided by Xu Cai on 30 January 1960 is "exposure material from Xu Cai, 30 January 1960," *Li Xin Rape Case*.

[9] See, for instance, the reports compiled on Li during "labor reform" (*laogai*). These assessments also highlight his temper. He appears to have relentlessly picked fights over trivial issues, a trait which can perhaps be linked to his autocratic and violent rule in the village during his time in office.

moved to Xu Village with his father in his early or mid-twenties after their previous home, the neighboring Song Village, was sacked by bandits in the early 1940s. Li's résumé thereafter indicates a rapid rise to prominence underpinned by strong political performance during the process of collectivization in the 1950s. After organizing a mutual aid group, a preliminary form of agricultural co-operative, in 1953, he joined the Party in 1954, and by 1955 he was leading the village's agricultural advanced co-operative. He began his last role, brigade secretary, when the post was created after communization in 1958, and he continued to work actively until the rape conviction and other charges brought about his spectacular dethronement.

Sexual abuse by cadres was not unusual in the early PRC, and the GLF, which placed control of scarce grain resources in the hands of a select few officeholders, was a fertile ground for predatory behavior. Despite the increasing involvement of rural women in productive and political life in this period, clear patterns of discrimination continued, and male elites by and large maintained their accustomed dominance. As Yang Bin and Cao Shuji have persuasively shown, women in Mao's China were vulnerable to a pernicious "institutional trap" which enabled abusive male cadres to extract sexual services in exchange for basic necessities: patriarchy writ large in the state bodies that were closest to their everyday lives.[10] The emerging population of female cadres was also vulnerable to abuses less extreme but nonetheless pernicious, with the nominal privileges of their offices often failing to translate into political voice. Many found themselves compelled to continue depending on male counterparts, often relatives or acquaintances, even in the New China.[11] Male cadres' power to demand sex in exchange for material benefits comes to the fore in a case noted by Ralph A. Thaxton, in which a male cadre slept with at least five different local women during the GLF. Ironically, when confronted with the circumstances, some local male residents argued that the very fact of the cadre's power – his ability to favor the women with food and job assignments – made it less likely that the encounters were abusive. For them, there must have been a willingness on the part of the women to sleep with a young, handsome, divorced man in a position of authority under conditions of famine.[12]

Power dynamics in the villages of the late 1950s, in short, made them frequent sites of abuse. In Li's case, the rape allegations came from four

[10] Bin Yang and Shuji Cao, "Cadres, Grain, and Sexual Abuse in Wuwei County, Mao's China," *Journal of Women's History* 28, no. 2 (2016): 50.
[11] For the burden of female cadres see Gail Hershatter, *The Gender of Memory: Rural Women and China's Collective Past* (Berkeley, Los Angeles and London: University of California Press, 2014); Kellee S. Tsai, "Women and the State in Post-1949 Rural China," *Journal of International Affairs* 49, no. 2 (Winter 1996): 493–524.
[12] Thaxton, *Catastrophe and Contention in Rural China*, 237–238.

victims, named in the records as Ma Xiuzhen (thirty-five, production team leader), Gao Yuanrui (forty-four, also a production team leader), Su Guihua (forty-four, on the staff of the local public dining hall), and Yang Ying (nineteen, platoon leader). Zhang Fan, with whom Li carried on an affair that was by all account consensual, was forty-seven at the time of the investigation and worked as a warehouse keeper. The backgrounds of the women, predominantly middle-aged and married, differentiate them from the victims in Yang and Cao's study, who were primarily unmarried and between the ages of sixteen and thirty-six.[13] Nineteen-year-old Yang Ying stood out in this respect, and she appears to have been especially vulnerable: her husband and all the rest of her family, fifteen people in total, had moved away to the northeast of China sometime previously, leaving her alone in the village. Otherwise, the case appears to fit the pattern outlined above. The victims had all been promoted by Li Xin, and they had, to varying degrees, formed relationships of dependency with him. Ma Xiuzhen, for instance, was promoted by Li after he deliberately dismissed the previous holder of her post, and the deputy team leader Xu Cai reported that she had "kept up a sexual relationship with Li Xin up to this point."[14] In this moment, at the height of the Great Leap famine, food also played a role: Li and the four victims appear to have gathered regularly at Zhang Fan's house to divide up grain stolen from the team storage depot.[15] It seems to have been in this context that Zhang Fan intimated to Li that the other women had agreed to sleep with him.[16] To what extent Zhang's "offer" to Li reflected a premeditated decision by the five women is unclear.

So far, so familiar. Yet a number of points in the archive file suggest that this was not an open-and-shut case. The fifth victim, Xu Lan, who accused Li of attempted rape, described his attack on her occurring at her home in June 1958; the testimony of her mother (who was absent at the time) supported this date. Yet another witness, and Li Xin himself in his confession, dated the incident to the fall of 1957, almost a year earlier. Li's confession, moreover, is exceptionally vague, admitting little more than that he "held [Xu's] hand" and "talked nonsense."[17] Xu's own

---

[13] Yang and Cao, "Cadres, Grain, and Sexual Abuse," 41.

[14] "Exposure material from Xu Cai, January 30, 1960," *Li Xin Rape Case*, L County Archive, 53-3-830-52.

[15] "Evidentiary material from Xu Wu, 30 January 1960," *Li Xin Rape Case*, L County Archive, 53-3-830-56; "Interrogation material of Li Xin, unspecified time," *Daosuan Case of Xu Quan*, L County Archive, 53-3-1520-101; "Verdict of Zhang Fan, 3 April 1960," *Daosuan Case of Xu Quan*, L County Archive, 53-3-1520-17.

[16] "Interrogation material of Li Xin," *Li Xin Rape Case*, L County Archive, 53-3-830-70; "Interrogation material of Zhang Fan," *Xu Quan Rape Case*, L County Archive, 53-3-1520-104.

[17] "Interrogation material of Li Xin," *Li Xin Rape Case*, L County Archive, 53-3-830-75.

testimony does include some detail, but again there is little conclusive. Describing the incident, she is recorded recalling,

As soon as he came in, he "hit" [*za*] me, and I gave him a dressing down: "You bastard, you're up to no good. This isn't like when you've come to the house before ... I thought you were better than this." He wouldn't let me talk about it, but that's the truth. Then he left.

It is uncertain – and the files do not clarify – exactly what Xu was describing when she referred to Li "hitting" her, and we have little more to go on for this allegation.[18] The lack of specifics is common to the other cases as well, with the statements of both the victims and Li never exceeding a couple of lines and conveying little more than the time of alleged attacks (between 1957 and 1959), the location, and the fact that the rapes were, in each case, preceded by a threat from Li. The narrative is nearly identical in each case: patterned, unadorned, and brief.

Formulaic confessions and witness statements are by no means conclusive proof that Li's alleged crimes did not take place. But leaving aside the question of what actually happened to Ma Xiuzhen, Gao Yuanrui, Su Guihua, Yang Ying, and Xu Lan between 1957 and 1959, the sentence Li received, and the fact that he was prosecuted at all, suggest that there must have been something unusual about his case. In the absence of a formal criminal code (which would not be implemented until 1979), legal definitions of the act of rape were not set in stone, but in general the bar for prosecution seems to have been a high one in the early PRC. One key document, the May 1957 "Directive from the Supreme People's Court and the Ministry of Justice on Adjudication in Current Urban Trials of Various Types of Criminal Case," asserts that the essential component of the crime is resistance on the part of the victim, rather than absence of consent: rape, it asserts, refers only to "sexual intercourse [either] carried out when a woman is incapable of resistance as a result of violence, duress, or other means, or that takes advantage of the woman's being in such a state that resistance is impossible."[19] The same provision underlines that rape can occur against a background of "exploitation of

---

[18] "Visiting records from Xu Lan, April 14, 1960," *Li Xin Rape Case*, L County Archive, 53-3-830-76.

[19] Zuigao renmin fayuan he sifabu, "guanyu chengshi zhong dangqian jilei xingshi anjian shenpan gongzuo de zhishi" (Directive from the Supreme People's Court and the Ministry of Justice on Adjudication in Current Urban Trials of Various Types of Criminal Case), May 24, 1957, at www.law-lib.com/lawhtm/1949-1979/1232.htm, accessed July 29, 2019; see also Xing Ying, *Cunzhuang shenpan shi zhong de daode yu zhengzhi: 1951–1976 nian zhongguo xinan yige shancun de gushi* (Morality and Politics in the History of Justice in a Village: The Story of a Mountain Village in Southwest China, 1951–1976) (Beijing: Zhishi chanquan chubanshe, 2009), 67.

a superior–subordinate relationship in the workplace, or a parental relationship," calling for perpetrators in such cases to be "severely punished."
Yet the focus on active resistance (something that scarcely appears in the
short, patterned statements in Li Xin's case files) suggests that, even in
these cases, something more than lack of consent was required. In practice, the situation was even less favorable to complainants, with sexual
allegations against cadres tending to be treated as, at best, supplementary
evidence in investigations of political and economic errors.[20] Thaxton
identifies that punishments for sexual offences were light and in one case
an accuser was forced to kneel and apologize to the alleged perpetrator.[21]
Even when the threshold for rape and attempted rape was met, other
offenders in the same period are known to have received sentences ranging from one to three and a half years' imprisonment.[22]

How, then, are we to account for the apparently unusual treatment of
Li Xin's case? It is, of course, possible that Li was guilty of everything of
which he stood accused at his trial in spring 1960, and that the detailed
circumstances of the crimes, omitted from the archive files, brought the
sentence within the usual bounds under the law at the time. Yet the files
themselves suggest that something else was at work. Li's case unfolded
against a backdrop of deep politicization in China's legal system. As part
of the so-called "Judicial Great Leap Forward" (*sifa dayuejin*), legal
cadres had been required to dispose of cases at a much higher tempo
since 1958.[23] To promote the interests of the GLF, they were expected to
expose the misdeeds of four categories of enemy – landlords, rich peasants, counterrevolutionaries and bad elements (*di fu fan huai*) – through
close contact with "the masses."[24] In plain language, this approach meant
that "judicial work groups," sent down to the countryside by the authorities, interrogated offenders jointly with local power holders, consulted
them on sentencing, and frequently made decisions with an eye to the
reaction of the local population. The theory went that, threatened with
exposure of their crimes by the masses in face-to-face meetings, inveterate

---

[20] Yang and Cao, "Cadres, Grain, and Sexual Abuse," 43.

[21] Thaxton, *Catastrophe and Contention in Rural China*, 249, 238.

[22] Jerome Alan Cohen, *The Criminal Process in the People's Republic of China, 1949–1963: An Introduction* (Cambridge, MA: Harvard University Press, 1968), 266–268, 347, 415–416.

[23] Lianjun Liu, "'Dayuejin' zhong de renmin sifa" (People's Justice in the "Great Leap Forward"), *Zhengfa luntan* 5 (2013): 142–153.

[24] "Wang yuanzhang zai zhongji fayuan yuanzhang, sifa juzhang zuotanhui shang de fayan" (Speech by Court President Wang at the Forum of the Presidents of the Intermediate Courts and the Directors of the Justice Department), May 8, 1958, *Zuigaoyuan, gaoyuan, zhongyuan 1958–1963 nian wenjian* (Documents of the Supreme Court, High Court, and Intermediate Courts, 1958–1963), L County Archive, 53-2-6-57.

offenders would be sure to admit their guilt.[25] It was a system designed to bring swift results. It was also open to misuse.

In Li's case, it is striking to note the extent to which the victims were supported by the masses, in the form of the elite of Xu Village. Members of the dominant Xu lineage combined to produce thirty-five "exposure materials" against him in just two days of investigation; by contrast, as noted above, the evidence from the victims themselves was by and large scanty, showing little sign of any particular determination to pursue justice against Li. Given the lack of strong testimony from the victims, it seems plausible that it may have been the weight of material provided by the village elite that doomed Li. Despite its limited utility as evidence, these reams of accusations must have clearly showed the investigating cadre which way the masses leant. Li had no choice but to promptly plead guilty, and no detailed investigation was carried out before he received his sentence.

The sense that politics was at play in Li's conviction is leant added weight by the outcome of a post-conviction review of his case in 1962, when the worst excesses of the GLF had passed. One rape charge was removed from the record entirely; of the remaining four, two were described in the files as lacking evidence "sufficient for the adjudication" reached in the original case.[26] The court, however, declined to reduce Li's sentence, and he would die of liver disease a number of years later, still incarcerated. In recent interviews, local cadres asserted that his family had appealed for him to be rehabilitated, but objections in the village had made this impossible.

The Case of Xu Quan: A Crime of Reseizure

One allegation against Li Xin stands out as being of a nonsexual nature: that of protecting a "class enemy" named Xu Quan. Xu was investigated at the same time as Li, on January 29–30, 1960, and his case, recorded in a second archive file, helps capture the course of events that led to both men's downfall. As a result of official enquiries, Xu was sentenced to ten years' imprisonment for "reversing the reckoning" (*daosuan*); that is, taking back property that had been confiscated under land reform. In its original form, this crime – "reseizure" for short – could be committed only by those classed as landlords, but the definition was later expanded to include "rich peasants" also. Reseizure cases are common in the judicial

---

[25] Jerome Alan Cohen, "The Criminal Process in the People's Republic of China: An Introduction," *Harvard Law Review* 79, no. 3 (1966): 487.
[26] "Court Review, 27 October, 1962," *Li Xin Rape Case*, L County Archive, 53-3-830-23.

files, especially in the years 1955, 1958, and 1960, but the literature on them is fairly limited.[27]

Rooted as it was in the CCP land reform program, "reseizure" was predominantly a political crime, a point made clear by its designation as a form of counterrevolutionary activity. Reseizure cases provided a means to continue the negotiation of property rights in the countryside after the formal end of land reform. Because of their political nature, they also offered a ready means to bring disfavored groups to heel or to reclassify them within the new social hierarchy. A case study from our very own L County in 1955 suggests that an allegation of "reseizure" could arise from fairly ambiguous sets of facts. The grey area between the CCP's land policy and traditional forms of property rights and land trading rules was a fertile ground for such cases.[28]

In Xu Quan's case, the charges were wide-ranging, including seizing two pieces of land in 1947 and three trees in the 1950s, as well as allegations that he had corruptly obtained his post as production team leader by exploiting the adulterous relationship between his wife Zhang Fan and Li Xin. Zhang Fan herself was convicted of embezzlement and adultery; she received a sentence of six years.

As with Li Xin, the circumstances of Xu's case appear to be more complex than the judicial system's open-and-shut treatment of him would suggest. The history of Xu's supposedly corrupt appointment is described in Li Xin's confession, which paints a rather different picture of the verdict:

I was a group leader [for mutual aid] in 1954, while Xu Quan was the head of the village. In 1955, the [agricultural] co-operative was established and then turned into an advanced co-operative in the autumn. At this time, Xu came to the office and asked me if he could change his class status, since he was the village head when the co-operative was established and had never been struggled against in the

---

[27] Two recent Chinese studies address the issue. Hu Yingze and Feng Xi illustrate how houses allocated during the land reform could be returned to the original owners in later periods in both legal and illegal ways. See Yingze Hu and Xi Feng, "20 shiji wuliushi niandai tugai fangwu fenpei jiqi bianqian yanjiu: yi shanxi sheng yongji xian weili" (Housing Allocation in the Land Reform and Its Evolution in the 1950s and 1960s: A Case Study of Yongji County in Shanxi Province)" *Kaifang shidai* 5 (2019): 130–151. Meanwhile, Li Lin sheds light on property disputes in general between 1950 and 1965. See Li Lin, *Shehui biange shiqi de caichan jiufen yu susong shijian: Y shi fayuan 1950–1965 nian minshi dang'an shizheng yanjiu* (Property Disputes and the Practice of Litigation in the Period of Social Transformation: An Empirical Study Based on Civil Archival Files from Y City Court between 1950 and 1965) (Beijing: Shangwu yinshuguan, 2018).

[28] Wenyu Jing and Shuji Cao, "Tudi chanquan yu 20 shiji 50 niandai de 'funong daosuan': Yi Shandong L xian Li Xuhai daosuan an wei zhongxin" (Land Ownership and "Reseizure by Rich Peasants" in 1950s China: An Investigation of the Case of Li Xuhai in L County, Shandong), *Zhongguo jingjishi yanjiu* 4 (2019): 56–68.

meeting on rich peasants [*funong hui*]. The township head told me that that Xu could be treated as a middle peasant, but he did not mention changing his class status. [However,] I changed Xu's class status to middle peasant after coming back. Thereafter Xu became close to me ... In 1956, shortly after being founded, four groups in the co-operative privately distributed approximately ten thousand *jin* of grain. Xu Quan did not join this private distribution. He had often said that poor peasants were not reliable, and at that time I was convinced. I thought that the co-operative was established for the poor peasants, but [I questioned] why they did such a thing. In 1957, Xu was selected as group leader, and after the harvest he became the production team leader.[29]

Li's account suggests little out of the ordinary: in fact, it fits the general pattern of cadre appointments in this period exceptionally well. During collectivization, rural cadres at the grassroots typically came into office via a procedure known as "approval by the masses and authorization by the Party." This system, which gave the official's constituency and his superiors a say in selection, was designed to strengthen the authorities' links to the grass roots, avoiding the promotion of those focused on narrow, local interests in favor of those whom both the villages and the higher levels of the state could agree on. Personal relationships between superior and subordinate could play a significant role in nominations, but not to the exclusion of all else: a nominating brigade secretary whose preferred candidate failed to fulfill their official duties could expect to be punished themselves.[30] What tended to arise under these circumstances was essentially a clientelist relationship, which bound subordinates to superiors and thus encouraged the implementation of policies and orders from above.

This appears to have been the situation with Xu Quan's appointment. He and Li already had a good relationship, good enough that Li helped him change his class status when the struggle against rich peasants, the category into which he fell, intensified in 1955. Xu had displayed some ability as a leader in his previous role, winning him prestige in the village. In this context and given the insubordination Li had faced from those under him in the past, Xu was a reasonable choice for the position for which he was selected in 1957. While they admitted to other offences, albeit in a vague and insubstantial way, both men's interrogations confirm that Xu's relationship with Zhang Fan began only after his appointment, suggesting that there was little substance to the suggestion that Xu obtained his post corruptly through her. It seems likely that this allegation

---

[29] "Interrogation material from Li Xin, time unspecified," *Xu Quan Reseizure Case*, L County Archive, 53-3-1520-99.
[30] Jean Oi, "Communism and Clientelism: Rural Politics in China," *World Politics* 37, no. 2 (1985): 254–255.

was prosecuted mainly to add force to the charge that Li Xin had sheltered a class enemy.

There are also difficulties with the main case against Xu, that of reseizure. He was said to have taken three trees for his personal use: two elms, one of which he sold in 1955 and the other of which he used as material for his mother's coffin in 1959, plus a third tree taken in October that year, which he was supposed to have put to personal use. These allegations were fundamentally problematic, since the regulations governing land reform suggested that trees should not be confiscated in the first place. Yet, in a context of resource scarcity, supposedly exempt property, such as trees, bricks, and even clods of soil, could become objects of redistribution and fierce contention. Changing power dynamics in the villages, coupled with an often arbitrary approach by successor leaders to the handling of confiscated property, only intensified these conflicts. In Xu's case, the two elms he was accused of acquiring had been in limbo for some time following land reform: as the former president of the local peasant association confirmed, they "were confiscated but not distributed to households."[31] This is a common feature in reseizure cases. Property that had been confiscated but, for whatever reason, had not been distributed was supposed to remain in the care of the peasant association. However, following the end of land reform after 1953, these bodies fell into decline, with village governments and Party organizations replacing them as the primary centers of local power. In the process, ownership of the confiscated properties in their possession often became controversial. Documentation from reseizure cases suggests that leaders in the new political organs regularly disposed of such properties to their personal connections.

Given this background, it is notable that no one seems to have raised any immediate objections to Xu Quan selling one elm tree in 1955, nor to the fact that the second remained untended for over a decade, despite being in a prominent location in the village. It seems that no one else, and certainly no official body, was felt to have an especially strong claim to them. The case of the third tree is particularly interesting, as it seems not to fit the pattern of a reseizure case at all. From the files, it appears that the tree was transferred to Xu Quan only in 1959, after the communization process in which land, livestock, and forests – the primary factors of production in rural society – were brought into collective ownership. Since the tree was in communal hands when Xu acquired it, the acquisition cannot, by definition, have constituted the crime of reseizure, which could be made out only for

---

[31] "Evidentiary material from Xu Fang," *Daosuan Case of Xu Quan*, L County Archive, 53-3-1520-47.

confiscated, not collectivized, property. Encroachment on the collective's holdings it may have been, but if we accept the regime's definitions as serious, it was not a counterrevolutionary act. The fact that Xu Quan was convicted despite the apparently dubious nature of the charges points to the quality of reseizure as a political crime adaptable to the exigencies of the moment. This is further underlined by a final allegation against Xu: that he reclaimed 3.2 *mu* (around half an acre) of land that had been confiscated from his family when they were assessed as "rich peasants." In Xu Village, the land reform took place in 1947, well before the CCP took final control of Shandong from the Nationalists, and it was at this point that Xu was first stripped of the land. Shortly afterwards, however, he regained it. In November 1947, the Nationalists took back control of the village and reversed their rivals' policy, directly telling the new owners "you got it wrong."[32] The land was Xu's once more. However, two years later, following the CCP victory in the Civil War, he handed it back again. It was this brief period when he held the land for a second time that formed the basis of the charge. There is little evidence of any class hatred or counterrevolutionary purpose in Xu's actions over the land; rather, he appears to have done little more than allowing politics to happen around him. In the hyper-politicized environment of the GLF, that was enough.

To understand just how unconvincing the charges against Xu were from a legal perspective, it is helpful to remember that, in the early PRC, the holdings of "rich peasants" like Xu were supposed to be protected from confiscation. Article 6 of the Agrarian Reform Law of June 1950 stipulates that land owned by rich peasants, whether cultivated by them or by hired labourers, is to be protected from infringement, along with their other property. Even small quantities of land rented out by them were supposed to be preserved.[33] It was only, later, during the period of collectivization of agriculture, that rich peasants were officially labeled "class enemies" alongside landlords. In short, cases of reseizure brought against rich peasants were essentially *ex post facto*.

A further complication is added by the fact that, while the legitimacy of property ownership was determined by a person's class status, that status itself was not necessarily static or objectively determined. Describing

---

[32] "Evidentiary material from Xu Zhong, January 29, 1960," *Daosuan Case of Xu Quan*, L County Archive, 53-3-1520-50; "Evidentiary material from Zhao Ruxiang, January 29, 1960," *Daosuan Case of Xu Quan*, L County Archive, 53-3-1520-51.

[33] "Zhonghua renmin gongheguo tudi gaigefa" (Land Reform Law of the People's Republic of China), in Zhonggong Zhongyang wenxian yanjiushi, ed., *Jianguo yilai zhongyao wenxian xuanbian* (A Selection of Important Documents since the Founding of the People's Republic of China), vol. 1 (Beijing: Zhongyang wenxian chubanshe chuban, 1992), 336–345.

three major, national revisions of class labels – during the Remedial Course in Democracy of 1960–1961, the Four Clean-Ups of 1964–1966, and the final reassessment in 1979 – Jeremy Brown demonstrates that labels were often changed based on apparently extraneous factors. Rather than focusing narrowly on the formal classification criteria, grass-roots cadres might apply inconsistent standards, draw on long-ago events, to support a change or act based on a person's recent misdeeds.[34] Less well-studied but also important in this connection was the "Transforming Backward Towns" (*gaizao luohou xiang*) campaign of 1954–1956, also known as the "Remedial Course in Land Reform" (*tugai buke*). This movement not only saw large numbers of class labels reconsidered; it also expropriated additional properties from "rich peasants" and "land-lords" to "complement the needs of poor peasants."[35] While the Central Committee attempted to limit the reach of the program by underlining that it was not intended as a means to "accomplish the tasks of socialist transformation" wholesale, it also emphasized the necessity of depriving "landlords" and "rich peasants" of their properties in order to "solve current problems in living and production and promote initiatives for joining the agricultural co-operatives."[36]

In L County, the Transforming Backward Towns campaign and the Agricultural Co-operatization (*nongye hezuohua*) movement were carried out simultaneously during late 1955 and 1956, driving the county toward a socialist transformation of agriculture. By the end of June 1956, twenty-two "backward towns" and 135 "backward villages" had been "trans-formed," with 634 out of 672 identified "landlord households" and 425 out of 522 "rich peasant households" dispossessed or forced to forfeit property. Of these, fully 107 "landlord households" and sixty-one "rich peasant households" were newly classified as such as part of the process.[37]

---

[34] Jeremy Brown, "Moving Targets: Changing Class Labels in Rural Hebei and Henan, 1960–1979," in Jeremy Brown and Matthew D. Johnson, eds., *Maoism at the Grassroots: Everyday Life in China's Era of High Socialism* (Cambridge, MA and London: Harvard University Press, 2015), 51–76.

[35] "Zhonggong Zhongyang guanyu gaizao luohouxiang gongzuo de zhishi" (Instructions of the CCP Central Committee on Work to Transform Backward Towns), August 1, 1954, in Zhongyang danganguan and Zhonggong Zhongyang wenxian yanjiushi, eds., *Zhonggong zhongyang wenjian xuanji* (Selected Documents of the CCP Central Committee), vol. 17 (Beijing: Renmin chubanshe, 2013), 1–7.

[36] "Zhonggong zhongyang guanyu gaizao luohouxiang gongzuo wenti gei zhejiang sheng-wei de pifu" (Reply of the Central Committee to Zhejiang Provincial Committee on Work to Transform Backward Towns), March 9, 1955, in Zhongyang danganguan and Zhonggong Zhongyang wenxian yanjiushi, eds., *Zhonggong zhongyang wenjian xuanji* (Selected Documents of the CCP Central Committee), vol. 18 (Beijing: Renmin chu-banshe, 2013), 278, 281.

[37] "Luohouxiang gezhong shuzi tongjibiao" (Statistics from Backward Towns), in Zhonggong L xian weiyuanhui bangongshi, ed., *L xian luogai bangongshi guanyu luohou*

These changes in class status had serious consequences. Inter alia, shifts of class label could transform legal ownership into criminal reseizure overnight. In fact, the bulk of reseizure cases in L County involved a change of class status. In one case, a man named Sun Mingshu experienced three shifts in his class label, each time accompanied by loss or reclamation of his assets, between the 1940s and the 1960s.[38] During land reform, he was classified as a "landlord" and lost his property; later, he succeeded in converting his class status to "middle peasant" and won it back. He was returned to "landlord" status during the Transforming the Backward Towns campaign, but again he successfully reversed the verdict and received his property back. When he was reclassified as a "landlord" for the third time in 1960, he was sentenced to eighteen years' imprisonment for numerous reseizure crimes. Finally, he lodged an appeal against his classification in 1966, and the court ordered his release pending a new trial to determine his status under the auspices of the Four Clean-Ups campaign.

In Sun's case, the difficulties with his class status lay in the complexity of the classification system itself. The criteria for determining class were various, ranging from the amount of land possessed to the division between land let to tenants and land worked directly by the owner, as well as the so-called "exploitation rate" (the level of exploitation that the person being classified had either committed as a "landlord" or been subjected to at their hands).[39] The interaction between these complex elements often made it possible to classify the same person in multiple ways. For instance, although Sun's family had owned more than thirty *mu* of land before the land reform, double the average for his village, they lacked sufficient labor force to work it because his father died early; moreover, since the land was pawned rather than rented, the exploitation rate was very low.[40] This equivocal situation made it easy for his class status to shift with the changing political winds.

xiangcun gezhong shuzi de tongji (Statistics from Backward Villages and Towns by the L County Office of Transforming Backward Towns), L County Archive, 2-1-39-21, 2-1-39-27. The L County Gazetteer notes a different number: twenty-two key towns and 109 "generally backward villages." See L xianzhi bianzuan weiyuanhui, ed., *L Xianzhi* (L County Gazetteer) (Beijing: Xinhua chubanshe, 1997), 20.

[38] *Daosuan Case of Sun Mingshu in 1960*, L County Archive, 53-3-1520.

[39] "Zhengwuyuan guanyu huafen nongcun jieji chengfen de jueding" (Decision of the State Council on the Classification of Rural Class Status), in Zhonggong Zhongyang wenxian yanjiushi, ed., *Jianguo yilai zhongyao wenxian xuanbian* (A Selection of Important Documents since the Founding of the People's Republic of China), vol. 1 (Beijing: Zhongyang wenxian chubanshe chuban, 1992), 382–407.

[40] Pawned land was not considered to be tenanted, so the landowner was not held to be exploiting those who worked it. The distinction built on the traditional system of "dual ownership" (*yi tian er zhu*, lit. "one field, two owners"), under which the pawnee was held

This is the background against which to consider Xu Quan's conviction. The allegations against him assumed that he was really a "rich peasant," a status which we have already seen he was able to have revoked in the mid-1950s. How supportable was this assertion? In an interview in Xu Village, the former Party secretary, who had known those involved in our drama personally, insisted that Xu was really a "middle peasant." According to him, only two households were classified as "rich peasants" during land reform in the village, and Xu Quan's was not one of them. For him, this made it impossible that Xu could have committed the crime of which he was convicted; as he put it, "how could Xu Quan possibly commit reseizure?" Instead, the offence that mattered to him was the embezzlement of grain that Xu had been involved in when he served as production team leader.[41]

Clearly Xu was never regarded as an emblematic "class enemy," since whatever his true classification, he had not been struggled against as a "rich peasant." Xu's exploitation rate is missing from the archive files, but with respect to the amount of land he owned it seems that he is unlikely to have qualified in the "rich peasant" category. Xu Fang, sometime president of the peasant association, reported that Xu had lost thirty *mu* of land to confiscation,[42] but this seems an outlandishly large number. A survey of five villages in L County in 1948 suggests that average land possession per capita was 2.8 *mu*: ten *mu* for "landlords," eight *mu* for "rich peasants," 4.5 *mu* for "upper-middle peasants," three *mu* for "middle peasants" and 1.5 *mu* for "poor peasants."[43] Thirty *mu* of confiscatable land (that is, land above the average possession rate per capita) would have placed Xu comfortably in the landlord bracket, yet no one seems to have suggested that he belonged to that class; and if he had lost a full thirty *mu*, why did he only recover a paltry 3.2 *mu* when he had the chance to do so?

Even under interrogation, Xu confessed to having lost only five *mu* during land reform. This would suggest that his family of two had around 2.5 *mu* of land per head more than the average for the village at that time, for a total of 5.3 *mu* per head. That would place him in the upper-middle peasant band: better off than many, but not a class enemy. When Li Xin

to own the topsoil on payment of a deposit (in Shandong, half of the land's value), while the subsurface soil remained in the hands of the pawner. The pawnee was not hired by the pawner and was not liable for rent. See Shuji Cao and Shigu Liu, *Chuantong zhongguo diquan jiegou jiqi yanbian (xiudingban)* (Traditional Chinese Land Ownership Structure and Its Evolution (revised edition))(Shanghai: Shanghai jiaotong daxue, 2015).

[41] Interview with Xu Fangxiu, May 27, 2018, Xu Village.
[42] "Evidentiary material from Xu Fang, January 29, 1960," *Daosuan Case of Xu Quan*, L County Archive, 53-3-1520-47.
[43] L xianzhi bianzuan, *L Xianzhi*, 112.

officially changed his class status in the village during the Transforming Backward Towns campaign, it became, on paper at least, entirely legitimate for Xu to reclaim his confiscated property. How are we, then, to understand his conviction for reseizure on this basis? And, in light of his limited property holdings, how are we to explain the eventual determination in 1960 that Xu was indeed a "rich peasant"? It seems clear that the case was, at least to some degree, constructed for political purposes.

Eruption: Factional Conflicts and the Socialist Education Campaign in Late 1959

What were the underlying dynamics that led to Xu Quan and Li Xin being convicted on charges that appear to have been massaged on the one hand, and taken far more seriously than comparable cases from the same period on the other? Here it is helpful to turn again to the files of evidence collected against them in early 1960.

The over sixty items of "exposure material" against Li and Xu provide a rich seam of information on latent contentions in Xu Village in the late 1950s. Notably, over 80 percent of these materials were provided by only six people, all of them leading figures in village life. Even more suggestively, five of the six were members of the same social group – the third subbranch of the elder branch of the Xu lineage – while the sixth came from the closely related fourth subbranch. They were Xu Cai (deputy leader of the Sixth Production Team), Xu Yu (sometime vice president of the peasant association, Sixth Production Team), Xu Yin (Xu Quan's successor as leader of the Sixth Production Team), Xu Wu (leader of the Fifth Production Team), Xu Rui (brigade treasurer, Fifth Production Team), and fourth subbranch member Xu Tian (sometime member of the peasant association, Sixth Production Team). A closer examination of their evidence suggests that whatever Li Xin and Xu Quan's crimes may have been, it was factional struggles among village elites, embodied in lineage and intra- and inter-team relationships that led to their downfall. In this connection, it is interesting to note that very little of the six men's evidence concentrates on the sexual and property crimes of which Li Xin was chiefly accused. Instead, corruption and abuse of power are their primary focus.

With the start of the GLF in 1958, the "people's commune" (*renmin gongshe*) became the basic unit of rural administration. The creation of these communes, organized into subunits of production brigade and production team, was in one sense a tremendous blow to the traditional power structure of the countryside, shifting the center of gravity from familiar villages and towns to a novel formation that generally stretched across numerous settlements. Yet despite this radical change, familiar units such as family and lineage continued to play an important role in social relations.[44] Jonathan Unger argues that the exacerbation of rural conflicts during the Cultural Revolution was generated by a confluence of "hostilities that were grounded in tradition and those engendered by the state," which "intersected and played off each other."[45]

Though the changes under communization were supposed to fuse villages into larger bodies, in practice this happened only in the administrative realm. Five villages made up Li Brigade, but the accusations against Li Xin came only from Xu Village, suggesting that it had not been possible for Li to expand his social network, power base, and corrupt activities beyond his home place. It is notable that, having originally come to Xu Village from a neighboring settlement, Li was able to rise to prominence as an outsider. This put him in a dual position: less able to maintain a strong support network than his fellow villagers, but also less constrained by kinship ties. The lack of blood relations to keep onside perhaps freed Li to favor the Party's interests over local interests, helping him to pursue collectivization and the GLF more proactively than otherwise. It may also have made him more able to exploit his position to demand sexual services, in large measure from the wives of members of the Xu clan, to which he had no kin obligation. Of course, in the long run, this abuse deepened those same clansmen's hatred of him and provided an opportunity to bring him down.

If the claims of abuse provided the opportunity, it appears to have been Li's leadership that supplied the motive. In the files, Li's proactivity in the pursuit of Party policy emerges as one of the defining traits of his time as brigade secretary, and not one that the dominant Xu lineage approved of. His aggressive attitude to revolutionary politics was in sharp contrast to the way things were usually done; as two interviewees put it years later, in Xu Village, "the family is big, and folk are modest. No one is willing to offend anyone else."[46] Li's outsider leadership won him plaudits from the center during the GLF, with his brigade praised for reported high yields. For instance, at a cadres' convention organized by the county committee in November 1959, each unit was required to report its output in order to fix the size of the quota for the state's annual grain purchase. Li's brigade was honored with the prestigious "first-class red flag" (*yideng hongqi*) for reporting an outlandish 490 *jin* of grain per *mu* of land, quadruple the

---

[44] Anita Chan, Richard Madsen, and Jonathan Unger, *Chen Village under Mao and Deng* (Berkeley: University of California Press, 1992).
[45] Jonathan Unger, "Cultural Revolution Conflict in the Villages," *China Quarterly* 153 (March 1998): 83, 90–94.
[46] Interview with Xu Fangxiu and Xu Qingxiang, May 27, 2018, Xu Village.

normal figure.[47] Committing to meeting the resulting high quota would inevitably have intensified food shortages, and perhaps it would be more likely to have been done by someone without local kin ties. As Yixin Chen points out, the handing of leadership roles to outsiders was a common feature under the GLF, allowing more radical policy approaches and generally exacerbating the famine.[48] Both production team leaders in the village may have been Xus, but it was Li who controlled local life during his tenure, a state of affairs his increasingly desperate fellow villagers seem to have been determined to end by early 1960.

If politics – and the desire to be rid of an outsider leader seen as excessively, even dangerously, radical – brought down Li Xin, in Xu Quan's case intra-lineage conflict seems to have loomed large. Xu came from the fourth (and second-largest) subbranch of the main branch of the Xu lineage. His subbranch was in constant competition for power with the largest subbranch, the third. (The first and second subbranches were small and relatively less important.) It is perhaps unsurprising, therefore, that the most vehement attacks on Xu came from Xu Cai, the vice team leader, who hailed from the third subbranch. His successor as leader of the Sixth Production Team, Xu Yin, was another member of the same subbranch, as was his brother, who headed the fifth. The fall of Li Xin and Xu Quan shifted power along two axes, from an agent of the state to a more locally minded leadership and from one subbranch of the Xu lineage to another.

Another locus of conflict to consider is the Sixth Production Team itself. From the start of the GLF onwards, the patron–client relationship between Li Xin and Xu Quan allowed the two men to effectively control this team. Their infringement of the collective interest resulted in constant dissatisfaction among team members, particularly those from the village elite, about Li's and Xu's monopoly on resources. As food grew scarcer during the famine, theft, a recognized counteraction for ordinary peasants facing hunger,[49] became more and more common among the

---

[47] Of 379 production units (brigades) in L County, forty-four were honored with the designation "marshal" for reporting over 500 *jin* of grain per *mu*, while seventy-two were awarded the "first-class red flag" for 400–500 *jin*. Li Brigade was at the top of this latter rank. "Hongqi bang" (List of red flag honorees), "Dahui kuaibao" (Conference Bulletin), in *Guanyu 1959 nian 11 yuefen zhaokai de siji ganbu dahui shang de kuaibao, dazibao, hongqibang, zhongdian renwu de cailiao (3)*, L County Committee (Bulletins, Posters, Lists of Red Flag Honorees, and Key Figures from the Four-Grade Cadre Convention held in November 1959 (3)), 2-1-150-15, 2-1-150-84. According to the county gazetteer, the average yield of all kinds of grain was 100–140 *jin* per *mu* in the 1950s. L xianzhi bianzuan, *L Xianzhi*, 115.
[48] Yixin Chen, "When Food Became Scarce: Life and Death in Chinese Villages during the Great Leap Forward Famine," *Journal of the Historical Society* 10, no. 2 (2010): 132–134.
[49] Wangling Gao, *Zhongguo nongmin fanxingwei yanjiu (1950–1980)* (Counteraction by Chinese Peasants (1950–1980)) (Hong Kong: Xianggang zhongwen daxue, 2013).

cadres, who had the advantage of being able to steal directly from warehouses rather than from the fields. This practice often required the involvement of multiple administrative staff members, who together managed collectivized life.

In the Sixth Production Team, Li Xin's authority made the process a fairly simple one. The brigade secretary was able to have a room in Xu Quan's house designated the team storage depot, with Xu's wife as its keeper. According to Xu Cai, the vice leader of the team, who submitted almost half of the "exposure materials" found in the files, Xu Quan and his wife regularly took grain from the store for themselves, for Li Xin, and, less often, for the female cadres in their circle (who were Li Xin's alleged victims). It seems to have been impossible to catch Xu and Zhao in the act – no surprise since the thefts would have taken place in their private home. Instead, the evidence of their conduct was sought in the amount of grain they had had milled, as well as the presence of a few hundred *jin* (that is, a few hundred pounds) of flour in their house. This was held to be proof of theft on the basis that, had the flour been simply a legitimate share of the collective's rations, it would already have been eaten (a not unreasonable conclusion given the dearth of food elsewhere in the village).[50]

Leaving aside the specifics of Xu's thefts, the extent of the factional conflicts at play in his case is made clear by the treatment of similar actions by others, all of which are mentioned in the files. Stealing from the collective had evidently been a strategy across the team in the early days of the famine, with its cadres taking part in a concerted effort to distribute the collective harvest privately. However, once relations deteriorated, Li Xin and Xu Quan alone were held responsible. Similarly, the record indicates that Li Xin was able to gain preferential access to resources not only from Xu Quan but also from other team cadres. Only in Xu's case was this activity used as the basis for a bribery conviction. For other team cadres, essentially the same fact pattern was deployed as evidence of Li's despotic leadership style.

Lineage and intra-team conflict, then, played a clear role in the downfall of Li Xin and Xu Quan. A final, closely related aspect to consider is the level of resource conflict between teams. Frequent changes in methods of resource allocation under the system of people's communes provided opportunities for teams with access to power to gain at the

---

[50] It is worth noting here that, however much he may have stolen, Xu Quan was not living a wildly extravagant life. He is known to have suffered from starvation-induced edema for two months in the autumn of 1959, and he was to die of edema and pulmonary disease just a few months after his imprisonment. For him, theft appears to have been a survival strategy first and foremost.

expense of the less well connected. In the early days of the GLF, almost all private property was collectivized without compensation under the so-called "wind of communism" (*gongchan feng*). Reflecting the contemporary slogan that the organization of agriculture should be "first large-scale, second publicly owned" (*yida ergong*), the seizure was accompanied by a shift in the basic unit of accounting upwards to township-sized people's communes, which were to organize production and distribute rations to rural families in place of their lower-level predecessors. This change was short-lived, however: recognizing the corrosive effect of the massive communes on rural production, the central leadership signaled a turn to "a smaller-scale collective ownership system" (*xiao jiti suoyou zhi*) at the Zhengzhou conference in March 1959. From this point, power was to be delegated downwards again, with two new levels of administration below the commune – production brigades, which often spread across one or more villages, and smaller production teams, which were to act as the new basic accounting unit.[51] This change required the redistribution of previously communized resources. In Xu Village, the population was first organized into a temporary "production camp," which brought the whole community together to cultivate collectivized land and participate in various infrastructure projects, then split into two production teams between which the land was divided. This process of division was an obvious site of contention, a moment when individual or group interests could be furthered under the guise of neutral administrative decision making. The cadres of the newly formed Fifth Production Team suggested distributing the land by drawing lots – a sign, perhaps, of desperation in the face of the inevitable. In the end, despite an even split in the quantity of land allocated, Li Xin was able to insist that the most fertile areas be handed to his Sixth Production Team, resulting in an appreciable difference in crop yields between the two teams.[52] Personal grudges among the cadres came to the fore at this time. For instance, Xu Wu, the leader of the Fifth Team, denounced Li Xin, suggesting that Li had prevented him from joining the Party out of concern that, as a potential member of the brigade Party committee from outside his client base, Xu would undermine his power in the village. Ultimately, Li Xin's partiality

---

[51] "Zhengzhou huiyi jilu" (Zhengzhou Conference Minutes), in Dangdai zhongguo nongye hezuohua shi bianjishi, ed., *Jianguo yilai nongye hezuohua shiliao huibian* (A Compilation of Historical Materials on Agricultural Co-operativization since the Founding of the People's Republic of China) (Beijing: Zhonggong dangshi chibanshe, 1992), 530.

[52] "Exposure material from Xu Rui, January 30, 1960," *Li Xin Rape Case*, L County Archive, 53-3-830-46.

provoked antagonism which not only disrupted his rule but also sent him to prison.

Having surveyed this intensification of local conflicts during the GLF, it only remains to ask what the immediate trigger was for the start of the criminal cases. Here, once again, the archive files help us. Each of the female victims' testimony refers to a pivotal commune meeting in mid-January 1960, during which they "had been fully educated" and "their consciousness had been improved." It was in the aftermath of this trans-formative experience that they found themselves able to "tell the truth" and "pin their hopes on the government to get justice."[53]

The origins of this pivotal moment can be traced back to the Lushan conference in summer 1959. At this meeting, Mao Zedong ordered criticism of so-called "rightist opportunism"; this was followed by the relaunching of the SEM in the countryside, a move intended to inten-sify the struggle between the two alternative roads of socialism and capitalism, promote the core policies of the moment (the "Three Red Banners," namely the "General Line for Socialist Construction," the GLF and the people's communes) and set the stage for the formulation of China's production plan for 1960. In L County, the renewal of the SEM was the occasion for a massive convention of cadres and activists between November 9 and December 7, 1959, with 4,808 delegates in attendance.[54] Following the convention, meetings at the commune level conveyed the center's instruction and gave local residents a forum to express opinions. In the commune neighboring Li's, this process generated a remarkable 36,456 comments between December 25, 1959 and January 7, 1960, reflecting the immense momentum the new phase of the GLF had gathered, as well as the depth of the contradictions at the grassroots level by this stage of the movement.[55] This moment of mobilization provided an opportunity for the masses to express their grievances, but the primary goal for the organizers was to attack the supposed rise of right-wing ideology and thereby retrench the GLF.

---

[53] "Exposure material from Guihua," "Exposure material from Xiuzhen, January 31, 1960" and "Exposure material from Yuanrui, 31 January 1960," *Li Xin Rape Case*, L County Archive, 53-3-830-35, 53-3-830-36, 53-3-830-37.

[54] "Dahui kuaibao" (Conference Bulletin), January 10, 1959, in *Guanyu 1959 nian 11 yuefen zhaokai de siji ganbu dahui* (The Four-level Cadre Convention in November 1959), L County Committee, L County Archive, 2-1-150-40.

[55] "1960 nian 1 yue dahui zongjie cailiao" (Summary of the January 1960 Conference), in *Zhengfeng, sanfan yundong cailiao, minbing gongzuo zongjie* (Summary of Rectification, Three-Antis Movement Materials and Militia Work), Y Commune Committee, L County Archive, 27-1-10-74.

In Li's commune, the equivalent meeting began on January 15, 1960. Several cadres in Xu Village seized the opportunity to launch a premeditated attack on Xu Quan, and Li Xin, attempting to suppress dissent in his usual dictatorial style, found himself embroiled in the struggle. There seems to have been a clear sense that the two men's positions had become vulnerable, and the allegations against Li were made ten days after the meeting, when, supported by other cadres, the female victims went to the commune to file suit.

One of the questions that emerged above is the issue of why Li and Xu faced the charges that they did, rather than more easily made allegations of abuse of power. As we have seen, the reseizure charge against Xu was facially implausible, and the rape claims against Li stand out for the seriousness with which they were handled, whatever the underlying facts. To be sure, in some cases the SEM did uncover wrongdoing by local cadres, including sexual crimes,[56] but it was also a chance to struggle against antagonists, in which charges could be concocted and individuals could be arbitrarily labeled "class enemies" or subjected to criminal punishment. All the evidence in this case points to such a power struggle having been at least a large part of the picture. From this perspective, the accusations of rape and illegal reseizing were extremely useful to Li and Xu's enemies, because, despite its seriousness, the level of corruption of which they could credibly be accused left them liable only to administrative penalties or internal Party discipline. To foreclose the possibility of their regaining power and seeking revenge, criminal sanctions were needed. Ironically, Li Xin himself seems to have been alive to this dynamic, apparently responding to the cadres accusing Xu of reseizure with a pointed remark that "we can simply dismiss him [Xu Quan]. Do you want him arrested?"[57] From the perspective of Li's victims, the rape allegations also had a certain instrumental utility. As members of Li's faction, if he became vulnerable, so did they. It seems plausible to suggest that their "improvement of consciousness" at the January meeting was, at least in part, a case of seeing which way the wind was blowing. Their claims turned them from being Li's partners in crime to being his victims and the instrument of his downfall. And, of course, if the allegations were true, this was the perfect moment to make them stick. As for the other

---

[56] See also Jeremy Brown's study in which a rape offence was reported during the Cultural Revolution . Jeremy Brown, "A Policeman, His Gun, and an Alleged Rape: Competing Appeals for Justice in Tianjin, 1966–1979," in Daniel Leese and Puck Engman, eds., *Victims, Perpetrators, and the Role of Law in Maoist China: A Case-Study Approach* (Munich: De Gruyter Oldenbourg, 2018), 127–149.
[57] "Exposure material from Xu Yin, January 30, 1960," *Li Xin Rape Case*, L County Archive, 53-3-830-47.

local cadres, they were fully aware that their accusations against Xu Quan exposed him to criminal liability. Their pursuit of his case and their support for Li's accusers suggest a determination to take the two men down once and for all.

If my reading of the record is correct, the criminal cases against Li Xin and Xu Quan resulted primarily from the impact of the campaigns of the day, which had given rise to an environment of hyper-politicization. They emerged from a context in which the system of people's commune, the major administrative innovation of the GLF, had rendered rural communities increasingly closed and involuted, offering leading local cadres new opportunities to abuse their position for personal and factional gain. With few alternative sources of power to draw on, individuals became increasingly dependent on state-backed collectives, whose uneven distribution of benefits became a matter of life and death as famine set in. This backdrop produced a factional power struggle among local elites, the proximate trigger for which was the rebirth of the SEM. In this way, the political campaign, one of the Mao-era party-state's primary tools of policy implementation, provided both the spark and the vehicle for the working out of local conflicts. It is important to highlight the extent to which, as in Xu Village, judicial punishment and campaigns went hand in hand. Campaigns regularly spawned large numbers of criminal cases, which offered a means to regularize and to worsen the punishments faced by their targets.

A key learning from this case study concerns the way in which the implementation of campaigns, as well as judicial punishments, produced contingency. At the local level, some of the effects of campaigns could run against, or orthogonally to, the state's original intentions. Moreover, campaigns were not just a path by which the state achieved or failed to achieve its own goals. Seen from below, they provided a framework for individuals at the local level to exercise their own agency, creating opportunities and imposing constraints through which people worked for their own purposes. They could be exploited to secure sexual favors or a change in class status; they could also create conditions of suffering, whether by opening individuals up to punishment for deviancy or by imposing more generally damaging ills, of which famine and the attendant struggle to survive were not the least. Campaigns also provided a path for the state to use rural contention to push its power down to the grass roots, an effort which generated an extraordinary amount of violence.[58] At the same time, a decentralized judicial system with limited safeguards

---

[58] Zhu Xiaoyang, *Zuiguo yu chengfa: Xiaocun gushi (1931–1997)* (Offence and Punishment: The Story of a Village (1931–1997)) (Tianjin: Tianjin guji chubanshe, 2003).

and poor practices of evidence gathering and case making allowed campaign-induced conflict to spill over into criminal punishment for key local figures. In Xu Village, as was doubtless the case elsewhere, the locals who set their leaders' downfall in motion may have simply wanted to rectify the problems they faced by bringing two corrupt cadres to justice. However, the convergence of campaign-style politics with politicized legal enforcement seems inevitably to have ratcheted up the stakes to a point where only one endgame was possible: a bitter struggle followed by brutal and – for Li Xin and Xu Quan – ultimately fatal punishments.

11 How the CCP Has Failed to Obtain Control over China's Collective Memory on the 1950s

Anja Blanke

After Mao's death in 1976, his successors led China not only into an era of deep political changes and transitions, but also into a time of uncertainties. The beginning of the reform and opening policy in late 1978 ended the "era of high socialism" that had shaped China since the 1950s.[1] Within just a few years Deng Xiaoping and his supporters laid the foundations for China's unprecedented economic rise. This was followed by a period of a historical coming to terms with the "historical mistakes" (*lishi cuowu*) of the "era of high socialism" of the CCP.[2] This also meant that some of the actors who were responsible for "historical mistakes" during the Mao era played a key role in this process of historical revision of the past. Apart from an official judgment of Mao's achievements and failures, as well as an assessment of the Cultural Revolution (1966–1976), it was particularly important for China's leaders to find an appropriate way of dealing with the "historical mistakes" of the 1950s in order to maintain the Party's legitimacy. Therefore, how to manage the official historiography of the 1950s was among the most sensitive questions that the CCP had to deal with as it attempted to come up with a convincing narrative of the 1950s. One reason for this was the fact that Deng Xiaoping himself was responsible for carrying out the Anti-Rightist campaign (1957–1958), in which

[1] Jeremy Brown and Matthew Johnson referred to the "era of high socialism," amongst other things, as politicization of everyday life. Jeremy Brown and Matthew D. Johnson, "Introduction," in Jeremy Brown and Matthew D. Johnson, eds., *Maoism at the Grassroots: Everyday Life in China's Era of High Socialism* (Cambridge, MA: Harvard University Press, 2015), 6.

[2] "Historical mistakes" are here defined as severe political misjudgments by the CCP, the consequences of which have caused substantial harms to large parts of the Chinese population or to particular groups in society. This was usually accompanied by a considerable negative impact on the development of the whole country and of socialism. Concrete examples are the Anti-Rightist campaign (1957–1958), the Great Leap Forward (1958–1962), and the Cultural Revolution (1966–1976). For a differentiated view of the term "historical mistake," see Anja Blanke, *Der Kampf um Chinas kollektives Gedächtnis: Offizielle und inoffizielle Narrative zur Kampagne gegen Rechtsabweichler (1957–58)* (Berlin: De Gruyter Oldenbourg), 48–50.

hundreds of thousands Chinese intellectuals were killed, jailed, or persecuted.[3] At the end of the 1970s, most of the so-called rightists who had been wrongly convicted and sentenced to re-education through labor were still in the *laogai* system.[4] Therefore it was necessary for the CCP's leaders to establish an official frame of historical reference that simultaneously grounded the party-state in the early to mid-1950s while accounting for the Anti-Rightist campaign and, even more sensitively, for the Great Leap Forward and its aftermath in order to keep the public discourse on 1950s China under control.

The CCP has followed a dual approach in dealing with the mistakes and injustices of the past: first, according to Daniel Leese and Puck Engman, after 1978, China's political leaders have initiated the "revision of unjust, false, and mistaken verdicts" of the Mao era. Between 1978 and 1987, millions of political victims were "rehabilitated" (*pingfan*) or their verdicts have been at least "corrected" (*gaizheng*).[5] Second, in March 1980, the CCP started to work on the "Resolution on Certain Questions in the History of Our Party since the Founding of the People's Republic of China." It was drafted under the guidance of the Politburo of the Central Committee and of its Secretariat, with Deng Xiaoping and Hu Yaobang presiding over the work. During the process of drafting the resolution, the challenge was that, on the one hand, the Party couldn't entirely deny their own and Mao's mistakes; on the other hand, it was particularly important to emphasize the Party's and Mao's historical merits in order to make use of the legitimizing strength of the CCP's history in the future. In doing so, Deng Xiaoping and his followers aimed to end the critical discourse on the "historical mistakes" of the past, within both the Party and society. The ultimate goal was to ensure social stability and unity as a foundation for economic development and "Socialism with Chinese characteristics" (*Zhongguo tese shehuizhuyi*).[6] The resolution, which was adopted by the Sixth Plenary Session of the Eleventh Central Committee of the Communist Party of China on June 27, 1981, was to establish the basis

---

[3] On Deng Xiaoping's role during the Anti-Rightist campaign see Yen-lin Chung, "The Witch-Hunting Vanguard: The Central Secretariat's Roles and Activities in the Anti-Rightist Campaign," *China Quarterly* 206 (2011): 391–411.

[4] *Laogai* 劳改 – "reform through labour." The *laogai* system was still in use after 1976. See Nan Richardson, ed., *Laogai: The Machinery of Repression in China* (New York: Umbrage Ed, 2009).

[5] Daniel Leese and Puck Engman, "Introduction," in Puck Engman and Daniel Leese, eds., *Victims, Perpetrators, and the Role of Law in Maoist China: A Case-Study Approach* (Berlin and Boston: Walter de Gruyter GmbH, 2018), 14–15.

[6] Tony Saich, "China under Reform, 1978–2000," in Tony Saich, ed., *Governance and Politics of China* (Basingstoke: Palgrave, 2001), 52–55.

for a collective memory in line with the Party's grip to power on a long-term basis.[7]

However, maintaining the control over China's collective memory soon turned out to be an extremely difficult task, as it has always been highly contested. Since the beginning of the memory boom in the 1990s, the CCP has been confronted with a flood of unofficial publications on post-1949 history challenging the official narrative of the resolution and shedding a different light on "historical mistakes" such as the Anti-Rightist campaign or the Cultural Revolution.[8] Members of the Red Guard generation began to turn a critical gaze on the history of the CCP; historians started to discover questionable events of PRC history more precisely; and witnesses, victims, and/or their relatives began talking about history and sharing their own memories of the "historical mistakes," resulting in an unofficial historiography as well as in the creation of alternative memorial sites in memoirs and publications of other types. Thus they were struggling against the forced forgetting of the Party and refusing to be constrained by the official narrative.

Furthermore, this was fostered by the relaxation of the CCP's heavy-handed and all-encompassing control in the 1980s, but particularly in the 1990s and 2000s, when private spheres were allowed to emerge, distinct markets began to flourish, and China opened up to the Western world. Under these circumstances, it is not surprising that different scientific

[7] Broadly speaking, "collective memory" refers to how certain groups remember the past. Following Maurice Halbwachs, it encompasses both individual memories and certain representations of the past such as official texts (like the 1981 resolution), commemorative and physical ceremonies (in China the National Day of the People's Republic of China is celebrated annually on October 1; it commemorates the founding of the PRC in 1949 by the CCP). Individual memories and certain constructions of the past can influence each other mutually, since individual memories are associated with the present and with the group's identity. See Maurice Halbwachs, *On Collective Memory: Edited, Translated, and with Introduction by Lewis A. Coser* (Chicago: The University of Chicago Press, 1992). From the CCP's point of view, China's collective memory has a normative dimension as well, which includes the selective forgetting of some aspects of certain events that are here defined as "historical mistakes." According to Danièle Hervieu-Léger, a normative dimension to memory "characterizes any collective memory which forms and endures through the process of selective forgetting, shifting and retrospectively inventing. Of its essence fluid and evolutionary, collective memory functions as a regulator of individual memory at any moment. It even takes the place of individual memory whenever it passes beyond the memory of a given group and the actual experience of those for whom it is a reference." Danièle Hervieu-Léger, "Religion as a Chain of Memory," in Jeffrey K. Olick, Vered Vinitzky-Seroussi and Daniel Levy, eds., *The Collective Memory Reader* (Oxford: Oxford University Press, 2011), 383.

[8] A memory boom has taken place not only in China, but also in many other parts of the world; this was triggered by the end of the Cold War. See Susanne Weigelin-Schwiedrzik, "Introduction: Writing History into Broken Narratives," in Susanne Weigelin-Schwiedrzik, ed., *Broken Narratives: Post-Cold War History and Identity in Europe and East Asia* (Leiden: Brill, 2014), 1–18.

discourses as well as different kinds of memories and voices began to circulate.[9] All this had a lasting impact on China's collective memory. In other words, basically, the CCP has never been able to take full control of its own past. This is problematic because the official historical canon and its implementation in China's collective memory play a pivotal role in the CCP's efforts to maintain its legitimacy. Not least due to the fact that this legitimizing canon is based on the narrative that the CCP ended the "century of humiliation" in 1949, this narrative needs to be protected from an escalating discourse about the CCP's "historical mistakes" and weaknesses. Therefore, especially after the 1989 student protests that brought a profound legitimacy crisis to the surface, the CCP is struggling to win the battle for China's collective memory.

Using the example of 1950s historiography, this chapter aims to analyze why the CCP has not succeeded in dominating China's collective memory. In doing so, I will identify four main reasons for the Party's failure: first, a weakness of China's official historiography of the 1950s can be seen in the 1981 resolution itself, due to its vague phrases, leaving too much room for reinterpretation of history; second, the phase(s) of intellectual and academic freedoms in the 1980s (and after) had a long-lasting impact on the development of intellectuals' independent ways of thinking and the training of young historians and of some independent intellectuals, who participated in unofficial historiography in the coming years; third, the CCP was not able to overcome inner Party disagreements on the question of how the Party should assess its own "historical mistakes"; fourth, memories cannot be suppressed permanently. This is to show that the historiography is an ongoing process that is not yet completed, and that China's current president Xi Jinping's politics of history has led the CCP into a dead end since this political approach attempts both to suppress alternative views on post-1949 history and to finally establish official narratives on a long-term basis.

The Weaknesses of the 1981 Resolution

One of the most important and essential objectives of the resolution was to reach an agreement on the assessment of the past both within the Party and in society. On the one hand, on the surface it should include some kind of analysis of the rights and wrongs in the history of the CCP since 1949; on the other hand, Deng Xiaoping set high value on not going too much into detail when talking about the mistakes and failures

---

[9] Timothy Cheek, David Ownby, and Joshua Fogel, "Mapping the Intellectual Public Sphere in China Today," *China Information* 32, no. 1 (2018): 109.

of the Party or of leading cadres. During a meeting of the drafting group on March 19, 1980, Deng made clear that instead of providing a real in-depth analysis of the mistakes of the past, the resolution rather should make a decisive contribution that common views will be reached, so that the Party and society can look forward to a promising and success-ful future together:

> As I said before, it is better to write it in broad outline and not go into too much detail. The purpose of summing up the past is to encourage people to close ranks and look to the future. We should try to ensure that when this resolution is adopted, the thinking of Party members and non-Party people alike will be clarified, common views will be reached and, by and large, debate on the major historical questions will come to an end. Of course, it will be difficult to avoid debates over the past completely. However, such discussions may be conducted in connection with the ongoing work in each period in the future. For the present, we should work with one heart and one mind for China's four modernizations, and all of us should unite as one and look forward. But that's not so easy to achieve. We must do our best to work out a good resolution so that we can reach a consensus and not let major differences arise again. Then, even if the past is brought up, people won't differ significantly in their views. They will stick to talking over the content of the resolution and the lessons to be learned from past experience.[10]

He puts emphasis on the collective and the consensus. In doing so, he also stresses the Leninist ideal of collective leadership that was grad-ually introduced in the 1970s and that has become the political key of his leadership since 1980.[11] Despite the fact that the resolution includes an analysis of mistakes and failures of leading cadres, Deng and his supporters were determined to adhere and develop Mao Zedong Thought in the resolution for their own political needs. They didn't take over the overall and the origin version of Mao Zedong Thought, but they extracted what they could make use of as legitimiz-ing strength. That's why they haven't renounced Mao Zedong com-pletely. Therefore the agreed formula says: Mao made gross mistakes, especially during the Cultural Revolution, but his merits outweigh his mistakes.[12] Ultimately, Deng and his supporters let the past serve the current elites' politics.

---

[10] Deng Xiaoping, "The Selected Works of Deng Xiaoping: Modern Day Contributions to Marxism–Leninism," at https://dengxiaopingworks.wordpress.com/2013/02/25/remarks-on-successive-drafts-of-the-resolution-on-certain-questions-in-the-history-of-our-party-since-the-founding-of-the-peoples-republic-of-china.

[11] Angang Hu, *China's Collective Presidency* (Berlin and Heidelberg: Springer Verlag, 2014), 44–48.

[12] The conclusion derived from this says that Mao was 70 percent good and 30 percent bad, but this verdict does not appear verbatim in the resolution.

Lastly, the final version of the resolution is a consensus paper that is shaped by vague phrases and an incomplete historiography reflecting the lowest common denominator within the Party. Susanne Weigelin-Schwiedrzik underlines that the 1981 resolution neither had a great deal of authority nor was able to prevent further discussions on the history of the Party: "Indeed, instead of dominating the interpretation of history, the CCP has increasingly been unable to hinder alternative interpretations from entering the discussion."[13] I argue not only that the resolution was unable to prevent an alternative discourse on the "historical mistakes" of the CCP, but also that its vague phrases rather have left too much room for interpretation and maybe unconsciously even promoted a reinterpretation of history in the following decades. This becomes particularly clear if one looks at official assessments of the "historical mistakes" of the CCP during the 1950s.

The example of the assessment of the Anti-Rightist campaign in the resolution illustrates that it touched the "historical mistakes" of the 1950s only on the surface. The relevant section says,

Nineteen fifty-seven was one of the years that saw the best results in economic work since the founding of the People's Republic owing to the conscientious implementation of the correct line formulated at the Eighth National Congress of the Party. To start a rectification campaign throughout the Party in that year and urge the masses to offer criticisms and suggestions were normal steps in developing socialist democracy. In the rectification campaign a handful of bourgeois Rightists seized the opportunity to advocate what they called "speaking out and airing views in a big way" and to mount a wild attack against the Party and the nascent socialist system in an attempt to replace the leadership of the Communist Party. It was therefore entirely correct and necessary to launch a resolute counterattack. But the scope of this struggle was made far too broad and a number of intellectuals, patriotic people and Party cadres were unjustifiably labelled "Rightists", with unfortunate consequences.[14]

It says clearly that the campaign itself was correct, but that its expansion was a mistake. In other words: the Anti-Rightist campaign was not classified as a "historical mistake." This is a strong contrast to other campaigns such as the Cultural Revolution that were considered mistakes within the official historiography from the beginning. The limits of the memory framework laid out in the respective section of the resolution require that the official

---

[13] Susanne Weigelin-Schwiedrzik, "In Search of a Master Narrative for 20th-Century Chinese History," *China Quarterly* 188, no. 1 (2006): 1071.
[14] "Resolution on Certain Questions in the History of Our Party since the Founding of the People's Republic of China," at www.marxists.org/subject/china/documents/cpc/history/01.htm.

historiography should not call the campaign into question. Although their assessment is not uncritical at all, the authors avoid an in-depth discussion of concrete consequences or responsibilities of the mistakes made during the campaign. Rather, they created some sort of universal ritual incantation letting people know what they can and cannot say in official sources. It gives a lead that one must never criticize the Party or its policies, but only faulty "implementations." The authors don't name names or mention the number of victims, not least because the resolution's focus should lie on the Party's merits. In doing so, due to its vague phrases, the authors of the resolution have, perhaps unconsciously, created a space for a more critical reflection of the events in 1957 and 1958 – even within future official publications on the history of the CCP. This has also been made possible by the fact that since 1989 the Party and its historians have realized that the official historiography cannot stand still and has to develop, albeit within certain boundaries of the resolution.

Thus, in the coming years, even some Party historians would make use of this scope for criticism created by the authors of the resolution. This is to say that they could adopt a more critical approach in the assessment of the Anti-Rightist campaign within the realm of official historiography – without stepping out of the official memory framework. This becomes apparent, for example, in the official *Biography of Mao Zedong* (2003) that has been edited by Party historians Pang Xianzhi and Jin Chongji and published by the "Central Literature Research Office of the CCP" (Zhonggong zhongyang wenxian yanjiu shi). The respective section on the Anti-Rightist campaign clearly exceeds the respective section in the resolution in both the quantity and quality of its criticism. This becomes clear when the authors refer to the consequences of the campaign:

The escalation of the Anti-Rightist Campaign had unfortunate consequences. Hundreds of thousands of upright, talented intellectuals and Party members suffered undeserved grievances, humiliation, and persecution, and their families were suffering as well. In retrospect, many of the slanderous Rightist words were only a sharp yet well-meant criticism leveled at specific shortcomings and mistakes in the Party's work, or even just a criticism of a particular grassroots unit or leader. Unfortunately, such criticisms served as evidence for the persecution. The intensification of the campaign led to terrible consequences for the nation's political life, the opposite of Mao's intention in launching the Rectification Movement: rather than invigorating the political atmosphere, the Anti-Rightist campaign inflicted huge damage on the "Two Hundreds" guideline. It was a tragic lesson.[15]

---

[15] Xianzhi Pang and Chongji Jin, *Mao Zedong zhuan*, di 2 ban (Beijing: Zhong yang wen xian chu ban she, 2011), 1676, my translation.

The author's critical take on the consequences of the campaign is also reflected in the wording. Whilst the authors of the resolution are only talking about "unfortunate consequences" (*buxing houguo*), Pang and Jin, though using the phrase "unfortunate consequences" at the beginning of this section, are also talking about undeserved grievances of the victims, and they claim that the Anti-Rightist campaign was a "tragic lesson" (*tongxin de jiaoxu*) for the Party.[16] However, their description of the negative consequences of the campaign remains incomplete – they describe neither Deng Xiaoping's role in the campaign nor the victims' destiny in the *laogai* system. Needless to say, the Mao biography also applies to the canon of his merits and not to his or the Party's mistakes.

Looking at the assessment of the Great Leap Forward in the resolution, one will come to a similar conclusion. Although the authors of the resolution admit that the Great Leap Forward, unlike the Anti-Rightist campaign, was a mistake "which caused serious losses to our country and people,"[17] they again remain vague in their analysis of the concrete negative consequences of the campaign:

It was mainly due to the errors of the Great Leap Forward and of the struggle against "Right opportunism" together with a succession of natural calamities and the perfidious scrapping of contracts by the Soviet Government that our economy encountered serious difficulties between 1959 and 1961, which caused serious losses to our country and people.[18]

Felix Wemheuer takes the view that the resolution "fails to give a convincing answer to the question of responsibility; final judgments remain elusive."[19]

Again, due to its vague phrases and assessments, the resolution has created space for a more critical take on the "historical mistakes" of the CCP. In the Mao biography, it becomes clear again that the authors have made use of the wide frame of the resolution by providing a more in-depth analysis of the causes of the errors that Mao and his supporters committed in the late 1950s; they take a more critical approach. Of course, Pang and Jin share the resolution's view on many points, for example that Mao became arrogant after a series of victories, and they even relativize many mistakes he made, and some aspects were left out of their analysis, like the great famine.

---

[16] Guanyu jianguo yilai dang de ruogan lishi wenti de jueyi (Resolution on Certain Questions in Our Party's History)," at https://web.archive.org/web/20160208225118/http://news .xinhuanet.com/ziliao/2002-03/04/content_2543544_3.htm, accessed February 28, 2020.
[17] Ibid.   [18] Ibid.
[19] Felix Wemheuer, "Dealing with Responsibility for the Great Leap Famine in the People's Republic of China," *China Quarterly* 201 (2010): 193.

However, they are more outspoken than the authors of the resolution in describing and analyzing the consequences of the Great Leap Forward:

> That the Great Leap Forward made some achievements is undeniable; but they came at a huge price. The Great Leap Forward and the people's commune movement did damage to productive forces and inflicted disastrous losses on the country and the people. This was a serious mistake committed by Mao Zedong and the CCP.[20]

This again becomes clear in the wording they are using. Whilst the resolution is describing the consequences of the Great Leap Forward as "serious difficulties between 1959 and 1961, which caused serious losses to our country and people," Pang and Jin call the Great Leap Forward a "bitter lesson" (*yanzhong jiaoxun*). In doing so, they characterize the mistakes of the Great Leap Forward and their consequences as part of a torturous history and a long way of learning:

> It would be another twenty years of torturous history, having assimilated lessons from both positive and negative experience, before the Party managed to recombine emancipating the mind and seeking truth from facts, restoring and developing the Party's ideological line in seeking truth from facts.[21]

The phrasing of the new resolution that was published in November 2021 is at least as vague as that of the resolution of 1981. The assessment of the "historical mistakes" is in fact an affirmation of the 1981 resolution's summary:

> Regrettably, the correct line adopted at the Party's Eighth National Congress was not fully upheld. Mistakes were made such as the Great Leap Forward and the people's commune movement, and the scope of the struggle against Rightists was also made far too broad. Confronted with a grave and complex external environment at the time, the Party was extremely concerned about consolidating China's socialist state power and made a wide range of efforts in this regard. However, Comrade Mao Zedong's theoretical and practical errors concerning class struggle in a socialist society became increasingly serious, and the Central Committee failed to rectify these mistakes in good time.[22]

Thus the resolutions from 1981 and 2021 by no means were truth and reconciliation campaigns. Generally speaking, both resolutions need to be understood in terms not only of establishing the parameters of official history, but also of reinforcing current elite politics. However, their

---

[20] Pang and Jin, *Mao Zedong zhuan*, 1809, my translation.
[21] Ibid., 1808, my translation.
[22] Resolution of the Central Committee of the Communist Party of China on the Major Achievements and Historical Experience of the Party over the Past Century, 2021, at https://english.www.gov.cn/policies/latestreleases/202111/16/content_WS6193a935 c6d0df57f98e50b0.html.

construction of the past doesn't offer a firm basis for the CCP's attempt to control China's collective memory.

Phases of Liberality and Academic Freedoms from 1976 to 1989

Another factor contributing to the fact that the CCP has failed in its attempt to control China's collective memory can be seen in the phases of relative openness from 1976 to 1989. This decade was not only affected by China's economic awakening, but also by phases of intellectual and academic liberalization that created space for alternative views on the "historical mistakes" of the CCP.

Shortly after Mao's death in September 1976, some intellectuals started criticizing his mistakes publicly. Furthermore, the "educated youth" (*zhishi qingnian*) gradually returning from the countryside to the cities, some of them disillusioned by the Cultural Revolution, started criticizing Mao and questioning the CCP. These intellectuals' and Red Guard generation's critical voices soon were followed by demands for more democracy.[23] Many former Red Guards had experienced the Cultural Revolution as an awakening of their own political awareness that visibly and gradually rose to the surface after 1976. This became particularly apparent during the "Democracy Wall Movement" (*minzhu qiang yundong*) from November 1978 to December 1979, in which the activists not only called on the government for socialist democracy and institutions, but also criticized the "historical mistakes" of the CCP.[24] Although the movement was suppressed by the government in late 1979, China's political leaders were unable to stop the critical view of the past by some intellectuals and former Red Guards. Additionally, the government didn't deviate from its liberal political approach, so a critical examination of the history of the CCP was still possible – to some extent it was even possible to generate debates on Mao's failures in the *Renmin Ribao*, the official newspaper of the Central Committee of the CCP.[25] Merle Goldman argues that during the early Deng years "the intellectuals had lost the fear that had formerly incapacitated them" because "with a few

---

[23] Merle Goldman, *From Comrade to Citizen: Struggle for Political Rights in China* (Cambridge, MA: Harvard University Press, 2005), 27–30.

[24] Lauri Paltemaa, "The Democracy Wall Movement, Marxist Revinionism, and the Variations on Socialist Democracy," *Journal of Contemporary China* 16, no. 53 (2007): 610–2.

[25] Jean-Philippe Béja, "Writing about the Past, an Act of Resistance: An Overview of Independent Journals and Publications about the Mao Era," in Sebastian Veg, ed., *Popular Memories of the Mao Era: From Critical Debate to Reassessing History* (Hong Kong: Hong Kong University Press, 2019), 23.

important exceptions intellectuals were generally not imprisoned, ostracized or subjected to personal disgrace."[26] Soon after 1981 it became apparent that the Party had failed to end critical discussions on their "historical mistakes" with the resolution. As a matter of fact, due to the political situation, critical debates on Mao and the CCP's mistakes and failures continued within civil society. However, this does not mean that these political liberalities were accompanied by unlimited intellectual freedom. For example, in 1983, when Deng was concerned about the spread of Western-inspired liberal ideas possibly creating doubts about the future of socialism, he initiated the Anti-Spiritual Pollution campaign.[27] Indeed, as Timothy Cheek notes, "intellectual life in the 1980s may not have been monolithic but it was not free."[28] Nevertheless, unofficial narratives that were created and spread in what was just under thirteen years would have a lasting influence on China's collective memory and on future debates. Additionally, these phases of a relatively liberal climate shaped parts of the intellectuals in a way that had an enormous impact on their publications in the 1990s and 2000s. Various types of texts and literature that would challenge official narratives emerged and spread in the PRC: fiction, memoirs, reportage, and academic literature.

In the following decades, some former Red Guards would contribute to an unofficial historiography on the "historical mistakes" of the CCP. One of these is Hu Ping, who became famous for his essay "On Freedom of Speech" ("Lun yanlun ziyou"), published soon after the suppression of the Democracy Wall movement. This essay not only contains demands for more democratic freedoms, but also includes a warning message that the "historical mistakes" after 1949 should not be repeated.[29] In 1987, he benefited from China's opening to the West and moved to the United States. Influenced by Western ideas and concepts he became a well-known democracy activist.[30] Influenced by his experiences during the Cultural Revolution, phases of liberality in 1980s China, and new impressions in the USA, in his later work he took an alternative view on certain historical events, such as the Anti-Rightist campaign or the Cultural Revolution. For example, in 2004 he published the historical report

---

[26] Merle Goldman, "Politically-Engaged Intellectuals in the Deng–Jing Era: A Changing Relationship with the Party-State," *China Quarterly* 145 (March 1996): 37.

[27] Richard Baum, *Burying Mao: Chinese Politics in the Age of Deng Xiaoping* (Princeton: Princeton University Press, 1994), 156–63.

[28] Timothy Cheek, *The Intellectual in Modern Chinese History* (Cambridge: Cambridge University Press, 2015), 230.

[29] Ping Hu, "On Freedom of Speech," at www.guernicamag.com/on-freedom-of-speech, accessed February 28, 2020.

[30] Siling Luo, "An Exiled Editor Traces the Roots of Democratic Thought in China," at www.nytimes.com/2016/10/29/world/asia/china-democracy-hu-ping.html.

Internal 1957: The Bitter Sacrificial Altar, which is based on both interviews with eyewitnesses and his own historical analyses. Contrary to the 1981 resolution, Hu's book, which even got official permission for publication within the PRC by the Chinese authorities, deals with the suffering of the victims during the campaign. Beyond that, he describes the Anti-Rightist campaign as a turning point in the history of the PRC. In doing so, in derogation from the official historiography, he stresses the special significance of this event for China's development.[31] According to Mechthild Leutner, Hu's book attracted much attention in the PRC. Two years after the book was published, there were still 250 Chinese Internet pages available that contained information on this book.[32] Many years later, in 2016, he published *Why Did Mao Zedong Launch the Cultural Revolution*, which fell victim to Xi Jinping's new conservatism in the politics of history. Unlike former works, this book was censored within the PRC and was published only in Hong Kong and Taiwan. This, again, underlines the relevance of Hu Ping's competing narratives for the CCP; as Cheek, Ownby, and Vogel note, "the party does not censor what it does not think is significant."[33]

Since the 1980s, eyewitnesses or victims of the campaigns have played an increasingly important role in the emergence of an unofficial historiography on 1950s China in the PRC by sharing their traumatic past experiences in memoirs, fiction, novels, and reports. In this respect, the so-called "wall literature" (*daqiang wenxue*) that was created by the writer and former rightist Cong Weixi, launched a flood of publications of individual memoirs. Already in 1979, shortly after he was released from the *laogai* system, he had published the novella *The Blood-Stained Magnolias under the High Wall* (*Daqiang xia de hong yulan*), in which he deals with his traumatic experiences during re-education through labor.[34] Basically, the CCP tolerated such forms of publication as long as the foci of these texts were on the authors' reappraisal of their own traumas and didn't call the CCP's legitimacy into question. However, these texts shed a different light on 1950s China and challenged Party historiography. These narratives obtained sustained relevance not least due to the fact that some of the authors became well-known writers in the PRC.

---

[31] Ping Hu, *Chanji: 1957 kunan de jitan* (1957: The Bitter Sacrificial Altar) (Guangzhou: Guangdong lüyou chubanshe, 2004), 2.
[32] Mechthild Leutner, "Parteigeschichte Pluralistisch? Neukonstruktionen Der 1950er Jahre in Historiographie und Literatur Der VR China," in Mechthild Leutner, ed., *Rethinking China in the 1950s* (Berlin: LIT, 2007), 81.
[33] Cheek, Ownby, and Fogel, "Mapping the Intellectual Public Sphere in China Today," 110.
[34] Eva Müller, "Cong Weixi," in Volker Klöpsch and Eva Müller, eds., *Lexikon der chinesischen Literatur* (Munich: C.H. Beck, 2004), 61–62.

Beyond that, the education of young intellectuals, who later became professional and public intellectuals, for example as university professors, was influenced by this phase of relative academic freedom and independence of Chinese universities. Especially in the early 1980s, students and young scholars have increasingly become concerned with Western ideas and concepts spreading in Chinese universities since China's opening up. In this regard, the growth of civil society was accompanied by a re-emergence of independent intellectuals.[35] Furthermore, after 1976, post-1949 history, including the "historical mistakes" of the CCP, has temporarily played a rather subordinate role in the universities' curricula.[36] Disregard for the spread of the official canon as well as the development of independent thought among young intellectuals may have had a significant influence on their later work on post-1949 history that would challenge the official narratives. Some members of this generation of public or professional intellectuals, born in the 1950s and educated at Chinese universities after the end of the Cultural Revolution, were influenced enormously by the political changes in this phase and by China's opening to the West. Over the years, they became part of a globalized academic world, were traveling to conferences at Western universities, and beyond China's borders became well-known and respected historians or political scientists. Public and professional intellectuals like Xu Jilin, Shen Zhihua, Wang Hui, or Yang Kuisong became "the key voices in this struggle to define and tell China's story."[37] In other words, although they have been working within the system, they did not merely recite official narratives, but challenged the Party historiography and acted relatively independently for a long period of time (this might have changed after Xi Jinping's takeover). Some of them would take a critical approach in their academic texts when dealing with the "historical mistakes" of the CCP during the 1950s and later.[38] However, it should not remain unmentioned that hardly one of them chose to openly oppose the CCP.

---

[35] Cheek, *The Intellectual in Modern Chinese History*, 326.

[36] Kuisong Yang and Wennan Liu, "Studying the Chinese Communist Party in Historical Context: An Interview with Yang Kuisong, October 17, 2015," *Journal of Modern Chinese History* 10, no. 1 (2016), 67–86.

[37] Cheek, Ownby, and Fogel, "Mapping the Intellectual Public Sphere in China Today," 110. For a compilation of different types of intellectual see Cheek, *The Intellectual in Modern Chinese History*, 332–337.

[38] For example, for a critical take on the Campaign to Suppress Counterrevolutionaries (1950–1953) see Kuisong Yang, "Xin Zhongguo 'zhenya fangeming' yundong yanjiu" (Investigations on the Campaign to Suppress Counterrevolutionaries in New China)," *Journal of Historical Sciences* 2006, no. 1 (2006): 45–61; Kuisong Yang, "Reconsidering the Campaign to Suppress Counterrevolutionaries," *China Quarterly* 193 (2008): 102–21.

In short, the liberal political phases between 1976 and 1989 contributed to a destabilization of the official canon on 1950s China within China's collective memory. It is more than likely that unofficial narratives published between 1976 and 1989 had a greater influence on China's collective memory than the official framework that was fixed in the resolution by the CCP. Although political leaders were able to set an end to this liberal political approach after the student protests in 1989, they were unable to undo the development of independent and critical ways of thinking within parts of this generation of intellectuals or to stop the spread of unofficial narratives on 1950s China. This is also shown by the memory boom and the founding of unofficial history magazines such as *Yanhuang Chunqiu* in the 1990s.

Inner Party Disagreements on the Assessment of the Past

Another aspect contributing to the CCP's inability to obtain full control of China's collective memory is a continuing disagreement within the Party on the question of how to deal with the past in an appropriate way.

These disagreements were already indicated during the drafting process of the resolution. There are protocols of at least nine meetings and conversations of the drafting group, demonstrating how difficult it was to find unity within the Party. On June 27, 1980, Deng Xiaoping expressed his dissatisfaction with the assessment of Mao's and the CCP's mistakes in the first draft of the resolution:

I have gone over the draft of the resolution. It is no good and needs rewriting. We stressed at the very beginning that the historical role of Comrade Mao Zedong must be affirmed, and that Mao Zedong Thought must be adhered to and developed. The draft doesn't reflect this intention adequately. The passages dealing with the events before 1957 are all right as to the facts, but the way they are presented – the sequence and especially the tone of presentation – should be reconsidered and altered. We have to give a clear account of Comrade Mao Zedong's contributions to China's socialist revolution and construction. Mao Zedong Thought is still in the process of development. We should restore and adhere to Mao Zedong Thought and go on developing it further. Comrade Mao laid a foundation for us in all these respects, and the resolution should fully reflect his ideas.[39]

In October 1980, the draft was discussed by 4,000 Party members. During the meeting they expressed their different points of view on the resolution's historical assessment without achieving a consensus. Finally, Deng Xiaoping urged them to reduce the circle of discussants in order to bring the internal arguments to an end.[40]

---

[39] Deng Xiaoping, "The Selected Works of Deng Xiaoping."   [40] Ibid.

As a matter of fact, Deng's approach of setting parameters and dampening discussion of the historiography was not sufficient to prevent alternative views on dealing with the CCP's past from appearing in inner Party circles on a long-term basis. It is almost impossible to precisely retrace the details of inner Party debates due to a lack of access to relevant records, but there are some indications of ongoing dissent on the official interpretation of the past.

For example, the former high-ranking Party officials Li Rui, Mao's personal secretary in the late 1950s, and Li Shenzhi, a former foreign-policy adviser under Deng Xiaoping, have contributed to a critical approach in dealing with the "historical mistakes" of the CCP since the 1990s. Between 1991 and 2016 Li Rui and Li Shenzhi published several articles in the history magazine *Yanhuang Chunqiu*, which was founded in 1991 and taken over by government officials in 2016 due to its critical approach to dealing with the past. Initially, the journal was founded as a form of democracy promotion, as Jean-Philippe Béja argues.[41]

Their alternative view of the CCP's history becomes particularly apparent in their articles on the Anti-Rightist campaign, in which they repeatedly emphasize the necessity of learning from the mistakes of the past. In an article that was published in 2002, Li Rui describes the Anti-Rightist campaign as a turning point in the history of the PRC that laid the foundation for the following catastrophe of the Great Leap Forward:

In retrospect, after 20 years of reform and opening up, it has become quite clear to me: first, the Anti-Rightist campaign changed the line of the 8th National Party Congress and led to a return to the path of class struggle. Second, speaking was criminalized, so that the ensuing Great Leap Forward proceeded without any criticism. Third, some ideas for strengthening the socialist democracy and the socialist legal system, as well as some ideas that would have contributed to the development of productive forces (such as the introduction of foreign capital and the training of cadres in specific professions), were criticized and consequently turned wrong into right, damaging the development of socialist democracy, and the legal system jeopardized the development of productive forces. Fourth, some people spread lies and betrayed friends; promoting and rewarding those who are inflamed and those who have influence leads to the moral decline of a society. This was a large-scale reversed elimination of the cadres, reducing their average moral and professional level, which caused damage to the cause. When talking about the role of the Anti-Rightist struggle in history, we must start from this perspective in order to come closer to reality.[42]

---

[41] Béja, "Writing about the Past," 29.
[42] Rui Li, "Fan youpai zhong xinwen jie 'Di Yi Da an': 1957 Nian Xin Hunan Bao Ren (The "First Case" in the Press during the Anti-Rightist Campaign: The *New Hunan News* Reporters in 1957)," *Yanhuang Chunqiu* 9 (2002): 2, my translation.

This critical assessment of the Anti-Rightist campaign's role in history was also shared by Li Shenzhi. He argues that the Anti-Rightist campaign even led to a reshaping of social classes:

The only new thing about it was the fact that by proposing "contradictions among the people" and the Anti-Rightist struggle as a model for dealing with "contradictions among the people," Chairman Mao invented a model that classified the people not by their production relationship, but by their ideology. Later, this became a standard of classification into classes with or without Mao Zedong Thought; the former is the proletariat, and the latter is the bourgeoisie. This is how many Communists who were vanguards of the proletariat suddenly became right-wing elements of the bourgeoisie. This is why many of them appeared as "three anti elements" (anti-Party, anti-socialist, anti-Mao Zedong Thought) during the Cultural Revolution, although there were only few who really dared to "oppose."[43]

Thus the official version of the past was in a way attacked from within the Party. Consequently, articles just like these, published in a journal with a monthly circulation of 200,000, presented an enormous challenge to the official narratives on "historical mistakes" such as the Anti-Rightist campaign.

Another aspect that can be interpreted as a sign of inner Party disunity is the leak of internal documents on the CCP's politics of history. In June 2013 the Communiqué on the Current State of the Ideological Sphere, Document No. 9, which was circulated within the Party in April 2013, was leaked by the Chinese dissident journalist Gao Yu.[44] It included "seven things that should not be discussed" (*qi ge bu yao jiang*) at universities and in the media, amongst them historical mistakes by the Party, i.e., promoting historical nihilism. It defines historical nihilism as an attempt to distort Party history and the history of New China.[45] Beyond that, in 2017, internal minutes from a discussion of a speech by Xi Jinping to the Central Party School in 2017 were leaked to Western media. In the discussion the panelists should have expressed their support for Xi's attempts for a more conservative course on dealing with the "historical mistakes" of the Party.[46] On the one hand, these documents

---

[43] Li Shenzhi, "Mao Zhuxi shi shenme shihou jueding 'yinshe chundong' de?" (When Did Mao Zedong Decide "to Put the Snakes Out of Their Holes"?), *Yanhuang Chunqiu* 1 (1999): 11, my translation.

[44] Gao has been sentenced to seven years in prison for leaking state secrets. See China's pathetic crackdown on civil society at www.washingtonpost.com/opinions/chinas-pathetic-lockdown/2015/04/22/bddf8fdc-e548-11e4-905f-cc896d379a32_story.html, accessed February 28, 2020.

[45] "Document 9: A China File Translation: How Much Is a Hardline Party Directive Shaping China's Current Political Climate?", at www.chinafile.com/document-9-china file-translation, accessed January 5, 2017.

[46] *China Digital Times*, "Dang shi youxie jiushi buneng dui laobaixing jiang" (Parts of History Cannot Be Discussed with the People), at https://chinadigitaltimes.net/chinese/

indicate the president's determined effort to regain control over the discourse on the "historical mistakes" of the CCP and on China's collective memory, not least because this went along with increasing censorship measures since his takeover. On the other hand, the fact that high-ranking Party officials must have passed the respective internal documents to a whistleblower suggests that Xi and his supporters are still facing the challenge of inner Party disagreements on the assessment of the past.

Memories Can't Be Suppressed

After the violent suppression of the student protests in 1989, the CCP was confronted with a severe legitimacy crisis. Accordingly, China's political leaders reacted with strict censorship measures and therefore with a restriction on intellectual freedom in order to set an end to the spread of adverse ideas and narratives. Zhao Suisheng even describes the phase from 1989 to 1991 as the most repressive years in post-1949 China.[47] Despite these measures, the Party was unable to hinder witnesses from sharing their past life memories with their relatives or friends due to the simple fact that individual memories can't be suppressed. Generally speaking, the Party won't be able to get full control of the past and thus of China's collective memory as long as witnesses of "historical mistakes" are still alive. According to Jan Assmann, after an average of forty years, individual memories can become part of so-called "communicative memory": "After forty years those who have witnessed an important event as an adult will leave their future-oriented professional career, and will enter the age group in which memory grows, as does the desire to fix it and pass it on."[48] This also explains the memory boom on 1950s China during the 1990s and the numerous publications of memoirs from former rightists and other witnesses, such as Harry Wu's 1994 memoir of his time in the *laogai* system, *Bitter Winds*, or Li Zhisui's biography *The Private Life of Chairman Mao*. Even though these publications were censored by the Chinese authorities, they came into circulation in the PRC by illicit means. Especially the latter was in high demand on the black market due to a growing interest in the details of Mao's life and work.[49] Therefore

---

2017/12/李小申-党史-有些就是不能对老百姓讲, accessed February 1, 2019. Unlike Document No.9, the authenticity of this leak is controversial.

[47] Suisheng Zhao, "Deng Xiaoping's Southern Tour: Elite Politics in Post-Tiananmen China," *Asian Survey* 33, no. 8 (1993): 284.

[48] Jan Assmann, *Cultural Memory and Early Civilization: Writing, Remembrance, and Political Imagination* (Cambridge and New York: Cambridge University Press, 2011), 36.

[49] Margaretta Jolly, "The Exile and the Ghostwriter: East–West Biographical Politics and the Private Life of Chairman Mao," *Biography* 23, no. 3 (2000): 487–9.

adverse narratives of these kinds may be able to exercise a long-lasting influence on China's collective memory.

Since Xi Jinping's takeover and the launch of the "war on historical nihilism," which should have set an end to the spread of alternative views on the "historical mistakes" of the Party, censorship measures once again have been intensified significantly: the Party has limited access to historical archives and shut down VPNs, which allowed internet users to circumvent the "Great Firewall of China." Wide scopes of historiography that had been tolerated during the Hu Jintao era have fallen victim to this repressive political approach, as we saw in summer 2016 with the takeover of the history magazine *Yanhuang Chunqiu*. The war on historical nihilism has expanded gradually and has continued to intensify over the last few years. It also addresses China's generations Y and Z, who were born after the reform era began. Party history, Marxism, and Socialism with Chinese characteristics were not essential for them when they were growing up. In the light of recent political developments, a profound re-education of China's youth in the field of political theory and history is mandatory to secure the CCP's legitimacy on a lasting basis. First of all, this re-education is carried out in institutions of higher education, but also in popular culture and the media in order to win over China's youth.[50]

It nevertheless seems questionable whether these measures are sufficient to finally gain control over China's collective memory, as China can't be closed hermetically. This goes hand in hand with the increasing mobility of Chinese students studying abroad, getting access to unofficial narratives on "historical mistakes," and picking up ideas at Western universities, which in turn they can potentially import to China. Although the Xi administration is not able to eliminate alternative views of the CCP's past, the leaders can try to make these competing narratives irrelevant not only by ideological education, but also by patriotism and materialism. As long as the CCP's history remains a legitimizing story of success, as long as standards of living continue to rise, and as long as the Party can identify itself with patriotism while deploying the formidable surveillance at its disposal, then they may have a chance to dominate China's collective memory.

---

[50] One example of this is the Chinese television show *Marx Got It Right*, which was produced on the occasion of 200th anniversary in 2018 of Marx's birth for CCTV (China Central Television) and which was promoted on Communist Party websites. CCTV, *Makesi shi dui de* (Marx Got It Right), at http://news.cctv.com/special/Marx, accessed August 30, 2018.

Conclusion

The CCP has failed to obtain control over the collective memory not only of 1950s China, but also of other sensitive events between 1949 and 1976, due to both external and internal factors. Some of these were out of the CCP's control, such as the erratic flows of individual memories. Other factors, such as the vague phrases in the resolution that created space for criticism or inner Party disagreements on the assessment of the past, possibly could have been avoided. It was naive to assume that the historical assessment of the resolution would set an end to the political and social discourse on the "historical mistakes" of the CCP and its (former) leaders. Rather, creating an official canon is a long process that needs to be adapted again and again to respective political and social developments.

Although the 2021 resolution theoretically left as much room for reinterpretation and critique by Party historians as the 1981 resolution, the opportunities to take a critical view of Party history have been increasingly restricted since Xi Jinping took office.

However, it is more than questionable whether Xi Jinping and his conservative supporters can ever succeed in the "war on historical nihilism" that was launched after 2012, not only due to the simple fact that memories can't be completely suppressed, but also because the success of this political strategy of dealing with the "historical mistakes" of the past is dependent on China's ongoing rise. As soon the CCP's story of success stagnates or crumbles, the Party at any time can become the object of criticism voiced by civil society. This potentially can generate a domino effect resulting in a critical public debate on the CCP's mistakes of the past, which in turn can challenge the legitimacy of the actual political leaders. Therefore it appears that this political approach of dealing with the past is leading the CCP's conservatives to a dead end. This became particularly clear with the outbreak of the coronavirus pandemic, which brought to light a growing dissatisfaction with the weaknesses of China's authoritarian regime, resulting in mismanagement at the beginning of the crisis in Wuhan.[51]

---

[51] Klaus Mühlhahn, "Kränkelndes System: Chinas Regierung und das Coronavirus," at www .cicero.de/aussenpolitik/china-regierung-corona-virus-system-kritik, accessed June 12, 2020.

12   Postscript

Rethinking China under Mao

Klaus Mühlhahn

The Chinese state that came into being in 1949 not only consciously self-fashioned itself as new and breaking out of a painful and humiliating past. Ambitious state initiatives sought to reconfigure business ownership, landholding, marriage, the organization of work and daily life, the very understanding of one's self, one's community, and one's past. Mostly, the new People's Republic of China was above all simply new: A "New China" (*xin Zhongguo*) in a new era. China should be remade by eliminating the ills of the past, creating a new culture, a new society, new classes, and new ethnicities. A new calendar was drafted, and new international alignments were shaped. New practices were promoted and an enthusiasm for everything new was carefully cultivated. After 1949 many things and projects built on renewal as the central idea.

Three decades later, at the end of the 1970s, however, the hopes for renewal had been shattered. The Cultural Revolution revealed that the efforts of creating a new China had ended dramatically in chaos, internal strife, confusion, isolation, and destruction. In 1978 a complete reversal took place as China embarked on a path of opening and market liberalization under one-party rule.

The history of the PRC is, then, a history of aspirations and betrayals; of new beginnings and hard landings; of experimentation and failure; of alternating periods of construction, destruction, and reconstruction; eventually, however, based on the forces of capitalism, but without denouncing the socialist system. Ambitions and confidence, tempered by anxieties about legitimacy, led to a frequent restarting with new models, only to discard those models in a violent and painful process, and replacing them by alternative approaches, causing leadership struggles, frequent policy changes, and system crises.

Western observers have found it difficult to create a consistent narrative, let alone a coherent explanation, of the history since 1949. This accounts in part for the tendency to divide PRC history into two: the horrors of the Maoist prehistory, and the rise of an economically liberated China since 1978. Overall, the PRC continues to defy common assumptions and models

275

derived from Western historical experience, including that of the Soviet Union – the fact is that China's path is not easily likened to other countries. In our history books, the PRC has become many things – next superpower, last communist totalitarian state, world's biggest capitalist economy, a threat, a systemic rival, and an anachronism – all at the same time.

This chapter provides an overview of the burgeoning historiography of the People's Republic of China, especially of the early period between 1949 and 1978, and suggests how we might integrate such work into narratives of the Chinese past and present. In working through the research of the past thirty years the findings not only help us identify new areas of research; they also rephrase some of the initial questions. The chapter will highlight areas in which reconsidering PRC history seems especially necessary: violence, and social transformation.

The State of the Field

A great deal has been written about the PRC. The various approaches may be reduced to three powerful, competing narratives.

The first – derived from Marx's writings – became the official credo of all Communist regimes: workers and peasants, led by a communist party, overthrew the evil and exploitative GMD government, liberated China, and embarked on the path to "communism." Communism was an ideal condition where the Chinese people would not only enjoy material abundance, but would also live in the most perfect democracy, harmonious, self-regulating and with no man subordinate to another. It was also a rational system and would come about as the result of the laws of historical development. This story, of course, was the centerpiece of Marxist–Leninist–Mao Zedong thinking, but there were also numerous Western works on China written by Marxists and Maoists in the West that followed that narrative and enjoyed a wide readership, such as the very popular books by Han Suyin, for example.[1]

The second narrative might be called the "modernization" story, in which the CCP were not so much heroic liberators as rational, technically minded modernizers, committed to developing a poor and backward China. Though undoubtedly and regrettably violent in their early stages (explained as largely inevitable given the enormous resistance the CCP faced and the

---

[1] See, for instance, the two laudatory volumes on Mao Zedong by Han Suyin titled *The Morning Deluge: Mao Tsetung and the Chinese Revolution 1893–1954* (Boston: Little, Brown & Co., 1972) and *Wind in the Tower: Mao Tsetung and the Chinese Revolution, 1949–1975* (Boston: Little, Brown & Co., 1976). For a discussion of Han Suyin's work and life, see Feng Cui, Alex Tickell, and Han Suyin, "The Little Voice of Decolonizing Asia," *Journal of Postcolonial Writing* 57, no. 2 (2021): 147–153.

huge economic and social changes that were needed), the CCP eventually abjured extreme repression. Empirically oriented scholars such as Elizabeth Perry, Wang Hui, or Lin Chun argue that the violent excesses of the regime have to be balanced against the undeniable achievements. Elizabeth Perry, for instance, has maintained that it was during the height of Chinese authoritarianism – the Maoist era – that the foundations of contemporary growth were laid. To Perry, Mao's revolutionary regime must not only be blamed for the violence but also credited with important gains in improving the quality of life for much of its populace.[2] Lin Chun, in her book *The Transformation of Chinese Socialism*, follows a similar line of argument. Mao Zedong and Deng Xiaoping were both revolutionary nationalists and modernizers, determined to catch up with the West.[3] Needless to say, that this view is also increasingly adopted by the Chinese government since Opening and Reform. On the eve of the conclusion of the 18th National Congress of the CCP in November 2012, Xi Jinping explained, "Since the founding of the CCP, we have united and led the people to advance and struggle tenaciously, transforming the impoverished and backward Old China into the New China that has become prosperous and strong gradually. The great revival of the Chinese nation has demonstrated unprecedented bright prospects."[4]

The third narrative might, perhaps, be called the "repression" narrative, and is popular amongst determined critics of Chinese communism. The "repression narrative" portrayed the PRC as an all-powerful state apparatus that coerced citizens into willful obedience and acceptance of the new order.[5] The theory of totalitarianism held sway, especially over scholarship interested in the Party, institutions, and ideology. In general, this theory suggested that totalitarian regimes share certain traits, and adopt similar designs. Western research also emphasized the large number of people who are said to have been victimized by the rule of the CCP. In books by Dikötter or Jung Chang, Mao Zedong is portrayed as a "madman" or "monster" who ruined the country.[6] Liberation is depicted as a tragedy

---

[2] Elizabeth J. Perry, "Studying Chinese Politics: Farewell to Revolution?", *China Journal* 57 (2007), 1–22.
[3] Lin Chun, *The Transformation of Chinese Socialism* (Durham, NC: Duke University Press Books, 2006).
[4] *BBC News China*, at www.bbc.com/news/world-asia-china-20338586.
[5] Jeremy Brown and Paul Pickowicz. *Dilemmas of Victory: The Early Years of the People's Republic of China* (Cambridge, MA: Harvard University Press, 2007).
[6] Frank Dikötter, *Mao's Great Famine: The History of China's Most Devastating Catastrophe, 1958–1962* (New York: Walker & Co., 2010). Frank Dikötter, *The Tragedy of Liberation: A History of the Chinese Revolution, 1945–1957* (London: Bloomsbury Paperbacks, 2013). Jung Chang and Jon Halliday, *Mao: The Unknown Story* (New York: Knopf, 2005). See also Gregor Benton and Chun Lin, *Was Mao Really a Monster? The Academic Response to Chang and Halliday's Mao, the Unknown Story* (Abingdon and New York: Routledge, 2009).

wreaking havoc on society and destroying numerous lives. During the Great Leap, Mao and the Party ignored the emerging catastrophe of the famine because of dogmatism, selfishness, and stupidity. Dikötter reveals in great detail how people in China during the first three decades of the PRC suffered, died, or struggled to survive. He states, "As these books show, the first decade of Maoism was one of the worst tyrannies in the history of the twentieth century, sending to an early grave at least 5 million civilians and bringing misery to countless more."[7]

It seems to me that each of the narratives discussed above tends to miss the complexity of China's state structure and history. Nobody, not even in China, seriously advances the first narrative anymore, but also the second and third narratives seem incomplete and unbalanced. Historians have always been divided about the merits of theories of totalitarianism. Most of them are not very enthusiastic about totalitarianism as an analytical tool. For many, the totalitarian model – with its claim of a monolithic, efficient state and of a dogmatically held, mind-altering ideology – is too mechanistic and does not describe, much less explain, social reality in those systems. Because the concepts and ideas behind totalitarianism had a polemical, and ideological, quality, historians came to see them as a distinct product of a Cold War mentality. Rethinking the history of the PRC makes it unavoidable to move beyond simplistic uses of totalitarianism.

On the other hand, both the communist utopian narrative and the modernization narrative tend to disregard and downplay the frequent violence of the period. Overall, repression, violence, and terror were relegated to mere footnotes in a story that was marked by the leadership's determination to create an egalitarian socialist society and modernize China. The use of violence, terror, and deportations was far too widespread, too systematic, claiming too many lives, to be entirely overlooked and discounted. Simply ignoring the repressive and violent dimensions of PRC history will certainly not help. We have account for both: the extreme violence usually associated with totalitarianism and the flexibility and complexity of the Chinese state structure and the political system that allowed it to modernize China as effectively as it did. Hence our main task is to draw up an accurate and empirically sound account of the working of the PRC in all its parts and as a whole. With much empirical work having been done, this now requires careful consideration of the relative weight of research foci. But in order to do just that, we also need to rethink the concept of totalitarianism or better its analytical values. It is reasonable to

---

[7] Dikötter, *The Tragedy of Liberation*, xiii.

argue that China historians failed to fully appreciate the depth of thought invested in the unpopular idea.

Beyond Totalitarianism

Two of the leading theoretical thinkers on totalitarian regimes, Hannah Arendt and Carl Schmitt, have only recently shown up in the literature on China. Yet there is much to learn from them for a new approach to PRC history. For one thing, it will help us grapple with our ever-increasing wealth of empirical evidence, but they also have much to contribute to the ongoing debate on the understanding of the nature of the regime, a debate, frankly, that is not marked by many new ideas.

Arendt described totalitarianism as a contradictory political system in constant flux trying to be faithful to its original utopian visions that had carried the movement to victory, while at the same time establishing a government to rule over society and provide basic goods and services. She wrote,

> The totalitarian ruler is confronted with a dual task which at first appears contradictory to the point of absurdity: he must establish the fictitious world of the movement as a tangible working reality of everyday life, and he must, on the other hand, prevent this new world from developing a new stability ... at any price, prevent normalization from reaching the point where a new way of life could develop.[8]

For her, the totalitarian state is fundamentally "structureless," neglecting material or economic interests, denying profit motives, and pursuing nonutilitarian goals.[9] Arendt offers a complex understanding of totalitarianism that hinges on the inherent instability and the (self-perceived) lack of legitimacy of these regimes.

For Carl Schmitt, every dictatorship is in its most fundamental form tantamount to "a state of exception" (*Ausnahmezustand*). Looking back on the history of dictatorial government in Europe, Carl Schmitt distinguished between two forms of dictatorship.[10] A "commissarial dictatorship" was the declaration of a state of emergency in order to save the constitutional order in times of crisis and threat. It functioned as a temporary suspension of regular law, justified by moral right or

---

[8] Hannah Arendt, *The Origins of Totalitarianism* (New York: Harcourt, Brace and Co., 1951), 391.
[9] Ibid., 419.
[10] Carl Schmitt, *Die Diktatur: Von den Anfängen des modernen Souveränitätsgedankens bis zum proletarischen Klassenkampf* (Munich and Leipzig: Duncker & Humblot, 1928). Michael Dutton was perhaps the first to apply Schmitt to the Chinese revolution in his book *Policing Chinese Politics* (Durham, NA: Duke University Press, 2005).

constitutional provision. In this situation, the state of emergency was limited and carried out on the basis of law. In contrast, a "sovereign dictatorship" was the result of popular mobilization against an existing order. It was not intent on "saving the constitution," but rather aimed at creating a new legal and political order to replace the existing order. For Schmitt, a dictatorship is never simply a form of despotism or tyranny, but a means to reach a certain end, which is either the defense of the existing order or the creation of a new order. It marks a temporary stage of transition of power. The Marxist–Leninist concept of a "dictatorship of the proletariat" falls into the category of a sovereign dictatorship, since it strives to build a new political order and society.

Arendt and Schmitt, notwithstanding their obvious differences, provide us with a fruitful new way of theorizing PRC history. The elements from Schmidt's and Arendt's theories help us understand that under the condition of a revolutionary "structureless" state in a constant state of exception, assertions of existential threats then not only defined and identified real vulnerabilities and threats, but also became politically constitutive acts. The sense of being in a state of emergency, of course, was not even fictitious or metaphorical. Still after the establishment of the PRC in October 1949, there remained an estimated 2 million armed men not connected to the CCP or the Red Army in China; 600,000 of them were the GMD rearguard. In 1949 China was divided into six military regions and the country remained under what was essentially military control until 1954. The CCP faced numerous other challenges to its rule and was weary of internal and external threats to its security. In the 1950s, the effects of World War II and the Civil War were evident everywhere: tens of millions of refugees uprooted by the world war and the Civil War moved across the country and flooded into the cities.[11]

The military conflicts had destroyed China's great cities, devastated its countryside, and ravaged the economy. Years of fighting as well as frequent changes of the ruling power and the administrative structure had brought about the collapse of social and political order. The need to defend the revolution internally and externally was portrayed as making inevitable the suspension of regular life. Revolutionary struggle became tantamount to emergency and exception. Since the new state saw itself as under siege or still at war and was distressed by anxieties about popular acceptance, security issues became of overruling importance. This discourse caused the state to reimagine individuals and groups in a way that pushed security concerns

[11] Between 14 million and 20 million Chinese died first in the "war of resistance to the end" against Japan and then in the ensuing Civil War. Another 80 million to 100 million became refugees. See Klaus Mühlhahn, *Making China Modern: From the Great Qing to Xi Jinping* (Cambridge, MA: Harvard University Press, 2019), 312–313.

into the foreground and at the same time devalued notions of procedure and legality. It established powerful new contexts to construct threats to the social body of the Chinese nation and as a result to produce new forms of political subject. It allowed the CCP to maintain a dictatorial rule whereby the "state of exception" evolved into a lasting "paradigm of government" in China that was invoked time and again. Mass campaigns and movements were de facto declarations of a temporal state of emergency.

Hence the idea of a "state of exception" was very much on the minds of most CCP leaders. This becomes very clear when one rereads policy documents from the 1950s. When Mao spoke about enemies of the people, he was quite aware of tension between the supremacy of sovereign power and the rule of law. On the one hand, leaders argued that in order to be compelling, the regulatory power of the state must be grounded in the law, especially the constitution, rather than in arbitrary orders from above. Yet, on the other hand, they acknowledged that the need for the use of "extraordinary power" (*feichang daquan*) made necessary the suspension of the law. The state needed to be able to resort to unregulated violence against enemies and traitors.

The conditions of structurelessness and emergency created a pervasive atmosphere of crisis and insecurity. This was made worse by the lack of legitimacy that marked the rule of the CCP from the very beginning. Following the definition of Marc Suchman, I understand legitimacy as "a generalized perception or assumption that the actions of an entity are desirable, proper or appropriate within some socially constructed system of norms, values, beliefs and definitions."[12] Legitimacy is not event-specific; rather it needs to be "generalized." Also legitimacy is not a property or resource, but rather a condition reflecting that the entity is based on relevant rules, laws, normative support, or alignment with the cultural framework. It is a symbolic value that justifies the actions of an entity by giving a normative approval to practical imperatives.

The CCP won victory on the battlefield aided by a rapid collapse of the GMD forces as well as assistance from the Soviet Union. Whatever sympathies it might have enjoyed among certain groups in the population, on the eve of the revolution the CCP did not have general social acceptability or credibility. Most reports from that time indicate that the majority of the population viewed the CCP with no more than curiosity.[13] The

---

[12] Marc C. Suchman, "Managing Legitimacy: Strategic and Institutional Approaches," *Academy of Management Review* 20, no. 3 (July 1995): 574.

[13] Conditions varied in this huge and heterogeneous country, of course, but in the cities the CCP mostly faced an indifferent and rather skeptical population. This is vividly demonstrated for Shanghai in the brilliant book by Zhang Jishun, *Yuanqu de dushi: 1950 niandai de Shanghai* (A City Displaced: Shanghai in the 1950s) (Beijing: Shehui Kexue Wenxian Chubanshe 2015), 21–23.

lack of general acceptance was also one of the reasons why Stalin and the Soviet advisers constantly urged the CCP to enter a "coalition government" with the "democratic parties" in China and to work within the existing political structures and institutions.[14]

In addition, the CCP came to power not by invoking socialism, communism, or Stalinism, but by dangling the concept of New Democracy. This concept promised that the CCP, while claiming leadership, would co-operate with the main political and social forces in China. More precisely, the new People's Republic was to rest on a broad social base, for the workers and peasants were to be part of a "national united front" which included the petty bourgeoisie and the national bourgeoisie. In accordance with this formula, indigenous Chinese capitalism (capitalist forces and classes not tied to the external imperialist order) was to be allowed to evolve in order to hasten modern economic development. Mao declared that China must utilize all factors of urban and rural capitalism that are beneficial and not harmful to the national economy: "Our present policy is to regulate, not to destroy, capitalism."[15] The CCP went to great lengths to accommodate and include all remaining groups and institutions. This policy was pursued because the CCP was very well aware of the challenges it faced in governing China and the lack of credibility deriving from its violent assumption of power.

When the Party decided in 1949 to gradually discard the slogan of New Democracy and instead began to stress the need for class struggle, it only exacerbated the lack of legitimacy and credibility: this, then, was a state and government that claimed to serve the people yet lacked any mandate for the radical transformation it was pursuing from those it was governing for. With the push toward socialist transformation, the CCP departed from earlier assurances and faced growing mistrust. Since the Party was almost by default unsure of its backing in society, it was fully aware of the risks and challenges it faced. It lacked input legitimacy as well as normative legitimacy. The Cold War conflict and later the conflict between China and the USSR created additional outside pressures that further increased feelings of vulnerability and pervasive nervousness. Hence the new government needed to strictly control society and to constantly mobilize the people in support of the state. At the same time, it was also under intense pressure to prove its dedication to the welfare of the people (output legitimacy).

This provides a useful framework for interpreting the history of the PRC as well as the problems it is still facing. The profound impact of

---

[14] Alexander Pantsov and Steven I. Levine, *Mao: The Real Story* (New York: Simon & Schuster, 2012), 356–358.

[15] Quoted in Mühlhahn, *Making China Modern*, 416.

vulnerability, distress, and security concerns permeated the PRC body politic and shaped a society with a comparatively low degree of institutional structuration. In the following I will demonstrate how this approach can yield new insights, focusing mainly on two areas: violence and social transformation. In order to be concise, I cannot provide full detailed empirical evidence.

The Dynamics of Violence

It has often been suggested that state violence and terror were essential elements in the totalitarian formula of rule. Moreover, the phenomena of the labor camps or of mass campaigns targeting large groups of the population as a manifestation of state violence convey the unmistakable message that Mao's regimes were bent on violence and mass murder. With the opening of the archives, more and more evidence on the violence has been produced. To be sure, this is all necessary work, which national history cannot and should not escape. But what, if anything, is captured by the notion of violence? What is to be gained from historicizing violence?

Of course, a history of violence and terror is only complete if not only revolution, but also war, is included in the story. The year 1949 was hardly a completely new beginning separating the period of war and violence from a period of reconstruction and purely ideological conflict. The victory of the revolution was the climax of more than thirty years of war, revolution, and violence. Chinese society in the years of the Cold War was deeply affected by the violence of World War II, much like European countries, which, after 1945, continued to be affected by the experience of the war having been fought on their own territories, or by the fear of imminent invasion.[16]

The various wars that were fought on Chinese soil or along its borders from the 1920s to the 1960s should be seen as manifestations of "total warfare."[17] The totality of it makes sense if we understand it – in both practical and ideological terms – as a life-and-death struggle. The question of mass violence has to be placed in this history of total warfare. The immediate question concerns the murder and persecution of any and all "enemies of the people" or "Han traitors" in an environment of political and social cleansing. But the more general question concerns the nature of war, which in China was rarely ever confined to

---

[16] Ian Buruma, *Year Zero: 1945 and the Aftermath of War* (New York: Penguin Press, 2013).
[17] For an in-depth discussion of the concept of total war in China, see Hans van de Ven, *China at War: Triumph and Tragedy in the Emergence of the New China* (Cambridge, MA: Harvard University Press 2018), 6.

military conflict or guided by politics. It seems that in their animosity, the many parties that were involved in the business of war in China (Japan, the CCP, the GMD, the USSR, the USA) seem to have assimilated rather than moved apart. Thus it can be argued that one side acquired the techniques and attitudes of the other – although we need to be careful in identifying what those traits were. I would suggest that an altogether more complex and entangled approach is needed, one that transcends a comparative or generic perspective. A focus on transfers of techniques, ideas, and emotions will reveal that violence and hostility were shaped by a peculiarly hybrid exchange that created a culture of violence beyond victory and defeat.

The socialist project was designed to defend society against its enemies within. Discourses and practices of exclusion and exception allowed the state to enlist its own citizens to fight against the enemies within, to police themselves, and to protect the socialist order. The question of loyalty or betrayal began to override concerns of transparence, accountability, and justice, opening the way for violent excesses that were conducted and permitted by the state. The discourse of struggle produced disenfranchisements, persecutions, and internments; it ultimately also justified the liquidation of those deemed uncorrectable or dangerous to socialism. Hence the notion that socialism must be defended condoned a moral right to annihilate those outside. Based on Hannah Arendt, it would seem that the turn to crushing force was a reflection of the weakness and fragility of CCP rule rather than the result of total power.

The obvious multicausality and multidimensionality of the violence in the PRC makes necessary a broadening of the field of inquiry. The most important area of debate is now less whether violence was deployed or the number of victims than the nature and the purpose of the violence which the regime exercised and in which society participated. There is a clear need for proper contextualization and historicization, in order to avoid the simplistic impression that violence emerges only out of the arbitrary rule of dictatorship. Confronting these issues, there are two aspects that can be explored. First is the social embeddedness of violence; second is the ideological imperative to order a multiethnic empire. The key proposition is that violence, while mostly state-driven, was deeply embedded in Chinese society. This raises the question not only of the nature of social violence, but also of how and why this propensity for violence developed within Chinese society.

Essential questions remain unanswered and need to be addressed: did terror – or, at least, certain kinds of terror – enjoy popular support? Was it self-vindication? A means of social mobilization and ideological identification? Could the regime count on popular participation? Is there an overarching pattern of violence?

Creating New China

While totalitarian models overwhelmingly focus on the state, the "regime," or the "system," the study of society became a subject of research in its own right relatively late. Yet as several chapters in this volume demonstrate, recent research, rather, started from another angle: where and how was the new state that came into being after 1949 produced, maintained, internalized, or broadened to encompass formerly unaddressed groups in society?

Timothy Mitchell has called this the "state effect": the various kinds of work required to install the effect of an activist, transformational state standing apart from and above something called "society." We have to recognize the fuzzy, shifting, and constantly refigured boundary between what we conventionally divide into state and society, asking about the distinction between the state apparatus on the one hand and a more diffuse state presence, awareness of the state, and self-fashioning with state norms in mind on the other. We can take the state seriously, but not take it for granted. The chapters by Julia Strauss and Anja Blanke explore the contingency, the unevenness, the many kinds of continuous human labor and everyday practices required to make the new state seem natural. In the course of the 1950s "the state" inscribed itself into society, ceasing to be an external, peripheral presence. Instead the state and the Party often sought to be embodied in a familiar neighbor such as a woman leader, activist, or labor model.

While earlier work mostly was interested in the social role of basic class categories – workers, peasants, and so forth – what is perhaps more fascinating and significant is the capacity of social classification to generate social realities rather than simply reflect them.[18] "Ascribing class" is, of course, only one dimension of this process; ascribing nation – ethnic, racial, or otherwise – and generating a new sense of Chineseness was even more important in PRC history.[19] In this context the chapters in this book by Shuman and Johnson should tentatively also point to the transnational quality of these ascriptive categories. Class, after all, is a universal category, whereas ethnicity is categorically not. What should be emphasized,

---

[18] Jacob Eyferth, *Eating Rice from Bamboo Roots: The Social History of a Community of Handicraft Papermakers in Rural Sichuan, 1920–2000* (Cambridge, MA: Harvard University Asia Center, Distributed by Harvard University Press, 2009).

[19] A brilliant application of Mitchell's state effect can be found in Gail Hershatter, *The Gender of Memory: Rural Women and China's Collective Past* (Berkeley: University of California Press, 2011).

however, is the effectiveness of the nation remade in war to create distinct postwar national identities. It is highly ironic that it was not only war, sacrifice, and humiliation at the hands of imperialism that ultimately ascribed identity, but also the universal ideals of class diluted into Chinese nationalism.

The construction of class and nation was highly effective in the transformation of Chinese society. We do not yet fully understand how this project of constructing identities worked, what social and individual needs and desires it produced and what impact it had on the self-fashioning of individual identities.[20] Nor do we have a strong sense of timing. Finally, we do not know how to evaluate contingencies – the role of scarcities, rationing, hardship, natural or man-made disaster – or, equally important, the proclivity of people to not get involved in anything at all, let alone in such onerous schemes as self-fashioning. It seems evident, though, that social groups, rather than merely being a site of regime action, are actors in their own right, as is demonstrated by the chapter of Aminda Smith. We need to fully understand the practices of those groups and actors and their strategies of societalization (*Vergesellschaftung*) before we can begin to fully fathom the legacies of PRC history. Just on the horizon of this kind of history we also discover that, much as the local and particular dominates, these social actors partake in a wider world that is partly made up of fantasies and projections, but is partly also the product of transnational practices.

Several chapters in this volume, for instance those of Zhang Jishun and Ruan Qinghua, argue that the regime intended to create a new collective subject, an entirely modern, illiberal, and self-fashioned personage. They point to the long intellectual tradition of imagining this kind of subject, the initiatives to create such personalities, and, in an exemplary fashion, the kind of striking conversion experience that real persons underwent in becoming "new men." While these labors of self-transformation differed in significant respects, the point is to highlight the ways in which the PRC was literally embodied in the lives of people. That discipline was central in this project is noteworthy, not least because it suggests a site where ascribing class, creating bonds of belonging, and transforming the self intersect in a telling fashion.

Hence we have to depart from the older literature that spoke of society "under" Mao, and explore the extent to which the government left deep and lasting imprints on the social construction of China. In

---

[20] See Michael Geyer and Sheila Fitzpatrick, "Introduction: After Totalitarianism – Stalinism and Nazism Compared," in Michael Geyer and Sheila Fitzpatrick, eds., *Beyond Totalitarianism: Stalinism and Nazism Compared* (Cambridge: Cambridge University Press, 2008), 1–38.

order to place the state on a more stable footing, the CCP invested enormous energies into the construction of the social and the individual, by transmuting social ascription into projects of self-fashioning and identification.

But as the chapters by Jing Wenyu and Jeremy Murray remind us, there is another, equally important, though less studied, dimension: there is evidence pointing to societal bonds fracturing and to the rise of conflict across society, as well as to the construction of new bonds based on new social categories. But at the same time there is also evidence suggesting that bonds of family and friendship did not disappear but actually strengthened, as did workplace connections. All this suggests that the resilient powers of society should never be underestimated. However, we do not yet fully understand the nature of this capability or the impetus that leads some of these efforts of togetherness to identify with the state and others to turn against it.

Conclusion

This postscript represents an attempt to reconsider the history of the revolutionary People's Republic of China. While bits and pieces of the older master narratives remain popular in the literature, the generalizations of those narratives have been eroded by recent research that presents the PRC as an extraordinarily diverse and complex history.

The PRC inherited indisputably difficult circumstances from the previous regimes: bombed cities, broken dikes, land-hungry peasants, refugee movements across the country, and foreign relief dollars. It had to expend an enormous amount of energy, with varying degrees of success, to re-educate, reconstruct, or eradicate, through means of coercion and persuasion, a pre-existing world of capital and maritime connections. There were capitalists, Christians, Buddhists, liberal intellectuals, and other followers of value and faith, whose successful reconstruction appeared to have long eluded the Party and the state. Meanwhile the USSR displaced the West as the premier model of progressive modernity. To build such a New China (again with varying degrees of fervor and success) required an equally significant amount of investment in the forms of cultural capital and political energy. New China inscribed itself into society and everyday lives.

Still, beyond new campaigns and productions there were memories and aspirations, institutionalized or diffused, open or underground, informing subject positions and eluding Party directives. The "Old China" held on in bits and pieces. The "New China" struggled to be born. In retrospect, the early PRC is an era of contestation that seemed to have required the invasive use of governing technologies such as thought reform and rectification campaigns. The CCP, then, did have to contend with a China in existence despite growing Party power or the expanding reach of the state.

Above all, under these conditions of uncertainty and anxiety the Party resorted to "the state of exception" to impose its power won on the battlefield. The critical decisions laying the basis for the state of exception were all made in a state of anxiety and vulnerability. The "state of exception" is an umbrella term for the "structureless" form of revolutionary dictatorship that gathers beneath it those emergency categories while emphasizing that this state has as its defining characteristic that it transcends the borders of the constitutional – in other words, that it faces no limits to its power.

Index

All-China Sports Federation, 78, 83
anti-localism, 124, 153, 156, 166, 168, 174
archives, x, 1, 3, 11, 12, 72, 83, 97, 100,
    105, 157, 215, 223, 273, 283
authoritarianism, 225, 277

Bai Yang, 200, 204, 206
bipolarity, 18, 22, 29, 43
bureaucracy, 7, 9, 10, 20, 78, 104, 111,
    122, 128, 129, 130, 131, 133, 134,
    139, 150, 151, 221, 231

campaigns
    Anti-Rightist campaign, 3, 5, 207, 256,
        257, 258, 261, 262, 263, 266, 267,
        270, 271
    Campaign to Suppress
        Counterrevolutionaries, 123, 125, 136,
        137, 139, 140, 142, 143, 221, 268
    Cultural Revolution, 1, 3, 5, 7, 48, 49, 58,
        70, 93, 96, 124, 129, 139, 156, 158,
        161, 173, 199, 201, 202, 204, 211,
        248, 253, 256, 258, 260, 261, 265,
        266, 267, 268, 271, 275
    Great Leap Forward, 1, 2, 3, 5, 6, 49, 58,
        64, 129, 159, 172, 175, 197, 208, 209,
        231, 232, 238, 254, 256, 257, 263,
        264, 270
    Hundred Flowers movement, 202
    land reform, 2, 5, 8, 10, 75, 102, 104,
        123, 125, 129, 136, 137, 138, 139,
        140, 141, 142, 143, 145, 146, 147,
        148, 149, 150, 153, 157, 166, 170,
        190, 232, 233, 239, 240, 242, 243,
        244, 245, 246
    rectification campaign, 7, 288
    Resist America/Aid Korea, 6, 136
    Socialist Education Movement, 231,
        233, 252, 254
Chen Yuchan, 161
Chiang Kai-shek, 148

Chinese Academy of Science, 63
Chinese Communist Party, 2, 5, 9, 12, 17,
    20, 30, 38, 47, 56, 63, 73, 80, 97, 121,
    127, 128, 129, 135, 136, 151, 154,
    157, 158, 168, 195, 196, 197, 213,
    232, 268
Chinese People's Political Consultative
    Conference, 30, 97
Chineseness, 19, 95, 285
class status, 240, 241, 243, 245, 247, 254
class struggle, 138, 264, 270, 282
coal, 6, 8, 10, 20, 44, 45, 46, 47, 48, 49, 50,
    51, 52, 53, 54, 55, 57, 58, 59, 60, 61,
    62, 63, 64, 66, 67, 68
Cold War, 4, 10, 11, 12, 19, 22, 23, 25, 26,
    27, 29, 30, 31, 32, 35, 36, 37, 38, 39,
    41, 42, 45, 47, 55, 62, 64, 66, 67, 70,
    73, 77, 78, 85, 99, 100, 115, 116, 258,
    278, 282, 283
collective memory, 256, 258, 259, 265,
    266, 269, 272, 273, 274
Comintern, viii, 67
consumer population, 176, 177, 178,
    182, 192
counterrevolutionary, 10, 123, 138, 139,
    143, 221, 223, 240, 243
criminal cases, 232, 234, 252, 254
cultural diplomacy, 99, 111, 115

Democracy Wall movement, 265, 266
Deng Xiaoping, 38, 39, 40, 256, 257, 259,
    260, 263, 266, 269, 270, 272, 277
Ding Ling, 164
Document No 9. 271

factional struggles, 232, 247
Feng Baiju, 154, 160, 166, 167, 169
film industry, 99, 103, 114, 196, 197, 198,
    200, 205, 207, 208, 210
filmmakers, 102, 103, 105, 106, 107, 108,
    200, 201

289

gazetteers, 12, 158, 159
gender equality, 8, 164, 173
Geneva conference, 37, 38
grass roots, x, 3, 141, 180, 199, 201, 205, 214, 221, 222, 226, 232, 241, 244, 252, 254, 262
Guangdong, 1, 46, 124, 154, 159, 160, 166, 267
Guangzhou, 1, 125, 154, 158, 160, 161, 167, 169, 267
guerrilla forces, 153, 154
Guomindang, 8, 17, 31, 70, 73, 105, 121, 127, 128, 129, 135, 136, 138, 139, 228

Hainan, ix, 8, 10, 37, 124, 153, 154, 155, 156, 157, 158, 159, 160, 161, 162, 163, 164, 165, 166, 167, 168, 169, 170, 171, 172, 173, 174
historical mistakes, 256, 257, 258, 259, 261, 263, 264, 265, 266, 268, 270, 271, 272, 273, 274
historiography, viii, 9, 12, 256, 258, 259, 261, 262, 266, 267, 268, 270, 273, 276
Hong Kong, xi, 64, 70, 73, 75, 76, 85, 93, 96, 103, 104, 105, 114, 116, 133, 166, 224, 231, 249, 265, 267
Hu Ping, 266
Huang Hongjiu, 69, 70, 72, 74, 85, 87, 88, 95
Hungary, 30, 36, 39, 42, 49, 52, 84, 91, 92, 93, 109, 110, 112
hyperinflation, 128, 136

identity, x, 77, 98, 110, 135, 156, 168, 181, 199, 258, 286
Indonesia, 33, 69, 73, 76, 85, 88, 91, 96, 101, 109, 110, 114, 115
industrialization, 7, 20, 36, 44, 46, 62, 64, 175, 192
intellectuals, 2, 8, 13, 129, 167, 205, 257, 259, 261, 262, 265, 268, 269, 287

Japan, 12, 23, 32, 33, 63, 64, 73, 75, 103, 107, 110, 112, 114, 157, 172, 181, 207, 280, 284
Jiang Qing, 208

Khrushchev, 29, 30, 36, 38, 39, 40, 41, 42, 43, 115
Korean War, 6, 7, 10, 17, 35, 99, 100, 104, 105, 107, 110, 112, 116, 170

landlord, 8, 13, 122, 123, 129, 137, 138, 139, 145, 146, 147, 149, 150, 151, 177, 182, 192, 209, 238, 239, 243, 244, 246
leaning to one side, 17, 100

legitimacy, 5, 38, 77, 99, 115, 145, 178, 182, 196, 243, 256, 259, 267, 272, 273, 274, 275, 279, 281, 282
letters and visits, 196, 197, 213, 214, 215, 216, 217, 218, 219, 221, 222, 223, 228, 230
Li Ming, 196, 198, 199, 200, 201, 202, 203, 204, 206, 208, 209, 210, 211
Li Rui, 6, 270
Li Xin, 233, 234, 236, 237, 238, 239, 240, 241, 242, 246, 247, 248, 249, 250, 251, 252, 253, 254, 255
Liu Qiuju, 161
Liu Shaoqi, 31, 32, 33, 39, 41, 106, 219
Luo Ruiqing, 137, 138, 139
Lushan conference, 252

Mao Zedong, 3, 4, 17, 30, 31, 32, 33, 34, 35, 36, 38, 39, 40, 42, 62, 97, 101, 156, 164, 172, 176, 198, 201, 202, 206, 207, 208, 210, 212, 213, 214, 218, 227, 252, 260, 262, 264, 267, 269, 271, 276, 277
Maoism, xi, 3, 115, 116, 222, 227, 230, 244, 256, 278
Maoist China, 2, 231, 253, 257
Marxism, 106, 260, 273
mass line, 59, 130, 195, 196, 197, 214, 215, 216, 217, 223, 224, 225, 226, 227, 230
Military Control Committee, 177, 178, 179, 180, 181, 182
Ministry of Foreign Affairs, 64, 97, 111, 112

Nanjing, 3, 138, 139, 140, 226
National People's Congress, 92, 95
nationalism, 13, 98, 99, 286
New Democracy, 136, 282
New Fourth Army, 156, 198, 200, 214
New Marriage Law, 5, 153
north China, 6, 10, 128, 129, 138, 139, 140, 142, 144, 147, 149, 213, 220, 221
North Korea, 33, 35, 84, 107, 108, 110, 111, 112

Olympics, 71, 74, 75, 76, 77, 78, 80, 81, 83, 89, 92, 93, 95
oral history, 72, 158
overseas Chinese, 19, 73, 74, 75, 85, 88, 93, 95, 96, 114, 162

People's Liberation Army, 37, 80, 102, 124, 127, 160, 174, 200
performance, xi, 48, 134, 148, 150, 152, 235
planned economy, 5, 7, 9, 20

policy implementation, 125, 128, 130, 133, 141, 144, 150, 152, 254
Politburo, 31
PRC history, 1, 2, 3, 4, 11, 13, 23, 68, 73, 95, 215, 258, 275, 276, 278, 279, 280, 285, 286
producer population, 177
propaganda, ix, 17, 81, 95, 97, 102, 103, 104, 105, 106, 107, 108, 109, 110, 111, 113, 114, 115, 116, 117, 147, 160, 162, 180, 207, 209, 215, 216, 218, 224, 227

Qiongzhou Strait, 153

refugees, 121, 123, 138, 179, 180, 181, 182, 183, 190, 280
regime consolidation, 36, 127, 132, 140, 150, 152
relocation, 176, 188, 190
resolution, 42, 104, 145, 190, 257, 258, 259, 260, 261, 262, 263, 264, 266, 267, 269, 274
revolutionary transformations, 5, 10, 11, 12, 196

Shandong, 2, 46, 154, 165, 179, 182, 232, 240, 243, 246
Shangguan Yunzhu, 205, 206, 208
Shanghai, x, xi, 1, 2, 7, 12, 76, 91, 100, 102, 103, 105, 107, 110, 122, 123, 125, 128, 131, 133, 137, 138, 139, 141, 143, 144, 145, 146, 148, 175, 176, 177, 178, 179, 180, 181, 182, 183, 184, 185, 186, 187, 188, 189, 190, 191, 192, 197, 198, 200, 201, 202, 203, 204, 205, 206, 207, 208, 209, 210, 246, 281
Shi Hui, 199, 207, 208
Sino-Soviet relations, 22
socialism, 3, 4, 5, 6, 7, 8, 10, 11, 18, 19, 20, 32, 34, 38, 40, 42, 46, 73, 79, 98, 112, 116, 191, 195, 252, 256, 266, 282, 284
socialist camp, 19, 22, 24, 25, 27, 28, 29, 31, 35, 39, 40, 42, 43, 67, 100, 111, 113, 115
speaking bitterness, 142, 148
sports, 19, 70, 71, 72, 74, 75, 76, 77, 77, 79, 81, 83, 84, 85, 87, 89, 91, 92, 94, 95, 96, 132
Stalin, 17, 19, 30, 31, 32, 33, 34, 35, 36, 38, 40, 42, 43, 98, 99, 110, 115, 282
state building, 94, 108, 116, 128, 130, 167
struggle meeting, 137, 142, 143, 146, 151
Sunan, 122, 123, 127, 128, 135, 136, 137, 138, 139, 140, 141, 142, 144, 145, 147, 148, 149, 150, 151

Taiwan, ix, xi, 11, 12, 35, 36, 37, 41, 43, 70, 75, 76, 77, 83, 93, 110, 117, 127, 154, 267
Tang Xiaodan, 200, 203
Third World, 4, 7, 24, 82, 84, 115
Tian Ran, 200, 209
totalitarianism, 277, 278, 279
transnationalism, 10
triangularity, 22, 23, 24, 26, 27, 29, 35, 40, 42, 43, 66

USA, 7, 18, 23, 24, 25, 26, 27, 28, 29, 30, 31, 33, 34, 35, 36, 37, 40, 41, 42, 43, 52
USSR, 7, 17, 18, 19, 20, 23, 24, 25, 26, 27, 28, 29, 30, 31, 32, 33, 34, 35, 36, 37, 38, 40, 41, 42, 43, 47, 50, 51, 52, 54, 55, 56, 59, 60, 61, 66, 78, 79, 282, 287

violence, 137, 139, 143, 145, 146, 147, 148, 149, 150, 151, 152, 157, 171, 237, 254, 276, 277, 278, 281, 283, 284, 285

Weltanschauung, 6
witnesses, 3, 258, 272
women fighters, 10, 124, 153, 156, 158, 161, 173
women's rights, 153
World Festival of Youth and Students, 69, 72, 74, 82, 83, 84
World Trade Organization, 40
Wu Chuanyu, 69, 70, 74, 77, 84, 85, 87, 88, 89, 91, 92, 95

Xi Jinping, 12, 68, 72, 197, 214, 259, 267, 268, 271, 273, 274, 277, 280
Xinhua News Agency, 102, 218
Xu Quan, 233, 234, 236, 239, 240, 241, 242, 243, 246, 247, 249, 250, 253, 254, 255
Xu Village, 232, 233, 234, 235, 239, 243, 246, 247, 248, 251, 253, 254, 255

Yan'an, 32, 130, 157, 164, 198
Yanhuang chunqiu, 3, 269, 270, 271, 273

Zhang Shunyou, 212, 213, 220, 221, 223, 224, 227, 228, 229
Zhao Dan, 200, 203, 205, 207
Zhao Ziyang, 166
Zhou Enlai, 37, 38, 53, 55, 93, 115, 116, 173, 209

Ingram Content Group UK Ltd.
Milton Keynes UK
UKHW020125010623
422685UK00006B/20